TGB

Oct. 12, 1978

I spoke to Dad this morning as usual, oh man I love him. He wakes me up every morning at 6:00 or 6:30. It's such a nice thing, to hear from him every day. I may not get up when he calls, but we do talk. Sometimes I'm so half asleep, I can't even remember what I said. But what matters is that I talk to him. I went to an extra lab tonight, to make up for the one I will miss on Wed. I miss Mom too. I'm getting into school. I miss Althea & the guys. I hope they write me.

Love,
Star.

Success, Success,
Success, Success,
Success, Success,

You'll read this someday, how will you be, what will you look like, married, huh? Oh Steven.

The Guttenberg Bible

A MEMOIR

Steve Guttenberg

THOMAS DUNNE BOOKS
ST. MARTIN'S PRESS
NEW YORK

This is a true account of the author's life. However, the names and identifying characteristics of certain individuals have been changed to protect their privacy, and dialogue has been reconstructed to the best of the author's recollection.

THOMAS DUNNE BOOKS.
An imprint of St. Martin's Press.

Printed in the United States of America. For information, address St. Martin's Press, 175 Fifth Avenue, New York, N.Y. 10010.

www.thomasdunnebooks.com
www.stmartins.com

ISBN 978-0-312-38345-9 (hardcover)
ISBN 978-1-250-01152-7 (e-book)

First Edition: May 2012

10 9 8 7 6 5 4 3 2 1

To my Mother and Father, Ann Newman and Stanley Guttenberg,
who let me go to Hollywood with three hundred dollars
and all the education I needed.
Everything important to survive in this world,
I learned at your kitchen table.
I love you and hope you allow me back in the house
after you've read this.
Your Loving Son,
Steven

Acknowledgments

It is with respect and admiration that I thank everyone who helped get this book published.

My agent and friend, Andrew Muser, was the first to recommend that my stories of starting out in the business could be fodder for a book.

Superagent Mel Berger of William Morris Endeavor listened to my tales and told me to write forty pages, and he would see if someone was interested.

Publisher Thomas Dunne took a liking to my writing and believed in me and my intent—thank you for this opportunity.

I thank everyone at Thomas Dunne Books and St. Martin's Press for their great and gentle guidance.

My brilliant editor, Peter Joseph, took me through the forest of writing, trimming, and publishing, all with patience and encouragement. Thank you.

My dear West Coast family Al and Jill Segel, who laughed at my stories and said that I should write them. You kept laughing and encouraging me.

My brothers Joseph Pappalardo, Howard Borris, Woody Harrelson, Rick Clemens, and Adam Segel, who read the draft and gave me fortitude.

Gavin and Patti MacLeod were so enthusiastic.

To Dick Guttman, David Rambo, Ted Heyck, Erik Seastrand, and all those people who read a little and couldn't read all of it, thank you.

My appreciation and love go to Michael Bell, for navigating the Hollywood waters for me, giving me maps of all the sinkholes, and showing me how much fun and what a sense of artistic accomplishment one can have as an actor.

And thank you to everyone who is part of my adventure in Hollywood. It's just too funny, if you think about it.

THE FIVE STAGES OF AN ACTOR:

1. Who is Steve Guttenberg?
2. I want Steve Guttenberg.
3. I want a Steve Guttenberg type.
4. I want a young Steve Guttenberg.
5. Who is Steve Guttenberg?

T
G
B

Chapter 1

"You are the last guy I would pick to be a movie star."

That's what an agent said to me when I was sixteen.

He was a friend of my godfather, Michael Bell. You may not have heard of Michael as an actor, but you have definitely heard his voice. He is one of the preeminent voice-over specialists. In the '70s, he would come from Hollywood to visit my family's house in Long Island, New York, bringing with him rented sports cars, beautiful girlfriends, and plenty of money in his pocket. When people would ask me what I wanted to be, I would look at Michael and his life and say, "Whatever he does!" He was a star to me. This guy was an inspiration to a kid from Massapequa.

In 1975, Michael made an appointment for me to visit his agent's New York office. I flew through Penn Station and ran twenty blocks to the skyscraper where I assumed my dreams would come true. I met two female agents and one older vice president of the agency. They were complimentary about my head shots, and I explained a bit about the theater experience I had in Long Island. Then, as if my dog had died, the VP asked the ladies to leave so he could speak to me alone. This started to give me the creeps. My first creep-out in show business, with more coming.

"I'm going to give you a gift," he said, "something that I would give my own son."

This is going to be good! I thought to myself.

Instead he said, "Get out of the business, get out of this office, and become something else. Forget being an actor. You don't have the look, you don't have the talent, and your name is ridiculous. I'm telling you this for your own good. This is a tough, competitive business that you have no place in. Take my advice, walk out these doors, no, *run* out these doors to Penn Station, get on the train back to Massapequa. You are the last guy I would ever pick to be a movie star."

I swear I didn't hear a thing he said.

On June 24, 1976, I graduated Plainedge High School, and already knew what I wanted to do. I had a girlfriend, of whom I was very fond, and could have stayed in the New York area, gone to college, and had a calm, normal life. But I had other things in mind.

Two days later I was on a plane to Los Angeles. I had three hundred dollars in my pocket, salami from my mother, and my father's briefcase. Michael met me at the gate. We walked outside and Los Angeles hit me. The sunshine, the air, the energy.

We got to Michael's car, a green BMW, and drove to his house. All the way we couldn't shut up. It was all new to me, and I asked about each and every thing I saw. Michael is a chatterbox, too, and couldn't help but give me the 411.

"That's where James Dean auditioned for *Rebel,* that's Beverly Hills, that way is Malibu where the stars all have beach houses, and over there, along those mountains, is Mulholland Drive, where I live. Oh, and so does Jack Nicholson, Marlon Brando, and Warren Beatty."

We took the 405 freeway and got off on the Mulholland exit. After passing mansion after mansion overlooking the cliffs, we got to his place. He pointed across the street to Ernest Borgnine's house.

"*McHale's Navy*? That guy?"

"Yep, but we in the acting business like to refer to him as the Academy Award winner for Best Actor for *Marty.*"

We drove down Michael's driveway, and there it was. A mansion overlooking the San Fernando Valley. We walked along a path that seemed right out of a movie. For that matter, so did everything I saw from then on.

I had two weeks to try and become a working actor. After that, I would be going to Albany University to study and enter the real world. But who knows, two weeks was a long time and anything could happen.

At dinner that night Michael suggested I take his extra car, a 1974 Pacer, and drive around Hollywood, look at the studios, and read *Variety.* "Just don't do anything dangerous or your parents will kill me."

The next morning I was up early to start my career. I bought *Variety,* which was exciting in itself. I drove past Warner Bros. in Burbank, then NBC. I took off to see Universal, then Twentieth Century-Fox, MGM in Culver City, and then the grande dame of them all, Paramount. That famous Bronson Gate made immortal in *Sunset Boulevard.* I could see in my mind William Holden and Gloria Swanson standing there, beckoning me in. And I noticed the guard smiling and waving people through. The card-punching clock for employees, and beyond the gates the famous Nickodell Restaurant where it looked as if starlet after starlet was coming in and out.

My stomach even now has knots in it, remembering my excitement. The feeling of freedom, of possibilities! I drove home and dreamed of driving onto that lot.

That night I told Michael what I did, and he said, "You have thirteen days left." He would bring me to his agents, Cunningham in Los Angeles, and introduce me. "You never know what can happen."

The next day we went to the agency and he introduced me to Vic Sutton, Rita Vennari, and Marcia Hurwitz, three agents there that agreed to "send me out" if something came up. Send me out! That was as good as being told I won the lottery. After that, I called them every day, twice a day. I was polite, but persistent. I knew I had a short amount of time to make a dent in Hollywood.

Meanwhile, I learned how to sneak on the Paramount lot. That feat would be impossible now, with the advent of sophisticated security. Even then it wasn't easy, but it was possible. That is one of the lessons that Hollywood taught me. Dreams aren't easy but they *are* possible.

In those days, there was one guard at each gate. For two days, I stood outside watching the people go in and out. On the right side of the gate was a time clock. Most of the Paramount employees had to take their cards out of a rack, punch in the time they arrived, and then walk on the lot. They would always finish the routine with a wave to the guard and a "Hi, Sam."

I mustered up my nerve. I had prepared by wearing my only sport coat, a corduroy number that I thought made me look older. I carried my father's briefcase and walked across Melrose Avenue with a handful of "co-workers."

I watched the guard let in a car and waited my turn to punch my card. Of course I didn't have one, but I hadn't thought of that! When my turn came I saw a group of blanks, slipped one in the slot, and heard the *punch*. I turned to Sam and waved, he waved back, and I was in.

I was in! I was on the Paramount lot! To the left were the studios for *Happy Days, Mork & Mindy, Laverne & Shirley,* and *Little House on the Prairie.* To the right were the executive offices and the movie sound stages. Everywhere I looked was opportunity, excitement, and my dreams coming true.

On that first day it felt like I walked a hundred miles on the ten-acre lot, and perhaps I did. What blew me away was the lot's self-sufficiency. Since then I've seen it on all movie studio lots. They have their own furniture store, which is the prop house; a clothing store, the wardrobe department; their own fire station, hospital, and construction shop. Whatever you need, it's there. It's all perfectly private, with its own rules, laws, and culture. That's what makes shooting on a lot so exciting. The real world's boundaries are gone, and you can make your own universe. Which I suppose is why artists thrive behind those gates and can dream up whatever they want. I think it was John Ford who called the business "a dream-catcher."

I left after nightfall and drove home knowing that I had accomplished something special. I told Michael what I had done and he laughed and encouraged me to keep going. "Do whatever it takes, kid. You've got to have chutzpah!"

The next day, I parked my Pacer off of Melrose, put on my jacket, grabbed my briefcase (that had nothing but two *Variety*s in it), and gathered my courage. I waited for a few of my "fellow employees" to walk across the street and I followed. Lo and behold there was my card, no name but exactly where I had put it the day before. This time I mimicked one of the other workers and read a *Variety* while walking in and giving a wave to the guard.

This time he waved back, but also waved me over. I gave a look of amazement and impatience. I looked at my watch and thought *I'm going to be late.* Late for what, I didn't know. But I knew I had to give the appearance that I belonged.

"Hey, I've never seen you before," the guard said. "Who are you? Where do you work?"

"Um, um," I stammered. I'd been caught and I started to sweat. I do that when I'm nervous. I can gush buckets. "I'm going to see my father."

"Oh yeah, and who is your father?" He knew I was up to something. I looked down at my *Variety.* All I could see was *President of Paramount Makes Boffo Deal.*

I looked at the guard and with all the earnestness I could grab said, "I'm going to see my father, Michael Eisner."

The guard couldn't believe this if he tried. "Michael Eisner has little kids, not someone like you."

At least the sport coat is working, I thought. *I'm looking older.* "Well, I'm his stepson, and I'm here to visit him."

The guard shook his head and said he would have to call Mr. Eisner's office to see if I was telling the truth. "What's your name, young man?"

And my first improv began. "Sure, I'll give you my name, but I want to know *your* name. Because I'm late as it is and you know what a stickler he is about time, and since I'm going to be late, I want to tell him who it is that made me even later! That's right, buddy boy, my Dad is not in a very good mood today and I'm not taking the brunt of his wrath; what's *your* name?"

The guard started stammering. "Um, um, you go on in. And say hi to your Dad."

I smiled ear to ear. "Will do! Thank you!" I walked on the lot, swinging my briefcase, acting like I owned the place.

From then on that guard thought I was Eisner's son, and every time I saw him I told him how much my "Dad" liked him. I can only imagine that every time Eisner went through those gates the guard thought he was on the president's good list.

A couple of years later I was working on *Players,* a Paramount film for Robert Evans and Anthony Harvey (the director of *The Lion in Winter*), and Eisner visited our set in Cuernavaca, Mexico. As I shook his hand I asked if he knew the story. He said he did and praised me for my unconventional methods of getting on the lot. Thank goodness he thought it was funny. Little did I know that ten years later I would film one of the biggest hits he ever had at Disney, *Three Men and a Baby.*

For the rest of my two weeks, I got up and had my "jobs." One was calling the agents twice a day to ask if there was anything in commercials coming up for me. The other was making my way over to the Melrose gate of Paramount, punching in, and wandering around the lot.

One of my first memories of my Paramount exploration is visiting the *Happy Days* set. And when I say "visit," I use the word loosely. "Sneak on" is a better description. I remember standing behind the director's chair, hearing Garry Marshall, the creator of the series, shouting out orders in a strong Bronx accent. I thought to myself that his was probably the model voice for Fonzie. Seconds later, in walked Henry Winkler. He hugged Garry and said without a trace of an accent, "I'm doing Shakespeare next week and my throat is getting sore!" *The Fonz doing Shakespeare?* I thought. *And where is the tough accent?* Henry is a Yale graduate, a classically trained actor, who can do anything that is put in front of him. But at that moment all I saw was The Fonz, and he had someone else's voice.

I spent all my time on the lot and before I knew it my time was up and I was supposed to go home. But I had caught the acting bug. The night before I had to leave I asked Michael, "If it's all right with you can I stay a little longer?"

"Of course it is, I'm proud of what you've done so far. You've got balls, kid."

The next hurdle was to ask my Mother and Father if I could stay. I knew that was going to be a tough phone call. I had never been away from home this long and I had college coming up in August.

"Mom, Dad, can I stay here in California just a bit more?" I asked when I called them. There was a silence on the other end.

Finally, I heard my father growl, "Why, Steven?"

"I just think I can do something with the acting. I really think I can, Dad. I just need two more weeks."

There was more silence. There had never been that much silence in my house.

"You can stay, but only for two more weeks. But then, Steven, you have to get home," my father said sternly. "You have school coming up, and I want you enrolled."

But I wanted to stay as long as I could. Two weeks turned into two months. Paramount became my home away from home. I would wander the lot from early morning till late in the evening, often sleeping in offices. I would sneak home at 5 or 6 A.M., shower, check in with Michael, and go back out. I would eat, sleep, and dream Paramount. Every sound stage had a phone on it and I used these to my full advantage. I would call the operator and ask to be connected to any of the numbers I needed. I would call the agency, call my friends in New York, and most important call my parents, promising to be home soon.

My favorite stage was the water set, which could be filled with tons of H_2O so that boats could be put in it. It was often empty, so I used it as my first "office." One day I came in and there was a full submarine set in there. Who was on the top deck but Charlton Heston and Christopher Reeve. Heston was in a nasty mood that day and was storming around the set. He walked up to me, in my trusty sport coat and briefcase, and yelled, "Do you work for Universal?"

I stammered like Jackie Gleason and answered the only way I knew how. "Yes, sir, I work for Universal."

"Well, you tell those assholes if they don't fix this script, I will, and you don't want me doing that!"

Geez, Moses is pissed off, I thought. *I've got to do something.* "I will, sir, and I'll do it right away."

He looked at me with those eyes, those amazing eyes, and I was stupefied. "Well, go on son, get it done."

I tell you, for a few moments I believed I did work for Universal. I opened my briefcase and scribbled some gibberish on a piece of paper and ran off. I looked back and he was smiling at me, with a big movie-star grin. Chris Reeve came up behind him, put his hand on his shoulder. I strode out of the stage. This had to be a good day for me: Charlton Heston said "asshole" to me. Things must be looking up.

I also found myself haunting the Bing Crosby Productions bungalow. The offices at Paramount were unlocked then, and I would roam them all, but Bing's offices were the most fun because they had golf carts. I would take one and tool around the lot. It sure beat walking and I could easily hide from or outrun the security guards, who did their nightly rounds on bicycles.

I would drive by the Lucille Ball makeup building often and stop to explore. The building was empty except for a few offices used as storage space. Some of the offices hadn't been touched for years. It was in one of them that I found a call sheet for a Humphrey Bogart film. I also found an office on the top floor that had a beautiful view of the courtyard. *Hm,* I thought, *this could be a great office for me to work from.*

But it was empty, and what is an office without furniture?

One evening I took my golf cart over to the prop department, and found a young prop assistant putting the finishing touches on a wagon for *Little House on the Prairie.* I had already filled out a phony requisitions form from the *Happy Days* set, asking for a desk, a few chairs, and other office supplies.

"What is this stuff for?" the prop master asked.

"We're putting in a desk for a new set, Mrs. Cunningham is opening a dress shop." Dress shop? I thought. Couldn't I come up with anything better than that?

He looked at me. "And who are you?"

"Set Design."

"Why do you have a Crosby golf cart?"

"Hey, pal, if this is a problem I'll have Garry Marshall's office call down, I'm late as it is." It seems that everything in the film and television business is always running late, and people understand this.

He groaned and pulled a beautiful desk, chairs, lamps, and even an ottoman out and said, "I'm closing up. Okay if I leave it here and you transport them yourself?"

I loaded up my furnishings and lugged them up the three flights of stairs to what would be my office. I sat behind my desk, opened my Dad's briefcase, and took out my *Variety* and *Hollywood Reporter.* I imagined myself making deals, sitting in story conferences, and even writing scripts in there. It reminded me of Bill Holden's office in *Sunset Boulevard.* I imagined myself getting phone calls, and . . .

Wait a minute! I thought. I had no phone!

The water stage was a stone's throw away. My father has a degree in electrical engineering and had taught me a thing or two about wiring, so I spliced the telephone wire leading to the stage phone and strung a line up the side of the building to my office. The next day I waited until the young prop man was closing again and asked him for a phone. No requisitions form needed this time, he knew me.

Back at the office I hooked up the phone and it worked! To the operators it seemed as if I was calling from the stage, which was fine for me. They even got to know my voice and I got on a first-name basis with them. They were sweet, as many of the bolts in the show-business machine tend to be.

Two months in Hollywood and I had my own office, with a phone. I had my feet on the desk, and was requesting an outside line like a pro. I know it sounds a bit rascally, but that's what show business is made of. Guys like me finding cracks in the wall when the doors are shut. Hollywood legend has it that David Geffen would steam open envelopes in the William Morris mail room, and Steven Spielberg had his own office (on the sly) at Universal when he was starting out. The business is full of these stories.

Michael would encourage me to keep going. "You have to live this business twenty-four hours a day. Eat, sleep, and dream it if you want to make it." And I did. But August was coming up quickly, and with it my deadline to be out of California and up at Albany State.

Chapter 2

Then *it* happened.

I would call Vic at Cunningham two, maybe three times a day, asking, "Anything I can go out on?" Every day I got the same answer. "No, Steven, but if there is we will call you."

Finally I got a message on my answering machine. "Steven, this is Rita, we have a commercial audition for you tomorrow, call us back." Rita Vennari was Vic's agent partner. She now owns her own agency.

A commercial audition! Oh my G-d! I couldn't call soon enough. I asked the operator to connect me with Cunningham and gave her the number.

"Is this Steve?" she asked.

"Yes, is this Margie?"

"It sure is, doll, how's the day going over there on the water set?" The operators always liked to chat but this time I was in a hurry.

"Margie, things are busy as bees over here, but I have to get in touch with this company, Faye Dunaway needs to speak to them." Always use a big star's name, I'd learned.

"Right away, Steve, and tell Faye we all loved her in *Chinatown*."

"Will do, Margie. Have a great day."

The receptionist at Cunningham answered. I was so excited I forgot Rita's name and forgot mine. I had to hang up, get myself together, and call again.

Both Rita and Vic got on the phone; they were laughing as they spoke. "Steven, we have a Kentucky Fried Chicken commercial audition for you, tomorrow. Can you make it?"

"Can I make it? Yes, yes, yes! That's why I'm here! Where? When? Thank you, thank you!"

They gave me the address, and the time, and I think they were as happy as I was. Agents go through as much rejection as their clients, sometimes more, and when a client gets something, anything, they are really excited and relieved.

I hung up and just danced around my office. Kentucky Fried Chicken! This could be the start of something big! I grabbed my briefcase and raced to the gate. I ran by the guard.

"Why're you in a rush? You never leave the lot before nightfall."

"Big meeting tomorrow, I have to prepare!"

"Break a leg! See you tomorrow!"

I ran across Melrose to my Pacer and couldn't get my keys in the door quickly enough. I raced home, and burst in the door.

"I got one! I got an audition!"

Michael was lying in the sunroom reading a novel. "What, what did you get?"

"Only the greatest fried chicken company in the world wants to audition me! Me!"

We sat that night for hours. Michael counseled me on what to wear, and what goes on at one of these interviews. I slept that night with one eye open, bounced out of bed early, and got dressed as if I were going to a military parade. Everything was perfect. I blow-dried my hair till my hand hurt from rolling my brush. Michael gave me a pep talk and out the door I ran.

The address was on Sunset Boulevard, right in the heart of Hollywood. Finding a free parking spot in Hollywood was always a challenge, but luck was with me that day. I grabbed my head shots and went in. But I wasn't prepared for what I would see.

The office had what looked like a hundred actors, all ages and all types, sitting, walking in circles, and talking to themselves. One of the other guys was Timothy Busfield, who is now an accomplished actor, director, and producer. I noticed his red hair and after that I would spot him at many auditions.

I didn't know what to do as I looked at this menagerie. Then the casting director, a vivacious woman named Debra Kurtzman, came out and noticed me standing there.

"You. Have you signed in?" She pointed to a list where the actors put their agent's name. I added mine and sat down in a daze. This was all too much. Luckily, I sat next to an older actor who had to have been an angel.

"You look like you are lost, are you?"

"It's my first audition."

"Well, I'll get you through it. You have a great smile, and that's what they want. So just smile, no matter what happens in there, just smile."

"In there?" It sounded like a gas chamber.

"I'm telling you, just smile. And one more thing." He pointed to a bookshelf. "Take your pride, and put it on that shelf. Just put it there, and pick it up when you leave."

Eventually, Debra came out and called, "Steven Gluberman?" I looked around, as did everyone in the room. "Steven Gluberman?"

Debra was just about to move on when my angel looked at my pictures and saw my name.

"Hey, that's you."

"It is?"

"He's right here," he shouted, and pointed my way.

Debra turned to me and said, "All right, come on in, Mr. Gluberman."

I got up from my seat and walked toward that door as if I were going into some kind of fiery hell. I remember sweating. Gone was my excitement, gone was the bravado. I did not want to be there.

The door opened. Beyond it, seated at a long table, were what seemed like twenty people, all with pens in their mouths, papers in their hands, and looking completely impatient.

"This is Steven Gluberman."

I was able to squeak out my correct name: "Guttenberg."

Debra said, "Yeah, okay, sorry, Guttenberg." It was pronounced like "gut" back then.

Then I remembered what my angel said to me. Smile. And that's what I did. I just smiled and didn't stop smiling till I left the office.

They asked me to tell them a little about myself. I can't remember what I said but I know I kept smiling. If I had described the Hindenburg disaster, I would have kept smiling. They asked me to do an improvisation of being at a football game and eating Kentucky Fried Chicken and being really happy. And boy did I ever improvise! I was cheering and smiling and eating and laughing. The director finally yelled, "Cut!" The advertising guys thought I was funny. I shook everyone's hands and walked out smiling.

Debra told me to wait for a while. I thought I did something wrong. I sat next to my angel and he asked me how it went. Before I could answer, Debra called him in. I sat waiting and he came out in less than a minute. He smiled at me and said, "Don't forget what I told you; you have a great smile." And he was gone. I never saw him again and I owe him a great deal. He's why if I can ever lend a hand to someone starting out in this business, I do.

I waited for about an hour until everyone had gone in. They kept behind eight people. Four boys, four girls. Debra told us they would play some mix-and-match, putting different actors together for improvisations.

It felt like a scene out of *Spartacus* when the Romans put the gladiators in cells with slave girls and watched what happened. I smiled and laughed and pretended to devour chicken with all the gusto I had. At the end of the day, Debra told us to all go home. We would know later today or tomorrow.

"Mr. Gluberman, you done good," she told me.

"It's Guttenberg."

"Whatever it is, you were good. Do you have a SAG card?"

I shrugged. I didn't know what that was. It sounded terrible.

"A Screen Actors card, are you in the guild?" I shook my head no. "Well, that is going to be a problem. Go home, Mr. Guttenberg, I'll call you."

Instead I drove to Paramount. I walked into the studio, passing the guard.

"Hey, how did your big meeting go?"

"Okay, I guess." Then I remembered I was Eisner's son. "You know how these Hollywood things go."

"Yes, I do, but keep your chin up, it's a game, a big game." I got the best advice from the most unlikely sources.

That day I wandered around the lot; the audition really took it out of me. By nightfall I drove back to Michael's house and walked into my room. And there on my nightstand was the answering machine with its light blinking. I had two messages. I furrowed my brow and pressed Play.

"Steven, it's Mom. I usually hear from you and I didn't get a call today. Is everything all right?" The machine beeped and played the next message.

"Steven, this is Vic and Rita, call us, we have news."

My fingers couldn't dial quick enough. I looked at the time and saw it was seven o'clock. But someone picked up. "Hello, Cunningham and Associates."

"Hello, is Rita or Vic there?" I was pacing.

"This is Rita."

"It's me. Steven Guttenberg." I felt like I was waiting for lab results.

"Oh, I was almost out the door. Steven, they want you, they loved you. You are shooting a Kentucky Fried Chicken commercial next Thursday!"

Oh my G-d! I fell to my knees. "No, no, you're kidding! You can't be, are you serious, really, really?" I went on like that for about five minutes and finally Rita had to stop me.

"Yes, yes, but you aren't in the guild so they are going to have to Taft-Hartley you."

"What is that?" Like a SAG card, it sounded terrible.

"Don't worry, you just have a good evening and we'll talk in the morning. I got to run. Congratulations, Steven, you are a working actor."

I didn't want this moment to end. They wanted me! I got a job! I was officially in Hollywood! Now I had to figure out what a SAG card was and how to get one.

I called the agency at 10 A.M. on the dot. That, I'd learned, is the earliest you can call anyone in an office in show business. I got Vic on the line.

"Man, you're up early. Now we are going to have to Taft-Hartley you, which means that you can work in this commercial if the Screen Actors Guild lets you. Then you have thirty days to join the union for five hundred dollars. If you don't pay the fee by the end of that period, you can't join and you are on the outside looking in again."

Five hundred dollars? I had never seen five hundred dollars, much less had it. "Uh, Vic, I don't have five hundred dollars."

"Don't worry, you'll make three hundred for the day, and you can get two hundred somewhere, can't you?"

I swallowed hard. I wanted that SAG card, whatever it was. "Yes, I can, no sweat."

"The spot is shooting at the Rose Bowl on Thursday. They'll pay you seven dollars and fifty cents to bring your own wardrobe. And one more thing."

"What's that?" I was hoping it wouldn't be that the Taft-Hartley was going to cost five hundred dollars.

"You will be shooting with the Colonel."

"What Colonel?"

"The Kentucky Fried Chicken Colonel. You know, with the white suit and the goatee."

"Oh my G-d. You're serious?"

"I am, Steven, and I have a feeling this is only the beginning for you." He hung up the phone. No good-bye, no nothing.

I sat back on my bed and thought, *The Colonel. My first job and I'm working with a star!*

My next phone call was to my parents. They were excited and proud of me, although my father did pour some water on the fire. "You know, Steven, this doesn't mean you can stay out there indefinitely. I still want you coming back to school."

"Yes, Dad, I know. I'll be back for orientation before my birthday." I understood his feelings about this business and respected what he wanted. Yet I just knew that I should stay with it.

The next morning I rolled into Paramount extra early. I had more than a spring in my step. The guard noticed and yelled to me, "Hey, what's with your energy today, you look extra excited, something going on?" Everybody in Hollywood wants to know what everybody else is doing.

"Oh, just got some things going, and I'm right on track." I punched my card in the time clock with a flourish and bounded onto the lot. I even went to the commissary that day, treating myself to an expensive breakfast. It was there that I saw Michael Landon for the first time.

I was in line when I heard a familiar voice. "Mary, I'm extra hungry today, the ride in from Malibu was a bear. Can you give me my oatmeal pronto?" I turned around and it was him. Little Joe from *Bonanza,* Papa from *Little House.* This guy was handsome, charismatic, and everything a star should be. I watched him get his breakfast and walk around the room saying hi to everyone. He worked it like no one I have ever seen. And everyone loved him.

I walked over to a table and sat alone, trying to look busy reading my trades, all with one eye on Mr. Landon. He sat at a table with lots of crew members, all eating and laughing and having a good time. *One day,* I thought, *I would like to be at a table like that. One day I won't be alone here.*

After I finished my breakfast, I brought my tray over to the counter and put it down. When I turned I bumped right into him. I went one way, he went the same. "You want to dance?" he chuckled to me.

"Uh, no, I uh . . ." What do you say to Michael Landon when he asks you that? He patted me on the shoulder and walked off to shoot his hit TV series.

Up in my office I looked out the window at the *Little House* set as I called Rita for my next set of instructions. "Steven, the union has agreed to Taft-Hartley you, and you have one month to join the guild."

"Okay, do I have to pay all at once? Can I pay in installments?"

"Steven, this is not a layaway plan at Sears. This is the Screen Actors Guild and they are serious as anyone can be. Just get your ass down to Sunset Boulevard and join the guild, *today.* Then call me when you have done that."

I needed five hundred dollars. Time to call home. I picked up the phone and called the operator again. "Hi Margie, it's Steven."

"Well, good morning, Steven, how's everything in bigshotland? Did you say hello to Ms. Dunaway for me?"

I hated to keep this ruse up but I knew I had no choice. "Yes, I did, and she told me to tell you a big hi back."

"Steven, I never do this, but could you ask her for an autographed picture? She is one of my favorites, and I always see her on the lot and am too afraid to approach her." I heard the other operators whispering. "For that matter, would you ask her for five pictures? The girls would like some also."

How on earth am I going to be able to get five signed pictures of Faye Dunaway? I sighed, "Margie, she is a very busy woman, I myself only get a few minutes around her each day."

"Pretty please, Steven. We are cooped up in this room all day and never get to mingle with the stars."

I couldn't say no. "Sure, no problem, I'll talk to her as soon as I see her."

"You are a sweetheart! Girls, he said yes!" I heard the operators laughing and giggling. "Now what can I do for you?"

I gave her my parents' number and she connected me. I knew I was going to have to deliver those photos if I wanted to keep up my free phone calls.

My mother answered and asked me about the commercial. She was a lot more excited about it than my father.

"When do you start? Where is it filmed? Are they nice people? Will they feed you?"

"Mom, it's really neat, I get to film at the Rose Bowl in Pasadena!"

"Where they have the parade? With all the beauty queens and the floats? Will you get to see them? I love that parade, it's always such beautiful weather."

"I don't know about that, Ma, but I will get to meet the Colonel of Kentucky Fried Chicken. The Colonel himself!"

My mother almost fainted from excitement. "Oh my G-d. This is too much! Stanley, he's going to be starring with the Colonel!"

"I don't give a shit if he's starring with Doris Day, he's coming home for school."

"Mom, I have something to ask you. I need five hundred dollars to get my SAG card."

"What the hell is that? Oh my G-d, Stanley, he wants plastic surgery. What the hell could be sagging on you? You're not even eighteen!"

"No, Mom, it's a guild card. I have to join the Screen Actors Guild."

"Oh my G-d, they want him to join the Screen Actors Guild! Do you know what that means?"

I heard my father grumbling in the background. He didn't like any of this. He wanted his son home.

"Mom, I need to borrow five hundred dollars."

Silence.

"They want you to pay five hundred dollars to join a group? They should pay you! Your uncle joined the Elks and it wasn't but twenty-five dollars for a lifetime membership. Tell them to shove it up their ass. You are not throwing away five hundred dollars on a subscription to some actors group."

"But Mom, if I don't join, I don't get to be in the commercial, and I don't get to see the Colonel."

"Let me talk to your father."

I held on as I heard their muffled conversation. It was not good.

My mother got back on the phone. "Is there any way you can get a temporary card, and if you decide to go through with the acting thing you can join in full later?"

"I don't think so, Mom, it's an all-or-nothing deal."

"Hold on." More muffled discussion. "Okay, your father is going to send you the money, but Steven, it sounds awfully expensive to join a club."

"It's not a club, Ma, it's a guild."

"Whatever you want to call it, it's pricey. I'll have your Dad mail it today."

"Could you Western Union it to me? I think I need to pay them pronto." I thought I would use a Hollywood word.

"Pronto? What's pronto?"

"Right away, Mom, as soon as you can."

"Okay, Steven, I'll go and wire it to you. But this still sounds funny to us."

I heard my father yell, "It sure does!"

"Thank you, Ma, I love you."

The next day I picked up the money my parents sent, and went to the Screen Actors Guild, which at that time was on Sunset Boulevard. When I approached the steps I noticed a few very attractive women standing on the corner near the building. I thought that they must be starlets also getting their SAG cards.

The office's lobby had trash on the floor and reminded me of a DMV. I thought that there would be glitter and sparkle. I thought everyone working there would be beautiful. I signed my name on a waiting list and sat down. Finally a heavyset woman called my name.

"Steven Glutterberg." *Why can't anyone get my name straight?*

"That's me."

"Well, big whoop, Mr. Gluttenheimer. Get up out of your chair and follow me."

This definitely wasn't turning out how I expected. We walked to a cubicle and I sat down across from her. She had my records from the production company.

"So, you want to join the guild. It looks like they want you for a commercial, is that right?"

"Yes, it's a Kentucky Fried Chicken—"

She cut me off. "Look, I know you are sooooo excited about becoming an actor and this is your first job. Am I right?" She knew it was. "I'm going to shorthand this for you. I don't give a rat's ass if this is *Gone with the Wind* and you're Clark Gable. Do you have your money?" I pulled out my wad of bills. "You are smarter than most of the thespians I get here. Most don't have the money with them, and by the time they get it their job is lost. Give it here." She counted it out. "Wait here while I do a check on your name."

"Why do you have to do that?" I had been caught driving without my license in New York a few months before. "If driving without my license is a problem, I had it, I just forgot it in my other pants when I—"

She cut me off again. "No, you little fool. I have to check if there is anyone in the guild with your exact name. But looking at yours, I highly doubt it. If there is, you have to change it. So start to think of another name for yourself, right now, pronto." There's that lingo again. She got up and left me for what seemed like an hour. Maybe she went and had lunch.

I started to worry about my name. Was there another Steven Guttenberg in SAG? If I had to change my name what would I change it to? I always liked the name Johnny. I liked that. Or Johnny Storm. Johnny Smart. Those were movie-star names. They sounded pretty good. I was almost hoping that she would come back and tell me there was a Steven Guttenberg so that I could become Johnny Macho.

She slid into her seat, interrupting my daydream. "Nope, not a single Guttenberg in the guild. You're in. Congratulations. Here is your temporary card." She handed me what looked like a library card.

"That's it? Is there some sort of ceremony?"

"You've got to be kidding." I just kept looking at her. "You're not kidding, are you? No, there isn't a ceremony, no trumpets, and no confetti. You are in the Screen Actors Guild. The statistics are this: ninety-five percent of our members don't work and haven't in years. Most of that five percent that are lucky enough to work make less than five thousand dollars a year. So if you're thinking that you will be John Wayne, forget it. You have a better chance of getting hit by lightning, which by looking at you I think you might enjoy. Now get out of this chair because I have fifty other people waiting to join the ranks of the unemployed."

I got up. "Thank you, I didn't know that stuff."

She lit a cigarette and took a long drag. For the first time she had a softer tone in her voice. "I used to be an actress until I got kicked around for a few years and wound up here. I always think that by giving you newcomers the bad news early, I'm doing you a favor. You're going to get used and abused more than you know. This is one of easiest moments you'll have. Break a leg, kid."

All the way to Paramount I thought about what she said. And then I forgot about it. I had to.

Thursday came quickly. I picked out two outfits like Rita had suggested. I had a red T-shirt and jeans for a casual look, and then my trusty sport coat and my only pair of dress pants. I couldn't believe it, my first real job in Hollywood.

Before I left that morning Michael came out to wish me well. "Just don't be nervous, and try and keep the sweating to a minimum."

"You can tell I sweat when I'm nervous?"

"Steven, my dogs can tell you sweat when you're nervous."

He was right. As I went up the driveway I repeated, "Don't be nervous, don't be nervous."

As my Pacer and I approached Pasadena I saw what I thought was fog. *It's summer and there is fog,* I thought, *strange.*

I found the parking lot for the Rose Bowl and saw the location vehicles. It's a pretty awesome sight to behold for the first time. There must have been ten huge trucks. Most of the crew was milling around the catering truck. My Pacer made the turn into the lot and a chubby production assistant stopped me. "Whoa there, cowboy, extras park over there. And you're late." He pointed to a grassy field about a half mile away.

I started to stutter, "I'm in the commercial, I am an actor."

"Yeah, well, extras over there."

"No, no, I'm in the commercial. I'm starring with the Colonel."

"What's your name?" I told him. He checked his list and laughed. "Oh, you're the Taft-Hartley." He waved other people right by.

"Yeah, I'm in SAG," I said proudly.

"Well, let me give you a piece of info. You are not in SAG, you are on probation. And if you screw up today, you are right back where you started. How you like them apples?"

"I don't know, I guess I won't screw up."

"We'll see, just follow the blue line to the PA over there. You can park with the other 'actors.' "

I started to drive and stopped. "What's a PA?"

"You are new, aren't you? This is going to be a fun day, I can just tell. PA is a production assistant. Don't tell anyone else you don't know that, I'm doing you a favor by telling you." He looked my car over. His nose wrinkled. "Is this a Pacer?"

"Yeah."

"I thought they recalled these, like the Corvairs."

"No, we're still allowed to drive them."

"Hmmm. See that guy over there near the honey wagons?"

"What's a honey wagon?"

He pulled his cap off and wiped his forehead. "Man, this *is* going to be a long day. Just follow the blue line."

"Thank you." I pulled away looking for the blue line. In the rearview mirror I saw him laughing.

I followed the blue line to a skinny man with a baseball cap who waved me over. "Park in the third spot."

I did, grabbed my clothes, and walked over to him. "Hi, I'm Steven Guttenberg."

"Good for you. You have the third hole in the honey wagon."

"Honey wagon?"

"Geez, you're the Taft-Hartley. You don't know your ass from a donkey's ear. A honey wagon is a dressing room. You are the third room, which we call holes. Got it?"

"Got it." *Dressing room? I have my own dressing room!* I walked over to the honey wagon and found my hole. No more than thirty square feet. It had a makeup table, a small bed, and a rack for clothes. It was a palace to me.

I shut the door and hung up my clothes. Immediately there was a knock. "I'm coming in," someone sang. The door opened to reveal a woman with pins in her mouth. I couldn't believe how clearly she could speak around those pins. "Good morning, sunshine, I'm Rosie, and you are?"

"I'm Steven Guttenberg."

She looked at her list. "Of course you are, you're the Taft-Hartley."

"Why does everyone keep calling me that?"

"It's a joke on every set, kind of like a virgin." *They know everything,* I thought to myself, *even my sexual experience.* "Let's see what you brought." She looked at my two outfits and just laughed. A few pins flew out of her mouth. "These look like your mother picked them out." *How did she know?* "I'll be right back, just sit tight."

In a flash she returned with a bunch of shirts and pants. "Here, try these on, pronto."

"Okay." I waited for her to leave.

"Well, go ahead." I didn't move a muscle. "Oh, now don't be shy. We wardrobe people are like doctors, there isn't anything we haven't seen."

"I would like to put them on in private, is that okay?"

Rosie laughed the rest of the pins out of her mouth. "Yes, yes, I understand, Taft-Hartley." She shut the door behind her and yelled, "Hurry, sweetheart, we haven't got all day."

I pulled the clothes on. They were very hip, and much more expensive than my own. I opened the door.

"Now that looks good on you. Turn around." I did as she said. "Nice tush, those will do fine."

"You think so?"

"Yes, you have a fine tush."

"No, the clothes, do they look good?"

"Of course they do, I just costume-designed you. Now just don't kill the Colonel and you won't be fired. See you on the set." She closed the door.

There was a pounding on the door. I opened it to find the skinny PA. "Let's go to makeup, and do you want breakfast?"

"No, I ate already."

"You came having had, that's a good sign, the sign of a pro."

"Having had?"

"Yeah, 'having had breakfast.' It means you are prepared." We walked to another trailer. He pounded on the door and yelled, "Stepping up!"

He opened the door and I walked into the makeup trailer. The energy hit me hard. There was music playing, four or five chairs filled by actors and actresses in various stages of readiness. There were cute makeup and hair girls. The trailer was air-conditioned and there was incense burning. The atmosphere was a one eighty from outside. The grand marshal of this party was Raoul, the head makeup artist. He was wearing a muumuu and had his hair in pigtails. "Welcome, welcome. Come on in, gorgeous. This is our space, the artists' oasis. You can be yourself here. No PAs allowed. Now sit here and I'll start to make you presentable."

He stood back and gave me the once-over. "I like your color but your hair is the pits."

"I styled it all morning. I kind of think it looks like Vinnie Barbarino in *Welcome Back, Kotter.*"

"Well, this isn't Welcome Back anything and it looks more like Bozo the Clown. First we'll put some base and eyes on you, then you'll go over to Cynthia for reconstruction of your locks." He started to apply thick pancake to my face, then delicately did eyeliner, lashes, and eyebrows. "You have very fine eyebrows, Cary Grant had them too. It's a sign of royalty."

"Love Machine" by the Miracles came on the radio and Raoul yelled, "Let's do the hustle!" He grabbed one of the makeup girls and started to dance.

Someone banged on the door and opened it up. "Stepping up!" This was an older, grizzled-looking man in white khakis, a multipocketed vest, and a checkered work shirt. "What the hell, Raoul, it's eight o'clock. I need everyone dressed and ready to shoot in a half hour." This was the first assistant director. He was obviously in charge. Someone cut the radio.

"Yes, William, everyone will be ready, just cool your jets."

"It doesn't look like anyone is even near ready."

"That's because you are an assistant director and I'm the key of this department. Now, William, leave us be unless you want some lipstick and eye shadow, pronto." He was the only one in the trailer not intimidated by the AD.

William knew he was trumped. "Okay, darling, but we only have the Colonel for two hours. Could you hurry it up for me?"

"Only if you say 'pretty please with brown sugar on top.'"

William gritted his teeth. "Pretty please with extra sugar on top and a cherry."

"A cherry, oh William, you will have all eight of them in twenty-five minutes. Now scoot."

Someone put the radio back on and exactly twenty-five minutes later everyone was finished. What a difference makeup and hair makes. The actors and actresses in the chairs looked completely different from when I first came in. Everyone sparkled, including me with my new hair.

There was a van waiting to take us to the set. The chubby production assistant I had met in the parking lot took one look at me and said, "You look very pretty, Taft-Hartley, just don't screw up."

"Thanks." I climbed in first and sat way in the back. I forgot that I tend to get nauseous in hot cars or buses. This van smelled like a hundred people had sweated in it. Also the driver was eating hard-boiled eggs, which didn't help. I kept breathing through my mouth so I wouldn't smell anything. I didn't want to vomit. That would definitely be screwing up.

The Rose Bowl looked very different than I remembered from the college games on television. It was empty except for us filming there. The stands I'd seen filled with eighty thousand fans now had one small section with about fifty people in it. Those were extras. The crew was set up on the field in front of that section. There were cameras, reflector cards, a coffee and snack cart, and a host of director chairs. As my van's group approached the set the assistant director walked over to meet us. The crew members broke from our pack and it was just us actors. There were four girls and four guys. The women were dressed like college students, although they were all over twenty-five. Two reminded me of little birds. Of the guys there were two older men and another young guy like me.

"So, my pretty little things. You all look beautiful and coiffed," the AD said, and yelled to Raoul over at the coffee cart. "Nice job, Raoul, a man of your word." Raoul lifted his Styrofoam cup in a toast. "Marty, they're ready."

Marty, the director, was looking in the lens of the camera and held up two fingers. I remembered him from the audition. He started up toward the stands. "Now everyone follow me, I want to place you."

Marty started placing us in various positions among the extras. I sat next to a very kind-looking older lady. The space on the other side of me was open. She whispered to me, "We've been sitting here since five A.M. with not as much as a drink of water. Thank G-d I brought tea." She pulled up a thermos.

"You want me to get you something?"

"Oh no, if you do and they think it is for me I'll get fired. I'm fine. The name's Lillian Adams, and you?"

"Steven, nice to meet you."

"A pleasure."

The chubby PA interrupted us. "Hey, Mr. Taft-Hartley, no talking, please." He silently mouthed, "You're screwing up."

Marty took over. "Okay, folks. Good morning. Now, you are all at a football game. Basically what I want is cheering and laughing and a good old American good time. I'll be taking the camera and putting it in different positions during the day, picking out different situations. So pretend you are with your friends, your classmates, your parents, or anything you can think of. I need lots of improvisation and basically I want you to have a good time. William, is he here yet?"

The assistant director yelled back, "Flying in!" I thought it was amazing that a plane was going to land on the football field. Maybe it was going to be a helicopter.

Someone yelled, "There he is!" A Cadillac was driving toward us, and parked right next to the camera. The PA opened the door and, slowly, very slowly, a leg dressed in perfect white stepped on the ground. Then another. A cane hit the ground with a thud. The driver came around and reached in to help out the man himself. The Colonel! He was dressed in his trademark white suit. Several advertising executives went over to greet him. The Colonel looked like he didn't have a clue what was going on but he was enjoying it. He waved to the crowd and almost fell over.

Marty came over. "Harland, great to see you. You look terrific!"

"I feel like a mound of dust. The hotel had music playing all night."

One of the ad men yelled, "Yeah, but you're still finger lickin' good!"

The Colonel looked at him as if he wanted to put him in a pressure cooker. "Let me sit down a spell."

Marty prodded him, "Harland, we only have you for a little while. Can we work for a few minutes and then take a break?"

"Sure, but give me a little coffee to get me going."

A coffee cup flew into his hand almost as soon as he said it. He took a sip and Marty started walking him toward the stands. He took a step or two and stopped to rest.

I was shocked by how old and frail he was. He looked tired, and it was only the beginning of the day. I turned to Lillian. "Wow, he looks a lot different than his picture on the chicken box."

"The man's been through a lot. He doesn't even own the company anymore. He's just a puppet."

Marty was bringing him my way. The Colonel was leaning on his cane, which had a gold handle with a chicken on it. He was breathing hard and starting to sweat. Marty was holding him up and looking desperately for somewhere to plop the Colonel.

"You." He pointed at me. "Anyone sitting there?"

"No." *Oh my G-d, he's going to put the Colonel next to me.*

"Help me with Harland, will you . . . what's your name?"

"Steven Gu—"

He interrupted me, "Yeah, I remember, Gluberman."

"Guttenberg."

"Whatever, help me sit him down."

I leaped from my seat and grabbed the Colonel's arm. I remember how skinny his little arm felt.

He sat with a harrumph. Marty bent over. "We'll get you out of here as soon as possible, Harland."

"No problem, Marty, I'm fine as long as I'm sittin'." He turned to me. "Thank you, son, I had a friend named Gluberman, from Tallahassee, in the chitlins business, any relation?"

"I don't think so, sir, I'm from New York." I didn't dare correct him on my name.

"Yeah, he was an ex-marine that had a pig farm as big as this football field. I was in chickens, he was in chitlins. We called ourselves Chick and Chit. Get it? Chick and Chit!"

It was the first time he'd smiled since he came on set, and all the ad men standing on the steps laughed along.

"Yeah, it's finger lickin' good, Colonel!" one of them yelled.

The Colonel mumbled under his breath, "I'll give you a finger lickin'." And smiled back at them.

Marty yelled from behind the camera, "That's what I want to see, Harland, laughing and joking and you having a good time! Freddy, load 'em up!"

A prop man and two assistants descended on all of us with Kentucky Fried Chicken boxes and individual pieces of legs, wings, and thighs. One of the extras shouted, "Hey, this chicken's cold!" Lillian turned back to him and said, "Appreciate what you have, young man, lunch isn't for another four hours."

We all had chicken in our hands except the Colonel, but he seemed delighted to see his product out and about.

"All right," Marty shouted. "I want everyone to pretend to watch a football game. I'm going to have Phil and Randy run back and forth as if they were the players." I looked up and there were the two production assistants standing about twenty yards away on the football field.

There is something that happens on a film set when the camera is ready to shoot. This was my first time seeing it. The first assistant director asked everyone if they were ready. It got really quiet and more serious than I had seen it all morning. No one spoke, except for a transportation driver way in the back. William yelled at him, "Davenport, I want quiet!" The driver stopped talking in mid-sentence. "It's all yours, Martin. Set!"

The sound man called, "Speed!" The camera operator called, "Rolling." Marty said, "Action" and pointed to us in the crowd.

I looked around and everyone was acting their asses off, screaming and rooting for these imaginary teams. I saw the two production assistants running back and forth; they were both out of shape, especially the chubby one. I started to yell and cheer, and it seemed to go on forever. But I didn't care, this was my first scene and I was loving it.

I turned to look at the Colonel. He had both hands on his cane and was smiling. One of the ad agency guys yelled, "Colonel, put your fist up in the air!"

He did and I felt his side leave mine. He started to fall over. I caught him just in time. I grabbed the back of his suit and had him by the coat-tails.

"Cut, cut! What the hell happened?" William pointed at me.

"I don't know, the Colonel started to fall over."

Marty and the rest of the crew flooded the stairs. The advertising guys all started to talk at once.

"Are you all right, Colonel?"

"Jesus Christ, son, why did you push him?"

"Oh my G-d, he's going to faint, someone get him some water!"

The medic ran up. "I have smelling salts, here, give him these."

I still had my grip of his coattails. Marty rushed up. "Are you all right, Harland?" They were wiping his forehead and holding his hands. I saw an ad man rubbing the Colonel's leg. "You can let go of him, Gluberman." I did.

"Oh, I'm fine, I just got a little off balance when I raised my arm. This fella here saved me from going over."

Everyone stopped and looked at me.

The ad man rubbing his leg said, "He didn't make you fall?"

"No, no. For goodness' sake, get off my leg. He saved me from rollin' in the aisle." He turned to me. "Thank you, Gluberman."

"Sure, Colonel, my pleasure." My eyes were as wide as everyone else's.

Marty leaned in to him. "Can we keep going, Harland?"

"Sure thing, just don't move, Gluberman."

Marty turned to me. "Can you handle that, Gluberman?"

"Sure, but can you call me Guttenberg? That's my name."

"Anything you want."

From then on I was gold. I looked at the chubby production assistant panting on the field and mouthed to him, "I didn't screw up."

The rest of the morning was like a song. Every time they had to move the Colonel, he asked me to accompany him. If it was to another section of the stands, I was there. If it was to sit in his director's chair, I was there. Some of the shots with me I was actually holding him from behind so he wouldn't take a face plant.

After two hours the Cadillac showed up and Marty begged for a few more shots. The Colonel complied for a few and then put his hands up. "I'm just plain tuckered out, y'all. Have ya got what ya need?"

"We do, Harland. Thanks for being such a sport. We'll see you in September?"

"I have a contractual obligation, and I won't shirk it. Next time put me at a picnic table with some old folks, this sports thing is way too exciting for me." He shuffled toward the car and turned around. "Where is that young fella?" One of the ad men, the one that kept saying "finger lickin' good!," ran up. "No, not you, ya little brown nose, him." He pointed at me.

I walked over and he shook my hand. "You take care now, son, what's your name?"

"Chick and Chit, sir." And he laughed. "Steven Guttenberg, Colonel."

"Right, I'll see you in the movies someday, I suspect. Just keep your nose clean, Chick and Chit!" He sat down in the backseat of the car, and was off.

I walked a couple of steps and noticed I was standing alone, away from the crowd. I turned around and William yelled, "Let's get back to work, we have two hours till lunch." He looked at me. "You too, Taft-Hartley."

We shot a lot of film in those two hours. We also ate a lot of cold fried chicken. The task at hand was to do all the setups that matched the close-ups of the Colonel. This is when I saw what a first assistant director could do. William re-created all of the extras' and the actors' positions that occurred while the Colonel was on set. He had a fantastic memory, and along with the script supervisor, he got every action that Marty needed to cut those sequences together.

The morning went smoothly and we broke for lunch. I ran up to Lillian walking through the parking lot. "Hey, want to eat together?"

"I would, Steven, but I'm an extra, and you are an actor. You eat over there." She pointed to a tent with a buffet under it. There were tables and chairs set up. "We eat over near that truck." She pointed to a man giving out box lunches. The extras were sitting on the concrete, on apple boxes, anywhere they could get their hands on.

"Well, I'll eat with you wherever you go."

"No, Steven, that's not allowed, I'll have to see you after lunch. But if you can steal me a dessert that would be nice." She walked away. It was the first time I saw the caste system of a set. There are the "haves" and the "have-nots." Today I was a "have."

I walked over to the catering truck and watched as the crew got their food. I got on the end of the long line. Just then the skinny PA came up to me. "You can cut in front of everyone if you want."

I looked at the hungry crew members and thought that just wasn't right. "No thanks, I'm fine."

"That wasn't a request. William wants you to have lunch quickly so we can get you to makeup."

"But it doesn't seem fair to cut the line, does it?"

"There is no 'fair' in this business. Just do as I say and you won't be on William's bad side, which believe me you don't want to see. Besides, actors always cut the line, it's normal." I took his word for it and walked up front to the window of the catering truck. The crew members let me in front of them, but they didn't like it, no matter how "normal" it was.

An energetic man with a chef's hat spoke to me in a heavy European accent. "What can I get for you, my friend?"

"Um, what have you got?"

He sighed. "Amigo, look at the menu." He pointed to a bulletin board.

From behind me I heard, "Come on, Gluberwitz, we don't have all day. Some of us work for a living." The crew was restless.

The chef chimed in. "Let me make it easy on you, we have delicious shrimp scampi, beef Wellington, and penne a la vodka, with not too much vodka. String beans, mashed potatoes, and homemade muffins. You can get salads and desserts on the buffet. Now, sweetheart, what would you like?"

A crew member shouted, "If you don't make up your mind I'm going to feed you Kentucky Fried Chicken." I'd had enough of that for sure, so I chose the penne.

"Good choice, *hombre,*" and he handed me a heaping plate. I walked over to the buffet, took some salad, and remembered Lillian wanting dessert. I took two pieces of cake.

I sat with the other actors and got to know them. They spoke about acting classes, theatrical agents, and how they knew someone that was making one hundred thousand dollars per year doing Toyota commercials. One of the older actors said, "If this runs national, we could make as much as five thousand bucks." I thought that was a fortune.

"That's nothing," one of the girls chirped. "I have a friend that did a Kellogg's and banked twenty-five thousand for one day's work. They made a print campaign out of it and gave her another ten for a buyout."

"What's a buyout?" I asked.

The other birdlike actress answered, "It's when they can use your picture indefinitely, and they give you a lump sum of money."

"They can hump you ten ways to sunrise," the older man added.

"Well, that sounds good to me, not the humping till sunrise, but the money." I still had to pay my parents back for the SAG card.

"You'll learn, sonny, getting a buyout can cost you more in the long run."

But I didn't know how much of a "long run" I would have. I was supposed to get back to New York for school in a few weeks.

The rest of the day was as exciting as anything I had ever done, though I did miss the Colonel being around. When the star is on the set, people step up their talent and behavior. Now the atmosphere became more relaxed, and shooting went smoothly. The last shot was at sunset, with me and one of the actress-birds eating a few wings and holding hands.

"Cut, that's a wrap, ladies and gentlemen." The crew and cast applauded and the set started to dissolve. I just stood there.

"Steven, you can go home now, it's all over." Marty was giving his walkie-talkie back to the sound department.

"We're done?"

"That's what 'wrap' means."

I got into the van and rode back to my hole. As I was undressing there was a knock at the door. It was Randy, the chubby PA. He was holding a clipboard and handed me a pen. "You have to sign out." While I did, I noticed he couldn't look me in the eye. As he turned to walk away he mumbled, "Sorry for giving you a hard time, it's something I have to work on."

"No problem, it's okay."

As I got into my car and entered the L.A. traffic I felt a bit deflated. I was sad that it was over. Being on a set is a real high, and it was my first taste of that drug.

When I pulled into the driveway Michael was out gardening. "Welcome back, Mr. Professional Working Actor! How did it go?" He was so encouraging and a terrific listener. After I unloaded on him, I went to my room and wrote everything down in my diary, then sat on my bed looking out the window wondering what was next for me. *Do I go home for college? Do I beg my parents to let me stay?* What was L.A. going to do with me?

Chapter 3

The next morning I overslept. Michael knocked on my door and opened it a crack.

"Get up, kid, I have something to talk to you about and you're going to like it."

"What?"

"I have been cast in a Universal movie called *Rollercoaster.* It's a big new 'Sensurround' flick about a madman in an amusement park. My friend is the casting director and she wants to see you today. There are lots of parts for teenagers and I told her about you. Now get dressed, we have to be there by nine."

"Oh my G-d, Michael! Wow! Why didn't you tell me last night?"

"One never interrupts a monologue."

I took the quickest shower on record and we jumped in his BMW. When we pulled onto Lankershim Boulevard, the first thing that I saw was a big black building. "That's called the Black Tower," he said.

"It sounds medieval."

"It's where all the Universal executives are officed."

"It looks a lot different from Paramount. It's kind of cold and scary."

"That's how they want it. They want to intimidate you. That's Lew Wasserman's style."

"Who's he? I know an Andy Wasserman from Massapequa. Maybe he's an uncle, maybe I can talk to him."

"Nobody gets to talk to Lew Wasserman unless you are very important."

"I'm important."

Michael laughed as we pulled up to the gate. "Yes, you are, Steven. He just doesn't know it yet."

The guard was a genial man with an Irish accent. "Michael, my boy, top of the mornin' to ya."

"Hiya, Scotty, how are you today?"

"Just fine, but it's only nine o'clock. The big man hasn't come in yet."

He looked through his stack of passes. "Oh, you're going to see Ms. Otto! Isn't she a looker!" He studied the pass. "*Rollercoaster,* that's big-time."

The Universal lot was impressive. There were rows of sound stages right in front of the guard gate, all busy with activity. We parked and walked toward the Black Tower.

"Now, when we meet Linda, let me do all the talking," Michael said.

"Okay."

"No, I mean it, Steven, this is a real casting office with a powerful casting director. Do you know the show *In Search of . . .*?"

"Yes, one of my favorites!"

"Alan Landsburg is the producer and is married to Linda Otto. He produces a lot of television so if you make a good impression she'll mention you to her husband." We entered the Tower and got in the elevator.

"And say what?"

"What?"

"And say what to Alan Landsburg?"

"You *are* green, son. She'll say something that puts you in a good light and possibly he'll give you a job."

"So I'll be using her to get to her husband to get me a job."

"In Hollywood, everybody uses everybody. You'll see."

The doors opened and a beautiful woman was standing there. "Michael Bell, you gorgeous thing." She gave him a big hug and a kiss right on the lips. I thought that was strange. Michael was telling me she was married.

"Linda, you look more beautiful than ever."

"And this must be your godson." I was hoping she wasn't going to kiss me. Maybe Michael didn't care what Alan Landsburg thought, but I did.

"I told you I would bring the little guy in. Steven, this is Linda Otto, one of the smartest people in town. Not to mention the most attractive."

"Oh Michael, stop . . . but don't stop, I love it!" They both laughed. I just stared at the huge diamond around her neck. It was the biggest stone I had ever seen. "Nice to meet you, oh, I'm sorry, I forgot your name."

I kept staring at the rock. Michael began to get nervous.

"Tell her your name, Steven."

"Is that real?" I pointed at her neck.

"It sure is, eight carats." She gave it a kiss. "Steven what?"

"Guttenberg." Out of nowhere I spelled it. "G-U-T-T-E-N-B-E-R-G!"

Michael gave me a look. "Remember what we talked about, Steven."

Linda looked at him. "And what was that, Michael?"

He sort of went pale. "I told him that you were a very busy person and didn't have time to fool around."

"Oh, but I do! It's all fooling around. Now come to my office."

Michael put his finger to his lips. We walked down a luxurious hallway furnished with antiques and into her equally well-appointed office.

I knew Michael wanted me to keep quiet but I couldn't help it. "Linda, I've never seen an office building with all this fancy stuff."

"Mrs. Wasserman picked out all the furniture in all the offices of Universal. Lew likes for her to be involved and this is her touch. Nice, isn't it?"

"It looks like a museum."

"We think so too, but who wants to argue with Lew Wassermann's wife? Not me! Sit, sit."

Michael fiddled with a pencil. "I told Steven that there might be something for him in *Rollercoaster.* Maybe a line or two?"

"Why not. Steven, do you mind reading a little for me?"

"Out loud?" I gave her a big smile.

"Yes, that's how it usually is done here." I don't think she liked that joke. She yelled to someone in another office. "Sylvia! Get me some sides!"

"I'm not really hungry, thank you." I thought I would take another stab at humor. She didn't smile at all. I thought Michael was going to take a stab at me with the pencil.

Her assistant ran in with a few sheets of paper. "Okay, Sylvia, would you mind reading with Steven?"

"No, not at all."

"But Linda, you didn't ask me if I minded reading with Sylvia." It just came out of my mouth. Linda looked at me. I think I saw smoke coming out of Michael's ears.

Linda let out a sigh. "You are funny, I'll give you that. Steven, would you mind reading with Sylvia?"

"It would be my utmost pleasure." Even Sylvia giggled. I looked the sides over and saw an arrow pointed at "Start." I slid my chair over near Sylvia. "Hey, this roller coaster looks tall and scary! You want to ride it?"

"No, it's way too big for me." Sylvia read like a robot.

"Oh, come now, it's just a roller coaster, what's to be scared of?" I put down the sides. "Can I say something?"

Michael was staring daggers at me. Linda sighed. "Sure, Steven, what would you like to say?"

"I just think that a teenager wouldn't say 'come now.'"

"So, let me get this straight, you want to rewrite the script?"

"Um, I don't know about that, but I know a teenager wouldn't say that."

Michael couldn't hold it in any longer. "Steven, just say the words on the page! This fine lady is giving you an opportunity to be in a major motion picture and I don't think you have any knowledge or business to discuss the text!"

"But I . . ."

"No buts, no ands, no nothing. Just read what you have!" Michael's face was as red as a tomato.

"Well, if you are going to yell at me, I need a moment to collect myself." I put my head down.

"That was great," Linda said to Michael with some awe in her voice.

"What was great?"

"That little improv, did you guys work that out at home?"

Michael looked at me, I looked at Michael, and we both started talking at once.

"Yes, no, I mean we did talk about things . . ."

"Well, we really didn't work the whole thing out, we kind of thought about a subject . . ."

"Well, I loved it. It showed range and imagination, and emotion. What do you think, Sylvia?"

Sylvia's mouth was hanging open. "I thought it was . . . interesting."

"I did too. Steven, do you think you can do that on a set with a camera and a hundred crew members watching you?"

"Sure I could, I just starred in a commercial with the Colonel."

"The Colonel, Elvis's manager? He is a pro and has been around forever. If you could work with him you could work with anyone. I didn't know he was doing commercials!"

"Um, I . . ."

"Well then, it's set. I'll find a part for you somewhere in this film. Michael, you have a rare find in this young man. Thank you for bringing him in."

Michael just stared at her. "Uh, yeah, I guess he is kind of special."

"I'll say. See you two on set." She gave him a hug and kiss and we both walked out.

As I walked down the hall I turned to Michael and started to speak. He stopped me.

"Not a word till we get outside."

We walked past the receptionist. "I was listening in, it sounded great!" I didn't say a thing, just smiled.

We walked out of the building. Silence. We got in the car. Silence. He put the key in the ignition and turned to me. "That was the biggest stroke of luck I have ever seen."

"Yeah?"

"If you ever do it again, I'll kill ya."

I wondered if he was serious. But I didn't want to find out.

The next morning I woke up extra early, stole out of the house, and drove to Paramount. I parked and, as usual, said hi to Sam the guard on the way in. He stopped me.

"Where have you been, Steve? We've missed you."

I wanted to level with him, but I knew I couldn't. "I've had a bunch of meetings off the lot, stuff I had to do. I'm going to be here for a few days, then it's back to Universal."

"Universal, our competitor! What are you doing there?"

I remembered Heston. "I'm working on a Heston film, lots of complications."

"The submarine picture? I see they're using our wet stage. I guess Uni doesn't have the facilities we do."

"Of course they don't, Sam, nobody has what 'The Mount' has."

"That's for sure. Have a nice day, Steven."

"You too, Sammy boy." I walked by him. *How long can I keep this thing up?*

As I approached my office I heard a voice barking orders. I turned and saw a rather large man in a three-piece suit coming toward me. He was short, but had to be three hundred or more pounds. His assistant was gorgeous, wearing the tightest pants I have ever seen. Behind them walked several well-dressed executives. The large man stopped and held court. "What I am saying is that she isn't a Carol Channing type, she is a Liza Minnelli type, and I want a Kim Novak type. If you can't do the job I will find another studio to do my pictures in and you will all be sorry we ever had this conversation. Am I making myself clear?"

His assistant chimed in. "Kim Novak, not Liza, not Carol."

The executives all spoke at once. "Yes, Allan." "Of course, Allan." "Whatever you say, Allan."

One of the women executives differed. "But Allan, what about using Raquel Welch?"

"What did you say?"

The whole crew took one step away from her. She visibly started to shake. "I said, why don't we use Raquel Welch?"

He sat his hand on his huge stomach and said, "You, what do you do?"

"I'm in development here, I'm a junior executive."

"Miss junior executive, what is your name?"

"Molly."

"Molly, like *The Unsinkable Molly Brown*."

The other executives took another step away from her. "I don't know."

"You never heard of *The Unsinkable Molly Brown*?"

"No, I don't think so."

"Well, let me give you an education. *The Unsinkable Molly Brown* was a 1964 MGM release, just about the time you were figuring out your Barbie collection and wondering why Ken had nothing going on down below. It was written for the stage by Richard Morris and adapted for the screen by Helen Deutsch. It starred Miss Debbie Reynolds as Molly, your namesake, and Harve Presnell as Johnny Brown. It got six Acadamy Award nominations, not to mention a Best Actress award for Miss Reynolds."

"I didn't know that."

"Well, you should know that, you should have an education in theater and film if you are going to be a 'junior executive,' much less working on one of my films. You are fired, my dear, and I'm doing you a favor." He huffed off, trailed by his disciples.

She looked after them and noticed me standing there. "Did you see that?"

"I did." I was dumbstruck.

"I'm finished, I'm through." She started to cry and sat on the stoop of the building.

"Why? Can't you get another job?"

"I've just been fired by the most important producer in Hollywood, Allan Carr. I'll never be able to professionally recover." I stared at her, not knowing what to do. "Don't ever piss him off."

"Okay."

"Do you mind? I'd like to be alone."

I walked up the stairs to my office. What kind of person could do that? What kind of business was this?

I called my agency and asked when I could get a copy of the commercial. Vic was a bit testy with me. "Steven, you just shot it. It takes time to edit and put the thing together. You just concentrate on getting more work."

"Are there any more auditions coming up?"

"Yes, in fact there is a Dentyne and a Pepsi in the next few days. We'll call you."

"Not if I call you first!"

"And I know you will, Steven." He hung up.

I called Michael to ask if he heard anything about the *Rollercoaster* job.

"Steven, you don't give anyone time to breathe, do you?"

"Yes, I do." I took a long, exaggerated breath. "I swear I don't want to be pushy, but have you heard anything at all?"

Michael laughed, just a little. "I am having a wardrobe fitting tomorrow, so I suspect you will be getting a call too if Linda really wants you for a part. Or she was just saying anything to get you out of her office."

"Would she do that?"

"Yes, Steven, and if she did, you got away unscathed. I've seen her take people apart."

I thought about Allan Carr and that poor woman. I believed him. "Well, if anything happens would you call me?"

"And where would that be, at Paramount?"

I realized if I had people calling the stage asking for me that wouldn't be too good. "No, um, better have me call you."

"No, Steven, you check your machine. That's what professional actors do, and you should do it ten times a day."

"I do it twenty."

"Steven, there is a point when you are no longer cute but aggressive and annoying. Watch that."

"I will, thanks." I knew he was right.

"I'm going to record a McDonald's. I'll see you later. And Steven, don't stay out too late, I don't want to catch shit from your parents. Bye."

I called my machine and, lo and behold, there was a message.

"Hello, this is Robert McAndrews. I'm the assistant costumer on *Roller-coaster.* I want to set up a fitting for you. You work on Wednesday so I would like to do it ASAP. Please call me at Universal."

Oh my G-d, it was real. I really was getting a part in the movie. I picked up the phone.

"Hi, I need to call Universal, please. Can you connect me?"

"Sure, is this the water stage?"

I knew something was coming. "Yes."

"Is Steven there?"

"Yes, this is Steven." I hoped I wasn't getting caught.

The voice got awfully charming. "Hi, I'm Mary Lou and I work next to Margie and she said you were getting Faye Dunaway's autograph for all of us."

"Yes, I did promise that and I'm working on it, she is just so difficult to pin down, you know?"

"Well, can I make a substitution for another autograph?"

This was getting complicated. "Um, sure, I guess so, but you know these stars are so busy, so hard to ask favors of. Who do you want for a substitute?"

"John Wayne."

"Are you kidding?"

"No, he's my favorite. I loved him in *True Grit.* Do you know him?"

"Yes, of course I know the Duke." It just shot out of my mouth.

"Oh my, you do know him. That's his nickname!" Everybody knew that was John Wayne's nickname. "When can you do it? Is he working with Miss Dunaway?"

"I don't know, Mary Lou, but I'll call his office and get it done. No problem." How on earth was I going to get John Wayne's autograph?

"Oh my word! I am so excited! I love you forever!"

"Thank you, Mary Lou. Can I speak to Universal, please?"

"Sure thing!" There was a beat.

"Universal Studios, may I help you?"

"Yes, the wardrobe department for *Rollercoaster,* please."

Someone picked up. "Wardrobe, Robert speaking."

"Hi, this is Steven Guttenberg and I'm returning your call."

"Oh, yeah, we need you in here for a fitting, can you come in today?"

I could come in anytime. "Sure, what time do you want me?"

"Three, three thirty? Just come to the main gate and Scotty will show you where to go."

I was writing it down. "Great. Hey, by the way, do you know what scene I will be doing?" I thought I could find out my role without calling the casting office and bothering them. I remembered what Michael said about being pushy.

"Let me see here." He sounded as if he was turning pages. "Yep, here it is, you are in a scene at Magic Mountain and you are entering a room."

"Um, I forgot, what are my lines?"

"Let's see, oh yeah. 'I'm sorry, Mr. Davenport. I was all over the lot, I couldn't find the key.' "

I scribbled as fast as I could. "Oh yeah, right. Hey Rob, who's in that scene with me?" As long as I was getting information, why not ask. He didn't sound as if I was being annoying.

More shuffling of papers. "It's . . . Bell, Guardino, Segal, and Widmark."

I knew it was Michael, but who were the others? "Michael Bell, right?"

"Yep, Harry Guardino, George Segal, and Richard Widmark."

I stopped writing and looked up. "*The* George Segal and *the* Richard Widmark?"

"Yep, no Fonda though, he's outside when this scene is going on."

"Hen—Hen—Henry Fonda?"

"The one and only, Mr. *Grapes of Wrath*. So we'll see you between three and—"

"I'll be there at three on the dot!"

I hung up and pinched myself. This couldn't be! The ringing of the phone pulled me out of my reverie.

"Hello?"

"Yeah, this is Eddie over in construction. You want me to bring the doors over now?"

I had told myself to never answer the phone. Since the line was spliced, it probably rang on the stage too. But today I forgot that rule. "Uh, I don't know, Eddie, can you call back?"

"Call back? Who the hell is this?"

"On second thought, let me go ask."

"Better answer."

I ran to the stage to ask the question and get back on the phone. The stage doors were open and a whole crew of carpenters and painters were working. I saw a large man with jet-black hair, who looked like he was in charge.

"Excuse me, but I have a message from Eddie in construction. Who can I give it to?"

"Which Eddie?"

"I don't know."

"There's an Eddie Jennton and Eddie Anderson."

"The one that wants to know if he should bring over the doors."

"The doors for the red set or the doors for the green set? I can't tell you unless I know which Eddie and which doors."

I couldn't believe my luck. "I'll be right back. Who are you?"

"Big Red."

I ran down the ramp, across the street, and up the stairs.

"Eddie, which Eddie is this?"

"Why are you out of breath?"

"Eddie, please, we have a lot going on here. Big Red wants to know which Eddie this is."

"Eddie Johnson."

"Eddie Johnson? There isn't any Eddie Johnson. There is an Eddie Jennton and Eddie Anderson, no Johnson."

"I'm new."

"Jesus Christ, Eddie, you are making this awful tough on me."

"I just want to deliver these doors."

"Okay . . . which gosh darn doors."

"The ones for the gold set."

"We don't have a gold set, we have a red set and a green set."

"Well, all I can tell you is I have doors for a gold set. I'm not going to get in trouble, am I? I'm just following the instructions I was given yesterday."

"Don't worry, Eddie, I'll take care of it. Hold on."

"Can you hurry? I have to get to Glendale by five."

"Eddie, I have my own problems. I have to get to Universal by three."

"Really, what are you working on?"

This guy had to be kidding. But I did want to boast, even if it was to the new Eddie. "Got something going on *Rollercoaster*."

"Really, I hear it's going to be big. It's with that new Sensurround system that Universal developed. My brother Ricky is working on it. Maybe you know him. Ricky Summers?"

That stopped me. "I thought your name is Johnson."

"Different fathers."

"Eddie, let me tell Big Red what's going on."

"You don't have to be nasty about it."

"I'm sorry, Eddie, got a lot on my mind. I'll be right back."

"Take your time, life's short."

I ran to the stage and found Big Red chewing a painter out. His cheeks looked like tomatoes. That explained his name.

"Excuse me, Big Red."

"Yeah, which Eddie is it?"

"It's Eddie Johnson."

"Who?"

"He's new." I couldn't believe this insanity.

"Oh, for the love of Pete, he's supposed to be on stage twenty-three. The gold set. And tell him pronto."

"Okay, I'll tell him. Sorry to disturb you." Big Red went back to chewing the guy out and I started down the ramp when I saw the stage phone. I wondered if my phone was a direct connection. I picked the receiver up.

"Hello?"

"Yeah, it's still me."

"Eddie, you are supposed to be on stage twenty-three, pronto." Now I was using the lingo.

"Wait a minute, let me look . . . oh geez, you are right. I had the damn thing upside down. Hope I didn't cause you any problems."

"No, no, it's fine, Eddie. Just deliver the stuff, and hey, how is the traffic out to Universal going to be?" Couldn't hurt to ask.

"It's a bear on the 101 but take Highland to Barham to Victory and across to Lankershim."

"Got it. Highland to Barham to Victory. I'll say hi to Ricky."

"Yeah, tell him I'm gonna go to Mom and Dad's on Sunday."

"Will do." I hung up. At least I got directions. I grabbed my briefcase and the trades and made my way to the car. I passed the guard as usual and he stopped me.

"Leaving early, Steven?"

"Yeah, gotta run down to Universal."

"Take Highland to Barham to Victory to Lankershim. Don't get on the freeway whatever you do."

"Thanks, Sam, got it." As I crossed Melrose I realized these must be inside Hollywood directions. I was finally on the inside.

My Pacer stood on line at Universal as I watched people wave to Scotty and drive on. It seemed he wasn't checking passes. I got my turn at the guard gate. With a wave I shouted, "Hiya, Scotty!" and began to drive through.

"Hey you, stop!" The gate arm fell across the hood of my car and Scotty banged the side of the door. "Where in heavens do you think you are going?" He was pissed.

"Um, I'm going to wardrobe for *Rollercoaster.* Don't you remember me, Scotty? I'm Michael Bell's godson."

"I don't care if you are Marlon Brando's godson. You stop here and check in."

My good mood changed to complete embarrassment. I looked in my rearview mirror and there was a long limousine behind me. An older gentleman with white hair and huge, oversized glasses with thick black frames was sticking his head out the window. "What's going on, Scotty?"

"No problem, Mr. Wasserman, just a little misunderstanding."

"Well, get rid of it."

"Yes sir, Mr. Wasserman." He whispered to me, "Right behind you is the most powerful man in Hollywood and possibly in all of show business since the beginning of time."

"Is that Lew Wasserman?" Wasn't Allan Carr the most powerful man in Hollywood?

"Yes, and every second that we talk is the most expensive second you or I will ever see. Now I'm going to let you on the lot without checking for your pass because if I don't, that six-foot-four monster is going to take both our heads off. Just drive on and don't let me hear you did anything else on this lot but go to wardrobe."

"Okay, Scotty, um, which way would that be?"

"Find it yourself, and don't call me Scotty. You've got to earn that."

There were stages on both sides of me. Stage after stage, much newer looking than the ones at Paramount. I slowed the car to ask directions of a man in a hat. "Excuse me, could you tell me where wardrobe is for *Rollercoaster*?"

"There's a roller coaster on the lot?" His voice was familiar, but I couldn't see his face well under the hat.

"No, it's a new movie starring Fonda, Segal, Widmark, and Guttenberg." I had to try it out, see how it sounded.

"Oh geez, nobody tells me anything. Wardrobe, let me see, oh yeah. Drive straight till the last stage and make a right. It should be directly in front of you." He leaned in to the Pacer. "Say hi to Widmark for me. Tell him Jack said 'Just the facts, Richard, just the facts.' He'll get a kick out of that." I looked at him and realized it was Jack Webb. *The* Jack Webb.

My voice cracked. "Will do, Mr. W."

"Jack, please, Jack. Would love to have a roller coaster on the lot though." He walked away and I marveled at him. The Jack Webb that was in my living room week after week on *Dragnet*.

"Thanks again, Jack." I had to call him that, I just had to. He gave me a wave. It made me forget all about the tongue-lashing I received from Scotty.

Sure enough, at the end of the stages I turned right and there was a huge tan building with a large sign, WARDROBE. I parked right next to a Rolls-Royce. *Things have to be getting better, I'm next to a Rolls!* I got out of my Pacer, making sure I didn't ding the shiny cobalt blue door. The window was open and I looked in. It looked like a hotel. I had never seen so much fine leather.

"Hey, what are you looking at?"

I knew that voice. I turned to see David Janssen from *The Fugitive*. He was standing close enough to touch. "Um, just looking at the car. I didn't touch anything!"

"Settle down kid, it's all right. Have you ever seen a Rolls-Royce before?"

I gulped, "No, sir." Jesus, he was standing right next to me. The Fugitive!

"It's all handmade in merry old England. If I had time I'd take you for a spin. But I got to scoot. You going in for a fitting?"

"Yes, I'm in *Rollercoaster.*"

"Oh yeah, isn't Widmark in that picture?" I could hardly speak. "Tell him Dave said 'Lick your lips.' He'll know what I mean."

"Sure, Mr. Janssen."

He laughed. "Dave, and kid, just remember, fake it till you make it." He smiled and started the car. It purred. He leaned his head out the window. "Hey, word to the wise, make sure Max doesn't stick you, his eyes aren't what they used to be." He looked over his shoulder and backed up. With a wave he was gone. I just stood there in a daze. *First Jack Webb, now David Janssen. I'm on a roll!*

I opened the door to the wardrobe department and the first thing to hit me was the smell. It was as if I had entered the largest old shoe on the planet. The place was dimly lit and enormous, filled with what looked like thousands of costumes.

"Hey, who goes there?" There was a voice, but no body.

"Steven Guttenberg, I'm here to see Robert McAndrews."

A little man holding several pairs of pants leaned over a railing about fifty feet up. "No problem, make yourself at home. There's coffee over there." He pointed to a regal-looking table with an antique coffeepot surrounded by fine china. "Hey, did Janssen leave?"

"I think so."

"Darn it!" And he disappeared. I went over to the table and admired the china. Even in the wardrobe department Mrs. Wasserman left her mark.

A good-looking man with blond hair appeared out of nowhere. I thought, in Hollywood almost everyone must be attractive Extending his hand he said, "I'm Robert, and you must be Steven Guttenberg."

"Hey, you got my name right."

"Sure, it's not difficult to read a cast list, and my grandfather always said that a person's name is the sweetest sound they can hear. Now, let's see what we have here." He checked a rack of clothes right next to the coffee.

I looked around. "How big is this place?"

"To give you an idea, it is about a football field long and half of one wide. It holds the largest collection of costumes in the world. Everything from *Gone with the Wind* to *The Rockford Files,* from Charlie Chaplin to John Wayne."

I thought about my promise to Mary Lou. "Is John Wayne here?"

"No, but we fit him for *The Shootist.*" He found a beige suit and took it off the hanger. "Here, go in there and try it on." He pointed to a dressing room.

I closed the door and wondered if John Wayne used this room too. "Do you know if he's coming back?" I met Jack Webb and David Janssen; maybe I could have a trifecta today.

"No, I think he's on his yacht this week, at least that's what I read in Rona Barrett's column." I opened the door and came out. Robert took a look at me. "Turn around." I did. "Yep, this will do fine, we just have to shorten the pants. How's the waist?"

"Great."

"Okay, Max! We need a little something from your magical hands!"

"Coming!" The little man whose voice I'd heard flew down the wooden staircase. He had pins in his mouth.

I stepped up onto a wooden box and he began to hem the pants legs. "You want cuffs?"

"I've never had them."

"Well, there's a first time for everything."

I felt a painful prick in my leg. "Ow!" I pulled my leg away. Dave was right.

"Sorry, sorry. It's the damn light in here."

Robert shook his head, pointing to Max's eyes.

"Janssen told me about you." They both laughed.

"Yeah, well, Janssen can't see too well either, have you seen his wives?" Max barked back. He stood up. "You look good in this suit, try and keep it when you're done."

"Can I do that? Wow, this would be my first suit."

"Maybe, we'll have to check with the designer, Mr. Miller."

Taking a chance on being pushy I asked, "Can I get a little tour of the place?"

"I would, buddy, but we have twenty actors to fit in three days. George Segal is supposed to be here in ten minutes. How about next time?"

I took the suit off and thanked the guys for being so kind. I pushed the door open and looked at the road leading to the building. I was going to see George Segal if I only waited. *How do I stall for ten minutes? Pop the hood!* I did and waited for almost twenty minutes. No sign of Segal.

Robert came out. "You okay?"

"Yeah, just a little problem with the fan belt." I had no idea what I was talking about.

"Let me see." Oh no. He looked at the engine, felt a few things inside, and said, “Try it now.” It started, of course. “There you go, these Pacers are the worst.” He noticed the hood. “You know you got a dent right here?”

“Yeah, I know.” Compliments of Scotty.

I got in and drove slowly down the road. No sign of the Dirtwater Fox. As I approached the gate my stomach twisted. There was Scotty standing outside. He stopped me. “Sorry about that little incident, lad, I had the boss right behind you. You forgive me?”

“Can I call you Scotty?”

“You can, son, you can.” He tapped the roof of the Pacer and I drove out with a big grin on my face. Things were looking up.

I arrived at Michael’s house and he was standing there with his arms crossed. How did he know about the hood? Did Scotty call him? “Steven, is there something you didn’t do? You didn’t tell your parents about the movie. Now they are all over me and are worried about you not coming home.”

“I’m sorry, Michael. I’ll call them.”

“Right now.” He wasn’t happy.

I sat on my bed and dialed. My father answered. “Hello?”

“Dad, it’s me.”

There was a beat. “Ann, it’s your son.” The unmistakable sound of him handing over the phone.

My mother got on. “Steven, what’s going on over there? Are you coming home?”

My father chimed in, “Oh, he’s coming home all right, that’s it!”

“Oh Stanley, be quiet. Now Steven, Michael said that you got a new job, and that you would have to stay longer, is that true?” She was being extra patient with me. This was a very bad sign.

“I was going to call you, Ma, really.”

“Well, your father is about to have a conniption and if you don’t explain to us what is going on you are on a plane today, no ifs, ands, or buts. Do you hear me, Steven? You’ve been out there long enough and we want you home.”

“Ann, he’s coming home, no movie, no nothing. He is going to college and that’s it.”

“Stanley, stop it, you’re acting crazy.”

“No, I’m not, this is crazy. California. I told you not to let him stay longer the first time.”

“Steven, you hear your father, what’s going on?”

"Are you going to listen to me or just yell at me?"

"Steven, you really aren't in a position to negotiate."

"Negotiate, ha!" My father was pacing, I could tell.

"Mom, I got another job. It's a movie called *Rollercoaster*."

"Oh, Stanley, it's a movie called *Rollercoaster*."

"I don't care what it's called, the only movie I want him in is *Steven Goes to College*. Give me the phone, Ann." I could hear them wrestling over the receiver.

"Back off, Stanley, or I'll take your arm off, I swear." She got calm again. "When would you be finished with this thing? Because your father really wants you to be in school come September. And so do I, Steven. This Hollywood crap is for the birds."

"I'll be home for school, I promise. I only work a day or two and I'll be done. But this is a really big deal for me, Mom, this could be my big break."

"I know, honey, but it's a very strange business, and we are very concerned about you out there." She sighed. "You really think this could be something special? What is the part?"

"I play a messenger or something and I'm in a scene with Michael. I have one line. A line in a movie with Sensurround."

My father perked up. "Sensurround? Like in *Earthquake* with Ava Gardner?"

"Steven, your father wants to know if Ava Gardner is going to be in the movie?"

"I don't know, Mom."

My father picked up the extension. "Steven, I'm upstairs. Is Ava Gardner on the roller coaster?"

"Dad, I don't know who is on the roller coaster. I think a nut is trying to blow it up."

"Do you think you'll meet Ava Gardner?"

"Stanley, Ava Gardner is not interested in you. Do you think if she dumped Frank Sinatra she'd go for you?"

"I don't know, Dad, but I met Jack Webb today."

"*Dragnet* Jack Webb?"

"Yeah, and David Janssen from *The Fugitive*. I saw his Rolls-Royce, I parked next to it."

"Stanley, oh my G-d, our son parked next to David Janssen, the Fugitive. I love him. What did he say?"

"Ann, if you think I have no chance with Ava Gardner you have less with the Fugitive."

"Shut up, Stanley. What did he say?" My Mom was into it.

"He said if he had time he would have taken me for a ride."

"That's it?" My Mom wanted more.

"And that I should tell Henry Fonda—no, tell Richard Widmark—that he should lick his lips."

My father screamed into the phone, "Richard Widmark? You met Richard Widmark?"

"No, Dad, he's in the movie."

"He's on the roller coaster?"

My mother cut in. "Who gives a shit about him, what did David Janssen look like? Was he handsome?"

"He was, Mom, and really smooth. Really cool."

"Oh, I knew he would be. I've loved him since *Dondi.*"

"He wasn't bad in *The Green Berets,*" Dad chimed in.

"Who gives a shit about *The Green Berets*? He had a very nice role in *C'est La Guerre.*"

"Mom, Dad, can we get back to the movie?"

"Yes, I just can't believe you met movie stars."

"Ava Gardner, that's some woman. When do you meet Richard Widmark?"

"I don't know, Dad, but I'll get his autograph for you."

"Nah, I'm not that interested. Ava Gardner is another story."

"Steven, when do you finish this thing?"

"Within two weeks, Ma. And then I'll come home."

"For sure?"

"Yes, for sure."

"Stanley, what do you think?"

My father sighed. "I don't know, all these crazy people out there with these crazy movies. Is Michael taking care of you?"

"Yes, Dad, I'm eating and not doing anything crazy."

"It's okay with me if it's okay with your father."

"Dad?"

"Okay, just two more weeks, Steven. Then I want you home."

"Thank you, Mom. Thank you, Dad."

"It's okay, dear, just keep your word. We love you and miss you very much."

"I love you too, Mom, I love you too, Dad. I'll call you first thing tomorrow."

"Good night, Steven, I'm hanging up now. Stanley, are you still on?"

"Yes." My mother hung up. "Steven, we love you and care about you. Just be careful."

"I will, Dad."

"Okay, and say hello to Ava!" He laughed and hung up the phone.

Whew, that was a close one. I sat on the bed, and thought about committing to this. Something inside me knew I had a shot at this business. I looked up and Michael was at the door, arms crossed.

"What did your folks say?"

"They said I can stay. I've got two weeks."

He smiled. "Congrats, kid. Now, you film in the next two weeks. I'll get the exact dates for you."

"I can get them too, no problem. I can call."

"You can!" He laughed. "This is getting good, now you know where to call."

"Yep, I'm paying attention. I think I can do this."

He looked at me quietly. "You have to think about this now. Do you really want to commit yourself to this? Because this is a seven-day, twenty-four-hour job . . . career. And this business is going to throw you around like a rag doll. There are things out there in the bogs that you could never dream of. Good, bad, and ugly. You have to ask yourself, are you ready in your heart?"

I looked at Michael and the seriousness of the moment gripped me. I was not yet eighteen and my teenage brain was attempting to decipher what was happening. "I think so."

"You think so? Well, you better have an attitude that works better than that."

"I do, I'm just stunned."

"Well, get over it and get on the ball tomorrow. Oh, and you're welcome." He was smiling as he walked out.

I took out my diary. This was going to be a good entry. I had started a diary for a few reasons. I wanted to chronicle this adventure, and have a history of what I was doing every day. Writing gave me some comfort, like what I was doing with my life was real and meaningful. It was such a dream to be in Los Angeles. I wanted to have it take some form. So every night, I recorded the day's events, adventures, and emotional ups and downs. I had something that said this life was worth it.

Chapter 4

I woke up on Saturday morning and got on my way to Paramount. On Saturday the studio was quiet, and I always found I could organize myself. Having my secret office gave me a place to make phone calls and plan things out on paper. I always wrote my daily plan. I felt that writing it down gave me something to follow. I was alone on this acting journey, and I think it was important to have the silence that being alone brings. Time to think. I would park at my usual spot across the street from the main gate, and wonder if I would ever be able to park closer. I already wanted a spot on the lot. I saw the convertibles and trucks that got on, and thought it was so cool that they could just bound out of their cars and enter the energy of the lot.

I walked across the street and saw a Mercedes pull up to the gate, and as I punched my card I saw who was driving. It was Ralph Malph from *Happy Days.* I didn't know him as Donny Most, all I saw was the funny best friend of Richie Cunningham driving a modern car, talking to the Paramount guard. *Happy Days*! One of my favorite shows. I watched him as his Mercedes pulled ahead into a primo spot not that far from the gate. Lucky duck. I walked through the gates and saw him taking out some golf clubs. Hollywood star, golf clubs, fancy car. That was the life.

I walked through the Western Town that day. It was always one of the treats on the lot. I could go from the Wild West to New York to old Victorian times in three blocks. Some of the buildings had working storefronts. I saw one of the streets set up for shooting. The equipment was all there, waiting for Monday. I saw signs for *Little House on the Prairie,* the Michael Landon-directed western. I imagined myself in the middle of a busy set with Landon directing me. Daydreaming again.

There was a message on my answering machine when I checked it. "Hi, Steve, this is Peter Burrell, second assistant director of *Rollercoaster.* Can you call me here at Universal and I can tell you your day out of days."

What the hell was "day out of days"? I finally had "pronto" down, and a whole other Hollywood term bamboozled me. I picked up the phone and asked one of the operators to connect me to Universal.

"What have you got going on over there?" she asked. "Some sort of coproduction?"

I didn't know what the heck a coproduction was. "Yeah, sort of. It's a film."

"Am I talkin' Swahili? I know that. What film?"

"*Rollercoaster.* It stars—"

"Yeah, yeah, I know it. My cousin Ernie is doing craft service, and I have a friend in accounting. They say Fonda is the nicest person. Have you heard that?"

Did everyone know about this movie? "Yeah, Henry is quite a guy."

"They call him Hank. If you see him call him Hank."

I liked talking to the operators. It felt good to talk to the one real part of my imaginary office.

"Universal Studios, may I help you?" Another operator now.

"Can I have Peter Burrell on *Rollercoaster*?"

"Am connecting."

These Universal operators were not chatty. Was that Wasserman's influence?

Pete got on the phone and it was official. I had a day, next Friday. "How are you getting here?" What was the correct answer? I wanted to be perfect.

"I have a Pacer."

"No, Steven, where in Los Angeles are you coming from?"

Another blunder. I needed to get the lingo. "From Mulholland near Coldwater."

"Okay, I'll have one of the PAs call you with directions."

"Good, thanks, Pete, I'll see you Friday."

"It's Peter."

I swallowed hard. "Sorry, Peter." There were a few beats of silence.

"I'm just messin' with you, kid. Call me whatever you want. Just don't call me and tell me you're late to the set. See ya."

I had a week to get ready. What I should get ready for I didn't know, but I sure as heck wasn't going to be late.

Driving back to Mulholland was always beautiful. I loved driving by all the shops on Sunset, the tattoo shops, the Comedy Store, the clubs, the discos. I would drive through West Hollywood, where Michael had a girlfriend who wrote for television dramas, and then get to the Beverly Hills Hotel. I'd make a right onto Beverly Drive, and there the atmosphere changes. The air gets lighter and the birds sing louder. When the road turns onto Coldwater Canyon the houses are more rustic but just as big and expensive. The intersection where Coldwater meets Mulholland didn't have a light then. Making the left onto Mulholland at rush hour was like threading the eye of a needle. It was the last moment before I would look up, see Ernest Borgnine's house, and then make the right down the steep driveway to Michael's. I told him about my day for *Rollercoaster.*

"How do you know it's Friday?"

"I spoke to Pete, Peter Burrell."

"Oh, he's great. I worked with him on something else. Might have been the *Night Gallery* I did." Steven Spielberg directed Michael in an episode of the Rod Serling show. "We work together that day so we'll drive together. I don't want you to be late."

"What happens when you're late?"

He stared at me. "All we have is time. That is all we have to make a film. And that time is finite and fleeting. We have to respect the producers, director, crew, studio, everybody involved in the making of a film. Just like the flapping of a butterfly's wings in Cairo can affect the weather in Oklahoma, a person being late affects the whole crew. Never, never, be late."

I nodded. Michael didn't turn away.

"Never be late. Got it?"

I knew he was trying to teach me. Michael knew what it took to survive as an actor.

That week I looked at my lines. They were simple and to the point, and the script went something like this:

INT. ACTION PARK CONTROL ROOM: DAY
The room buzzes with activity. Several of the policemen are at the table. The captain speaks up.

CAPTAIN

We have to find out what is going on in this guy's mind. Is he planning for something else?

The door opens and in come two detectives and the park manager.

PARK MANAGER

Don't worry, we have it all under control. Fellas, let me handle it. No need to make a big deal.

```
                    CAPTAIN
      It is a big deal, we have a maniac in
      this park. I want him found and put out.
```

Now I enter. My character walks with Michael toward Richard Widmark and the police. Then I had my first line.

I read it over and over. An actual movie script! It had been delivered to Michael's house. One script for him, and one page for me. He had the part of the park manager, and seeing him study his part was an honor. Michael is classically trained. He read the screenplay constantly, and had his own actor's workbench where he got prepared. Preparation in acting is such an important piece of the whole. Preparation gives confidence.

Thursday night before I shot, there was a knock on the door. I opened it to find a fellow who couldn't have been but a few years older than me. He was out of breath. It had started raining and he was soaked.

"I've been looking for this house up and down Mulholland. The sign is so small. Anyway, here is the call sheet. You Michael Bell?"

"No, I'm—"

"Glutterberg." Could anyone get it right?

"Yeah, but I'm . . ." I saw him looking over my shoulder. He wasn't listening.

"This sure is a nice house. You live here?"

"Yeah, with Mr. Bell, he's my godfather."

"I got a godfather too, he ran away with a prop girl." He looked into the den. "One day I'm going to be a producer and get one of these." He put up his hood and turned down the path. "Hey, I'm Joey. I'll see you on set."

"Are you a PA?"

"Yeah, why do you think I'm delivering call sheets in the rain? See ya."

Michael sat with me and explained what a call sheet is. It has all the information about the day's shooting, sunrise and sunset, the production phone numbers, and a list of cast and crew. It's daunting to read one at first. It looks like the guide for an airplane takeoff.

I spent the night before the shoot in my room learning my line. My discipline was weak and I had no idea what I was doing. But I knew to learn that line.

The next morning my alarm went off at four thirty and I jumped up. It reminded me of going crabbing with my friends and getting up this early.

But this was going to a movie set. And I had a line. And I knew that darn line.

There was a traffic jam on Coldwater Canyon on the way to Ventura. Traffic that early? A sign of things to come. As we came down the hill the view of the valley was exciting to me. But on the hot days, there was a brown fog above the buildings.

"It's smog, and it just sits there," Michael explained. "It's because of the mountains. And the emissions."

"Smog? Sounds like a band." I was really ignorant about this. Like most Americans in 1976.

Michael looked forward as he got to Ventura. He would just stop when he saw I couldn't grasp something. The sun started to come up and we were on the freeway. It was moving. We weren't late. And I knew my line.

When you pull up to a movie set, it is like arriving at an army base run by carnies. It is buzzing with people. We were met by someone who reminded me of the assistant director on the KFC commercial. "Morning. Who are you?"

"Michael Bell, and I have here Steven Guttenberg."

"I see Bell, but no Gluberwitz." He squinted at me as if I was crashing the party. "Is he a visitor? Because he needs to get an okay."

"No, he's an actor. Steven Guttenberg." Michael winked at me.

"Oh, yeah, here he is. Yeah, Michael, you are in a two-banger. And you, you got a honey wagon."

Michael went to his trailer, and I went into mine. It had a bathroom, which was an improvement on KFC. The suit I had tried on at Universal was hanging there, along with shoes, shirt, everything. This was a big deal. I never wore a suit.

I put on the suit and looked at myself. The pants were too short.

"Where's the flood?" A grip threw that at me while I was walking to makeup.

"I don't know." I looked between him and the PA that was taking me to the makeup trailer. The PA knocked on the door and opened it.

"Stepping up." More showbiz jargon. It's said so that your entrance won't be a surprise, in case, for example, someone is having their eyeliner done. Many of these sayings come from technical and safety necessities.

This was the second makeup trailer I had been in. So it was old hat for me. When I did theater at home, I had a difficult time with eye makeup, especially the liner. I was able to take my time with it then. Here, in Hollywood, there was no time for the irritation. I had to sit back and let the makeup artist scrape a pencil under my eyeball. It needs to be done, and fast. No blinking. No matter how it hurts. Get on with it.

I went back to my honey wagon. On the way the PA asked if I was hungry. I was always hungry then. He showed me the craft services table. I looked at this massive table with every kind of candy, cookie, cracker, fruit, meat, sandwich, drinks, and the pretty girl serving it all. Was I in heaven?

"What do you want?" The PA was talking into a walkie-talkie at the same time.

"Um, I'll take a cookie, and can I have some red licorice?"

"Yeah, anything you want."

I couldn't believe he said that. Here was a vision that any eighteen-year-old would embrace. "How much can I take?"

"As much as you want. Hurry up, they are going to need you."

I loaded up my pockets and went back to my honey wagon, but not without Michael seeing me.

"What have you got in your pockets?" All of my pockets were stuffed. It was obscene. "Steven, they give us food all day. Do you know that?"

"I just thought they wouldn't bring me back to it."

He sighed. "Have fun, kid, and I'll see you on set."

I sat in my trailer for three hours. I ate everything in my pockets and, of course, felt full and sluggish.

The door opened without a knock. "Hey, we want to walk you up in five."

Pulling my pants low, I brushed my hair and repeated the line. I kept repeating it as I sat for the next hour. Another knock on the door.

"Really sorry. This time it's for real, five minutes. Really sorry, Gluberwitz."

I sat for one more minute and he swung the door open. "You're on!" I walked quickly with him. "They want to get this before lunch." It was about eleven thirty.

We rounded a bunch of trailers. Thick cables lined the ground. As I got closer to the set the vibe of the people changed. The closer to the lights, the more I felt the excitement. You can feel it as you follow the black cables to the center of it all. As I walked on the set I saw someone just shining. He stood out. Tall, strong, silver-brown hair, a wide smile, and confidence oozing out of him. It was Richard Widmark. And what a presence. He was powerful, charismatic, and ready to work.

I got closer to the lights and the first assistant director met me. He introduced me to James Goldstone, the director. A lively and focused guy, he had some fine clothes on and looked very successful.

"You're Michael's godson, yeah? Linda told me about you." He tussled my hair. "Geez, how big is that fro? Anyway, let's have a good time, and we got— Len how much time before lunch?"

Lenny was a huge man. *Another assistant director?* I wondered. "Forty-five."

"Great, we can get this in forty-five. Len, where's Harry?"

Harry Guardino walked in. "I'm here, just on the phone with my wife. Where is Segal? Why am I here when Segal isn't here? I'm going back."

"If you're going back, I'm going back." Widmark laughed. They all started laughing. It was a joke that I later would hear all the time: "If he's not on the set, why should I be?"

I looked around. It seemed like a thousand people were going in and out of the "hot set." I got a bit dizzy. I had to blink my eyes a few times to get back to solid ground. I started to sweat. I felt it around the starched collar of my shirt and on my scalp.

Michael was talking to Guardino and I could see him watching Widmark. Everyone was. Widmark was such a powerhouse. He was a cinema icon, had won the Academy Award for *Kiss of Death* and starred in *Judgment at Nuremberg.* It was enough to make you just want to stare at him.

"Hey, Steven, come here and meet your fellow actors." Michael was waving me over.

I walked gingerly over the cables toward the bright lights. I felt the heat once I got on the set. It really was "hot." Michael ushered me toward Guardino. I recognized him from *Dirty Harry.*

"Harry, this is my godson, Steven. He is playing my assistant. First job too."

Guardino laughed and put his hand out. "Oh my, first time." He took a drag from his cigarette. "You're going to do great." He turned to Widmark. "Dick, this kid's a first-timer, be nice to him."

"I don't like first-timers."

My smile froze at a crooked angle. Did he just say that? Michael's smile was frozen too. Harry started to stammer.

"I don't like first-timers," Widmark growled again, and walked over. He grabbed my hand. "I love 'em." He broke into a gigantic smile and his eyes danced. "I do! I love 'em because we all were beginners once. This is going to be fun, kid. How many lines?"

"Two, or one big one." Sweat was running down my sideburns.

"Take the pause and take control of both the lines. Make them yours." He turned to the director. "Jim, when can we go?"

Goldstone was looking into the camera and with a squint said, "Two seconds, Richard." There was a lot of activity around the camera and the buzz on the set started to pick up. Someone yelled for rehearsal and the buzz lessened. Michael leaned in to my ear.

"Just do exactly what they say. No improvisation, no new lines. Just do your lines nice and easy."

"Okay." I had no idea what was going on, I just said it.

"What's your line?" Michael was fixing his collar. I mirrored him.

"Hey, it was tough to get these plans." I paused. "The park is huge."

"Don't pause."

"Yeah, but Richard Widmark said to take a pause."

"Yeah, well, Richard Widmark doesn't know you. Just do it in one breath and you will get it done. Don't fool around." Michael left me and walked up to the makeup lady. I felt a jolt on my arm.

"Come on, you're supposed to be outside for rehearsal." An attractive lady was pulling me. She was in incredible shape and pulled me like a rag doll.

As we approached the door a beach-bum type came up to me. He had shorts on, which I thought was strange to wear for work. Later I learned that crews love to wear shorts, even in the winter. He handed me some rolled blueprints. "Here you go, pal, these are the actual plans for some new rides on the tour. They are copies but don't mess them up, okay? Got them because my nudnick of an assistant forgot to get the real prop plans." He looked over his shoulder at a teenager shuffling his feet. Also in shorts.

"I didn't know I was supposed to get them, Dad," the kid said.

"We call me Phil here, not Dad," the prop man said.

"Okay . . . Phil." His son was holding in a laugh.

The woman opened a heavy metal door and pushed me outside. "Okay, you see this light?" She pointed toward a bare red bulb on a stand just outside the door. "When it goes on, you enter. Got it?" She was serious as hell. I didn't recognize that look then, but it was the look of raw, fierce ambition. "I said, got it?"

"Yes, when I see the light go on, I go in."

"Right, and make it pronto." There was that word again.

"Of course, pronto!" I laughed, thinking that I was in on a trade secret, the "pronto" club.

She shook her head. "Don't fuck it up, we want to go to lunch."

And the door shut. I looked at the bulb; it wasn't on. So I looked around and saw the exact opposite of what I was feeling. The vibe here was relaxed and most of the crew was at ease. The door cracked open and she popped her head out. "You ready?"

I was staring at a man spray-painting a board. "Huh, yeah, yes."

She frowned, then shut the door quietly.

And I forgot to watch the bulb. I watched a man eating a bag of pretzels. They looked great.

The door flew open. "Is something the matter?" It was her again.

"No, everything's fine."

"Then why didn't you come in?" She pointed to the bulb, which was bright red. It was blinking and flashing and doing everything but pulling my sleeve. "Do you think you could come in when it blinks, please?"

I felt completely stupid. "Yeah, I guess I was looking at something else."

"Well, this time just look at the friggin' light, okay, sport?"

"Yes, pronto."

She shook her head and shut the door.

I wasn't going to miss it this time. I stared at that bulb and I didn't take my eyes off it. I tried not to blink. No way was I going to screw this up.

It didn't go off. The door flew open.

"You fuckin' moron. Do you think you could enter, please?" A few other PAs surrounded her and I heard the first assistant director coming at me.

"What's the problem here, son? Cherry, what's the problem?" As she was about to throw all the blame on me a burly man in shorts made his way over.

"Our fault, Chief, someone kicked the plug out on the last take."

Take, I thought, *what does that mean?*

The assistant director shook his head. "Sorry kid, our fault." He looked at me. I could feel the sweat dripping down my face. "Are you all right, kid?"

"Yeah, I just sweat a lot when I get nervous and I was watching the light and it didn't go off. I swear I was watching it." I felt the sweat collecting in the armpits of my shirt under the nicest suit I had ever worn.

He put his hand on my shoulder. "Relax, kid, it's one line, and we'll have you outta here in a half an hour. Then we'll have lunch. You can eat with me at my table. How's that?" He saw that I was shook up.

I let out a sigh and a laugh. Cherry smiled and gave me a tickle on my ribs. "Yeah, sport, it's going to be fine." She whispered in my ear, "Really, Goldstone is pissed as hell, we are two days behind in ten days of shooting and you are a favor. So just get this done, 'favor.' " She pulled back and smiled what I learned was the shark smile. All teeth, no emotion, no caring.

A bell went off. "We're on a bell!" she yelled, and shut the door.

In about a second the light went off, I walked in to the stage, and there was the set in front of me. Full of lights and people, and everything was pointed at me. I walked in and said my lines. Perfectly.

Goldstone yelled out, "Do you think you could come over to the other actors, kid?" I noticed that I was about fifty feet from everyone else.

"Sure."

"That would be great, kid. Can we go again right away, pleeeeeeee-ase." It was the "pleeeease" that gave it away. They wanted to eat lunch.

I felt my arm rip from its socket as Cherry dragged me to the stage door. We went outside, she pointed to the light, she pointed to her watch, and she made a cutting gesture across her neck. I got it. I was going to get this crew to lunch and I was going to say my lines in the correct place.

It seemed like hours before the light went on. I almost missed it watching a showgirl in full costume walk by the stage, with five costumers around her. I saw the light in the corner of my distracted eye and grabbed the door and flung it open. I walked through the lights and stepped up to the immediate set and said my line, perfectly. Widmark looked me up and down and chortled.

"I think he's ready, Jimmy, and by my chronometer we got twenty-five minutes till *la comida*."

Goldstone smiled at me. Were those the same fangs I had seen on Cherry? "Soooo, let's put some powder on the kid and shoot this pronto."

"Pronto, sir."

The set started to buzz at a higher frequency. If you hang around sets often enough you can tell when they are gearing up to shoot even before you hear "We're on a bell" and "We're rolling!" Everybody gets a little more on their toes.

"Hey, sport, we're waiting." Cherry was standing by the open stage door with two ladies carrying what looked like travel bags. One was for makeup, the other hair. And next to them was a wardrobe assistant. So many people looking at me. Up and down. Scrutinizing every millimeter of my face, hair, and clothes. As I approached this gaggle, they literally attacked me with a soft powder for my forehead, and a comb through my Afro. The wardrobe lady was wiping my collar with what smelled like dry-cleaning fluid. I hadn't smelled that odor since my grandparents owned a dry-cleaning shop in Brooklyn. It was getting on my neck and beginning to sting.

"Um, excuse me, but I think that fluid is irritating my neck a bit."

She looked at me with steely eyes. "Yeah, well, if you didn't have makeup on your collar, and you kept the tissues in your shirt like we told you to, we wouldn't have to put seriously dangerous chemicals on your pretty little skin." That shut me right up. The rule is when you leave the makeup chair, the actor has tissues in his collar to keep the makeup from coming off his chin and getting on the shirt. I didn't know this and had used the tissues to wipe the sweat off my palms. Big mistake.

Cherry chimed in, "Next time, keep the f-ing tissues in. If there ever is a next time, sport." She smiled and showed me her pretty fangs.

"Oh, there'll be a next time." At that moment, I wasn't really sure.

"Oooookayyyy." And she shut the door.

I watched that light as if my life depended on it. At that moment it did.

A car went by with clowns in it. I didn't look. I heard a gaggle of girls behind me, walking with loud shoes, probably high heels, meaning these were probably showgirls in skimpy outfits. I didn't look. You could have blown up a car and I wouldn't turn my head. I was going to get this right.

I think I heard the light before it flashed. My hand was already on the handle, and I pulled it open. So hard that it made a bang that shook the building. But I kept going. I walked into the set, right up to Michael, and said, "It was rough to slev these, the . . ." Pause. Pause. "The paaa, is . . ."

"Cut!" A bell went off and the set was flooded with moving bodies. And a lot of them were coming toward me. First was James Goldstone. He was smiling. I let out a sigh and before I could utter a word, he cooed, "No problem, kid, happens to everyone."

"Me included and foremost," Widmark growled out of the side of his mouth while getting powdered by his very own makeup man.

"And one more thing, don't tear the door off the hinge. Mr. Wasserman will blow a gasket," Goldstone said.

"Okay, let's get back to it. Steven, back outside, and please put us on a bell!" the first assistant roared. And along came Cherry.

"Favor, we have twenty minutes to get your coverage, and hopefully some of your humble costars. So please, Mr. Actor, let's do this nice, and then let's all have lunch. Capisce?"

What the hell is capeesh? "Sure, but everyone flubs up, the director said so."

She did the sign for "lock your lips." The door slammed shut.

Again I stared at the light bulb. Behind me it sounded as if someone was giving out money. Hoots and hollers, but I didn't flinch.

The light went on, again I pulled the door open, much gentler than before, and walked in. Michael came up to me and gave me my cue.

"Cut!" There was a bell, and no movement this time. Only Goldstone. "Kid, where are the blueprints?"

I looked at my hands. The blueprints definitely were not in them.

"Here they are." Cherry sounded as if she'd discovered a new planet. "They were left outside, by the light bulb."

I couldn't move or breathe. But I sure could sweat. I was covered with makeup people, hair people, and dry-cleaning fluid.

"Kid, no problem, but I really want to get this before lunch." I saw a man in a dark suit standing by Goldstone's chair. He looked like a banker.

"I don't know what happened, I must have put them down when I went to tuck my shirt in."

"Does he really need those? Let's let him come in without them. It'll be easier." Widmark turned and winked at me.

Goldstone sighed. It was the first time I saw a superstar actor like Widmark play set politics. Smooth, very smooth.

"We need the plans for the scene, Dick." Goldstone was good at it too.

"Okay, plans it is. How much time we got?"

"Ten minutes."

"Then let's saddle up, amigos. My man here, what's your last name?"

"Guttenberg, Mr. Widmark."

"I like it. German. Okay, let's get Guttenberg outside, I got a feeling he's going to ace it. Right, Guttenberg?" He looked at me with those eyes that I had seen in film after film.

"Correcto, amigo." Where did I get off echoing his Latin flair? He laughed and turned away.

Again I felt a jolt and Cherry pulled me through the makeshift sound stage. She stood me straight up as the makeup, hair, and props people fiddled with my body. I noticed it was the prop man's son who was giving me the rerolled blueprints. He whispered to me, "Listen, you got to get this right or they're going to can you. I saw a guy yesterday get fired for sneezing during a take."

"What's a take?" I really didn't know.

"You're fucked, man."

"Let's go, Brandon, stop talking to the talent." His father stood a few feet back.

"Okay, Da— I mean Phil."

Everyone dispersed and I opened the door and looked back at the set. Everyone was looking at me and their watches simultaneously. Except for Widmark. He looked like he knew a secret. I smiled, no one smiled back.

I stood at attention in front of that door.

I went over my lines.

I held those blueprints fast.

I walked in and screwed it up again. And again. And again. The crew was grumbling. The men in shorts fifty feet above in the rafters were pacing. The director was talking with the man in the dark suit and they were both shaking their heads. They pulled the first assistant director over and he shook his head. And they all turned and looked at me. Not pretty. The director walked over to me. He put his hand around my shoulder.

"Kid, this is something I don't like to do." And with a little nudge we turned and started to walk off the set. I knew what was coming. Everyone did.

"Then don't do it." I turned to see Widmark lighting his cigarette. He took a long draw and blasted it into the air. The light picked up the smoke religiously. "If you do, the kid will be banged up for life. Lose his confidence. Can't fire him, Jimmy, not here, not in front of me. And with all due respect, Herr Director."

"We are at the six-hour mark, Dick. The crew wants to eat, and the line isn't that important." Goldstone held his ground.

Widmark looked around at the hungry souls and asked the first, "Can we get a waive from the crew?"

"We have to ask the shop foreman." The first assistant director looked at a very large grip. "Well, Dan?"

Dan was also in shorts and flip-flops. "Sure, but we got to eat soon, these guys have had a very long day as it is. We agree to waive the lunch penalty."

The set started to move again, everyone to their places.

"You got a reprieve, kid." Goldstone squeezed me a bit and walked to the camera.

I started to go to Widmark to thank him. He put up one hand and mouthed, "Later, amigo."

I would like to tell you that I got it right that very next take. But I didn't. It took another fifteen minutes that could have cost the company a ton of money if the meal penalty was enforced. But finally I got it.

Goldstone held his hands high in the air. "Cut and print and thank you, Lord." The set started to empty.

Two big hands grabbed my shoulders and I spun around. Widmark grinned at me.

"How did it feel, buddy? You still like it?" He started to loosen his tie. Michael looked over his shoulder at me with a big proud smirk on his face.

I said something ridiculous like, "Um, it was good. Thanks for helping me."

"*No problemo, caballero,* now let's get some lunchy." He turned to go and I yelled after him.

"Hey, Mr. Widmark, David Janssen told me to tell you—"

"To lick my lips, right? Tell Janssen to comb his hair." And he walked out the big double doors, just as they were opening and the light poured in. His cigarette smoke hit the light and made a halo. Like out of a movie.

"Pretty good, kid, now you have to do it again for us." Michael was taking off his jacket and handing it to a waiting wardrobe assistant.

"I thought I was done?"

"No, we have to do coverage on the other characters in the scene. Is that all right with you? Now save me a place in line, and remember, crew first." Michael walked toward his trailer.

Coverage? What the heck is that? I saw a few crew members walking toward a tent and I followed. They must know where lunch was.

Hollywood really puts out a first-class lunch for the crew. There was a tent bigger than any I had ever seen, except for the circus. Underneath were tables with every sort of epicurean delight that can exist. And a few feet from the tent was a food truck. Next to it was a barbecue. The amount of food that came out of the serving station was unbelievable. I started toward the window and I heard, "Crew first." A large man in a Hawaiian shirt with the requisite shorts on stared down at me.

"I know, I was just looking."

He slowly shook his head and I walked to the end of the line. And there was Harry Guardino. Michael joined us.

"Your son, Michael?"

"No, godson."

"He did good. You did good, kid. Just don't lose it for my coverage." He laughed. "Just kidding, I nod a lot during the scene, so it doesn't matter what happens. But you can hold the script if you want. Always used to make me feel better when I was a young actor off-camera."

Michael and he started to talk about New York. I thought about my Father. And I wondered where Ava Gardner was.

"What can I get you?" A smiley face poked out of the serving window of the truck. I looked at him blankly. "Um, I know you have a lot on your mind, but would you kindly choose an entrée, there are about a hundred people who still need to be fed."

I looked over my shoulder and sure enough, there was a line as far as I could see. "Hey, Favor, could you move it along? We only have an hour for lunch." I could always count on Cherry to point things out to me.

"Actually it's an hour from the last person in line, so it doesn't matter that much." Harry laughed and shrugged his shoulders. "That's the only Screen Actors rule I know."

He and Michael got into a discussion of the Screen Actors Guild, and about actors getting paid residuals. The accounting methods in 1976 were much less accurate than they are now. While they talked I looked around at the carnival of movie-making that came to Six Flags to shoot that day. There were at least twenty or so ten-wheelers, and 150 crew. There were at least that many lookieloos and all the park employees. And they were watching us eat lunch!

"Okay, hot stuff, what's your pleasure?" I looked up and there was another face staring at me from the opening of the truck.

A crew member from five or six people back yelled, "Come on, kid, read the menu, you can do it."

I started to sweat. "Give me the . . ." I froze up.

"He'll have the almond chicken, Marcel." I knew that growl. Widmark. "Kid, you gotta get that sweat thing checked. I knew a guy that the Duke called the Human Sweater. Makeup once used a whole box of tissues on him on *Rio Grande*." And he walked off with a grin.

"It doesn't get better than that, Steven. You got the star of the movie taking care of you." Michael gave his order and I took my tray. I walked over to the salad bar, which was as elaborate as any catered affair. I loaded up my tray with as much as I could carry and found a place to sit with room for Michael and Harry. Maybe Widmark could get me a picture of John Wayne for Mary Lou.

During lunch, the different departments sit with their own. There are the smattering of departments that mix, but pretty much you will find the ADs with each other, camera, makeup, wardrobe, grips, all sitting together.

"Hey, sport, you aren't going to spill on that suit, are you?" A short and emphatic wardrobe lady shook her finger at me. "I only have one of those."

Michael put his tray down and mumbled under his breath, "Tell her you'll change for lunch."

"I'll change for lunch." She smiled and resumed her conversation with the wardrobe department.

I looked at Michael. "Thanks for the tip."

"Bring me back a Coke." He pointed at my tray. "Steven, don't take so much, they'll think I don't feed you."

I walked to my dressing room. There was a piece of tape that said DAY-PLAYER on the door window. I thought that it was an accomplishment to have a day on a movie. Especially a Universal film.

But there was a smell. I felt a tap on my shoulder and I turned to see a burly man with goggles on the top of his head and a lit cigar. The smoke from his cigar was overpowered by a noxious odor. "We gotta drain the tanks, it's right under your hole so I would get your stuff out of there or it'll reek for two weeks." He was holding an enormous hose and looking toward another man by a sewer truck.

"How long do I have?"

"About ten seconds."

I jumped up the steps, tore open the door, grabbed my stuff, and boom, there was a smell that would make hell seem like a florist's. I ran down the steps.

"I thought you said ten seconds."

"They were Hollywood seconds, cheap and fast." He and his partner laughed.

I walked to a separate honey wagon that had a men's room and changed.

"Steven, why didn't you leave your clothes in your dressing room?" Michael was just finishing his meal. A few of the crew were done eating also.

"I had to change in the—"

"Yeah, well, you only have a few minutes to wolf down that tray of food. You've got to get back to makeup for a touch-up, then back in your wardrobe and back on the set."

I felt someone behind me.

"Mr. G, would you mind coming to makeup a little early? We want to get a jump on Mr. Widmark's coverage." Cherry. What could I say? I was starving and the tray of food, colder now but still edible, was staring me right in the face. But so was Cherry. I figured it out quickly. Always say yes.

"Sure, can I put my food in something so I can eat it later?"

Cherry grabbed me by the hand and we scooted through the picnic tables. "Here's the deal. I'm on the edge of being fired. There are two other ADs that have more seniority over me and they need to cut someone this week. I don't want it to be me. So I want to ask you a favor."

"You want a favor from me?"

She said yes through gritted teeth.

"Let me get this straight, after torturing me all day you want me to do something for you?"

She turned all soft and feminine right in front of my eyes. "Widmark likes you. If he tells the front office that I am his favorite AD, then I can stay. If not, I go. And I want you to convince him of that."

I had no idea of the "what's in it for me?" routine. "Sure, um, now? Or do I go to makeup?"

"You go to makeup, but on the way is Widmark's trailer. Just poke your head in and say something."

We walked past truckloads of grips and electricians. Then I saw my first big-time movie star's home away from home. The trailer was about thirty-five feet long. It looked to me like a hotel. There was music playing, and I saw Widmark talking to someone on the step. They were in a very spirited conversation. Cherry nudged me.

"Go on, I need this job."

I leaned back. "No, no way. I know when not to interrupt someone, and now definitely is that time." I looked at her. "And another thing. I'm not your whipping boy, okay? You rode me all day, and I'm grateful to have this job, but you've got to give me a break."

I thought she was going to blast me. She just looked down.

"Okay." And she walked away.

I think Cherry had what many successful types in Hollywood have. The ability to change course in a second. Just want something so badly and then abandon it when need be.

I was carrying my wardrobe in my hands, and walked toward my honey wagon. Surprise, no odor. Not a whiff.

"They need you for a touch-up, Mr. Guttenberg." It was the same guy who had dropped off the script.

"Hey, remember me? You came to my house to deliver the script. And you got my name right." I was happy to see a familiar face.

"Yeah, I remember you." He hesitated, and looked as if he wanted to talk more, but looked over his shoulder and saw another PA waiting. "They need you now." He turned on his heels and walked away. Didn't look back.

That was another short lesson. Don't confuse friendliness for real friendship. I once heard if you want a friend in Washington, buy a dog. Perhaps that is true in Hollywood too.

The rest of that day was a blur of running to the set, waiting for the cameras to set up, and standing off-camera for hours waiting to say my one line. When actors have done their parts on-camera they then sit next to the camera and give lines to the other performers for their on-camera close-ups.

I have heard stories of actors not getting along with their costars and literally staying in their trailers while the script supervisor reads the off-camera lines. One of the most famous stories is one about the series *Moonlighting* in which Bruce Willis and Cybill Shepherd would not talk to each other, much less do off-camera lines. I have never been in that position, although sometimes I would have liked to talk to no one rather than some of my costars, and I'm sure they felt the same way. It's a shame that it happens, but sometimes personalities clash and huge arguments occur, wasting time and money. Sometimes it's easier for an actor to emote with a mop head rather than their costar.

But this time, all the actors were such pros that they made this process look easy. They gave each other abbreviated cues, they were able to skip mounds of dialogue and end up at the right line every time. As opposed to the carnival that accompanied the filming of my part, these actors ripped through the pages quickly. Michael, Guardino, Widmark, they all handled their close-ups with ease, and were able to help the director and camera crew get what they needed, while satisfying the emotional and physical demands of the scene. There was no drama, other than what was on the page.

Widmark was last. He sat smoking a cigarette until it was his turn. When the camera was ready, he set the cigarette on the edge of his chair, and did his dialogue. He was so on book that the cigarette never went out between takes. He took a drag, and shot his part. Two takes on each angle of the camera. With a smile and a good word to the crew.

"That's it, Dick, you want to try anything else?" Goldstone stood with his hands on his hips, awaiting instructions.

"I'm happy, but if you don't mind, let me do one for the cheap seats." Widmark smiled, the crew giggled. He made them a bunch of adoring fans.

They geared up for one more. Goldstone rolled the camera, and quietly said, "Action." Widmark did it in his own time, and it was a lot bigger than the two previous takes.

"I like that one, Goldy, can you make sure the cutter sees that?"

"That's the one we are going to use, Dick. And thank you, everybody."

The first AD yelled, "That's a wrap!"

The crew started to disband, similar to a club crowd seeing the lights come on after last call. Widmark had an assistant or someone taking him off-set and Michael gave me the eye to say good-bye to him.

"Mr. Widmark, I just want to say . . ." I stumbled, and started to sweat.

"You say, 'It was a pleasure to work with you,' and you shake my hand, kid." He took my wet hand in his. "But you've got to get a handle on your perspiration, amigo." He laughed and turned to go. "And if you see Janssen, cancel that hair dialogue, he's touchy about his locks."

On the way home, Michael kept telling me what a good job I did, and that this could be just the beginning of my career, if I wanted it. I think he was more excited than I was, if that was possible.

Chapter 5

The next morning I was up early and on the phone with my parents.

"Did you meet Ava Gardner, what was she like?" I could hear my father rubbing his hands together, waiting for a juicy story about his favorite actress.

"Um, I didn't meet her, Dad."

"What? I thought she was going to be on the roller coaster."

"No, I wasn't on the roller coaster, Dad. I was in an office scene."

"An office scene? What the hell were you doing in an office scene? I thought you were supposed to be on a roller coaster. Ann! Pick up! This whole thing was a bunch of malarkey. He wasn't in a movie with Ava Gardner, he was in an office scene."

"Stanley, the office scene was in the same movie. All the actors don't do all their scenes together. What is wrong with you? Your son was in a big-time movie with Richard Widmark and George Segal."

"I don't like Richard Widmark. He has given me the willies since he threw that poor old lady down the stairs in her wheelchair. But George Segal? You didn't tell me that. *Where's Poppa?* was great. Was he on the roller coaster?"

"No, Dad, he plays a detective."

"George Segal as a detective? I don't know."

"Stanley, we're not talking about whether you like George Segal or not, this is Steven's big break."

"I don't know about that, Mom."

"You are the best, always remember that. And who are you to tell me that this isn't your big break? You are my son and I think this might be the beginning of something."

"When are you coming home for college?" my father said quietly.

"Soon, Dad, I just want to try a little more."

"Okay, but orientation is around your birthday, and I want you up there."

"I will be, Dad."

I hung up. Michael stuck his head in my room. "Steven, come into the kitchen, I want to talk to you."

What could this be? I walked into the kitchen. Michael had a serious face on. "I want you to get a job."

"A job? Where do I get a job?"

"Get on your bike and ride up and down Ventura Boulevard until you come up with something. If you are out here, you are going to work, as an actor or a waiter or selling encyclopedias."

"But my father wants me home."

"Well, if you want to go home, go. If you want to stay, get a job."

I stopped at every possible employment opportunity on Ventura. Finally I found a job as a waiter at Farrell's Ice Cream Parlour on Van Nuys Boulevard. I made about eight dollars in tips my first day. A fortune for me. I soon got a second job on Ventura at The Sports Fan. I finally started to make enough money so that I could afford gas for the Pacer and use it to go on what seemed like thousands of auditions for commercials. I started to get a lot of them. So many that although Cunningham and Associates didn't sign me, the agents took me to lunch. That's a good sign, it means you've got something going on.

Vic, Rita, and Marcia Hurwitz (who is a big shot at the Innovative agency now) took me to Hernando's Hideaway in the Beverly Hilton Hotel, a watering hole of the rich and famous. And lo and behold, who was sitting two tables from us but Warren Beatty. As I ate my Cobb salad, I couldn't help but stare. Vic had to tap me on the shoulder.

"Steven, you have to put the salad in your mouth, it's falling all over the table and floor. You can't do that at Don Hernando's."

"Sorry, but that's Clyde sitting over there, as in *Bonnie and*. He is just so perfect."

"Yeah, well, he lives here, and if you keep staring, Don is going to throw us out." He motioned toward the impeccably dressed man near the maître d's booth. Even Don looked like a movie star.

I did everything I could not to look at the most handsome man onscreen next to Paul Newman, ate my salad, and listened to the agents talk about everything but me. I soon learned that the conversation doesn't have to be about you and your career. Just the fact that you are at the table with your reps is all the attention you need.

At the end of the lunch we walked out to the valet stand.

"Steven, give us your ticket." Vic was handing his to the valet.

"I don't have a ticket, I parked on the street."

Marcia smiled at me. "You parked on the street, where did you find a spot?"

"Near Santa Monica Boulevard."

"You walked ten blocks to the restaurant? No one walks in L.A."

I did. There was no way I was going to pay the valet to park my car when all I had to do was hoof it for fifteen minutes.

"Next time valet it, you were sweating for half an hour," Vic shouted as he got into his Mercedes. "You almost made my chicken into chicken soup."

They drove off and I watched the line for valet fill up. Lunch is an important ceremony in the entertainment business of L.A. So much so that the vehicle one has could be the difference between a deal or going back to the office empty-handed. My Pacer just wouldn't cut it in the long line of foreign cars. American cars aren't the auto of choice among the movers and shakers. Except for one man, Jeffrey Katzenberg, who is famous for, among other things, driving a tricked-out Ford Mustang.

I walked the ten blocks to my car. There was a ticket for fourteen dollars. Ten times what the valet would have cost. And three and a half hours' work at Farrell's.

I commuted between my Paramount "office," work, and the myriad commercial auditions and shoots so much that I started to live out of the Pacer. I was hardly home, but Michael didn't mind. He believed in a 24/7 work ethic for an actor. It really is the only way to make it in Hollywood. Perhaps in anything.

Michael had agents from a now defunct agency called ACM, run by Paul Woodville and Edgar Small. He introduced them to me after my success in commercials. That is the way it is in Hollywood, one piggybacks on the success of other jobs. Now that I was picking up some steam, they agreed to meet with me.

"Kid, you got no credits, no look, and a dreadful name." Edgar always had a cigar in his mouth.

"But I know I'm good. I can act, I can do something."

"Will you change your name?" Paul was an ex-actor himself.

"To what? It's my name." At that point in my life my name was still pronounced with a "Gutt" as in "cut."

Edgar stared out the window of their Sunset Boulevard office. "Something less ethnic, yet strong, something like John."

Paul jumped in. "Yeah, and a last name that means going somewhere, like a trip, like an adventure. Yeah, like John Adventure!"

"Johnny Adventure." Edgar made smoke rings.

"Johnny Adventure. Look at him, he's Johnny Adventure." Paul clapped his hands. "No, shorter, Johnny Venture!"

Edgar laughed. "Like Rock Hudson, like James Dean. Johnny Venture, I like it."

"But I already registered my name with the Screen Actors Guild as Steven Guttenberg, and it cost me five hundred dollars."

"Steven Guttenberg isn't a marquee name, kid, you gotta think bigger."

"I really don't want to change my name, it's on all my papers, my license."

Both their faces showed such disappointment. Edgar took a long drag on his cigar.

"Well, it is a famous name, Johannes Gutenberg," I said.

"The printer; he wasn't an actor. I still like Johnny Venture!" Paul said it with such gusto, I started to like it.

Edgar was staring out at the Cock 'n' Bull restaurant across the street. "Hey, there's Jack Lemmon, he looks good."

"What if we shortened Steven to Steve?" Paul was searching.

"And his last name could be Lemmon? Steve Lemmon?"

"What about Steve and we pronounce Guttenberg with a 'goo.' Steve *Goo*tenberg."

"I like that. It's classy, yet real. Paul, you're a genius. Okay with you, Steve Gootenberg?"

"Yeah, I guess so, can I keep the spelling? The line at the DMV is always a mile long."

"Sure, why not. Steve Gootenberg it is. Now let's go have some lunch at the Cock, maybe we can sign Lemmon."

"Good idea, I'm starving." Paul shook my hand. "Congratulations, Steve Gootenberg."

They both went past me and out the door.

"Want me to join you for lunch?" I was starving too.

Edgar popped his head back in the office. "Not till you get a job. But good try, kid. We aren't officially representing you yet, but once you book something, we'll negotiate it. Now go out and hustle. And remember you aren't Steven anymore, you're Steve."

And I sat in the smoke-filled office with my head shots in one hand, and my new name in the other.

From my car, parked up a hill off of Sunset, I could see Edgar and Paul pitching Jack Lemmon. They were much more animated than when they spoke to me. They were on the hustle. They were pouring on the charm.

And Lemmon wasn't buying. He kept waving them away. They didn't budge. That's the persistence that one needs in the business. On any level.

Persistence can get you through brick walls. Not everyone is going to buy on the first time. You have to go back and back. And meet. And be talked about. And be recommended. And not be afraid to cold-call.

One of the most powerful casting directors at the time was Hoyt Bowers. He cast all of Paramount's films and television shows. His office was just a few precious feet inside the Bronson Gate but millions of miles away for most unknown actors. Of course, my secret office was just a movie studio block away.

One day, I approached his office. There were about fifty Native American actors in full war paint standing in front. I navigated my way through the tribe and found my way into the entrance of his office. I overheard his secretary on the phone.

"We need more Indians, double this amount. And more feathers, aren't Indians supposed to have lots and lots of feathers?" Pause. "But we didn't order an exotic tribe, we ordered something that Clint Eastwood would shoot, an everyday tribe." Pause. "Because Mr. Bowers wants more Indians, and more feathers, that's it."

I rounded the corner and saw the first multitasker of my life. This woman was typing a letter, talking on the phone, drinking coffee, smoking a cigarette, and motioning me in. She slammed the phone down, and without looking up she sang through her clenched teeth, "What can I help you with, dear?"

"I would like to see Mr. Bowers, please. I'm an actor."

The coffee cup, the cigarette, and the typing all stopped in unison.

"How did you get in here?" She took a drag from her cigarette. Not looking at me.

I knew this wasn't a good question. "I had another appointment on the lot."

She started typing again. "And who were you here to see?"

I said nothing.

She sighed and took another drag. "I suggest you take a walk out that Bronson Gate while I'm still in a good mood."

"Can I talk to Mr. Bowers for just a minute?"

"You've got balls, I'll give you that. But now I have to cut them off." She picked up the phone and dialed. "We've got an unwanted visitor, Pat, could you please come in here?" She went back to her typing, smoking, and coffee drinking. Never looking at me.

I pulled out my head shot. "Can I leave this with you?"

I felt a hand on my shoulder, a large one. "Son, you have to come with me."

This was the biggest security guard I had ever seen. I turned around and I was looking at his belt.

"Sylvia, you want this picture? Should I file it?"

"Sure, with the others." She motioned toward a pile of photos. It had to be taller than the security guard.

"Put it up there, son." I tried my best to put it on top but couldn't reach. The guard took my picture and gently laid it on top. "All these dreams, all these dreamers. What's your dream, son?"

"Right now? To meet Hoyt Bowers."

It wasn't the manhandling when he threw me out the gate that bothered me. It wasn't my attaché case being thrown onto Melrose Avenue. It wasn't even the Native American actors getting one more whoop in.

It was that Sylvia never looked at me. That I didn't even have a chance. I needed to figure that out. And I needed to meet Hoyt Bowers.

Vic Sutton had left a message on my answering machine. "Steven, we have another appointment for you. Can you do a Travolta imitation?"

I called back. I said I could. I also told him my name was now pronounced "goo."

"Who told you to do that?"

"My new agents. Well, they aren't my official agents, but if anything happens they'll negotiate it." When the words came out of my mouth I realized what a strange deal that was.

"Steven, these are agents who won't sign you, but if you get anything they will take the commission?"

"I think so." I started to sweat.

"And will they submit you for anything?"

"I don't know. Maybe." I had no idea what the deal was with Paul and Edgar. I was just glad they were talking to me.

"You have to get things straight with people in this business. It's all verbal here. It's a relationship business, Steven. I mean 'Steve Gootenberg.' "

I sat with my diary that night and wrote what Vic told me. I had no idea what it meant. But I did know I could do a Travolta impression.

The audition for the *Welcome Back, Kotter* board game commercial was packed with Sweathog look-alikes. There were Barbarinos, Washingtons, Epsteins, and Horshacks. I looked as much like Travolta as I looked like Robert Redford. But I could do a mean imitation.

"Steve Gartengerg?" They called me in for my turn.

"Gootenberg." I liked the sound of it.

The room had a few people in it. They wanted to hear my Travolta. So I went into it. I swung my hips, smiled, laughed, and even played the game with the director. I got the job. When I found out, I called my parents.

"I got another job, Ma. It's a commercial for the *Welcome Back, Kotter* game."

"You're going to be on *Welcome Back, Kotter*! Stanley, he has a starring part on *Welcome Back, Kotter*!"

"Mom, it's the game."

"What game, they have a game?"

"I haven't heard of a game for that show." My father was listening in.

"Dad, it's not out yet, that's why they're doing a commercial."

"When do you film this thing?"

"Next Thursday."

"And how much longer do you want to stay out there?"

"I don't know, Dad. I got another job, so maybe I can do something out here."

It got quiet. "I'm very happy for you. Where are you doing it?"

He didn't want to like it. But like most of us, the glamour was tempting. I'd been there for two months already, but he was still worried about my staying in Los Angeles. And with good reason. My father knew more than I thought he did.

"You'll be back for August, to go to school, right?"

"Yes, I think so, Dad."

"You think so, or will?"

"I will." I didn't know if I could keep that promise.

The shoot was a few days away and I used that time to get an appointment with Hoyt Bowers. My office gave me an advantage, I hoped, including an inside line.

"Margie, could you get me Hoyt Bowers, please?"

"Got something going with him?"

"Maybe, do you know him?"

"Just enough to know no one gets to see him unless you are a big-time mucky-muck. I'll connect you."

I put on my best professional agent voice and started to rehearse what I would say. "Hi, this is the ACM agency, and we were wondering if we could get an appointment with Mr. Bowers for one of our newest young actors. Hi, this is the ACM—"

"Why are you repeating yourself?" I recognized Sylvia's voice.

"Oh, sorry, I didn't know you were on," I stammered and was back to my own tone.

"Then why were you talking? Who is this?"

I hung up. That went well.

Thursday rolled around quickly. I had to get up at four in the morning to leave at five to arrive in Sylmar by six thirty. Sylmar is north of Los Angeles, up the 405 freeway. Even at five in the morning there was traffic. I rehearsed my lines over and over while reading the directions and eating breakfast. Not surprisingly I had my first encounter with the Highway Patrol.

I pulled over. I had learned from my father, who had been in the NYPD, to stay in your car and be polite. I did the opposite and approached the squad car. Luckily the cop entertained my coming toward the window.

"Did you say get back?"

"Is a duck's ass watertight?" He still used the loudspeaker.

"Is a duck's ass what?" The freeway was buzzing past us.

He pushed me back with his door. "Go back to the car, please." He shooed me toward the Pacer. I got back in.

"Do you know you were driving under the speed limit? License and registration, please." I pulled out the necessary documents, and of course started to sweat. I looked at the clock. It was 6 A.M. I had a half hour to get to the set.

"I'm on my way to Sylmar, I'm shooting a *Welcome Back, Kotter* game commercial."

"What *Welcome Back, Kotter* game? They have a game?" His face softened, the glasses came off. "Me and the missus love that show. I didn't know they had a game. Do you have an extra one in the car?"

I didn't, of course. But we got into a discussion about how his wife was a schoolteacher and loved the show. He didn't give me a ticket after I promised to send him a copy of the game.

"Will Gabe Kaplan be there?"

"If he is, want an autograph?" His face lit up. Another autograph promise.

He drove off with a wave and I wiped the sweat from my forehead. Sweating already.

I drove through a suburban neighborhood in Sylmar. It was quiet until I came to the private home that was our set. Ten-wheelers lined the cul-de-sac, and I was guided toward a parking spot. A PA approached my Pacer.

"They still make these?" He had a baseball cap on. Did they all?

I ignored the put-down. "I'm Steve Guttenberg, here to play Barbarino."

"I'll bet you had problems on the hills." He laughed and pointed me toward makeup. It's there that I met my first actor friend, John Starr. This guy took over the makeup room, which is a feat in itself. He was playing Horshack, the nerd, and was completely prepared.

"I've been watching tapes of the show, writing background stories on my character, and have been living like Horshack since the day I got the part. I asked for a copy of the game, got it early, and have been playing it since last Wednesday. What have you been doing?"

That stopped me in my tracks. In fact most people in makeup stopped their primping and looked at John.

His makeup artist laughed. "You've been preparing for this? It's a commercial."

"It's a role that I take seriously. Like all my parts. Don't you agree, Travolta?" He laughed the horse bray of Horshack and turned toward me.

I gave him my best Barbarino impression. "I agree with you, Arnold, I just don't understand what you said."

The AD came in. "Stepping up! We have a rehearsal in ten, can I have the meat?"

I looked around the trailer for food. John whispered to me, "We're the meat."

"And I need you in ten. Let's shoot this sucker and get out of Sylmar."

One of the things that I remember most about this shoot was an actor named Thomas Carter. Tom played the character of Washington. He had fire in him. He wanted to be in all the shots, he improvised, he came up with new lines. He gave the director new ideas and things to choose from. A lesson to me. Come prepared, and prepared to come up with new stuff. Add to the scene, add to the story.

Yes, this was a commercial, and albeit a small one, but I took away important lessons from both these actors. John has since gone on to be a television executive, and Tom is an accomplished director, with *Coach Carter* and *Save the Last Dance* among his credits. I also realized that Sylmar wasn't so bad after all. I left the set and walked to my Pacer. I saw John on the way.

"If we get on the freeway now it'll be bumper to bumper," he said. "Let's grab a burger at Tiny Naylors. I've even got a coupon."

"I can't tonight, I'm waiting over at Farrell's. Got to be there by eight."

"Then here's my number. Call me. I have these pizza parties and I invite the most interesting people. You might be one of them." He turned and headed toward a vintage Mercedes. "And don't forget to call, you need some actor friends."

I showed up to Farrell's that night with my makeup still on and my hair blown out Travolta style.

"You look like a bad version of Tony Orlando." The busboy didn't mince words.

"Travolta. I'm supposed to be John Travolta. In a commercial."

He looked me up and down and squinted his eyes. "Yeah, I think I see it, but his lips are bigger."

I spent the rest of my shift shuttling to and from the bathroom, staring at my lips in the mirror. In this business you can have a hundred professionals tell you how good you are, but if one busboy doesn't like you, it bothers you all day.

Back at Paramount I sat at my desk poring over *Variety* and *The Hollywood Reporter.* I would search the columns for possible projects that I would be right for. And lo and behold Hoyt Bowers was casting for *The Barbary Coast,* a television series starring William Shatner. Captain Kirk! This was a perfect opportunity to meet Bowers. I knew *Star Trek* backwards and forwards, that had to be a help.

"Hi, Margie, can I have Hoyt Bowers's office, please?" I had a plan.

"You and he have a relationship going now?" She and I were getting pretty chummy.

"Well, yes, we are working on a project."

"Is it with Ms. Dunaway?"

"Yes." I don't know how that came out of my mouth.

"Well, you'll be able to get that picture for us."

Uh-oh. "Of course I will. Now let's get Bowers on the horn so we can get working, pronto."

Margie giggled to the other operators, "Not long now, girls, Steve is working with Mr. Bowers and Faye Dunaway!" I heard cheers.

"Casting." Sylvia had a cigarette in her mouth, I could tell.

"Hi, Sylvia, it's Charlie over at *Little House.* We have a package for Hoyt, do you think you could trot on over here? It's from . . ." I looked over the production names for the show in *The Reporter.* "From Michael Landon."

"Can't Michael have some one trot it over here?"

"Confidential, you are the only one he trusts."

"Well, in that case, I'll be right over."

I knew I only had about fifteen minutes. The *Little House on the Prairie* set was across the lot and Sylvia looked like a fast walker.

I gathered my briefcase, put on my sport coat to look important, and bounded down the stairs. I rushed out the entrance and bumped right into a dapper man and a beautiful woman.

"Take it easy, kid, what's the rush?" His deep, melodious voice seemed to have its own reverb.

"I'm sorry, I . . ."

"I thought this building was empty, whose office is up there?"

"Uh, no one, I think I'm in the wrong place." I started to sweat.

"Where do you want to go?" The woman had to be a beauty queen.

"Mr. Hoyt Bowers's office."

"Hoyty Toyty." The man laughed. "Tell him Evans wants that list on his desk by two. And kid, don't go in that building anymore, it's not safe. Besides it's haunted by Gable and Lombard." The beauty queen laughed, he took her arm, and they were off.

Great, my office was unsafe and haunted.

I approached Bowers's office. Sylvia's desk was empty. His door was ajar and I could hear that he was on the phone.

"If we can't have Dunaway, we're going another way. Older, younger, I don't know. But don't waste my time." He hung up.

I knocked on the door and poked my head in. "Excuse me, Mr. Bowers? Can I have a minute of your time?"

"What the . . . Sylvia!"

"She's gone, sir, I think she went to the *Little House* set." I walked in. He just stared at me open-mouthed. "My name is Steven Guttenberg. No, let me correct that. I'm Steve *Goot*enberg and I wonder if I—"

There was a familiar hand on my shoulder. "Hi, son, we meet again." I turned to look at Pat's belt buckle. Did Bowers have a silent alarm or something?

Sylvia knocked on the door. "Him again? Sorry, Mr. Bowers."

This time Pat was somewhat kinder while tossing me out the gate. "Do you know how many actors are trying to see Mr. Bowers? Let me give you some advice I would give my own son. You look like a good boy. Find something else to do, anything, but just get out of show business. It's no place for a decent fellow like yourself. And if I find you here again I'm going to screw your head off and hang it from the Paramount sign. Have a nice day."

I walked from the Bronson Gate back to my car, wiped the sweat from my forehead, and went right back in the main gate, waving to the guard as I re-punched in. I was going to get my appointment with Bowers if it killed me. And judging from the size of Pat's hands, it might.

Paramount had a small gym on the lot. It was actually a historic landmark, where some of the first movies were filmed. I think D. W. Griffith used it as a sound stage. It smelled like sweat-soaked wood and had all kinds of antique exercise equipment. I started to use it as my personal gym. Very rarely would I see anyone in the building, other than two writers from *Happy Days* who used it as a place to work.

One day I went in at an unusual time for me, about eight at night. I heard a familiar voice down one of the dark hallways. There were other voices, but the loudest was one I recognized. I snuck down the hall and peeked into a small window. It was a sauna, and there was Michael Landon with a few of his cronies, stark naked, taking in the heat. I listened as he talked about Lorne Greene from *Bonanza.*

"Lorne loved bacon. He could eat bacon with anything. Ice cream, fruit, you name it."

I thought this was a perfect time for me to enter and learn something, even if it was only about bacon. So I took my clothes off in the hall, and sauntered in. The hot air hit me like a thousand-pound weight. I had never been in a sauna before.

"Close the door!" the whole gang shouted in unison. I chose a spot near the heater. Not a good idea.

"You're going to fry, kid, sit next to me." It was Merlin Olsen, the three-hundred-pound football player who was about to join the *Little House* cast.

"No, I'm all right." Sweating was my specialty.

I listened to Landon talk about directing, writing, and showbiz politics. Someone kept pouring more water on the coals. It got hotter and hotter. I must have passed out because the next thing I knew Landon was pouring ice-cold water on me as I lay naked on the gym floor.

"We almost lost you in there, kid. You got to know your limits." There he was, the star of *Bonanza* and *Little House,* naked as a jaybird and slapping my face.

I bounced up. "I'm okay, I'm okay." I wasn't, and fell down again. Olsen picked me up like a baby and sat me on one of the stools.

"Stay here and keep drinking water. Hydrate, hydrate." They must have forced about ten gallons of water down my throat.

I kept going to the gym, and sitting with them day after day. The people I heard stories about in that sauna ranged from Mae West to Charles Blühdorn, the owner of Gulf and Western, which controlled Paramount. Landon was a wealth of information. I even learned that Hoyt Bowers liked McIntosh apples.

My direction was clear. I stopped at a small bodega on Melrose and bought a bag of apples. My call to Sylvia was easy. I said that the on-set store had free cartons of cigarettes as a promotion for the secretaries. She couldn't get out of the office fast enough. Enter me, again.

"You are kidding, right? You're back again?" I knew Bowers must be ringing the silent alarm, so I had to do something extreme. I jumped on his desk and started dancing.

"I'm the Gucci of young actors but I'm stuck on a shelf at Woolworth's. Please give me a chance, give me five minutes to talk to you. After that you can have Pat throw me out the Bronson Gate and I'll never come back."

I felt the enormous paw on my leg and for the first time was face-to-face with Pat. "You're going to be a part of the sign now, son."

Sylvia ran in, out of breath. "No cigarettes, no nothing. You!"

Bowers must have been having a good day. "You have chutzpah, kid." He laughed. "I like that, now get off my desk and take a seat. Back off, Pat, it's charity day."

He gave me more than five minutes. We had to be in there for an hour. I told him all my dreams and he told me the realities. And he made a call to Fran Bascom at MTM Enterprises. He got me a meeting for a television movie called *Something for Joey,* based on the true story of football player John Cappelletti and his brother.

"Now get out of here so I can work. And don't do this to anyone else on the lot. You might find yourself hanging from the Paramount sign, and I wouldn't want to see that."

After that, I had Mr. Bowers in my corner for many years. I don't know why he was kind to me, but I will always appreciate it.

Chapter 6

I had no idea MTM Productions was named after Mary Tyler Moore, the television icon and one of its founders. I thought it was an offshoot of MGM until I went to the audition.

"Steve Guttenberg?" The casting director, Fran Bascom, pronounced my name the new way. We walked down the hall to the audition room. "Hoyt told me you have a lot of chutzpah and you might have talent. It's enough just getting in to see him."

The door opened and I immediately recognized the director, Lou Antonio. He was a guest star on one of my favorite television shows.

"You're the half black, half white character from *Star Trek*!" I blurted out.

Thankfully Lou had a sense of humor. He was an actor turned director, and there is something special about that combination. He had only one question for me. "Why do you want to be in this movie?"

I knew about John Cappelletti as a Heisman-winning football player from Penn State. The Cappelletti story, about John and his younger brother, who had physical challenges, was famous in college sports culture. I had read the script and knew that Geraldine Page was playing the mother. I knew that this was going to be a movie with integrity. But my answer was simple.

"If I don't get another job, I have to go back to New York."

"That's it? That's the whole reason?" Both Lou and Fran stared at me. "Nothing else?"

"Not the whole reason, but I think I'm really good, I'm dedicated, and I can add to your movie." I remembered Tom Carter, giving something more to the story.

"We'll get back to you, thank you."

The seven words an actor hates to hear. I put on my best face and walked out to my Pacer.

"Hey, Mr. Guttenberg." I turned and there was Fran at the front door.

"You've got a call-back. Monday, two thirty." She smiled and turned toward the door.

The four words an actor loves to hear. I had a call-back. A chance to show my stuff. That whole weekend I did nothing but work on the role of the little brother. The fact that it had maybe ten lines didn't matter, I studied those lines as if I were going to be doing Lear at the Globe. On Monday I was at MTM an hour early, sitting on the curb when Lou pulled up.

"Did you sleep here, kid?" He laughed and walked in.

I waited, and waited, and wasn't seen until four o'clock. I was the last actor in, and Lou and Fran gave me as much time as I needed for my reading.

"You sweat a lot, Steve. Are you all right?"

"Yeah, it's a nervous reaction." I started to sweat even more. Fran gave me some tissues, and I blotted my face. I left with half the tissues clinging to my skin.

Two hours later, on the pay phone at Farrell's, Paul Woodville said he would officially sign me as a client. "You've got a job, Steve Guttenberg, you've got a job." Four more words an actor loves to hear.

I was early every day I worked on *Something for Joey.* I watched the magnificent Geraldine Page, who later won an Oscar for *The Trip to Bountiful,* prepare for scenes, and improvise moments that weren't on the page. Marc Singer, who played John Cappelletti, gave me pointers on how to use the camera, and get some technique. And Linda Kelsey, who eventually found her way to Minnesota and its theater community, was like a big sister to me, making sure I was on my mark. But the real surprise on that show was the associate producer, Roger Young. He and I got along famously, and he was intrigued with one thing about me: the fact that there was a virgin in Hollywood.

"This just doesn't happen, no one is a virgin in this town. The second you step off the bus someone fucks you, literally and figuratively." He made it his mission to find someone to take care of business. It became our daily joke.

"Find anyone yet, Roger?"

"Not today, but I will." This went on for the whole shoot, until one day.

"Find anyone yet, Roger?"

"Yes, I did, Steve."

I swallowed my Adam's apple.

Roger had a friend, a divorced lady in her thirties who was willing to do a little charity work. On the day of the event I must have taken fifteen showers. Roger gave me her address and patted me on the back.

"Only one deal-breaker in this event, kid. You have to tell me all the gory details."

I arrived an hour early. The apartment was in the valley, in one of those hacienda-style apartment complexes. After getting lost (valley apartment complexes can go on for miles) I knocked on the door and a lovely woman ushered me into her crowded one-bedroom flat. A baby cried in the other room.

"You have a child?" She was a full-fledged adult, I realized.

"Just getting divorced, but don't worry, I have a babysitter." An older woman came out of the bedroom.

"I know what you're doing and I think it's disgusting," the old woman said. That gave me a lot of confidence.

"It's a favor, Cheryl. For Roger." More confidence.

I took her to a steak place on Ventura Boulevard. We didn't have much to talk about, except that she liked New Yorkers. When the waiter approached the table I ordered a beer. He asked for my ID.

"You're eighteen, you can't even order the rum-soaked babka." Even more confidence.

She finished her dinner in half the time I took. She had a favor to fulfill, and Cheryl was watching the baby. I was stalling as much as I could. I slowly ate my babka, which the waiter brought as, you guessed it, a favor.

She tapped her fingers on her third martini glass. "Shall we go? I need to get home."

I paid for the dinner and noticed the waiter smirking. Could he have known?

"You're going fifteen on a forty-five-mile-per-hour street." She was right. I had been fantasizing for years about doing the deed, but I couldn't get my foot to apply more pressure. She reached over with her high heel and pressed my foot to the metal. "Let's get this show on the road. Pronto."

We walked into her apartment and Cheryl was pushing a stroller back and forth. "Do you want me to take John Jr. outside for a minute?"

A minute! Is that how long she thought it would last? Zero confidence now.

Cheryl finally left us alone once the baby was asleep. My date made the first move.

"Let's go in the bedroom."

"With John Jr.?"

"He sleeps through anything."

And we did it. Funny, Cheryl overestimated the duration by thirty seconds.

On Monday morning there was a knock on my dressing room door. Roger wanted all the gory details. I gave him as much as I thought a gentleman should.

"Well, I got a good report about you. Only one thing, you've got to get that sweating under control."

Meanwhile, Michael was doing so well that he bought a beach house in Montecito. He called it "Los Residuales," after the fantastic amount of money he made from commercials. Living with him on Mulholland Drive was one thing, but Montecito was something else. On the same beach were James Brolin, Kenny Loggins, and Jane Russell. All I could think of when I met Russell was that Howard Hughes invented the underwire bra for her. They were the most famous breasts in history, and I got to have dinner with them.

Things started to pick up for me in commercials. The casting directors began to know me and there were even times when I would hear other actors in the waiting room whisper, "Guttenberg's here, we might as well leave now." I booked about twenty commercials my first year in Los Angeles, and sold everything from toothpaste to motor oil. The checks came rolling in. I had never seen that much money in my life. I even quit my job at The Sports Fan.

One day Edgar called me about a successful teensploitation company that has made sexy, scary, and comedic films for over forty years.

"Steve, can you drive a van?"

"A van? Like to the airport?"

"No, like with girls and pot."

"What?" Did he say what I thought he did?

"They're making a movie at this exploitation film company that was famous for cheerleader movies and teenage girl sleepover movies. They're seeing people for the lead role in a sexy teenage movie, you'd be great."

He gave me the particulars and I wrote them on a scrap of paper and stuffed it into my wallet, which was about the size of a baseball glove. That was my filing system.

The company's offices were in one of those smarmy Beverly Hills–adjacent neighborhoods. At the audition I was among about thirty actors my age, and thirty or so beautiful girls walking in circles and repeating the lines. It looked like a Busby Berkeley movie. I was called in and read my part. And something interesting happened. One of the producer types wanted to have me back for a second reading.

"Not only are you getting a call-back, the producer is having people to his house for the readings. This looks very good for you," my agent told me.

But the meeting at the producer's house was priceless. The house was in the Trousdale Estates, a ritzy area north of Sunset in Beverly Hills. The door opened to reveal a pleasant-looking man in casual clothes, not the producer I had previously met. He had me sit in an overstuffed chair in the living room.

"Steven, you're here. I'm so over the moon about you for this part. I'm not exactly sure if I can get it for you but I'm going to try."

"Great. Um, are there any other actors here?" I knew something was unusual about this meeting. Hey, I thought, it's Hollywood.

"No, you're the only one, and there was just one thing I was wondering about. Can you do push-ups?"

This was weird. "Sure."

"The part is a very strenuous role, I wondered if you could do some push-ups to show me your stamina." Even weirder.

For the next ten minutes I did push-ups in the hope that he would yell "You've got the part!" He didn't. And after he asked me to take off my shirt I headed for the door. "This is the only business that eats its young": credit Johnny Carson.

I didn't get cast in the film. An actor that I had known from the audition circles got the part I was up for. It also starred an actor who later became quite famous for a television series and several studio films that he acted in and directed. Sorry, no names, folks.

Paul and Edgar were wonderful people but weren't sending me out very often. In my meanderings around town I met an ambitious pair of agents, Nicole David and Arnold Rifkin. Arnold's catchphrase at the time was "I can sell sand to the Arabs." Nicole was a former actress who had starred on Broadway in *You're a Good Man, Charlie Brown*. They worked in one office at desks that faced each other, clients' pictures on the wall and a tinny radio playing behind Arnold's desk. They represented a bartender named Bruce Willis, who was also an actor. Rifkin-David later became so successful that their agency was bought by William Morris and Arnold became the president of that company. They had a lot more fire in them than Paul and Edgar, and I respectfully told Edgar that I was moving agencies.

"You'll never get anywhere with those two, they're five-and-dimers." Edgar blew smoke in my face.

"That might be, but I want to thank you for helping me get this far." I meant it. I felt bad that I was leaving.

"Don't let the door hit your ass on the way out." He didn't look at me.

Years later I saw Edgar at a party. He was still smoking his cigar. "I guess we screwed up by not paying enough attention to you." He was genuinely sorry for losing me as a client. Some people in Hollywood abandon their grudges, some don't.

Arnold and Nicole told me they had put me up for a pilot, whatever that was. It was a meeting and a reading. I sat in the waiting room of Warner Bros. casting for my turn to wow them. In walks a burst of energy and confidence. A handsome and friendly guy who had just filmed the starring role in *Roots.* LeVar Burton was the first actor I ever saw have a datebook. He had such a schedule that he had to write all his auditions in this expensive-looking calendar. I looked at my wallet, stuffed with paper. That datebook was an advantage. The casting executive, Barbara Miller, personally came out and ushered him in. It was like he was doing them a favor. And he was. LeVar had the power. It was the first time I saw power move the mountain.

The producers walked him out of his audition as if he were visiting royalty. I just stared at that leather-bound appointment book.

I wound up getting the pilot, called *The Last Chance,* and got to work with the director, Will Mackenzie, a former actor whom I recognized from *The Bob Newhart Show.* The first thing he wanted me to do was go to the Beverly Garland Hotel in Studio City and meet my fellow actors. Most of them were flown in from New York. They taught me about the "per diem." One of the actors, a tough guy from Brooklyn, explained it to me.

"It means we get cash money for traveling and staying 'on location.' The per diem is our daily allowance. I like to save it in a rat hole, and use my credit card to buy everything. Then I deduct all my expenses on my taxes, and I get to keep the cash. You gotta work this system." He was busy stealing soaps and towels and stuffing them in a gym bag as he spoke to me.

We filmed the show at the Paramount Ranch, which is a huge outdoor studio on the border of Malibu and Calabasas in the middle of a state park. There is enough room for a backlot, and they have a Western town there as well as dozens of sets, all waiting to be used.

The honey wagons were old hat to me, and I was starting to get comfortable on a set. Being able to sit in one's chair and use the time meaningfully is part of the game. What I found most exciting was watching other actors prepare for work. My cast mates not only had certain acting gifts, but their abilities shined brighter with the awareness of where the camera was, the lens the cinematographer was using, and the different setups.

The day that shooting ended on *The Last Chance,* I called Nicole and asked her what was next.

"Steven, most actors go to the beach and relax after a job. Why don't you take it easy, we'll call you when we have something."

That just wasn't me. But there was a conversation coming that I didn't want to have. I had to tell my father that I wanted to stay in Hollywoodland. First I tried it out on my mother.

"Oh, I think you have to tell him that yourself, Steven."

"But Ma, I think if you tell him he might think it was okay."

"I think you're dreaming, son. You have to do this one."

"He'll kill me."

"You should have had Ava Gardner call him."

"I don't know Ava Gardner."

"I knew it! I knew he was lying about knowing Ava Gardner." My father was on the phone.

"Stanley, how long have you been listening? You better not do this on my calls to my girlfriends."

"I don't, Ann."

"Dad, I have to tell you something."

"Don't tell me you're not going to college. Steven, are you going to college?"

"Dad, you asked me not to say it."

"I'm serious, Steven. Are you going to—"

"Not yet." There was a long pause.

"When?" My father was staying calm.

"Oh, Stanley, stop this interrogation. Let him do his thing out there and he'll come back when he wants."

"Steven, I think it's the wrong thing to do. But if you want to stay, do what you want."

"Thank you, Dad."

"Thank your Mother."

"Oh, stop this. Steven, you can stay out there as long as you want. But if you want to come home, just come home. Your father is being very good about this, aren't you, Stanley? I'm very proud of you."

"Steven, I don't want you staying out late out there. Get home at a decent time."

"I will, Dad."

"Steven, your sister wants to tell you something."

My sister Susan, who was eleven, got on the phone. "I saw that gum commercial that you did with that girl that was supposed to be your sister. That wasn't your sister. I'm your sister. That was weird."

And that was the "I'm not going to college" conversation. My father was a billion times more understanding than he threatened to be.

I went back to Paramount, where I had a good routine going. I would scour the trades, make my calls, sneak onto the various sets and scrounge lunch, go to the gym, and listen to Landon tell his stories. Then Arnold left me a message on my machine. "Steve, call me about Phil Silvers."

I called right back. "Phil Silvers? Bilko? *It's a Mad, Mad, Mad, Mad, World*? *That* Phil Silvers?"

"Yeah, he's doing a teen comedy called *The Chicken Chronicles* and you need to get to Ventura Boulevard as soon as you can. It's the last day that they are seeing people."

"A teen comedy? Isn't he a hundred years old?"

"He's playing the owner of a chicken take-out place. Just get there."

Walter Shenson, the producer of *The Chicken Chronicles,* had gained fame for producing the Beatles' movies *Help!* and *A Hard Day's Night*. His Rolls-Royce was parked in front of the casting office when I pulled up in my Pacer.

"You didn't hit my Roller on the way in, did you?" He loved that car.

"I don't have enough gas in it to hit a haystack. Is it a real one?"

" 'A real one.' You don't want this part, do you?" He had a smile on his face.

"I want to work with Phil Silvers, I want the part." I wanted any part.

Penny Perry was the casting director and she took a liking to me. She thought I was right for the lead, and I got the role of David, a teenager living in Beverly Hills during the Vietnam War. The script was written by Paul Diamond, the son of I.A.L. Diamond, Billy Wilder's partner on classics like *The Apartment* and *Some Like It Hot.*

Here is where I saw a bit of the Hollywood machine working. Arnold and Nicole were trying to get some of their other clients roles in the film, and since I was cast as the lead they had more pull. So much of the film business is based on leverage. I read with actress after actress, which isn't the worst thing in the world, especially for an eighteen-year-old with no social life.

Which was a problem. I was lonely in L.A. I could count my friends on two fingers. Michael, and John Starr from the *Welcome Back, Kotter* commercial. I needed to get out more.

Michael suggested I go to Gazzari's, a Sunset Boulevard disco that attracted a very "in" crowd. I hadn't been out in Hollywood much, and was excited about the prospect of meeting some new people. I blow-dried my hair until I had an Afro the size of a beach ball. My outfit was a Hukapoo-print polyester dress shirt with polyester green slacks that were tighter than an apple skin. To complete this costume I slipped into my wine-colored five-inch marshmallow platform shoes.

It was raining that night, one of those torrential downpours that L.A. is famous for, as I headed to the Sunset Strip. Sunset was really in its prime, with The Roxy, On the Rocks, and a million other places that had lines out the door. The Gazzari's crowd was the thickest. I parked a block away and walked carefully so as not to fall over in my platforms.

Every eccentric that roamed the 213 area code was desperately trying to get in. I circled the mob, popping my head up above the crowd, trying to be noticed. I squeezed my way toward the front and, lo and behold, I got the nod from the gatekeeper.

"East Coast platforms, you're in." He pulled me through the sea of wannabes and I entered the inner sanctum.

It was the ultimate in L.A. hot spots. The lights, writhing bodies, and pounding music made me feel as if I was among the city's royalty. But I still felt alone. All these people, cliques of every sort, and it was as if a spotlight was on me with a flashing sign that read "The Only Guy Here Without a Posse."

I ordered a screwdriver, which was the only drink I knew. Then she touched my arm. A very attractive African American girl with a dress shorter than I had ever seen asked me to dance.

"You can't move with a drink in your hand, put it down." Her voice was as velvet as the rope outside.

"Mind if I just dance the next song?" I had just paid for it with an hour and a half worth of tips.

"Yes, I do." And she pulled me onto the dance floor.

I had learned how to dance in my parents' living room from my friend Marty Weber. She was no Marty Weber.

"You do the New York Hustle, I like that." And she proceeded to

West Coast me around the floor. She was *very* friendly, which got my antenna up. We were dancing closer than was normal for a first dance. And then it hit me. In the form of a large hand on the back of my neck.

"You're dancing with my date." He moved his hand to my shoulder. "Come back to the table, LaTiqua."

I opened my mouth to speak but my dance partner cut me off. "I'm not your date anymore, fuck off, Elmo."

"Elmo? Like *Sesame Street*?" Definitely the wrong thing to say.

"You don't like my name?" That was a euphemism for "I have a reason to hit you." And he did.

The screaming and crying wasn't the worst part. I don't mean LaTiqua; she retreated to her table. I did most of the emoting, but the horrible part was being carried to the door by the bouncers. Both Elmo and I were thrown to the curb from a side door.

I tried to make nice. "Look, Elmo, I was asked to dance. I'm sorry if it isn't working out with you and LaTiqua; I have no interest in your girl. Let's just walk away from this and move on."

The side door opened and Elmo's three friends were also tossed out on their behinds. They were much smaller than him, but just as difficult to deal with.

"Well, fellas, I've had enough fun for tonight, I bid you a good evening." I knew this wasn't going to be the end of it, but I walked in the direction of my car.

They followed me, and I picked up the pace. I broke into a slow trot, trying to get my keys out of my painted-on pants and trying not to fall off my platforms. As usual I started sweating and my hands couldn't get a grip on the keys. I saw my Pacer and broke into a full run. I was a couple of feet away when I was tackled.

Kicking and screaming. They did the kicking, I did the screaming. The pummeling continued until I felt a hand in my back pocket, and my file cabinet of a wallet being pulled from its home. That inspired me.

I grabbed someone's head and started to hit it on the pavement. And now it was Elmo who was screaming and crying. The three friends picked him off the pavement and dragged him away.

All the way back to Michael's I bled on the car seats. Polyester doesn't soak up liquid like it should.

I snuck into the house and tiptoed back to my room. I thought I had made it when I heard a snicker.

"I take it you didn't make any friends."

Michael taped up my rib cage and cleaned the asphalt out of my arms.

"The face, they didn't get your face. Smart actor you are. But your parents will kill me if they find out. So let's keep this between you and me." And we did. Until now. I'm fine, Mom and Dad. And I still have my marshmallow platforms.

The Chicken Chronicles was my first starring role. What a difference there is between coach and first class. Being the lead means everything is better. Everyone from the crew to the supporting players treated me as if I was something special.

We were shooting in Hancock Park, one of the most affluent areas of Los Angeles. All the mansions were built in the '30s and '40s for Hollywood mucky-mucks. In those days Beverly Hills was the sticks.

The first day of shooting I arrived early. I drove up to the PA, who was the gatekeeper of ye olde parking lot. He had on the regulation baseball cap.

"I can't find your name on this list, are you sure you're on this picture?" The PA looked up and I recognized him at the same time as he recognized me. "Taft-Hartley?"

"Kentucky Fried Chicken? Randy?" My old nemesis.

"Schmuck, that's the star of the flick." The second AD pushed him aside and leaned into the car. "Sorry, Mr. Guttenberg, he's got his head up his ass. We have you parked near your trailer."

"Trailer?" Randy and I said it at the same time.

I was quickly escorted to a parking space next to a Winnebago that looked about ten feet shorter than Widmark's. "Get him breakfast pronto, Randy, and then walk Mr. Guttenberg to the set for blocking when he's ready. No, bring him over to Frank's trailer. And if you call him Taft-Hartley one more time you're history." The second AD walked off.

"You look like you lost weight." I felt sorry for Randy. He'd lost all his power.

"Thank you. I had the Dr. Atkins candies working for me. I still need a better attitude." This was the Hollywood caste system. Now he had to cater to me. It was an odd moment.

We stopped in front of my trailer. "I'll let you settle in, then I'll come get you to see the director. Five minutes, okay?"

I flopped on the trailer's couch, opened my script, and started to go over my lines. I'd learned to read my lines over a hundred times before I got to work. That's my personal way of memorizing, although a lot of actors I know also do that.

I looked around the trailer. I saw my wardrobe hanging in the closet.

Jeans and a shirt with nifty shoes. I knew enough to get dressed first and be as ready as I could before they called me.

There was a knock and the door was flung open. "Sandy Berke here to take your clothes on and off!" She laughed and came in, turned me around, and told me how good I looked. She ran out as fast as she came. But that's typical of wardrobe people and costume designers. I've never worked with a costume professional who wasn't pleasant to be around.

Randy walked me out toward the director's room in the honey wagon. On the way, Walter Shenson's Rolls-Royce pulled in front of me.

"Hey, Steve, good morning." He gave the keys to a set driver and walked over with his hand out to shake mine. "When I produced *A Hard Day's Night* with the Beatles I remember coming to the set, of course it was London, and I saw the guys gathered around the food truck. And I put my hand out just like this and shook all four, Paul, John, George, and Ringo. And I said, 'Fellas, this movie is going to change your life,' and I'm going to say it to you. Have fun, kid, and do a good job for me, will ya?" And he was off to meet the director, Frank Simon.

"Burrito? Oatmeal? Want to visit the caterer or go have makeup?" Randy was hungry.

"We need him now, jughead! Confab!" An AD was motioning for me to join Walter and Frank in their conversation.

"What's a confab?"

"It's when you and the big shots talk about the day's work. Don't you read the trades?"

I did, but forgot about "the confab." I made a note to remember that. Confab and pronto.

Frank Simon was a tortured talent. He wanted to elevate the film into something with higher aspirations, but he had to direct a teen comedy. He smoked nonstop.

"Steve, have you thought about the angst and deep import behind how David, your character, handles the drama of the film? I think he's trying to make sense out of his parents' distance from him, his confusion with the Vietnam War, and his curiosity toward women and their inner meaning." Frank looked at me and took a long drag off his cigarette. Walter poked his head between us.

"Frank, I want to make a teen comedy that makes a lot of money. The fact that it says something, that's terrific. But I want to make money, especially for Mel."

Mel was Mel Simon, a real estate magnate from Indianapolis, who wanted to be an investor in films. Ours being his first.

"Just make it good, Frank. Now, why aren't we shooting?" If there is one phrase that every producer has in his vocabulary it's "Why aren't we shooting?"

I looked up to see Lisa Reeves and Meridith Baer, my two gorgeous costars. I was a very regular guy in an extraordinary situation. I had five weeks in the company of women who were several years my senior, and extremely experienced with romantic scenes. These women were every boy's fantasy, including mine. And they were trapped on the set, with me! I remembered reading that Robert De Niro and Dustin Hoffman both said that one of the reasons for becoming actors was to meet girls. These fellows were correct. And when you are the lead, if you ask them to sit and talk, they sit and talk. If you ask them to go out after the wrap, they do. Anything for the star of the show. I could get used to this.

Day after day I arrived on set and had everything done for me. I even brought my laundry in and Sandy was kind enough to send it out with the rest of the wardrobe. The great part of this shoot was the amount of camera time I had. I learned the techniques of film acting while I shot. Matthew Leonetti, who recently shot *The Three Stooges,* was the cinematographer on our film. He was such a gentle, thoughtful man, as most cinematographers are. They are always the calmest people on set.

Twelve-hour days are the norm for filmmaking. They can even extend to fourteen or more. But that was no problem to me. A set is a wonderful place. And I started to do something that I still do to this day. I thanked every crew member I saw at the end of the day. Someone had told me that it is the crew that makes you look good, so I spent an extra half an hour shaking hands and laughing with the grips, electricians, and drivers.

About a week into the shoot I got a message on my machine from my mother one night.

"Steven, your father wants to talk to you." I dialed right away. Of course I didn't think about the three-hour time difference.

"Are you all right? Why are you calling this late?" I could tell my mother was sitting up in bed and putting on the light.

"I got your message, Ma, it sounded important." I heard my father rustle in the background.

"What the hell is he calling so late for? Goddamn Hollywood."

"Steven, your father wants to talk to you."

I stiffened. I was ready for anything.

"I'm not talking now, it's two in the morning!" My father was under the covers, his voice muffled.

"Stanley, enough already, I want you to talk to your son." A long pause.

"Steven, how are you? Are you all right?"

"Yeah, Dad, I'm okay, I just . . . just really miss talking to you. I really miss you."

Another long pause. "Your mother and I want to come out and see you. We want to see what this whole Hollywood thing is all about."

My mother chimed in. "Tell him whose idea it was, Stanley."

Another long pause. "I want to see you, Steven, I miss you very much. It was my idea. And who knows? It could be fun. We'll bring the girls and we can all stay at Michael's. And I really miss you. Did I say that?"

"Yeah, Dad, but I really like hearing it. I need it." I could hardly squeak it out.

"It's okay, Steven, it's okay."

"I just feel like I disappointed you and I—"

"It's okay, Steven, it's okay. Just calm down. It's going to be okay."

We both sat on the phone together not speaking for quite a long while. You could have given me a billion dollars, I wouldn't have felt better.

Chapter 7

It was a perfect California day when the family arrived at the airport. I scanned the crowd for the familiar faces of my clan. I saw my mother first, then I saw my father. My sisters, Judi, who was thirteen and Susan, who was eleven. My mother saw me first.

"There he is! Steven! He looks great, doesn't he, Stanley?" My mother and father hugged and kissed me. Only now do I realize how important that moment was. They hadn't seen me in over three months and it was everything for them to hug me.

"Is this Hollywood? Steven, I made you something." My sister Susan showed me a crayon drawing.

My mother smiled. "You look so good, Steven. I like your hair. Very *Welcome Back, Kotter.*"

"Let's go get your bags." I walked next to my father. A few moments went by, then my father grabbed my hand and held it. He smiled and kissed me on the cheek.

"You're always going to be my son, my gift from God. That's what I called you when you were born. You know that?"

My father is a tough guy, but when he gets soft and sentimental he always reminds me of what is important in life.

"I know that, Dad, I won't ever forget it."

He hugged me and I put my head on his chest. It had been so long since I hugged him.

With about a thousand pounds of luggage, we headed for the car. Michael stood waiting in front of the BMW. The ride back to Michael's was nonstop talking. I forgot how much fun it was to be with the family. I had missed them.

We pulled up to the house on Mulholland. "Stanley, kids, Steven, look at this, look at this!" My mother was having a conniption. "Oh my G-d, look at the private road, the plants, the flowers. Michael, this is a mansion!"

Michael and I settled the family in. When New Yorkers come to Los

Angeles for the first time, everything is a revelation. The topography, the sun, even the air is different. And everywhere there is a feeling of Hollywood. Even if you can't see it, you know it is there. Somewhere behind that hill over there is a movie star tanning poolside.

My father stood by the kidney-shaped pool looking over the expanse of the valley. When you are on the top of Mulholland Drive the view is incredible.

"It's very foggy. Very brown. Why is that? It's three in the afternoon and the sun is out."

"It's the smog. It's always there."

"Makes it hard to see things clearly." He stared out at the haze. "Do you like it out here, Steven?"

"I like it, I guess."

"Do you want to stay out here? Not go to school?"

"I want to make it. I want to be a success."

"Your mother doesn't tell you, but she worries about you. Every day."

"I'll be all right, Dad, I'm going to make something of myself. And if I don't, I have nothing to lose. I'll go back to school." That was a teenager talking.

"Just don't lose yourself, that's all you have, that's all we have. You understand?"

I nodded as if I did. But I really didn't.

The next morning, the alarm rang at five o'clock and the family was up. They were on New York time and I was used to getting up for my 6:30 A.M. set call. We piled into my Pacer and went to see me shoot a movie.

We approached the set, and all the trucks and hubbub. My sisters were jumping up and down in the small interior.

"Is John Travolta going to be there?"

"No, no, that was a commercial I did, this is a movie." We pulled up in front of my trailer. A driver took my car.

"Oh my, someone taking his car. Stanley, you see this?"

"I see, I see." My father wasn't impressed.

An AD approached us. "Anytime you want, hair and makeup is ready for you."

"This is my family, can you take care of them while I get ready?"

"Sure thing, Steve. Why don't we get you some breakfast to start, folks." My family had their mouths wide open. To them, I was just Steven, the kid that couldn't figure out how to match his socks. Here I was being treated like a star.

"Stanley, that's our son. That's our little son, with his own trailer. I heard Cary Grant has his own trailer. Steve and Cary Grant. Imagine that!"

"I'm imagining, I'm imagining." Still not impressed.

We were doing scenes at St. Vincent's hospital near Vermont Avenue. Some of it was closed for repair and that was where we were shooting. The first scene was in front of the steps that framed the entrance to the building. We were all waiting to shoot.

"What's the holdup? Why aren't you acting?" Judi was eating her specially made burrito.

"We're waiting for Mr. Silvers." The first AD was tapping his foot.

"Phil Silvers! Bilko?! Bilko is here today?"

"Mom, I told you he was in the movie."

"Yes, but I didn't think he was here today. Oh Stanley, I didn't do my hair. And my makeup!"

"Ann, you look fine." Even Bilko didn't impress him.

Suddenly a huge Fleetwood Cadillac lurched toward the set. Crew members scattered out of the way as it ran up the curb and stopped just inches from the camera. The door opened and a yellow and red western boot stepped onto the pavement.

"Help me get out, for Christ sakes!" Two grips pulled a rhinestone cowboy with the biggest ten-gallon hat you ever saw out of the caddy. It was Phil Silvers.

"Howdy, folks! Ah have arrived! How do you drive this thing?" He shook the grips off and spotted me. He was using a Texas accent. "Kid, help me walk up the steps. Let's shoot this turkey!"

"Phil, can I introduce you to my family?" My folks and sisters approached him warily. This was their first star. I didn't count.

"Madam, your son has a big career ahead of him. I told that to Frank Sinatra's parents and look where he went. Kid, get me a chair."

"Okay, let's shoot. Ready, Mr. Silvers?" Frank was lighting one cigarette with another.

"I'm conversing with the star's parents, except the father isn't talking. Haven't you seen me? Bilko? Sullivan? Movies?"

"I liked you in *Mad, Mad World*."

"I was great in that one, wasn't I? Better than Spencer Tracy and Milton Berle, don't you think?"

"I guess so. It was a good movie." My Dad wouldn't be impressed if an alien landed on the front lawn.

"Tough audience. Well, let's see what we can do today. Nice to meetcha." And the day started. What my father did get a kick out of was that Phil couldn't drive that boat of a car for the scene. It took him ten times to pull up to his mark.

Afterwards we broke for lunch. There was a rumor that Henry Winkler was shooting a film called *Heroes* with Sally Field somewhere in the same hospital.

"Let's see if we can find them. I love the Fonz." My mother was up for an adventure.

We didn't find that set, but something happened that made my father perk up. Everyone working at the hospital was excited about the two movies shooting on the grounds and was on a movie-star hunt. We were wandering the halls and stopped at the cafeteria for some coffee. As my father was waiting in line to pay, we noticed a few people staring at him, whispering. Finally, one of them mustered the courage to approach him.

"Excuse me, you're somebody, aren't you?" A man was pointing at my father. A woman approached.

"You're Barney Miller, aren't you? From TV." The woman was so excited as she searched her bag for a pen and paper. "Can I have your autograph, please?"

"It's him, it's him! It's Hal Linden from *Barney Miller*!" A crowd of doctors, nurses, and patients started to surround my father, giggling like a fan club.

And my father lit up. A smile as big as I had ever seen on him.

"No, no, I'm not him. I'm Stanley Guttenberg. That's the star, my son over there." He pointed toward me. Of course they didn't recognize me, I hadn't been in anything that was released yet. The crowd frowned at me and turned toward my father.

"Please, please, an autograph." Someone pulled out a camera. "Can we have a picture, please, Mr. Linden?" And it started. My father signed autographs and took photos with all his "fans." And he loved it. We all did. He felt a little of Hollywood, what it was like, what I was attracted to myself. He was so happy. He smiled and laughed as he ate it up. It is one of the stories that he tells over and over. And it is one of the greatest moments of my career.

I got closer to my father on this trip. He really enjoyed watching me work, and saw that he hadn't lost me to Hollywood. I was still his son, and respected and admired him more than anyone in my life. Michael had a an exciting, luxurious lifestyle and that gave me substantial motivation to make my way in the business. But my father's grip on reality, on the values that matter most, kept me aware that I had to keep ahold of myself.

My family visited the set several times during their trip. And I witnessed one of the surprising things that happens to set visitors. They get bored.

"When is something going to happen?" Judi would yawn over and over. Things move slowly during filming. There are lights to set, camera tracks to lay, and lots of plans to work out. Each setup can take thirty to forty-five minutes. To a civilian that is an eternity. I heard that Harrison Ford said, "There are two things you don't want to see made, movies and sausages. The pro gets used to it. Henry Fonda had a famous line: "I get paid to wait, I act for free." Michael Caine would sit in his trailer and play solitaire. Lots of card playing goes on while waiting. And storytelling. I think that is a treat, listening to show-business stories. Memories of actors, directors, and crew members that are told only on set. One of the best things a young actor can do on set is learn to be quiet and listen. But my family wasn't interested in stories. They wanted to see action. They wanted to see a two-hour movie shot in one day. Just sit in director's chairs and have the film unfold in front of them. Instead they saw about three minutes' worth of film shot in twelve hours.

"Is this all you do all day? It seems like there is a lot of sitting around." My father needed more stimulation.

"That's moviemaking, Stanley. These are artists, professionals."

Pause.

"Steven, when is something going to happen around here? I want a good explosion, a car crash. Isn't anyone going to get shot?" My mother started pacing.

"Mom, it's not that kind of a movie. It's a teen comedy. I think Phil is going to drive the Caddy up a curb later."

She looked at me. "I think we're going to go back to the house, swim in Michael's pool."

"There's crafts service." I pointed to a table laden with every food ever created. My family turned their heads in unison and their eyes bulged. To a civilian, the crafts service table is something out of a Willy Wonka movie. It is open all day, every day, and there is even a crafts service person to satisfy your every need. My father approached the table.

"What can I get you, sir?" Andy the CS person was busy making a quesadilla.

My father surveyed the table. "How much is that?" He pointed to the cheese sandwiches.

"Nothing sir, it's free."

"Hmmm, what about the sucking candy?" He rolled the Jolly Ranchers between his fingers.

"Free also, take as many as you want."

"And the breaded chicken?"

"Free." Andy was perplexed. "It's all free, sir, compliments of the producer."

"Everything? Everything on the table is free, as in no charge?"

"It's all goddamn free, as in no chargeee, *nada,* not a cent!" Phil was reaching for the Hershey bars. His ten-gallon hat was tipped to one side, practically falling off his head. He filled his plate with every snack he could get his hands on. "And we get as much as we want, pronto!" He ran away from the table as if he were stealing. This was one of the most successful stars in television, he probably made a truckload of money, and he still gathered as many freebies as he could. No matter how rich and famous a person is, the idea of getting something for free is impossible to resist.

It was around this time that I quit my job at Farrell's. I was on my own now, no real-world job. But I had a real agent in Rifkin-David. And that makes all the difference.

After *Chicken Chronicles* wrapped, I returned to my office at Paramount, this time feeling a bit more confident about walking through the gates. I punched my time card and swung my briefcase a little higher than I did before. The guard stopped me with his holler.

"Hey, Steve, we haven't seen you in a while, been on location?" I had no idea what that meant. *Location?*

"No, same location, still here in Hollywood."

He left the guard shack and approached me. This was never good.

"I mean 'on location,' on a film, somewhere exotic? Were you shooting in Asia, Europe? Man, I always envy you execs getting to travel like that."

"Oh, location, yes, on location." I started to get it. "Yeah, we were shooting an action pic, lots of blood and guts. Lots of . . . action." I knew too much talk would only get me in trouble.

"But where?" He looked over his shoulder to make sure no one was driving up. "Tell me something good. I never get the juicy parts, people just drive through. Were you with pretty girls? Starlets? I hear lots goes on when you guys go on location. Sex parties and stuff. Booze, broads. Give me some names. Come on, I'm starving here."

He was serious. Was I the only guy on the lot who was approachable? Reluctantly I spit out, "There were some parties."

"I knew it!" He slapped his hands together and did a little dance. "Tell me, pal, tell me everything."

Honk! A Ferrari with two men in suits at the gate.

"Hey, we have a meeting with Robert Evans, can you two discuss recipes some other time?" The driver wore a monocle. I swear, a monocle.

The guard turned toward him as if he just broke up the guard's first kiss.

"To be continued, huh? I knew it, I just knew all I heard was true." He hurried back to the guard shack.

I walked to my office knowing that I had to come up with a story for this guy. But what? I didn't know anything about being "on location" and nothing about wild parties.

The lot was busier than ever. There must have been two shows shooting. The Western Street had horses, wagons, and hundreds of extras, all dressed in 1800s costumes. There were even fiddlers playing. I walked across an alley and there was New York Street, complete with a scene being shot for a gangster film, with all the extras dressed as if it was the Depression. I heard "Action!" and two men with guns blazing charged out of a bank front, and "shot" a few of the extras, leaped into a getaway car, and sped away. Only they stopped about twenty feet away. Any farther and they would be on Europe Street.

On the other end of New York Street a modern-day lawyer show was shooting. The "lawyers" were walking down the courthouse steps and being stopped by "photographers." They posed for pictures and walked past the camera. One of them had sneakers on.

The director threw his hat to the ground. "We see the damn sneakers. Can I have actors fully dressed when we shoot, please? Or would he like to wear those sneakers home now?"

As I walked over to Europe Street, they were shooting a Parisian scene, something about a painter having an argument with his lover. This poor guy must have gotten slapped forty times in the twenty minutes I watched.

"Can't she just stage slap me? I'm dying here." The makeup lady kept putting ice on the actor's swollen cheek.

The actress shrugged her shoulders. "I just get so caught up in the drama of it all, I forget to hold back once it gets to the slap!" She started crying and ran off to the trailers.

Then I turned another corner and there she was. Sitting in a makeup chair, with several people around her. She was talking to a handsome actor about the scene they were going to film. The conversation heated up. The director joined in and there was some shouting. I don't know who started it, but Ms. Dunaway finished it. With class.

"Look, I know we have differences about this, but I need what I need. Let's take five minutes, we all relax and reconvene in ten minutes." She looked at the actor. "That means you, 'Ferocious.'"

The entourage gave her room. She turned her head to catch some of the sun. Just smiling and enjoying some quiet. The woman obviously needed some time alone. But it wasn't going to happen.

"Ms. Dunaway?" I stood there watching her.

"Yes?" She cocked her head to one side. "Who are you?" She looked around, but for a split second no one was watching us. She laughed. A wide, beautiful grin. "You're not supposed to be here, are you?"

I shook my head.

"You sneaked on the lot?"

I nodded.

"Well, I love that. Just love it. Are you an actor?"

I struggled with the words. "I am."

She shook her head, laughing, her hair swaying. "Good for you." Smiling wide and punching me in the shoulder. "Really admire that. What do you need?"

"Two pictures. Of you . . . and John Wayne."

"Do I know John Wayne?"

Don't all movie stars know each other? I thought.

"I just need one of you." I was looking into her eyes. There really is something different about movie stars' eyes. Female stars are even more powerful to look at. There is a reason the camera likes them.

She called someone over and with a wave of her hand had a few photos on a clipboard in front of her.

"To who?"

"Margie and Mary Lou. But Mary Lou really wants John Wayne. Not that you aren't better than John Wayne. It's just she likes John Wayne."

She started to sign, fast. "Here you go. It's the Margie, Mary Lou, and 'to whom it may concern' three pack. That will do you?" She handed me the photos.

"You're even more beautiful in person." I blurted it out. She smiled and touched my chin. For a moment. And then she turned away to get on with it.

The pictures all had a sweeping signature, and they were easy to read. Nothing fancy, just professional. But they were exactly what I needed, sans a John Wayne. Now I needed to know where they kept the operators.

Back in the office I had commandeered, I picked up the phone.

"Well, we haven't heard this extension for a while. Where have you been?"

"Margie?"

I heard a click. "And Mary Lou. Where's my John Wayne?"

"And my Faye Dunaway? We're beginning to feel forgotten. Remember, we knew you when."

"Where are your offices?"

"Below the administration building. Why do you ask?"

I showed up at the administration building lobby and asked the receptionist where the operators were.

"Downstairs, but no one really is allowed down there. Operators and executives only."

I walked down the stone steps. The receptionist called from the top. "Don't stay too long or it's my head. Follow the blue line."

There was a blue line that ran along the hallway. I followed it past a laundry room and a storage center to a sign: TELEPHONE AND COMMUNICATION CENTER. There was an arrow that had been decorated with rainbows, balloons, animals. I turned the corner and was smack-dab in front of what looked like someone's kitchen converted into a telephone bank. The décor was blue doily and angel food cake. The walls were lined with personal photos and telephone boards. Sitting in front of me were six of the friendliest faces I had ever seen. All talking at once into their headsets. Bells ringing, lights flashing, and cords flying in and out of the clip holes that connected Paramount to the rest of the world.

A rather large lady bent the ear without the headset at me. "You need something, dear?"

"I'm Steven Guttenber—"

"My John Wayne. You got my John Wayne!" A ball of energy swamped me. "I knew it, Mr. Guttenberg! You got my John Wayne. Let me see." Mary Lou grabbed the manila envelope and giggled as she almost tore it open.

"Let's see. There's nothing but Faye Dunaway."

The lady who had asked me who I was stood next to me. "You are the delightful Mr. Guttenberg. I thought you would be taller."

"Really, why?" Taller, why would I be taller?

"The distinctive voices are all taller. But you are fine." She touched the top of my head. "I'm Margie. The hog there is Mary Lou." Mary Lou had her hands on her hips.

"There's no John Wayne in this batch." She held the pictures out like cards.

"John Wayne, John Shwayne. Give me my Dunaway." Margie held it in her hands as if it were a diamond. " 'To Margie, Faye Dunaware.' " She held a beat. "Faye Dunaware? Did you get me Faye Dunaware's autograph?"

"Look at the picture." I pointed to the head shot.

"Oh my goodness, I got so excited I forgot to look at her . . ." She took a breath. "She's beautiful. Ms. Bonnie and Clyde. She kissed Warren Beatty, you know. I mean really kissed him."

"I would like to kiss Warren Beatty!" a young man yelled from the last telephone station. "Let me at him!"

"I would too," another girl yelled. "Oh, Warren!" She play-fainted.

Mary Lou held her photo. "But I wanted John Wayne."

I hustled back to the stairway. There at the top was the receptionist.

"What's it like down there?"

"You've never been?"

"They keep me up here. Operators and executives only. I talk to them on the phone. They sound nice. I've been here three years, they're only a few feet away and I've never met them. Isn't that weird?"

The months fly by in L.A., especially in show business. I had turned around and it was April of '77. I had been in Hollywood for ten months and had kept my out-of-school extension going. I found myself wanting to go back to my family and New York. I had just filmed the lead role in a movie, so why did I decide to leave? Maybe I sensed the danger. But I was eighteen, what did I know?

I called my parents. "Mom, I want to come home." Just like that.

I heard another extension pick up. My father. "Steven, did you say you're coming home?"

"Yeah, I don't want to stay here anymore. It's not me." There was a silence.

"The answer is no. You had your chance a few months ago. Your father and I have other plans, we're moving."

"Ma, are you kidding?" Too much silence. "Ma?"

"She ran up to tell your sisters. I'm really happy that you decided this, Steven. It's too far away."

"In lots of ways, Dad."

In California, I told Michael first. He thought it was a mistake.

"You'll be back. You love it too much."

"I don't know about that. Maybe I can be a dentist or something. Something so I'll have a guarantee about life."

"There are no guarantees in life. Just do what you feel inside. Just be happy. But you'll be back."

No way, I thought.

I drove to see my agents, Arnold and Nicole. Back in the day an actor could pop in without calling. No cell phones made things mighty different.

"Hi, Stevie, what's up?" Nicole asked. "Hey, we heard some news about the pilot."

"Jenny, get me Hoyt Bowers at Paramount," Arnold called out. "I'm calling Universal to see if anyone is in now. Steven, I'm sorry I'm so busy here. Just got some sales going on. Hello, yes, this is Arn— Yes, I'll hold. We heard about your pilot. They are thinking about it. It's on the bubble."

"What's a bubble?"

"NBC is considering having it go to series. We'll know in June." I didn't react.

"That's good news, Steven."

"I'm leaving the business."

They both stopped mid-sentence.

"Steven." Nicole had this charming smile on her face yet she looked as if I had slapped her. "What are you saying? Everyone wants to leave the business. I do, all the time."

"I want to leave it right now. I want to leave it about twenty times a day," Arnold laughed.

Their assistant Jenny yelled in from the outer office. "Who's leaving the business?" She walked in. "Take me with you."

The phones rang, another assistant called. "CBS casting on one, Lynn Stalmaster on two and—"

"Let me take Stalmaster." Arnold couldn't resist.

"No, Arnold, not now. We'll call them all back. They can wait." Nicole looked at me. "Where are you going?"

"Back to Massapequa." It sounded important and ridiculous all at once.

"Massapequa?" Arnold leaned forward on his desk. "What is he saying, Nicole? Why does he want to go to Massapequa?"

"Why do you want to go to Massapequa?"

I stammered, but got the guts to blurt it out.

"I've just had enough. I like it out here, but I want to go home."

And now the agenting started. "Now, let's think this thing over."

"I say stick it out with the rest of us. Who says you can escape?" Jenny walked out.

"Do you really want to leave all of this? How long have you felt this way?"

"A while. Every time I'm alone, which is a lot." An honest moment in an agents' office. Doesn't happen that often, but when it does, everybody notices.

"But there are so many things going on." Nicole cast a line. "They are casting for a cop show you could be very right for." My ears and ego perked up.

"I'm working on getting you in to see Coppola." Arnold slowly worked the lure. "And they are interested. Maybe they'll see you tomorrow. But it shoots in September."

"In September I'll be at Albany University."

"A SUNY school? The one upstate?" That look again, incredulous.

To their credit, Arnold and Nicole had a deep, time-consuming conversation with me. Very un-agentlike. But they finally let go. I walked away feeling I did the right thing.

I packed what little clothing and tchotchkes I had. Michael leaned against the doorway.

"You sure you want to do this? You were just getting the hang of it. In fact, I think you're pretty good." A compliment from Michael was rare. Yet, he too was probably agenting me. You don't take no for an answer. No one does in this business. And I was saying no.

Chapter 8

The summer in Massapequa was humid and rainy. The exact opposite of L.A. The neighborhood had a lingering smell of fresh-cut grass. I was back in my room, with the model airplanes and posters of astronauts.

Coming back was an adjustment. I had to fight off my slight addiction to the phone. I loved the action, making calls, getting messages. Very exciting, and very addicting. That's the rub of this business. You get in it for money and power and fame. Then if you are one of the lucky ones you leave with your winnings. You sit back at the beach or the pool or the penthouse. You watch TV, play golf, go to lunch, travel, spend time with loved ones. But at some moment, you think about the action. The calls. The messages. No one escapes that.

Soon, I was leaving home again. This time for college. I was going to start a normal life. Go to school. Get a job. Live like a civilian.

The school had a typical campus. It looked like a movie set. Everything was starting to look like a movie to me. That's not a civilian thinking.

Carey, my new roommate, was a skinny guy with a mop of yellow hair and the devil in his eyes. A few other guys started to drift in. One of them, Jack, carried a large piece of furniture, struggling under its weight as he squeezed it through the door.

"Hey man, we are going to get so high after we get this chouch in."

"A chouch?"

"Yeah, it's a chair and a couch in one piece."

And so we had a chouch. It reminds me now of my friend Woody Harrelson's invention of the round towel. Really good ideas that just need management.

I fell into student life easily. When young adults get together and have no adult supervision, it is mayhem. That's what I remember from Albany State. And the release of *The Chicken Chronicles*.

The release of a feature film is like a new religion trying itself out on the public. Either people believe in it or they don't. There is some publicity to get some word of mouth, and at the end of the day (a big Hollywood saying), you hope to get the people in the seats. Avco-Embassy, a newish Hollywood distributor, was selling and wanted me to help promote. Dick Guttman and Wally Beene, from the PR firm Guttman and Pam, called me. Or I should say called the suite.

Jack came by in between bong hits. "Someone from the West Coast on the line for you." He filled our room with smoke. "I think it's a chick."

"I'm no chick and I'm no spring chicken. Wally Beene here."

"Steven, it's me, too, Dick Guttman."

Big shots calling me. A bit of fuel for the addiction.

"Steven, they want you to do some publicity for *The Chicken Chronicles.* We are starting to get a lot of interest for you and we need you to start to publicize the film. And Walter Shenson's office is down the hall and I can't avoid him."

"What?"

"Steven, Wally is going to walk you through this, you're going to love this. Got to go, got a bigger star on the line."

"What?" The L.A. showbiz patter was fast, and I had been out of it.

"It's Wally Beene again. We're going to trot you out there and just let you rip. Talk about whatever you want to but always mention the picture. How much you love it and want everyone to know. And just have a damn good time. The rest will take care of itself."

"Because we'll be doing it all," said a perked-up English accent. It was Jerry Pam. If you were a British star you were represented by Jerry. He was a player, even drove a blue Rolls-Royce.

"Jerry? A big shot like you gets on the phone with me?"

"I didn't want to, I hate to slum it, but Walter Shenson is a good friend of mine and I want to help his picture. And I also think it would be good for you. What are you doing in that institution in, where are you? Upstate New York? That's bloody horrible. Guttenberg, get your ass back here and get back into Hollywood. We need you."

"You need me?" I thought about that Rolls-Royce. "How's the car?"

"Tell you what, Guttenberg, you do some press for Walter, sell this film, which shouldn't be too hard, the movie is bloody good. . . ." Always selling. "If you do everything, I'll give you a ride in my Roller."

I did every interview I was asked to do. Newspaper, radio station, and anyone else who would listen. It was starting. The hubris anywhere there is power, growing in our dorm room in upstate New York. Even Carey got a taste of it.

"You're doing what? You're going to be on the radio? Are you kidding me? What did you do again? I know you told me, but tell me again."

"I acted in a movie and I'm going to do some interviews."

"Can I use it to get girls?"

The line at the cafeteria each morning was the usual assortment of half-asleep teenagers, some dressed for the day, some eating and going back to bed. Carey and Jack sat down at my table.

"Who were you talking to this morning?"

"It was five forty. Don't ever speak the English language at that time again. Or any other tongue."

"It was for an interview. For the movie."

"Is it for *The Chirken Collidals*?" A skinny kid with thick glasses stood over the table.

"Yeah, no, it's *The Chicken Chronicles*. How did you hear about—"

"This morning. It sounded like a cool movie. I see everything. When's it coming out?"

There were a couple of girls eavesdropping about a table away. Carey saw this.

"Girls, come on over. Don't be shy." The two girls were giggling.

"How did you know it was me?" This was a new, sweet drug. Fame.

"It's here in the paper," one girl said. "A picture of you from the movie. You look younger."

"It was shot last year."

The girl giggled. "Can you sign this?" She put the newspaper in front of me. My picture, out of focus and smudged, but there was a resemblance. And my name was spelled "Glutenheimer."

"Can I sign it with my real name? Guttenberg."

"I'd rather you write the name that is in the paper, otherwise no one will believe I met you."

"Two Ts or one?" I couldn't read it.

"Two, I think."

And that was my first autograph. Steven Gluttenheimer.

As I continued my press blitz, I started to enjoy some celebrity on campus. The staring is the first thing you notice. People linger a bit longer on you. Their brain tries to figure out how they know you.

"School? No. Work? No. Laundromat? No. Where do I know you from?"

"I did the cooking segment on the channel eleven midday show. With the pork."

"Yes, that's it. What's your name?"

"Steven Guttenberg."

"No, that's not it."

But the good far outweighed the bad. Small gestures would pop up. A free beer at the Rathskeller Bar . . . actually that was the extent of the freebies. Other than an extra smile or two from a professor. And then . . .

I came back from class and Carey was standing outside the room, pacing madly. "There you are. Jesus, where have you been? I've had people out there looking for you."

"Yeah, man, everyone was looking." Jack stumbled into the conversation, holding his bong. "Have you gone in your room, man?"

"Go in there, go on in there." Carey was salivating.

The door to our room was closed. I peeked inside. The shades were drawn. I felt Jack pushing the bong at my back.

"You want to take this in there? It's my lucky bong."

"Sure." I took the bong and slowly entered the room, closing the door behind me.

"I'm in here." A female voice. I looked toward Carey's bed and there was the giggling girl. Under the covers, with just her blond bob sticking out.

"You're probably wondering why I'm here." She sat up, and her boobs just fell out of the sheets. She reached her hands toward me. "I saw you in the paper and I thought that was so incredible that you did that movie. *The Chirkin Something Story*. I think my cousin read the novel."

"It's *The Chicken Chronicles* and I don't think it was a novel." She still sat there smiling at me. And staring at me. It went on a bit longer than a normal stare went on. I got it.

"Why don't you come sit here by me. Maybe get those pesky trousers off."

"Let me get this straight. You want to be, have, do . . . You want to have sex with me because I'm in a movie?"

She took a moment to think about it. "Yes. Yes, I do."

I got weak in the knees. I had only been laid once. "Be right back." I opened the door and backed out while smiling back at her. "Her," no name.

The guys were waiting outside. "She wants to have sex."

"With all of us?" Jack stuttered.

"No, you numbskull. With him." Carey put his arm around my neck. "How are we going to handle this?"

I looked at the door and thought it over.

"No, not for me." Were those words really coming from my lips?

"You're shitting me. Tell me you're shitting me." Carey was incredulous.

"How can I do this? This girl is going to have sex with me because I'm in a movie. What has happened to her? No, I won't do it."

There was a round of pleas and cries, but eventually they calmed down.

"I'll take it from here, boys." Carey opened the door and poked his head in. "I'm Steve's roommate. . . ."

And so I saw it. Fame's raw power.

People, complete strangers, wanted to talk to me, hear my stories, and their laughs came easier. The willingness to listen to a celebrity, even a small one, is large. My tales of how the movie was made or even my take on the campus architecture were interesting. They just wanted to watch me move, up close. And I liked it. I saw how people walked away from me with my scrawl of a signature as if they had an ounce of gold. The addiction had grown.

Our suite became a hub for parties. Jack set up a bar and made mixed drinks. It was as classy as it could be until someone fell on one of the speakers.

"Hey, man, someone's on the phone for you," a guy in a Viking hat yelled at me during one of the parties.

I answered the phone in a drunken haze.

"Steven?"

"Yeah, it's me."

"It's Arnold. Steven, what the hell is going on there?" If he was calling, it was for something. He wouldn't call to chat.

I acted like I didn't care, but I did. "Hi, Arnold. I'm at a party, big blowout here." Beat. "I love it here."

"How would you like to audition for a really important movie? They saw *The Chicken Thing* film."

"*Chicken Chronicles.* Not *Chicken Thing.*" This was my movie, I had a stake in it.

He got smooth. "I tell you what, I can get you in there to meet Franklin Schaffner anytime in the next two days. And you'll have to read, and read well. I will send you the sides. What's the address?"

"But Arnold, I'm done with Hollywood."

"But this isn't Hollywood, it's Portugal, and Vienna, Austria. And it's *The Boys from Brazil.*" Silence. "You've heard of the novel?"

"No. It sounds like some strange movie. I'm not going to go there and do push-ups or anything for some weirdo producers."

"Steven, this is a class group. It's the Producer Circle in Manhattan. They are very upscale."

I thought about it as a tray of shots went by. A girl wrapped her arm around mine and we double-shotted whatever was in the glass. "No, no, Arnold," I shouted. "No movies, I don't want it now. I gotta go." I don't know if I ever hung the phone up, because I fell over.

I lay out on the couch in my suitemate's room. My eyes focused on a poster he'd put up. It was of a soldier saluting. George C. Scott saluting. *Patton,* directed by Franklin Schaffner.

From where did I know that name? Like a bombshell it went off in my head. Arnold.

"Greatest war movie ever told," my suitemate said. "Better than *Tora! Tora! Tora!*"

I stared at him. "You ever hear of Franklin Schaffner?"

"Only one of the best directors working today. You ever hear of a little movie called *Planet of the Apes*? *Papillon*? This guy is the real thing."

I stumbled to the phone. "Rifkin-David." I recognized Jenny's voice.

"Jenny, it's me. Steve. Steven." I wanted to get through to Arnold. *They haven't given the part away yet, have they?* The addiction.

"Oh, the runaway. You don't want to go to Manhattan and get to be in a movie?"

"I do, I want to. Is Arnold or Nicole there?" I had to get through.

"We're both on." People move quickly when there is money on the line.

I knew I had to get right to it. And I was still drunk. "I want to do it. I want to audition for *Planet of the Apes*."

Silence. "*Planet of the Apes* was done, Steven. Do you mean *Boys from Brazil*?"

"Yes, the one with the Schaffner director, him. I want to go to Papillon." I sat down, the room was spinning.

"You're not going to Papillon. If you get it, you'll go to Portugal."

"Arnold, what's wrong with him? He doesn't seem right. Steven, are you okay?"

"Can I meet on this?" Every actor, no matter how drunk, can say these words to his agent.

"Sober up. We'll send the sides." Every agent, no matter how drunk his client is, can say those words.

I took a train to New York and made my way to the Producer Circle Company's penthouse. This was a very rich and respected group of producers, mainly of stage, *Mame* being a jewel credit. They went on to produce films such as *The Shining* and, stagewise, *California Suite*. Marty Richards, a partner, won the Oscar for *Chicago*. I sat in the most luxurious three hundred square feet of waiting room I had ever seen. Mervyn Nelson, the dialogue coach, was speaking with two young men who looked a little like me, or I them. The part was for a Jewish hothead who was a fan of the Nazi hunter played by Lawrence Olivier. I had received the sides by mail from Arnold, and studied them meticulously.

Mervyn turned to me. "And you are Guttenberg?" He was an acting teacher in the city, and was known as a very fine actor as well. "Do you know the material you will be reading? Are you ready? Do you know you will be working with Olivier and Frank?" He rattled these questions at me. I appreciated how direct he was and nodded. "Then let's go in."

I walked into the office and was confronted by a tower of a man, Frank Schaffner. He was dressed as if he was going golfing. He didn't look like any director I had seen. I met producer Marty Richards, a very dashing and likeable man who had been a casting director before he started producing. He introduced me to the other producers. His wife, Mary Lea Johnson, sat there on a couch, looking like the beautiful and confident heiress of Johnson & Johnson that she was.

I walked out of the meeting and Mervyn grabbed my hands. "That was good. He liked you. Now go, and forget about it." He turned away and I did just that.

Back at school, Arnold called me and told me I had the job. Getting a job. I don't care how jaded a performer, we all like to be told we got the job. I spent the next few weeks getting out of the school that my father had gotten me into. And now I was leaving for what I still thought would be one last job and then back.

The limousine that came to get me was a bit much. I sat in the front for the most part. Sitting in back of a limo made me carsick, I discovered.

My family was waiting for me at the airport. "That's a nice car, Steven. You paid for that? No, they paid for that, right?" My father smiled.

We were met by an airport rep whose job it was to walk us through the airport. This was something I never knew existed. When there is work, the business treats you well. My parents and sisters and I followed this rep to the private lounge, where we found Mervyn Nelson and Marty Richards. They told my parents that I would be fine and they would look after me. My mother gave Marty some sour ball candy and hugged me. I kissed my sisters and then was walking up the gangway to the plane. For a few months I had eluded the business. Now I was in the bosom of it again.

I sat up the whole trip. I had never experienced first class, had never been to Europe, and didn't know that jet lag was going to hit if I didn't sleep on the plane. We arrived at sunrise, Lisbon time. I had been up the whole flight, eating everything that the stewardesses could bring. I took as many mini bottles of free booze as I could. They were prizes to me. So was anything I could take from the plane, including menus, silverware, slippers, and the toothbrush kit. Just the plane ride was enough excitement for a lifetime.

The flood of attendants, the limousines, and the police escort from the airport were overwhelming. We dropped Marty and his producing partner Bobby Fryer at the Ritz. It was where Gregory Peck and his family, and James and Pamela Mason were staying. It looked every bit the best hotel I had ever seen.

That's not where I was staying. The production company put me at the modest Hotel Tivoli, on Avenida da Liberdade. The window looked out onto the main thoroughfare where, the day I arrived, they were preparing for an anticommunist demonstration.

My own hotel room was another first. I started to steal the soap and towels as soon as I got there. Then I lay down for a few minutes.

Cut to me waking up in the middle of the night. The next night. I called down to the front desk, and they told me it had been thirty-six hours since I arrived. I'd slept a day and a half.

There was a blur of action. Someone called and got me coffee. Half asleep, I met the production office, the home base. I was walked around in my stupor from department to department. The heads of makeup, wardrobe, and stunts met me. I had no idea what anyone was saying.

And then I was led into Mr. Schaffner's office. He was surrounded by a small crowd of technicians, talking about some drawings on a bulletin board.

"Steven, come here, I want you to look at this storyboard. You ever see one?" I shook my head. "Then let me educate you. These are the drawings that I base the whole movie on. Every scene is illustrated.

"This fucking thing will have tension. That's the secret. Tension and release. You get me, Guttenberg?" He grabbed my shoulder. "You sleepy, kid? Kid?"

I had to sit down. They got me some water. The hours had caught up with me. Schaffner was kind and got a laugh out of my predicament. The ADs got me back to my hotel and I slept again.

I was woken up by the production office and took a cab to the Ritz.

There in the dining hall was the pre-filming party and there, near a mound of shrimp, stood James Mason.

Mervyn saw me standing alone and asked if I wanted to meet Peck. Yes, please. Gregory Peck in the flesh. Smiling and laughing and shaking hands. He was in animated conversation with Portugal's premier newscaster. Their Walter Cronkite.

"Greg, can I interrupt. I want you to meet the actor Steve Guttenberg. You're going to kill him."

I looked from Mervyn to Peck. I had forgotten Peck kills me in the film.

"Nice to meet you. I hope I don't kill you first. I hate that. When they schedule a killing or a kiss on the first day of production." He had a way of pronouncing everything as if it were wildly important.

At his side stood two beautiful women. His wife, Veronique, and his daughter, Cecilia. She was a little older than me and she was everything I wasn't. Bel Air, private schools, privileged background. The Peck family are a special breed. They were the tallest, best-looking people I ever saw in person, with an air of royalty, but were still very human. The best ability, I think, of classy people is being able to put others at ease.

The stunt coordinator, a dapper man from London, introduced himself at the bar. He was dressed impeccably, which got me to thinking that my wrinkled shirt, dungarees, and chukka boots were a bit casual.

José, Mr. Schaffner's Spanish-born first AD, slapped me on the back. He was firm even in a social setting. People on sets have a job, and it does bleed into their personal lives. A director likes to take control. His assistant director makes sure he gets what he wants. Right now, even at the party, José wanted to know if I was ready to work.

"You're not going to sleep away the morning, are you? We've got you boarded for day after tomorrow. You get your sleep, okay?" His smile hid a toughness. His grip on my shoulder was firm. "I need you to be there first. So there is no waiting when Mr. Schaffner and the big men come in." He cocked his head toward Peck and Mason. "And when Lord Olivier is around, then it has to be spotless. Everyone on their toes. You understand?"

I nodded. This was all very adult.

"And then tell this wanker to bugger off when you want." The stunt coordinator broke the tension.

José, who was only five feet tall, turned away and started a conversation with someone else on the crew. Parties in show business are not like parties in the real world. When my parents get together with people for a party, there is no agenda. José had an agenda. Get this movie done, and get another film with Schaffner.

Cecilia Peck was nice enough to introduce me to James and Pamela Mason.

"Young man, we should have you to lunch someday," James told me. Here was one of the biggest stars on the planet and he was talking to me. That dignified and encouraging accent, and the smooth-as-single-malt voice.

"What are you doing after the party?" Cecilia looked so fresh, had such positive energy, and she adopted me as her escort. We were out till after three that night. Her father had an early call and didn't like it. When we came back to their massive, ornate suite, we were still laughing.

"Cecilia." It was as if a lion were roaring. Not a happy lion.

I said my good-byes and walked down a hall built for kings, in chukka boots and all of nineteen. *People really live like this?* I wondered.

I was told to be in front of the hotel the next morning at 5 A.M. I was told several times, by several people on the production. Even José. I had a wake-up call, I set my alarm. Instead I awoke when someone banged on my door and said in an angry Portuguese accent, "Get fuck up. Get fuck up."

I fell out of bed, already dressed, stumbled to the van, and was the last one in. That means sitting way in the back. And getting the looks.

Next to me was a man who was sweating more than me. He looked at me. "I'm glad I wasn't the last. José hears about everything."

I sweated and felt carsick all the way to the set. José was there waiting for us.

"Mr. Guttenberg, please do not do that again. It can stick things up for us." I never was late again on that show; I even made sure I was in the van and on set first.

And the sets were incredible. That day's set was of a maternity ward that had two different looks. The first was a thriving Nazi nursery during the war and the second was the same space thirty years later. The artists were converting it. The magic these people create can't be discounted. The set dressers, painters, and constructionists create so much of the illusion.

"I would rather have this than a Picasso." James appeared next to me. "I love watching these men work."

"We have a Picasso, two in fact, darling. And I would rather have them." Pamela joined us and turned to me. "Would you like to have lunch with us? They won't be getting to you until the evening. You're here for a night shoot."

"I brought you in a bit early so I can make sure you are here. You don't mind, do you?" José had a sly smile on his face. "Have lunch, and then we get you ready. I need you at sunset. Exterior of the mansion."

I had a lovely lunch with the Masons. Pamela had actually brought it and they shared it with me. The older actor and the newbie.

Peck walked by, in character. He was playing Josef Mengele and looked every inch the villain. His hair was dyed jet black, as was his mustache. He said a terse hello. Was he angry at me for bringing his daughter home late? Or was he playing Mengele?

"Greg looks great, doesn't he?" James looked at him in awe. "His is the performance to watch. His is the one that will get the notice." It was later Olivier who got the nomination, and I know it disappointed Peck, even after he won a Golden Globe. "The Award" is still the Oscar. (Greg had one of the golden statues on his mantel at home.)

Greg, Jimmy. The insider code is calling people by their casual names. Here were these stars using nicknames as if they were stickball pals. My off-the-books name was Steven, rather than Steve. Could I ever get to the place where some young actor just loved to call me Steven?

I sat in makeup while Peck and Mason had theirs done in their trailers. Frank came in. "Steven, we are going to shoot this exterior about ten tonight, but I need you to be ready whatever time we choose. Can you do that?" I nodded, happy that he called me Steven. Little did I know my name was listed on the call sheet as such.

We wound up shooting at sunrise. I sat in the trailer till then, desperately trying to stay awake. When they called me, I had a burst of energy that carried me through the morning.

Schaffner wanted a plane to fly overhead in the same shot, and the film waited for the flight. Big movie, big stars, big director. They wait for the shot.

"I paint wiss zee light." Henri Decaë, the cinematographer, said to me as I stood by his camera. In Europe, the camera is king. The actors, no matter how important, always come behind the camera. Not so in the United States. Henri was lighting an area the size of a football field, and waiting for the planes. We had two that were going to fly over at about 7 A.M. I was ready, having been there since 3 P.M. the day before, compliments of José.

"We only have two shots at this, Guttenberg. I'm counting on you." Schaffner smoked his cigar. "Don't fuck it up."

He pulled out a piece of paper. "Ever see a shot list?" He unfolded a piece of yellow legal paper covered in numbers and drawings. He began to show me how a director plans his day. How many scenes and camera setups it will take. He listed the twelve hours of shooting. This was the last shot of the day. Three setups. "I can have you in the hotel by nine thirty, if we all get it right." He looked at José at his side, a pilot fish. "I want that plane, José."

"And you shall get it boss, twice." Away from the work, they were very different. José more independent and Schaffner much more of a folksy guy. But here they were working and playing roles.

I sat near the camera, waiting. Schaffner, José, and Decaë with a viewfinder, all waiting for the sun. And then the planes.

"When the sun rises it will happen very fast, please everyone be at your ready." Henri looked at me, pointed, and snapped his fingers. Schaffner came over and very quietly told me how he saw this shot. He explained what he was going to do with the camera, and how he wanted my part to be integrated into his vision. He was precise and very polite.

As the sun came over the back of the mansion, José got the crew ready to shoot, using three or four languages. I think that fluency was one of the reasons Schaffner used him again and again. The first AD had to communicate the director's vision. A good first can make or break a film.

"Action." Said through a cigar. "Camera." The camera started to dolly on tracks one hundred feet in length, and Henri moved the camera all the way. They got the plane. We wrapped at 7 A.M.

As the crew dispersed, one of the director's assistants approached me. Schaffner wanted to see me at his car. I found him in the front seat of a white Mercedes, smoking.

"Kid, you feel okay about the work?"

I started to sweat. Was I being fired? "I don't think I did much. But I liked it."

"That's what I want you to continue doing. Not much." I think he looked at me sweating and smiled. The car drove off. The good directors know so much, and they politely let it all go.

The van wound its way back to the Hotel Tivoli, which was surrounded by demonstrators, both anti- and pro-communist. They were forcefully arguing in Portuguese, and there were bottles and sticks being thrown. This was at ten in the morning. The whole day I didn't sleep, just watched the thousands march down the street. It was an odd juxtaposition. While people were fighting for their rights I was fighting for makeup.

Marty Richards hired a tutor for me to continue my studies. Albert was a grad student at Oxford who looked like Ichabod Crane. "Mathematics and physics is my suit. And travel for the pure enjoyment of it. We being so close to Morocco and all." He was as useful as I wanted, and I didn't want to keep up on my studies as much as I wanted to explore Lisbon with Cecilia. She had been in Europe many times before, and it was lucky for me to have such a genial and worldly touring companion. I was seeing things completely out of my experience, and she was part of that.

We also had an actor friend named David who played a chauffeur. He joked that the movie was about him. Only later did someone tell me how an actor reads a script. As he turns pages: "Bullshit, bullshit, me, me, bullshit, bullshit, bullshit, me." Whatever part an actor plays, he thinks the movie is really about him and his role.

We started to night shoot for a few weeks. If a film has a fifty- or sixty-day shooting schedule, the night shoots are their own little world. They can play with your body, hormones, mood, and health. Lunch is at midnight. "We're burning daylight" becomes "We're burning darklight."

There was a boy actor, he couldn't have been more than ten, who had to be in some of the scenes. He was from Lisbon, didn't speak any English, and José was his only connection. They were very close, and the care that José and the crew showed this boy was top of the line. It was hard for him to stay up, and I think if you watch the film, it shows on his face. But it worked, it feels true. I, on the other hand, still had no idea what I was doing on film, other than trying to be real. And summon the courage to do something special in a scene.

"You ever get killed on-screen?" I shook my head no. Schaffner was in a tan multipocketed photographer's jacket. He was so polite and firm, it was a good feeling being directed by him. "I want to go to the set, just you and me."

He brought me into the room where Barry Kohler was going to meet his demise. My character was going to bite the dust at the hands of some Nazis (very accomplished German actors) and Peck. Schaffner sat on the set's bed, smoking his cigar. He told me that this was where the character would make a small stand, and then be overpowered. He spoke so seriously about the situation that it was as if he were talking about real people. He explained what he thought everyone in the scene was thinking and he slowly showed me the staging that he had on his shot list.

"I get up every day at about three and look at the day's work, and make my schedule. The shot list is part of the day. I incorporate all the time it takes to put up and take down setups, the lunches and the breaks. Then I set the day for myself and show it to José at set. And then hope you can do what I want."

What does he want from me? I thought, and started to sweat.

"You sweat a lot, Steven. That's good for the character. Just match your sweat." He laughed. Matching is important. Shots from many angles, shot at different times, all have to look like the same moment. He could be sure I would be sweating all night. "We've got all of five hours to do this. You're in everything." He never mentioned Peck, or how obviously nervous I was.

Henri was tinkering with the lights, "Till they tell me to go away." The two very talented and gigantic German actors came on set. They were being talked through it with Schaffner. Then José gave them over to the stunt coordinator.

The set grew quiet. Everyone was working, but quietly. It wasn't a coincidence. Even Peck came on quietly. As quiet as a six-foot-three movie star looking like a wax-skinned Nazi could be. He had a few people trailing him, wardrobe, makeup, and a few PAs. He was in a white suit. And that white suit had to be perfect. So wherever he went in that suit it was as if he carried the future of the world with him. No attention was spared. And all the while he was looking at his script. Calmly assessing the set, being kind to everyone. He stayed in character, his dialogue coach nearby to catch anything if his accent was off. He conferred with Schaffner. Then he paced the floor while José got things together. Quietly, without any uncertainty, the sequence was shot. And Schaffner checked off the scenes. Smiling at me with his cigar in his teeth. "Now let's do away with Barry Kohler. Do you remember what we talked about?"

"Yes, and can I die with my eyes open?" I really thought that was a very noble way to bite it as a character, looking out to the next adventure. We had a bit of a disagreement. Here I am a pisher, and I'm telling Schaffner how I want to play it. We genially argued about it, and I wouldn't let it go. I knew it would be that special thing in a scene that I wanted. Really important to define my character.

He relented, but: "If you blink, I will *really* kill you."

We filmed to the minute for five hours. On time. And if you look at the scene where I get the knife to the stomach, I blink.

Schaffner cornered me at the premiere and we laughed about it. But I tell you, he had a slight glint in his eye.

I didn't see Albert, my tutor, for a few days. Then the production office called and said he hadn't picked up his check. "Quite irregular for that hooligan." The accountant was a no-nonsense Englishman. "If he didn't pick up his money, something's happened to him. Who knows what." I asked around. There was a brothel that was popular with the crew and I checked whether he had been there. The head madam said she knew many professors and couldn't tell if my educator had been there.

Olivier. I've heard it said that the bigger the star, the nicer. Not always true, but it sure was this time. He had an assistant or two, a driver, and a small group around him. They were all there to attend to Lord Larry. And so was everyone on the set, whether you knew it or not.

"Larry, please, dear boy, call me Larry," he told me modestly. "I just put on funny noses and do a few accents, memorize a monologue or two and I get round to it. I can sit off-camera for you, and you for me if you like." We did just that. We had telephone scenes together. The only lord on the set did actual off-camera work. I think about all the actors I have worked with that evaporate when it is their turn off-camera. Olivier kept the rhythm and gave just enough for his partner actor to work without blowing his own energy. He was not well at that point, and really toughed it out for this movie. His legs pained him, and he had to sit a lot of the time. Still, he had a brilliant attitude toward the work, treated every member of the set with respect, and didn't put himself above anybody. "Funny accents, that's all it is."

I remember driving off after the last time we worked together. I got in the van and looked out the back window. He waved good-bye to me as we drove away down a long road. He stood there till we rounded the bend. He got an Academy Award nomination for Best Actor for his role and mentioned Peck in every interview he gave about the nomination. Class and integrity.

I sat in my room the night we wrapped, after the party at a nearby casino, looking out the window at the Avenida da Liberdade, and thought about my experience on this film and the political demonstration. Down the block I saw a figure, limping unsteadily on a cane. As he came closer, I could see he had a bandage on his head and his arm in a sling. He looked up at my balcony.

"Hey, mate, I had a bit of trouble in Morocco." The story he told was that he had gone there for some recreational travel. He unwittingly found himself in an opium den. That's when the beatings started. He narrowly escaped with his life. His story made my curly hair straighten. It was full of everything, from a chase through the bazaar to being hung by his thumbs and whipped. He waited for my response.

"All that's missing is a magic carpet ride," I told him.

"I had one of those, too." He smiled wryly.

"What does that mean?" I said, smiling back at him.

"There are some things you shouldn't know, young man, but if the reward is big enough, the risk is worthy."

Cold. That's what driving up to Albany in January was like. I got out of the limo, and as the driver was getting my bags I saw my suite window, with my suitemates looking out at me.

Jack was the first to greet me. "Man, what was it like, did you nail any Spanish girls?"

"I was in Portugal."

"Portugal, Spain, fucking Panama, I love those Latin ladies."

Carey had long hair now. "Hey, I've been having more sex than in my entire life, which wasn't that much, but man, 'the friend's a movie star' really makes things happen."

We threw my bags into the suite and exchanged stories of the past three months. It was early morning when everyone left. Jack and I went to the food hall and ate breakfast.

"I'm leaving tomorrow. Going to California," I told him. I had gotten a call from Arnold the day before in Lisbon. He said that Jean Guest, a major casting director and head of talent for CBS, wanted me for *Billy,* a television series. John Rich, who had directed *All in the Family,* was the producer and director. The addiction was here to stay.

It was strange to pack up what I had at the suite. I had started a life here, walked away from the lights, the fast pace, the phone calls. But all it took was one taste and I was back in.

A week later, I stood at the gate with my family, waiting to get on the plane. And so my parents, my loving, understanding parents, had to let me go again. Before I flew out, my father gave me an Italian good-luck horn. "Keep this with you, it will keep you safe. But the best luck you can have is to use your head. Don't do anything you don't want to."

My grandmother escorted me to the door. She took my face in her hands. "Tatie, be a good boy. Don't take shit from anyone."

Chapter 9

Landing in L.A. was old hat now. I recognized the coastline, where the Santa Monica Mountains were, and where Michael lived. Not far from Universal and Warner Bros. That's where I wanted to live, but Michael had other ideas.

"You can have your old room, with one side deal. You have to get your own place soon. And your own car." I was being thrown out, for my own good. Michael knew that his house was a protection I had to grow out of.

I bought a used Toyota Corolla and Michael's friend was kind enough to take me apartment hunting. On Veteran Avenue, south of Wilshire, there was a small stucco monolith. The owners showed us a furnished studio apartment. The couch folded out to be a bed. "It's a bouch. A bed and a couch." So I had a "chouch" and a "bouch" in the same year.

"No parties, no noise, and no trouble. That's how we like it," the owners warned. "And your next-door neighbor is a very quiet grade-school teacher."

I slept there that night on the bouch, and woke up with a red mark on my back that took all day to disappear, only to return each night like an old friend. The mattress was a little thin.

I worked on *Billy* not far from the apartment. I took my Toyota through the gates of Twentieth and was actually on a studio lot legally. There was (and still is) such a thrill to drive up to the guard, and know your name is on the list. Or the best of all is to have the guard know you by face, and wave you in. Those are the egotistic treats of the business.

John Rich was a tough, no-nonsense director and fervent Democrat. His most prized possession was Nixon's signed letter of resignation, which he had somehow gotten and hung proudly in his office. He could be a curmudgeon but I was lucky to work for him. He was directing seven episodes, and Dick Clement and Ian La Frenais, who wrote some wonderful films, such as *The Commitments,* were writing all seven. I had the lead role, but Rich gave me no preferential treatment. He had been around the "actor monsters" that hit series had created and didn't like being pushed around by the talent. I wasn't going to become a monster, and he was going to see to it.

The very first day of production we were on set, ready to shoot, and he stopped the camera rehearsal. He pointed toward a man in a dark suit who looked like an executive.

"And who are you?" Rich crossed his arms over his chest. He was a big man, about 250 pounds.

"I'm Brad from the mail room." The man was being playful.

"And Brad, why are you here?"

"Eddie brought me." He motioned toward an affable crew member holding a large potted bonsai tree.

"And Eddie, do you always bring visitors unannounced?"

Eddie started sweating. *I* started sweating. "I guess I do."

"Well, I guess you are fired, Eddie, and you can take your friend Brad with you." Then Rich went into his thesis. "If I was your surgeon and while I was operating on you I brought my friend Brad from the mail room, would you mind?"

"I guess so."

"You guessed right. Why is it that every profession has boundaries, no one has friends come to watch them work, but in show business, everybody wants to visit?" He put his hands through his thick gray hair. "No visitors unless I say so. Now toodle-oo, gentlemen, we have a series to shoot." They scurried out and we got on with the day's work.

Later, he told me that he likes to fire someone right away if he can. It instills fear in the crew, and that will last the entire shoot. "It's good for them to be a little afraid. This is my ship, I know where it's going, and no one is getting in the way."

Even though Rich was irascible, he couldn't hide his soft side. He lived in Trousdale, an upscale (if that's possible) area of Beverly Hills. He had made a lot of money but had a frugal side to him. One that he said he developed as a kid growing up without money. "Don't spend everything. Save what you can, this is a fickle business." He drove the same car for years, wore the same clothes (expensive as they were), and lived modestly, except for the house. Houses in Los Angeles, especially in the film industry, are signs of success. Signals of things that have worked, which is rare.

We shot seven episodes of *Billy,* even one with Suzanne Somers. It was television, and things happen in a different way than film. The series has to perform for it to continue. I knew nothing about that. Maybe that was a good thing.

I watched the episodes in Los Angeles, and then flew to New York to surprise my parents and sisters. It was evening and I walked up the back stairs of our house. My mother was cooking dinner. I tapped on the window and she jumped.

Surprising my parents would become one of my favorite things to do. Invariably, I would sneak up on my mother, and make her have one of those moments. They always were delightful.

"The idea of the show is you are a dreamer?" My father watched with as much attention as everyone else, but was the most casual about it.

"And you get to see those fantasies acted out." My character was an ordinary guy who daydreamed like Walter Mitty. The show was based upon a film called *Billy Liar.*

He took a minute to decide. "I like it. Have you been wearing the horn?" He gave me a small smile. After that visit, he began calling me every morning at 6:30 A.M. in L.A. to hear what I was up to.

I started to go to The Groundlings improv classes. The Groundling Theatre was run by Gary Austin, Tracy Newman (who went on to create *According to Jim*), and Tom Maxwell. These people were on the cutting edge of comedy, and Michael had told me to join. In my first class were some of the most outrageous and competitive actors I had ever met. Phil Hartman and Paul Reubens were among my fellow students. In that class was also Victoria Carrol, who eventually became Mrs. Michael Bell. I would stare at Victoria like all the other improvisers in our class. She was the classic smart blonde, able to use her good looks as a weapon in scenes. All the platinum blondes on the silver screen, starting with Mae West, knew the business and their part in it. The beautiful blonde is an archetype, and if the look is marketed correctly, a fantastic career can be made.

Paul was a sweet, soft-spoken guy. I remember the first time I saw him stand on the tiptoes of his high-top sneakers and dance, which later became part of the Pee-wee Herman character. He was very, very funny. It was such a pronounced difference from his private self. I like Paul, and did some scenes with him that he was kind enough to choose me for.

Phil had a booming voice, and the ability to play buffoonish, self-important characters. When I see his work, whether it be *Saturday Night Live* or his film and television performances now in reruns, I see those tools from our class. He was the most likeable man you would want to meet. Something that I see time and again in talented artists. Along with true talent comes good manners.

"Good manners, that's all you have to have when on one of these talk shows." Wally Beene had suggested that I do a talk show, tell my stories and get some publicity. All for the possibility of being seen by someone who could give me a job. Wally had an in with *The Merv Griffin Show.* I met with a man named Murray, who was a straight-laced business type. He headed Merv's company, and said that Merv wanted me on the show. Wally then brought me downstairs to meet the booker, and got a lukewarm response. But he pushed the fact that Murray and Merv were in favor of me, and I was booked on the show, much to the booker's dismay. "Just don't do anything embarrassing," he warned.

The Merv Griffin Show was one of the longest-running talk shows on the air. He was famous for having the biggest stars and his casual and adoring manner was beloved by his audience. It was a show that catered to little old ladies and the family crowd. So of course I wore a skintight leather suit.

It was a two-thousand-dollar, little-too-snug Ponderosa getup. I got it on loan from *Billy* and promised not to get sauce on it. I looked ridiculous, but it gave Merv something to play on. I spoke quickly and too quietly. He kept repeating to the audience what I had just said, and was very kind in prompting me for the stories I was supposed to tell. There is such a thing as the preinterview, in which the booker gets on the phone with the guest and prods him or her to tell stories with a beginning, middle, and end. And there needs to be a payoff. So many times you can spend hours trying to get the right stories. In my pre, we came up with a host of stories that the booker felt comfortable with. I didn't remember any of them when it came time to tell them. Merv would give me a cue, and I would tell another story having nothing to do with the prompt. The booker stood on the sidelines pulling his hair out.

And Merv loved it. I was in my dressing room with Wally, and Murray walked in smiling. The booker tagged behind him.

"You didn't do one thing we talked about." The booker was holding his notes, exasperated.

"Doesn't matter, Merv liked him, that's all that counts," Murray said. And that is the truth about most shows that are dominated by one person. (Coincidentally, Jerry Seinfeld, a fellow Massapequan, was on that same show. We literally bumped into each other in the hall.)

Johnny Carson, on the other hand, did not like me. It was explained to me that he just didn't want young actors on his show. I accepted that until I saw him interviewing other young actors. The truth was that he just wasn't a fan of mine. But I have to appreciate that he let me go on with his guest hosts. David Letterman, Joan Rivers, Bill Cosby, even Jay Leno interviewed me on *The Tonight Show.* But not Johnny.

Well, I had Merv on my side and that led to *The Tomorrow Show* with Tom Snyder. Tom was a very bright interviewer, who put his guest in a chair across from him and did a one-on-one. Doing a stand-up with Merv seemed easy compared to sitting in front of someone, with nothing to lean on except my wits. No leather suit, no live audience to play off.

I was picked up in a limo, with a dark-suited chauffeur, complete with cap and gloves. I got into the back of this cavern with wheels, sat back, and tried to see through the darkened windows. It was about 8 P.M., and the show taped at 10. This was a Cadillac that floated along at sixty-five miles per hour. I started to sweat. The windows wouldn't go down.

"They've been stuck for a while. You want me to open a window up here?"

"Please."

"Boy, you look like you've been through the wringer and you haven't even started the show yet."

The chauffeur dropped me off at the studio, where Wally was waiting. The booker gave me a quite civilized preinterview. He went over all the material, and wanted me to be free to go wherever Tom went with the conversation.

"Are you going to sweat like that on the show? It's live, you know." The booker gave me a wad of tissues.

"Course not. The boy's got an automatic stopper. Once the cameras start he's cool as a cucumber." Wally was so at ease in these situations. He had been Elvis's publicist. He took me aside when the booker left. "Oh, he's just pickin' at anything he can, he's got to justify his salary. Just go out there and talk, and try to keep the sweat at a minimum. I don't mind being a bulldog here, but I can't be called a liar. There are enough of those between Beverly Hills and here." He held up an album, a scrapbook. Wally opened it and proudly displayed all my press clippings. "Here, my boy, is someplace to put all your stories. I call it 'The Guttenberg Bible.'" He was so proud of it. Wally was an authentic friend in a town of tinsel.

Tom smoked. He smoked before the interview, during, and after. He was very friendly before we taped, and made me feel comfortable.

"What's this I hear about you breaking in to Paramount Studios, commandeering an office, and calling casting directors yourself?" He was intrigued by what I had done and kept glancing offstage with an "is this guy for real?" look. I managed to keep the sweat under my arms and off my face. I didn't want Wally to be a liar.

It was like getting a shot from a doctor that you have been dreading. Before you know it, it's over. I was out of NBC and Wally was shaking my hand, telling me what a good job I did. My head was spinning. Tom's cigarette smoke added to my queasy stomach. Back in the limo, this time I wanted to ride up front. I felt silly being all alone in the back of the car, a phony playing the big shot. It was a rented ride, nothing more.

The chauffeur drove slowly and carefully. But the smoke and the nerves made me feel like all my stories were going to come up on me.

And they did. "Can you pull over?" He veered the Caddy over to the shoulder of the 405 and I opened the door and let all the free radicals out on the cement. I stood up and caught some of the cold valley air. *Is this going to happen often?* I couldn't take the nervousness, but I couldn't do without the business. I was hooked.

Chapter 10

I was still feeling uneasy and insecure about this decision to become an actor. It felt like a temporary thing. I loved the action, but knew, and still do, that it plays tricks on the mind. I started to dread the weekends. I wanted to avoid being alone.

A person who wasn't alone was one of my neighbors, a librarian. I would lay on my bouch, listening to her go through a physical competition every other night. I didn't know that lovemaking could be so brutal and, frankly, loud. At first I thought that she was being hurt, but after many hours of study, I realized she was enjoying it.

Twentieth Century Fox Television sent me out to promote *Billy.* Ten cities in twenty days. The treatment you receive when working for a big studio is fattening. The limousines, the first-class airfare, and the host of marketing and promotion people who are there just to make sure you are taken care of. Oh, and to make sure that the show gets as much notoriety as possible.

On this trip I would cash in my first-class tickets at the counter and travel coach. In those days, the airlines actually had real dollars at the counter and were able to give me a refund. I saved large sums of money and hid it under the rug.

One such stop on the ten-city tour was Chicago. The local CBS affiliate had a man named Gerald who was supposed to meet me. He waited for a while at the gate but when I didn't appear with the rest of first class he thought I wasn't on board. I caught up with him but I couldn't tell this guy that I cashed in for a seat near the lavatory. I knew there was a bit of the illusion that had to be committed to as a star.

"What do you like to do? Where do you want to go? Do you want to go out at night? Want to go to the clubs?" Gerald asked once we got in the limo.

"We can get you in anywhere," the driver added.

"Tonight we'll set you up in your suite, and we'll go for sushi tomorrow night." I agreed, but had no idea who Sushi was.

I hopped out of the limo at the luxury hotel like I owned the place. And everyone gave me the impression that I did. When I went to the trunk to carry my bag, the doormen jumped in and grabbed it from my hand. "We'll have everything sent up." I went along with it and tried to act naturally—except my heartbeat was 140 beats per minute and I was sweating. The bellman opened the door to a suite, something I knew nothing of. But I was a star on tour, who cares that I normally slept on a bouch.

The swirl of the attention and list of interviews was dizzying. The idea was to start at 6 A.M. with the radio DJs, who are so experienced they can do the whole interview for you. That's exactly what my first one did. We went to a studio on the outskirts of town. We were to start with the distant places and work our way back to the center, presumably to go meet Sushi. Gerry waltzed me into the studio and told me to "just have fun." The DJ and his sidekick took good care of me, guiding me through some questions and having me participate in some contests. I started to have fun with it, but it was the wrong fun.

"You didn't mention the show." Gerry turned from warm as sunshine to cold as a north wind. "You didn't get one plug done. You need to plug, plug, plug. Pronto." I walked out with my head down. I had no idea what plugging was. But I knew pronto.

"You don't stop talking about *Billy,* young man. You know we can talk about other things. Like knit one, purl two." I was on a knitting show at another radio station. My interviewer was ninety years old and waving needles as big as drumsticks in my face. But I wanted to give Gerry what he wanted, pronto, and it wasn't anything to do with knitting a sweater.

"That's what we want. When your host starts to veer the conversation to anything but the show, you turn it back. You keep control." Gerry started to drink at about 11 A.M., when he saw me getting a handle on the interviews. He had done this a thousand times. Only the cute girls working the halls interested him. The rest was just rote. Until the evening. We did our last drive-time radio slot and moved on to meeting Sushi. This was just beginning to become a fad, and the place was packed. Sushi had taken over.

Gerry had girls there from his office, and seemed very chummy with them, maybe overly chummy. "I'm going to have a little present in your room when you get back tonight," he said gleefully as he ate something that had tentacles on it. He fell backward, asleep on a huge pillow, as the party continued around him.

Later I put my key in the door and came into my suite. The maid had been there, all my clothes were cleaned and pressed and the curtains were drawn. There was a chocolate on one side of the perfectly made bed, and a woman on the other.

"I'm your little present. And I don't have a name." She was one of the waitresses at the restaurant that had served us lunch. I was speechless. Gerry had really done it. "Are you going to stand there or unwrap me?"

I would like to say that I did the right thing. Whatever that was.

On the way to the airport, Gerry had the most spectacular hangover I had ever witnessed. He didn't mention his present once, but wished me luck with the show. "You'll be back if you get numbers." Getting ratings was what it was all about. We didn't get them and he was right, I never went back.

No one called back. That's what happens when your show fails to get ratings. John, Ian, and Dick were the only ones to get in touch with me. The people from the studio were on to the next thing. We aired seven shows, they didn't get an audience, and I was back to zero. Instead of being at school with friends I found myself alone in my apartment, listening to my neighbor get her lights turned on by what sounded like an entire rugby team.

I did get recognized by a small number of people. I shopped every week at a grocery store in West Los Angeles, and once this very cute woman followed me from the peppers to the potatoes to the radishes, staring. I knew that I could have struck up a conversation with her, but turned away. But I liked watching her watch me. It was a different feeling than with that sweet misguided girl in my dorm.

Audition after audition. I saw the same guys. A few new ones, but mainly faces I recognized from other cattle calls. Because of *Billy* and CBS's Jean Guest being a fan, I was able to get better treatment during auditions. Just a smattering of preference. When I say preference, I mean the wait was forty-five minutes instead of an hour. But those minutes can add up.

Jean had a colleague, a brilliant and forward-thinking woman named Jane Rosenthal. Jane believed in me and we enjoyed each other's company. She was full of new ideas and went on to be very successful. She now is Robert De Niro's partner and cofounder of the Tribeca Film Festival.

Michael had a manager, Judy Thomas, whom he introduced me to. She was a charismatic hustler who introduced me to plenty of people. Her apartment was a melting pot of talent. There were singers and dancers, actors and performing artists. One of the actors she represented was Perry Lang, a towheaded charmer full of more energy than I was. He became a friend. He had done Sam Fuller's *Big Red One* and guest-starred on plenty of television shows. He had a Jeep. We would tear around the Hollywood Hills with complete abandon. Perry was a freewheeling type, completely opposite my uptight self. He lived in the woods in the outskirts of L.A. with a girl, I think it was Helen Hunt. Helen was a sensational person, and coincidentally also had a small part in *Rollercoaster.* (She was listed in the credits, unlike me. But of course she was, she was going to win an Academy Award eventually.)

One day Perry picked me up and was in an unusually anxious mood. The Jeep drove on two tires all the way to Judy's. He burst through the door as I tailed him, and there was Judy. "I love you and so does Steven Spielberg," she said. Perry had auditioned for the film *1941,* and got one of the leads.

That addiction! I felt it in my stomach as he hugged me and kissed everyone and everything in the room. He was going to get paid, he had a Jeep, he was living with a girl. But it wasn't me.

I couldn't stay home that night so I went to Paramount. I was still able to use the office and glean as much energy from the studio as I could. I visited every day I wasn't auditioning. Arnold wanted me to stop doing commercials, so the number of calls had been cut in half. Less action, and it depressed me.

I was on the underwater stage, just snooping around. I picked up one of the phones and asked for an outside line.

"Do you know that you have a doppelganger?" Mary Lou asked me with a sly smile in her voice.

"I do?" I knew this couldn't be good.

"Yes, and he was on a TV show called *Billy.* You little liar. You are an actor, you stole this office, you're using the phone illegally, and we know."

Silence. I started to sweat.

"I have the John Wayne photo."

"You better, or I'm going to climb those stairs to the executive suites and spill the beans."

"Please don't spill the beans."

There was a film memorabilia shop on Vine Street that sold photographs of everyone that was ever anyone. I asked the shopkeeper if he had John Wayne.

"The Duke? Not literally, but we have him in signature. Stop sweating in my shop, it causes mold." The place had shelves and more of Hollywood castaways. "We have several different shots, and he looks good in all of them."

I looked at cowboy shot after cowboy shot. They were all signed to different people. I needed a John Wayne photo signed to Mary Lou, I told him.

"I can forge it." That's what I needed to hear.

I drove back to Paramount, parked my usual block away, punched my card, and walked into the lot. She had wanted to meet me on the New York Street, which was being dressed as a New Orleans street. Only a few set dressers were there.

"Is it really him? Is he still alive?" She squinted at the signature. "It better be real. Where was he when you saw him?"

"He was at his home, on a horse." Lying through my teeth.

"He has horses at home? Well, of course he does, he is the Duke." She gave me a kiss on the cheek. "I won't tell no one, wasn't going to anyway."

"Why do they call him the Duke?"

But she was gone. I never spoke to her again. After that, I started to lessen my excursions to my office. Then I stopped going altogether. It just drifted away.

Steven Spielberg was casting the other lead in *1941* and Arnold and Nicole had gotten me an interview with the casting director's assistant. She pushed me up to the casting director, who liked me enough to recommend I take dance lessons, as there was a musical number. I took the lessons and practiced the routine. I did everything I could to win that part. But I was awful. When Spielberg saw me do the number on a sound stage at Universal, he was kind. I walked out of there thinking I had some worth, even though I had clobbered around the dance floor like a buffalo.

But I had a very good audition at Robert Evans's house around the same time. I had read articles about him in the trades. He is an icon, and still is one of the smartest and most charismatic guys working today. His house looked like something I'd dreamt up. The first time I drove my Toyota through those gates I thought this must be what Hollywood really is about. There were staff members buzzing about the place. He had a butler. I heard Mr. Evans's name forty-three times before I met him. And he didn't disappoint.

Bob came out to the makeshift set that was next to his famous tennis court, off the pool house converted into a screening room. He was followed by Dino Martin (of Dean Martin, father, fame) and Anthony Harvey, the director. Between Bob and Dino, no one could get a word in, or wanted to. Dino had lived a very public life, not only as Dean's son but as the singer in a successful pop band. He was blond, handsome, a professional athlete, a pilot, and a heartthrob. All I wanted was to be his sidekick.

In life, when a male meets another male, the common response is "Can I take him, or not take him?" In the audition for a buddy film it is all about "Can I befriend this guy? Can I act as if we are lifelong friends?" The filmmakers wanted to see who could create a friendship that was believable.

The *Saturday Night Fever* album played on the speakers surrounding the pool. The fountain (yes, a house with a fountain in the pool) sprayed a fine mist over the lounge chairs. A few feet away, there was another actor already auditioning. It was Jerry Hauser, a wonderful actor who had, among other roles, the lead in *Summer of '42.* Dino and Jerry sat down. They got along well. It seemed as if they knew each other. Another fellow auditioning was David Jolliffe, who had a lead role on the television show *Room 222.* I think one of them even had a guitar. Between these two guys, I thought I hadn't a chance. If everything was fair, I should have driven out of the gates. But it isn't.

"Guttenberg, get in there and show us what you got." Evans was friendly and encouraging. "You play guitar?" I shook my head. I knew I should have taken lessons when my mother gave me the chance. "Good, because Dino wants to be the only one who plays guitar." He gave me a wink. I sat down and we did the two scenes. Anthony Harvey had done *The Lion in Winter* with one of my favorite actors, Peter O'Toole, and I was eager to show him what I could do. Dino was as far away from me as a person could be. We were from completely different backgrounds. It was hard to see it mesh.

I drove out of there looking back at the people rushing to and fro. There were more auditions going on, and I saw other average cars with regular average faces coming in with the same awe that I had. There was a line of them around the block. Everyone wanted this part.

"You're going to Cuernavaca. Call us." That's all Nicole's message said. I got the part. The film was called *Players.*

Soon I was on a plane to Mexico, with a fancy rushed-through passport. In Cuernavaca, we stayed at a hotel called Las Mañanitas. The principals, including the very big star Ali MacGraw, were staying in sumptuous suites. I had a room and was glad to have it. At the hotel were two young ladies that were the most gorgeous women I had seen in person. Melissa Prophet (Miss California), and Rene Roman (Miss Indiana) were playing small roles in the film. What they also knew how to do was have fun. Dino befriended me; he saw from the first breakfast, when I was about to order something that would make me sick as a dog, that he had to show me around. Teach me how to survive Mexico without Montezuma's revenge. He had just broken up with Dorothy Hamill, the Olympic skater. He was a bachelor, and famous. The world was his oyster and he let me have a taste. Location can be one of the most attractive perks of being in the business. That security guard had been right.

Harvey would set up the scenes with almost nothing left to chance. He had his shot lists prepared months in advance, as opposed to Schaffner's morning ritual. He was a classical director working on a modern subject matter, tennis. *Players* was about a pro tennis star and his older and beautiful lover. My typical thespian outlook was I thought it was about the friendship that Dino's character had with Rusty, the part I was playing. I attacked every scene with a gusto that was totally inappropriate. This film was about how beautiful Dino Martin and Ali MacGraw were together and, oh yes, there was a best friend. I tried to create a character that you could read without words. I had read about Dustin Hoffman making a character work on-screen without words, that small techniques can eliminate the need for dialogue. I decided that I would try to make the physical tell the story. Sound could be cut, but if I could embody the character physically that would never be cut. I knew I had to spark a reaction in the audience. I needed to create my technique, and get noticed.

There was a scene in which Dino and I were at a filling station, and he was meeting Ali in her Ferrari. The scene was all about him and her. Not me. I spent the whole scene looking away, hopefully creating a moment that made Anthony use me as a cutaway as opposed to having me do the top of the scene and then vanish as scripted. I was the Greek chorus, I was the foreshadowing, but only *I* knew it. Anthony couldn't understand why I kept looking away, but he still used it in the editing of the film. Not all of it, but enough that you had to notice me.

Chapter 11

I got noticed. Jack Grossbart at the William Morris Agency had met me while I was working with one of his clients on *Billy.* He had called me several times to tell me that one day I would be ready for a powerful agency. The time had come and I was signed. The thing about agents or managers is you can't chase them. They want it to be their idea to represent you. They want that feeling of discovery, of seeing what someone else doesn't.

Leaving Nicole and Arnold didn't go as smoothly as the first time I left. Arnold was angry, and Nicole was hurt. I cried. I told them that I had to spread my wings, whatever that meant. But it was the best decision for the moment. Years later, they had a new company called Triad that eventually merged with William Morris. Everything connects.

"There's gold in them thar hills, and I'm going to prove it," Wally Beene laughed when I told him. "You are starting to get on these hound dogs' radar. They have to sniff you out. And Guttenberg, you are starting to become a delicacy. I know it. Just don't believe it all. Drink the sarsaparilla, but don't get drunk."

Jack was a television agent, and didn't cover the motion picture business. He introduced me to a tall, clever film agent, Steve Reuther. He had talent and a smooth-as-cream way about him. Someone told me that the names change, but the faces stay the same. I've seen Steve Reuther in many young agents.

Allan Carr was casting for his new musical, *Can't Stop the Music,* with Bruce Jenner, Valerie Perrine, and the Village People. The Village People were one of my favorite groups at the time. They seemed like a macho group of guys and I, like all the world, bought into it. Steve wrangled me an audition that was being conducted in the offices at the top of William Morris. Allan had produced *Saturday Night Fever* and *Grease,* both major hits. The agency would do anything for him, and giving him offices made it easier to get their clients in there.

I checked my messages from a telephone at UCLA that I had commandeered as my new Westside office. I would convince the operators that I had just gotten cut off, saving a dime.

"Put on a tight pair of shorts and get over to the office. Pronto." Steve was out to lunch when I called back, but I went home, put on a pair of skintight shorts, and drove over.

Jimmy, who ran the parking lot, was famous for getting the agents anything they needed. He knew where the bodies were buried, probably literally, and was treated far better than just a carhop. "You going to see Mr. Carr? I know you are. Nice shorts."

Steve had left instructions with the receptionist for me to meet Carr. I walked up to the penthouse floor and there were a hundred young men in short shorts. All looking like John Travolta. All with muscles. All with giant hair. And he picked me.

Allan, 350 pounds of cynicism and creativity, sat on a couch in a caftan, a flowing one-piece tent that covered almost all of his body. He sat with one leg crossed, the other on a special carpet that protected his expensive silk slippers. I tried not to notice that he wasn't wearing underwear.

"Turn around. Let me see your tush." I did. *Is this what I have to do to get a job?* "Steve Reuther represents you? I'll call Steve and make the deal. Do you have any aversion to wearing a sock in your pants? Enough." He clapped his hands like a sultan and his yes-men ushered me out.

"I don't know what you did, but you got the job. You're playing Jacques Morali, and Alan wants you to meet Valerie Perrine." Steve was there waiting. "Whatever you do, don't be alone with Allan, he's a grabber. This will be the weirdest experience you ever had, I guarantee it." He wasn't kidding.

I arrived at Valerie Perrine's mansion in Encino, an upscale portion of the valley. I walked up to the double doors and pulled on the huge knocker. I was greeted by two even bigger knockers, attached to Beatrice, a former showgirl. She was statuesque and naked except for the tiniest G-string. Next to her were two of the largest and most menacing looking mastiffs ever born. I was stunned.

"You are ze Guttenberg?" I nodded. "Come, come, Valerie is out by ze pool."

Valerie was an Acadamy Award nominee for *Lenny* and a former showgirl herself. She too was practically naked and covered in Hawaiian Tropic cocoa butter. She jumped up from her chaise lounge to hug me and her slippery skin caused me to fall over on her. The dogs perked up and rushed us.

"No, no, he's not food!" Valerie was kind enough to remind them. "He's my costar and you cannot have him."

I got my wits about me and was able to take in the grandeur of the place. The pool overlooked the valley, much like Michael's. But the house was a monster, there was a private chef, and there were men and women, also in practically nothing, sunbathing and covered in oil. It smelled like a coconut farm. I started to feel a bit shaky and of course started to sweat.

"Hey, kiddo, fancy meeting you here." It was Larry Mark, a marketing executive from Paramount who was in charge of the ad campaigns for *Players*. At last a friendly face. Larry put me at ease. "Eat something. The chef is from Ma Maison."

This nude scene, which, of course, was every young man's dream, was in reality too much for me. I backed out of the house, thanking Valerie and Beatrice for the pleasure.

I threw up in my car. So much for glamour.

Paramount was planning on a big premiere for *Players* in New York City. This meant a free trip home, where I could see my family and share with them some of Hollywood's finest. The event was to take place at the Ziegfeld Theatre. The only catch: the dress code was tennis white.

"What is tennis white? Is it white?" My father sat at the kitchen table.

"It's a form of white, Stanley. It isn't your T-shirt white, it's a more expensive white. Am I right, Steven?"

"I don't know, I don't own anything white except my underwear." I really didn't.

"Well, if this is going to cost me a dime, I'm not going. I don't need to spend money on some clothes I'll wear once and let them hang in the closet. I just won't."

"You'll wear whatever you're supposed to wear, this is a movie premiere, not a get-together in Brooklyn. It's about appearances."

"It appears to be expensive, and I'm not spending a dime." My father was firm.

Paramount reserved a room for me at the Plaza Hotel, and I dressed there. They bought me an entire outfit, all in white. They provided a makeup person, a hair person, and a chauffeur. My mother came in, dressed all in white. My father wore a tan suit and a grin on his face. "No one tells me how to dress. Not Hollywood, no one."

That night the entire theater looked like a Noel Coward dinner party.

The sports announcer Howard Cosell and his wife, all done up looking like an ice-cream man and his bride, sat next to my parents. Howard looked at my father and asked in his famous voice, "What's with your outfit, where's the white?"

"No one told me." My father shrugged. He whispered to me, "I'm the only one here that will wear his suit again." He was probably right. My white getup hung in my closet for years until I gave it away.

I flew back to California and started rehearsals for *Can't Stop the Music.* Rehearsals consisted of the director, Nancy Walker (a very talented character actress from the golden era of movies, but who was only famous to me for playing Rhoda's mother on *The Mary Tyler Moore Show*), watching the Village People being taught to act, me being taught to roller-skate, and Bruce Jenner being taught to take the film industry seriously. We were all horrible.

The rehearsal space was the Debbie Reynolds Studio in the valley, where our rival film, *Xanadu* with Olivia Newton-John, was also being rehearsed. It was being produced by Robert Stigwood, who had been partners with Allan on *Saturday Night Fever.* They had parted ways and hated each other, to put it mildly. But that didn't stop our two shows from mingling, especially the dancers.

Dancers, I found out, are an entirely different animal. They are probably the best athletes in the world. And they wear the tiniest of outfits, which suited me fine. *Xanadu* had American dancers. Not to be outdone, Allan had Hot Gossip, the British dance troupe, headed by Arlene Phillips, now one of the judges on the UK version of *Dancing with the Stars*. Hot Gossip were uninhibited in a way I had never seen. I watched them with my eyes as big as plates. Every time they did a routine, I fell off my skates, ran into walls, put food in my ear, and of course sweated. I didn't know what to do with myself. Then a friendly voice spoke to me.

"You like that? You're a funny one, Guttenberg." It was Gary Kalkin, the film's publicist. "You don't care about anything but the dancers, do you?"

"I care about Olivia Newton-John. And my relationship with her." And that was the start of a wonderful friendship and a routine we did for weeks. I pretended to be in a torrid affair with Olivia, and Gary played the doubting Thomas. It was probably the most acting I was able to participate in during rehearsal.

"Likeability and fuckability." Have you ever heard these terms in the context of selling a person? I heard them when I poked my head into

Gary's office while we were rehearsing. I was often lurking around. There is an old story about Humphrey Bogart roaming the halls of Warner Bros. and overhearing a conversation between George Raft and Jack Warner. Raft didn't want to do *Casablanca.* "Too many words." The story goes that Bogie hid around a corner waiting for Raft to leave and then poked his head in. "Hi, Mr. Warner." That's all it took. So I made sure I was always somewhere I could see something or hear something. I heard Gary on the phone, selling.

"This film has everything, it's sexy, funny, and has some star talent." He went on to describe everyone. "With Valerie you have fuckability, with Bruce Jenner you have a lot of fuckability and a good amount of likeability, with Steve Guttenberg you have a lot of likeability and I think fuckability, but a lot of likeability. With the Village People you have likeability and fuckability and it is rampant. It's the all-in-one chocolate shake of talent." He laughed. "I'm going to send you some photos and we'll have a clip in a few days."

I poked in. "I'm not fuckable?"

"You are, just not like Valerie and Bruce, and definitely not like the Village People. But you got it, I think the gay community will like you. And you know who runs this town." I didn't. But I smiled and agreed.

The filming was a gigantic endeavor. There were at least a hundred people on the crew, not counting the cast and production. We had costume designer Theoni Aldredge, of Redford's *The Great Gatsby,* Bill Butler, who shot *Jaws,* the editor John Burnett of *The Goodbye Girl, Grease,* and . . . *And Justice for All,* hairstylist Romaine Green, who has been on more Woody Allen films than you could name. This was an all-star crew.

It was a spectacle every day. One day Jane Fonda shows up, the next they film "the milk shake scene," with a set that cost a mini fortune. There were arguments and production stoppages. There was gossip and some sexy rendezvous on set. Bronte Woodward, the writer, visited the set, trying to keep things on track. Neil Machlis, the associate producer and production chief (he handled all the money for Allan and has gone on to be a very important producer) circled the film. And nothing could be done to make the whole thing hum. But to me, it was a big playground. I roller-skated down Broadway in the opening credits wearing frighteningly skin-tight jeans with a tight green shirt. They closed it for blocks and blocks. the shot started near the Colony record store and followed me for what seems like the Macy's parade route.

When we filmed in New York Allan had us headquartered at the

Plaza. It was *the* place in town, and I had to get as much free stuff as possible. It was thrilling being at a five-star hotel after eating Top Ramen for dinner every night in my studio apartment.

My twenty-first birthday occurred during the middle of production and Allan had my grandmother flown up from Florida, as well as my Mom and Dad and sisters brought in by the longest limo that BLS Limos had. We all attended the party at Elaine's, had an incredible feast, and Sammy Cahn sang "Happy Birthday." Sammy Cahn, who had thirty Oscar nominations and four of the statues on a table in the foyer of his home.

My mother and father were just going with the flow, enjoying all the exotic types. My grandmother was quiet, and that wasn't like her. I asked her what she was thinking. "Tatie, I just saw Sammy Cahn sing to my grandson. Oh, Tatie, you don't know what that means."

It all carried on until Allan announced, "We are all going to the most popular and famous disco in the world, Studio 54. Grandma, if you don't want to come we can have a limo take you home, but if you want to have a little fun, come along." He winked and had a laugh with her.

"Get the car, Allan, I'm ready to party." Allan took her arm and shepherded us into a caravan of limos like you have never seen. We all headed toward Fifty-fourth Street. I had my head out the window. I wanted to see the crowd outside the club from down the block. And it was a crowd.

Marc Benecke, the most famous doorman of all time, let us in. My family was escorted to the VIP section, where my mother immediately started a conversation with Andy Warhol and Bianca Jagger. My father sat on one of the couches, a bit uncomfortable. My grandmother was dancing. There was Liza Minnelli with her entourage and star after star. My mother schmoozing with Andy Warhol. The disco music boomed over the speakers. I saw my family boogieing with the best of them, even my father was persuaded to dance with Beatrice, Valerie's showgirl friend. He got up and slowly moved around, but by the second song he was shaking it like he meant it. Now I had seen everything. My mother, father, and grandmother all celebrating at Studio 54. The evening was perfect.

I was learning early that the best part of being famous was sharing it. There is nothing better than walking into a restaurant with those you love and having the maître d' showering you with compliments and falling all over himself to take care of your every whim. This is embarrassing if you are alone, but when you pass that special treatment to your family and friends, well, there isn't much better.

What *Can't Stop the Music* lacked in artistic merit, it excelled in fun. It showed me people and things that shocked me, but it taught me to tolerate the enormous weirdness that lay before me.

That summer while we were filming in New York, Martin Richards, the producer of *The Boys from Brazil* and a friend of Allan's, invited him and me to stay at his home in East Hampton and attend a lavish party there. I rode out with Allan in a ginormous limo. I had lived on Long Island for most of my life and never been to the Hamptons. But there I was sitting with the biggest, in both ways, producer in Hollywood. He had access to all kinds of drugs, which I wasn't interested in, but by the time we pulled into East Hampton, he was out there. The guy had an enormous appetite.

Marty's mansion by the sea looked like a hotel, with butlers, maids, chefs. (By the way, Marty recently won the Academy Award for *Chicago,* so he hasn't been idle.) I got to my room and there were clothes for me, all in my size. What the? Could these really be mine?

Then I was called to a lavish lunch at which the table looked like a Ritz Carlton buffet. In those days, seeing food like that was still new. I ate till I had to roll off the chair.

The next morning I woke to hear a hundred-person crew putting together an enormous tent for the party. I came down to see more food. Just more and more of everything.

The guests started to show up at seven. The Village People, Valerie, Bruce, and about three hundred of the Hamptons elite and social climbers were there. I got fairly drunk and found myself talking to a beautiful woman, an actress. The conversation led to looking around the house. A tour.

We found ourselves up in an attic room and one thing led to another. As we were discussing world affairs in walks someone who was a very big star. He was looking for this woman, and now he'd found her. With me. I'd had no idea she had a boyfriend, but that didn't solve matters. We were definitely caught with our pants down.

How I talked my way out of this, I don't know. I stumbled and stammered and somehow avoided a major ass-kicking. I had to get out of there as fast as possible. No need for this guy to come to his senses and punch me silly. I fumbled my way downstairs and found the limos. "To the United Nations Hotel and step on it."

I fell out of the limo when we got to the hotel, got into the elevator, and pushed my floor's button with a sigh of relief.

As I said before, there isn't anything better than sharing your fame with your loved ones. So before I'd gone to the party, I'd called my grandmother.

"Gram, I have this incredible suite at the United Nations Hotel. I'm going to a party in the Hamptons so you can use the room. Why not come in, meet some girlfriends, and see some shows. And buy anything you want, it's on me. Everything's on me."

"Tatie, I couldn't, it's your room, and it's such a fancy place."

"Nobody is fancier than you, Gram. I love you. Take the room, whatever is mine is yours, you know that."

"Can I invite a friend?"

"Anyone you like, Gram."

And I had one idea and she had another.

So, I drunkenly got to the room's door and knocked.

"Yes?" My Gram.

"Gram, it's me, Steven."

"Tatie, what are you doing here?" I heard a little movement.

"I was at the party but wanted to come back."

"Okay, Tatie, just a second." More rustling. And then whispering. I cocked my head. *Whispering?*

"I'll be just a second, Tatie." More whispering. The door opens and there is my sweet little Gram in a bathrobe. I walk by her and start to take my coat off. I opened up the closet and reached for a hanger. And there, hunched over inside, was the cutest little old man. He was frozen, one leg in the air, holding his slacks in his hands. Staring at me, not blinking.

Is that little old man having an affair with my grandma? I thought to myself. I had two choices: wake up out of my stupor or . . . just drop my coat and close the door.

And that's what I did. My grandma stood there, eyes as big as I'd ever seen them. "I'm tired, Gram, I'm going to go to bed." I flopped on the bed, and acted like I passed out. But I didn't. *Please, please let me pass out.*

I heard the closet open and two pairs of feet come toward the bed. Then, "You better get out of here. If he wakes up he'll kill you." I heard Gram pushing him away from the bed.

"He's out cold, he won't hear us."

Us? Us? No, please, please let me pass out.

My grandmother got him out of the room, thankfully. He begged and cajoled, but she was no pushover.

The next morning I got up and my grandmother came in.

"Hi, Tatie, how are you feeling?"

"I'm hungover, Gram, but feeling good. How about you?"

"I'm fine, nothing different. Everything the same." A twinkle in her eye.

"Okay, let's go get some free food, Gram." We had breakfast in the restaurant and traded hints. Neither of us was going to break.

This darn film had so many odd moments. I fell in lust with "Janna," one of the dancers, and made plans to visit her in London when we wrapped. Now, here is a lesson in life on location. When a film is in production, everything and everybody looks better. But after wrap, you go back to the real world.

When I got to London, I checked in to the hotel and rang Janna. She didn't answer. Odd. The next morning I called again. She answered but wasn't that pleasant and grudgingly made plans with me. I took a cab and found her house. Run-down and rough, like the neighborhood. I rang the bell and the door was opened by a six-foot-six, leather-bound, goth gentleman with a cockney accent.

"Aye, mate. Can I help you?"

I looked at the number on the door. "I'm here to see Janna?" *Was I?*

This made him a bit angry. He bellowed for Janna, I went back inside, and she slithered to the doorway. When we'd been on location she seemed fresh and clean and blond. Now she was dressed head to toe in black leather. At 10:30 A.M. All she needed was a mask and she was Catwoman.

"Right, you're here." She pulled a drag on her cigarette. "Right, well, uh, I have to tell you something." She looked at me with those blue eyes. The last time I saw them.

I flew back to Los Angeles for what would be an exciting few months. I had two movies opening, both *Players* and *Can't Stop*. They were rushing the opening of *Can't Stop* because of the imminent fade of disco and the return of rock again. I went on junkets that lasted for days. During these marathons it's possible to say things you don't mean, or want to say only off the record. I confided in one reporter who wrote all about it. I learned another lesson. The press wants the story. You are replaceable. Me, bitter? No. Jaded? Maybe.

As the junkets went on for *Can't Stop* the cast members started dropping out of the tour. We were flying from city to city, and every day we had one less Village Person. Then Bruce dropped out, then Valerie. And I don't blame them. If I had a brain in my head I would have fled too. But I was twenty-one, and ready for any free trip I could get my hands on. I ended up in Washington, D.C., at the Four Seasons Hotel with my publicist Steven Lewis Goldstein, basically touring solo and finding ourselves drunk in a hotel bar. It was there that a generous reviewer pulled me aside and broke the bad news—the film was a lemon. It was getting panned everywhere and I had better run for cover.

But I had two very good things that happened during this film. For one, I became a client of my business manager, Howard Borris.

There is a saying, "You can't make a living in show business. You can make a fortune, but you can't make a living." Believe it. When and if you are lucky enough to make money, it comes in piles. Business managers take these piles and divvy them up so you can live comfortably while unemployed and looking for work. You pay them five percent of your salary to do this. Tax deductible, of course, as they always remind you.

I originally met Howard when I was fourteen, the first time I visited Michael, when he lived in a bachelor pad off of Laurel Canyon. His first house, which Howard had advised him to buy. For years he had been Michael's business manager. Howard paid his bills, invested his money, and basically ran his life.

For the first couple of years I was in L.A. Howard did my taxes, but wasn't my business manager. My first year of being an actor I made about $7,500. He had told me to save my receipts so I could deduct them from my gross salary and reduce my tax obligation. I had no idea what that meant, but I collected my receipts and brought them to him in April. I had $8,500 worth of receipts.

"Steven, do you know how much you made?" I nodded my head yes. "Do you know you spent more than you earned?" Howard explained to me that he was basically a sheriff of the state, and that he had a responsibility to keep me honest. It was a good lesson in accounting, and the start of my fiscal education.

I was on the junket coming through L.A. and Howard visited me. He had never visited me. When a rep comes to see you, he is very interested in you. Beware the ones that don't visit.

I was sitting in a makeup chair and Howard came in and announced, "It's time for you to have some direction. You are making fifty thousand dollars on this film and you need to have investments."

The makeup man's ears perked up. "What do you think of investing in hot dog carts that have bikinied girls selling them in Century City?"

Howard didn't take his gaze off me but answered. "Restaurants are not a good investment but you could get laid if you owned the cart." The makeup man cocked his head. Free advice is free advice.

"So Steven, you have to direct all your fees to my office, and I will write your checks."

"And where will all my money be?"

"In my bank." Howard smiled.

"And what do I do?"

"You earn."

The best clients for a business manager are those that never call the office. That wasn't me; I bothered his bookkeepers with every question imaginable. But I started to learn about finance, which every actor should know about. I was interested in keeping as much as I could. Because every actor has his in and out times, no matter who you are.

The second fortunate occurrence was my meeting Rona Barrett on set. She was the preeminent gossip columnist, in the biggest newspapers and on television. As a good friend of Allan's, she was the only journalist to put a positive spin on the film. It was the only press that didn't make you want to crawl into a hole.

She took a liking to me, and gave me little gifts in the form of mentions. Being that she was the only game in town other than Army Archerd, the ink meant something. Rona was the first celebrity maven that took care of me.

Both *Players* and *Can't Stop the Music* came out . . . and bombed. The gray that falls over you, the film, and your career is maddening. So much work, with hundreds of people, for sometimes years at a time, all decided basically in one weekend. Hit or bomb. And they both were doozies. The very next day you have this muck all over you, and everyone takes a step back. And I can't blame them. If you stand next to someone who is hot you get heat, and the opposite is also true. I spent a lot of lonely times after the thrill of the Attention Tour. Allan was holed up at his house on Benedict Canyon, desperately trying to hold on to his power. He was alone, and seeing a mogul alone is very upsetting. They become human, and sometimes there isn't much human in there.

Robert Evans braved the soft opening of *Players* much better. He was very well liked in town, was able to spin it into other projects, and make lemonade out of the lemon. I admired Bob's ability to have a realistic outlook on this punch in the gut, while Allan couldn't accept it.

I had a friend, Chris from Massapequa. He was out in L.A. hustling in the young producer mode. He wanted to introduce me to a manager named Jay Bernstein. What was a manager? I didn't know, but Chris said he represented Farrah Fawcett and Suzanne Somers. That was impressive. They were some of the top stars in the business.

Chris drove me to Jay's place on Beverly Drive. "He has a Jacuzzi that fits twelve people." He winked. "You know what happens then? An orgy."

The door was opened by a butler who led us through a castle. It had to be 15,000 square feet. And he had a cane collection. Not a few. Hundreds of them. We walked into the den of a Great White Hunter, animal heads on the wall, where Jay sat on a leather couch holding on to a bejeweled cane. He had a goatee, glasses, and was very put together. The butler shut the door and Jay told me who he was. He was a preeminent self-promoter. A powerful showbiz guy. And he had a gun in an ankle holster. You have to think, why do you wear a gun? In show business? But it didn't matter to me. He could have worn a bazooka as long as he could move me up to the next level.

"Come with me, I want to show you something." He walked to the cane collection. "I have a unique collection of the world's canes. Everyone from the Marquis de Sade to President Nixon. I have all of them. And this." He pulled a fancy one out and pointed it at the door.

"Step back." He pushed a button and a six-inch blade came out of the center. "I like to think of myself as someone who gets things done. When I call the studios or the networks, they know that I have the Farrah-Suzanne machine. He who has that combo makes the rules."

He showed me around and presented me with the Jacuzzi. "Sits twelve, but stands as many as you could imagine." I could. I could imagine.

Jay introduced me to Larry Thompson, another manager he had teamed up with. They were very loyal to their clients. They went against type: even if the bigger client was on the phone, they would still concentrate on you.

Larry called me with an idea. Could I play Jimmy Craig, the Irish Olympic hockey goalie who became the famous flag-draped image of the 1980 Olympics? I could play anything, I said. "Just get me in the room."

"But you are Jewish, and Jimmy Craig is Irish." Steven Stern, the director, and Frank von Zerneck, the producer, looked at me as if I was nuts. "It won't work. Thank you for coming in."

That didn't mean a thing. I went to the barber and asked him to dye my hair red. Irishmen have red hair. He used lye to make sure the color stuck and did it at a cheap price. Everything about it looked good. It felt a bit crunchy, but I paid and went home.

That night I took a shower and my hair fell out. I don't mean a little, I'm talking about clumps. I looked in the shower drain and there was my head of red hair, and in the mirror was a bald twenty-two-year-old with a few wisps of maroon near his ears. I just about had a nervous breakdown.

The next day, I went through with my plan, which not only included having red hair (now just three strands of it) but had me dressed up in a goalie uniform complete with pads and helmet. I even had skates on. I strode into the ABC building in Century City and asked to see the *Miracle on Ice* people. I looked so insane that the casting director had to let me in to see Steven and Frank.

"What the hell are you doing?" Steven was very amused.

"You aren't going to hit us with that stick, are you?" Frank was laughing.

"No, I'm here to show you that I can play Irish." I took my helmet off and showed them my noggin.

"You shaved your head?"

"No, look at these hairs. They're red."

"You dyed your hair for a part you weren't going to get?"

"Not only did I dye it, I have it all in a box at home. It looks really good when I paste it to my scalp. Realistic."

A few moments went by. They stared at me, the casting lady stared at me, and I waited. Steven got up and walked around me. "And you did all this to get the part?"

In my best Boston accent, which I had gotten from a tape at the Samuel French bookstore, "I did, and I pahked my cahhr while wearin' the skates."

Steven touched my scalp. "Anybody have a comb?"

"I do." The casting assistant handed him one. Steven grabbed the strands and did a classic comb-over.

"Frank, I think this looks good. I think I could work with this hair." He smiled at me, and patted my head. "I have no choice but to give it to you. Anyone who would do this for a role deserves to have it. Now go home and grow as much hair as you can. We shoot in three weeks. And you are working with Karl Malden, an Academy Award winner, so bring your own comb."

I waddled around the room hugging everyone. I waddled out the door, down the escalator, and into the vast underground garage. And I forgot where I parked my car. It took me two hours of waddling down rows and rows of cars. But it was worth it, I had another job. I had another chance. I had another three weeks to grow hair.

Chapter 12

I'd got my little studio apartment settled. I was spending time at UCLA and Westwood was my home turf. It was at its peak then, a little college town catering to students and a small number of outside L.A.-ers. On the weekends it was packed. Food, girls, and action a walk from my apartment.

And Howard calls. "You need some deductions. You should buy a house."

There is a feeling you get when you make chunks of money. To see your bank account go from penny-pinching to having enough to buy something with walls and a roof is a major transition. The ego goes a bit cuckoo. *I'm buying a house.* I would use that whenever my ego needed it.

When I was in Mexico filming *Players,* I had an affair with a young lady who also lived in Los Angeles. We became close friends. She had an electric personality and looked like Ava Gardner. She was very social and had entrée everywhere. She knew all the big shots, the owners of sports teams, and Arab sheiks. She had expensive tastes and bought herself furs and diamonds, which filled her Hollywood apartment. More movie stars knew her than I could count. The big guys. The guys who you don't mention.

Effervescent, vivacious, and beautiful, she *was* Hollywood. A young struggling girl who got off the bus from Kentucky and used what she had to get ahead. She was famous for climbing over the wall of the home of a very important producer whom I would eventually work with. She jumped over in short shorts and introduced herself to the happily surprised impresario. They became fast friends. She later became a producer herself.

"Ava" introduced me to the clubs in L.A., to the nightlife that has its own celebrity. She could get in everywhere—except for the Playboy Mansion.

I met a reporter for *Variety,* Jim, who was a fan. He offered to get me an invitation to one of the theme parties, maybe the Fourth of July at the Mansion. It was all I could think of, I actually was going to the top of the hill. I could even bring a guest.

And wouldn't you know it, I could not attend. I auditioned for and got a guest role on *Family,* an ABC show. Of course I couldn't turn work down.

Ava asked if she could go, instead. She had never been there and wanted to work the crowd. It was a better party then, Hef was vital and personable and the crowds were smaller. He really circulated. You could really network with the elite there, and Ava wanted that.

"Can I come and bring someone and say it's you?" Ava was pushy even with me.

"But how?"

"I'll just say he's you, no one knows you, so what's the big deal?"

I took Ava's word for it. Not good. Lesson about to be learned: invitations to Playboy parties are NON-TRANSFERABLE.

I had a remarkable time on this ABC show. Ed Zwick, who later directed *Glory,* was a directing fellow from the American Film Institute and was the director's assistant. I got to soak up film technique from James Broderick, Matthew's father, and Sada Thompson, one of the most generous actresses in the business. My part was challenging; I played a villain. All was good on this side of town. Meanwhile Ava and, let's call him "Charlie," were on their way over to the Mansion to destroy my newfound Playboy credibility.

I came back to my new home from being as smarmy as I could muster on set and found a message on my machine.

"Steve, it's Ava. Charlie and I are waiting for a shuttle bus to take us to the Playboy Mansion! Ooh boy! Here, Charlie . . . say something."

"I am out of my mind excited, Steve. Hey, wait a minute, I'm Steve tonight!"

Ava got back on. "Hey, the bus just pulled up and there is a mob trying to get on. And everyone is in lingerie." Ava hung up. Those lucky devils. I had a 7 A.M. call time and had to be up at 5. So as I slept, my alter ego partied.

I shot another day at *Family.* The cast also included everyone's sweetheart Kristy McNichol. She was beautiful in an athletic way and a big star. It made me a bit giddy. There was something about working next to someone who was in all the gossip magazines that I couldn't ignore. I played my part but as I was saying my dialogue, I would think, *I'm talking to Kristy McNichol. There she is, in front of me. I think she likes me.* Nothing could be further from the truth, I don't think she noticed that I was there, but it didn't matter. Here was this beauty that the papers were talking about and she was in a scene with me.

I was about to do a scene that had me being particularly nasty and I decided to check my messages.

"Ah, Steve, this is Wally Beene here. You better call in, I got a word from Jim. What the hell did you do last night at Hef's place?"

What? What did I do at Hef's place?

"Guttman and Pam. Can I help you?"

"Hi, Carol, it's Steve Guttenberg."

"Oh, shit." I heard two or three extensions pick up.

"Steve, it's Dick. What happened last night? We have been getting calls all morning."

"Steve, it's Jerry. I spoke to Hef's office and they said you got into a lot of trouble last night. Hef is really pissed off."

An AD beckoned me to come to the set. I was frozen.

"I was working and then stayed home. I wasn't . . ." I realized who *was* there.

"Well, Jim spoke to Hef, and hoo boy, was he angry. He said you were grabbing the girls and leaped on the Viennese table. And they found you in Hef's kitchen in the refrigerator. What in Sam Hill were you thinking? What did you do that for?" Wally rarely got angry, and this was one of those few times.

The AD tapped my shoulder. "Finish this bullshit later. We have to rehearse and shoot." All ADs get inhuman at times.

"Can I call you back? I have to shoot. I swear I wasn't there."

Gerry came on the line, in his English royalty accent. "Well, old chap, it seems someone by the name of Steve Guttenberg was at the Mansion, and that Steve Guttenberg is banned from the estate, indefinitely. We need serious damage control."

I turned and walked toward the set as if I had been hit on the head. Try and concentrate when you know your boyhood dream was within your grasp, and someone just threw it in the river.

It was the best scene of the show for me. I focused on my dialogue and used Method to channel the feelings I was having about this disaster into the work.

When a player wraps on a show, before the entire show is finished, the AD announces: "Everybody, one of our guest stars is wrapped. Let's give Steve Guttenberg some applause." The cast and crew congratulated me and one of the grips called down from high on the rafters. "Hey, Guttenberg, I worked the party last night and you were the best thing there! I haven't seen so many bouncers kicking a guy out since I saw Ollie Reed at the Candy Store on Rodeo." There was a bit of an uncomfortable silence, and then the crew was on to another scene, another set. This stuff happens all the time in Hollywood, strange behavior. I got out of my wardrobe as soon as I could and raced home to get on the phone.

As I walked into my house the phone rang. It was Ava.

"Before you ask me what happened, it was a complete disaster and I had nothing to do with it."

"Ava, what happened?"

"The second we walked in, Charlie left me and the next thing I knew he was doing imitations of Hef using pretzel sticks as a pipe."

"That doesn't sound too bad." It really didn't. Seemed harmless.

"He was in the monkey cage in Hef's private zoo, and he was naked."

And it didn't get any better. The whole time Charlie was there he made a mess of himself. Or of myself. Ava said they threw him out, meaning he was put into a car and driven to the edge of the gates and tossed into the street. Lovely.

I sat in Wally's office at Guttman's on El Camino Drive. Wally leaned on the desk while Dick and Jerry paced.

"You don't know what this means," Jerry sniped at me. "Hef is a very powerful player and you ruined his party. Just not what you should do."

"I didn't do anything. It wasn't me."

He didn't look at me. "That's worse. You gave your invitation to some person you did not know. It's unforgivable."

"I think what we have is an opportunity." Wally smiled. He liked the game. "You or your double got a little over-anxious that night and let loose a little."

"A little? He drank Hef's Chateau Lafite from someone's shoe."

"This has been used forever. Mitchum in jail, O'Toole and that pack that roams Merry Old England. Sinatra is a loose cannon, the papers are full of rewarded bad behavior. Why shouldn't it be for our boy here?"

Dick loved it. "I agree with you, Wally. Jerry, this could be good."

Jerry got up and went to the door. "I think you guys have lost your minds, but I know where you are going and I've been there. I say do it, use it."

Wally and Dick concocted a plan to have the news of my/Charlie's bad behavior blamed on this role that I was playing. I was doing the Method and I couldn't leave the character on the set, brought it home, or home to the Mansion, and kaplooey. That was the plan.

It didn't work. They begged Hef. The call lasted about eight minutes.

Hef was polite to Dick, and believed that I was doing a role and couldn't get out of it. But I was still banned.

The William Morris Agency had been sending me out on teen films by the dozen. I wasn't tall enough, or short enough, or handsome enough, or average-looking enough. Then came an audition through a casting director named Ellen Chenoweth. She was looking for an early twenties cast to do a period comedy-drama. The film was called *Diner.*

I went on that audition like any other teen-twenties film and met Barry Levinson and Mark Johnson. Barry had worked with Mel Brooks and cowrote . . . *And Justice for All* with Al Pacino. He had written a script about growing up in Baltimore and was able to get financing through the enormously powerful and popular Jerry Weintraub. At the first audition, Barry and I talked for a long time. We talked about everything but the script. And then he asked me if I liked it. It's dangerous territory when a writer asks you about his script. Thankfully, I loved it, and saw that there was a depth in this material that I hadn't read anywhere else. It was literature. It wouldn't be a fluffy teen film about a bunch of friends pursuing girls. Only one car crash and no aliens. Just acting and filmmaking, and so the casting was central to the movie.

It was a good meeting but I didn't hear back from anybody about the role and thought that it had gone like the rest of the recent auditions. Then I got a call from Bernstein's office.

"Steve, it's Jay." I wondered which cane he was holding. Was it the one that could stab a person? "Larry is on with me too and wants to fill you in."

Larry spoke up, excited. "I was in New York visiting my client Barry White and got on a plane to Los Angeles and who do you think was on the flight?"

I was thinking about the fact that he represented the love icon. "*The* Barry White?"

"Yes, but that's not what is important. I was sitting three rows away from Jerry Weintraub. Jerry Weintraub the producer of *Diner.* And I thought to myself, 'Self'"—he chuckled—"'I got to go up and talk to him about Steve Guttenberg.' I mean the guy is just sitting there for five hours. So I picked a spot and went up to him and talked you up. He didn't know who the heck you were but he sure knows your name. If he doesn't remember a thing from the flight, he will remember your name. I said it about a thousand times." That's a devoted manager, saying my name over and over until someone remembers it. And Jerry did.

I was called in to have a screen test in New York. Kevin Bacon, Tim Daly, myself, and John Doe from the band X were put together to see if we had chemistry. We were hungry actors, strangers, trying to create the illusion that we were best friends. I walked away from it feeling that I did well, but still no call. I checked my machine as many times as Larry Thompson said my name to Jerry Weintraub. Nothing.

A few days later, my friend Mike Binder, a stand-up comic who now is a successful producer and director of films such as *The Upside of Anger* and *Reign Over Me,* was at my house. He was famous for practical jokes, like standing up in a restaurant when the bill came and shouting, "The baby is yours and I don't want to argue!" then running out and leaving me with the check.

The phone rang. Binder answered it. "No, he isn't, can I take a message." I tried to grab the phone, but he wrestled away from me. "Yeah, I'll tell him." He hung up the phone. "You just got a job in a diner. Back to waiting tables, huh?"

I called Larry back, then Jay got on the phone. They patched in my agent, Peter Meyer from William Morris, with his assistant listening on the other line. All the agencies started doing that after Sam Weisbord, one of the founders of William Morris, started having his assistants listen to his deals. Peter's assistant Elaine Goldsmith later became a successful agent, repping the likes of Julia Roberts, and produced some successful films. (Oh, she also was kind enough to type up some of my papers when I was in classes at UCLA.) It was the only way to learn the business, and is still practiced, so watch what inside jokes you tell.

Larry gave me the news. "They want ya. Which is real good. And Peter, I think you should tell him the deal."

"Steven, we have a good deal, and a good deal," Peter said. "They offer you thirty-five thousand and second billing, or thirty thousand and first billing."

I sat down on my stoop and had one of those moments. The moment when you know you have a job. That you have something to do for the next three months. You are on vacation from the hunt for food. You are getting paid. And maybe, just maybe, someone will see you in it.

I said my good-byes to a girlfriend or two, and set out for Baltimore. But not before lending my home to two friends I knew socially and had had some hedonistic fun with. Of course in my brilliant mind these were the guys to have housesit. Did I realize that the house cost real money? Obviously not.

The plane landed in Baltimore and a driver took me to a Holiday Inn not far from the Inner Harbor, a trendy mall. I met Tim Daly in the lobby. He had a box of cassettes that he was looking through and was smoking a cigarette. "We're supposed to be best friends in this. Let's go walk around."

We went to the Inner Harbor to shop and talk. In those days there was no Internet to know who anyone was, their credits, their profile. So it was really an opportunity to tell each other who we were and what we wanted. Wants are a very large part of acting, whether in a scene or in life.

Tim had several businesses, one as a contractor whose specialty was tile work. He was classically trained as an actor, looked like Superman, and was a really smart guy. We went well together that day, having a good time, two actors happy to have a job, and that giddiness made us bond. These bonds, especially when you are young, help the performance.

We got back to the hotel and found notes under our doors. There would be a reading tomorrow in Barry's room for all the cast. Ten A.M. pronto.

At nine forty-five I knocked on Timmy's door and found him smoking and organizing his script. He was meticulous in his preparation, having his character's scenes marked with thin pieces of colored paper. My script was in a binder and was well worn from my reading it again and again.

We walked toward Barry's room, which was identical to ours. There was no "I'm better than you" on this film, no "I get a suite and you don't." It was a small movie, with everything spent on the screen. We knocked on the door and I thought we were early. We weren't. The other guys were there ten minutes before we were. Sitting on the one bed and around the floor were some of the guys I met during the screen test, some I hadn't. Mark Johnson, the executive producer, was there, smiling and thrilled to see us.

"Tim, Steve, I want you to meet the other cast members, this is Danny Stern, he is playing Shrevie." Danny was tall, wearing the oldest clothes I had ever seen. I recognized him from the film *Breaking Away*. He had a distinctive voice, one that you couldn't help but like.

"This is Paul Reiser, he plays Modell." Paul was sitting cross-legged on the floor.

"I got the role shopping for underwear." We all stared at him. "Actually I went along with my friend, he was auditioning, I was waiting for him and Barry asked me to read. I really needed underwear, though." Barry loved him. He had made his role bigger because of Paul's talent.

A good-looking guy with thick blond hair smiled and laughed as he said hello. He was wiry and powerful, and friendly as all get-out. "Kevin Bacon. Good to meet you guys." Kevin already had lots of success in theater and in a soap opera in which he played a character known as Tim the alcoholic. Later we would be walking around and people would recognize him and shout, "Hey, it's Tim the alcoholic."

Barry looked at a beautiful girl sitting in a chair, waiting for her moment. He motioned toward her. "This is—"

"Ellen Barkin, nice to meet you." She had a strong handshake and overflowing charisma. Like the most popular girl in school. She was in incredible shape and really happy to be there.

Barry looked us over. A brilliant screenwriter on his first directing job. "We need one more. I saw him before, maybe he's wandering. Where is he?"

"John Doe?" I thought they hired the guy from the screen test.

There was a knock on the door. Mark stepped up to it and in walked Mickey Rourke. "I'm sorry, I didn't know where . . . I was looking around. . . ." Mickey has a bop to him, like he hears the sweetest jazz all the time. He smiles like he knows something we don't know. He had a leather jacket on with a white silk scarf. He took the jacket off and kept the scarf. He had style, and a pompadour of chestnut hair. He looked like Monty Clift. He shook everyone's hands and sat on the floor and opened his script, which was in a leather binder.

"Let's begin." Barry led with the stage direction and we read. The work came alive, and we played like we were in the same band for years. There was a little improvising, not much, mostly sticking to the page. Lots of playing with the elusive Baltimore accent. The script supervisor was there timing the read.

Barry smiled afterwards. "Felt good. Any thoughts?"

"I liked it, good job everyone." Mark gave us some kudos. It was an uneventful session, it seemed. But what happened was the best thing that can occur at a first reading. It was working.

For the next few days we all had a chance to get to know one another. Barry knew all the places to go. We had dinners at crab houses and restaurants that he had gone to for years. Barry took us from location to location, all together in the van, looking at where we would be acting. It gave us a sense of security, and we could mentally prepare. It was a van full of brilliant people. We all had something to say, we all started to define who we were for one another, and how much we would be able to be pushed. In those five short weeks we created a language that we all spoke.

The city of Baltimore really laid out the red carpet for Barry. He was a native son, a favorite of the mayor, and the city went out of its way to help make the film. There was a fancy party, Barry's parents were there, and he invited all the people that we were playing in the film. There is nothing better in this business than sharing it with those close to you. And since we were filming entirely in Baltimore, Barry got to spend months with the friends he had grown up with.

"I'm the character you play. I'm Barry's cousin." And indeed, there was the real Eddie. He had a thick Baltimore accent. He told me about Barry as a kid, how proud they were of him, and how excited he was to be making this film. It was a good way to start production.

The first day we got picked up in the van and brought to the wrong street. We walked up to a building that was supposed to be a billiards parlor; it was a sheet metal shop. No problem. We bounced back into the van and found the set one block away. We saw Barry near the catering truck. He told us of the time he was working at Universal and Jack Benny and he were at the coffee truck. He described Mr. Benny ordering in his slow and deliberate voice, pinching his pennies out of a change purse.

Barry was gifted at noticing the small things in people's behavior that gave them an identity. And how those characteristics could reveal or hide the person's real desires and secrets. That is one of the things that makes him a brilliant director.

The first scene we shot was Tim and me checking in with the owner of the pool hall, getting a table. The actor behind the desk was a first-timer, a civilian. Barry had nonactors playing in many of the scenes, and they were believable.

It is really true, a great director can make anyone look good. Especially with a talented cinematographer like Peter Sova. He had done a documentary called *Rockers* and was having a big start to his career. He was Czech, and had an unbelievable eye for film.

We were on to the next setup and Mark came over and said that Jerry Weintraub was there and wanted to meet us. It was like meeting a movie star. Jerry is about six foot four, handsome and Charismatic Galore. A mountain of a man with a wise and sensitive side. He made everyone feel like we were doing important work, that the studio was counting on us, and had high hopes for the film. Jerry was giving us the best gift a producer can give, the gift of confidence. Jerry knew we were young and nervous, and he wanted us to be in an atmosphere of freedom. Freedom from the studio and from tinkerings. He wanted us to be free enough to be those guys he recognized when he read the script. To add to the great movie that he wanted to produce.

We actors filmed around Baltimore every day, and at night we started to pal around. We all went to a health club that was a drive away from the hotel. Mickey, Kevin, Tim, and Ellen were regulars. I remember sitting in a steam room for the first time with the guys. Kevin used a loofah, which he said removed dead skin. A loofah? I had no idea. He was also the first person I ever heard say, "You can never be too rich or too thin."

I became very fond of Mickey. He had an outsider kind of attitude, but was very aware of everyone's feelings, even if it appeared he wasn't. We would sit in each other's rooms going over scenes and doing acting exercises. He was a student of Sandra Seacat from the Actors Studio, and he shared some of what she taught him about honesty in the work. At the same time another actor was getting a lot of the parts Mickey wanted in the business and he was very discouraged about that. He had just gotten married, one of the reasons he wasn't at the screen test, and was very much in love. But me being single, he accompanied me to a few clubs to listen to music, and we got to know each other through the music we liked. He was also a reader, he had a book near him most of the time. And the scarf. That white silk scarf.

I will forever remember the hairstylist, Christine George, and her bouts with Mickey about his hair. Christine wanted his hair neatly parted and clean. Mickey wanted a high pompadour. Their arguments were infamous, the yelling, the throwing down of brushes, the slamming of doors. Mickey eventually won. But Christine gave him a good fight. He would leave the room with his hair her way, and pump it up in his honey wagon to where he wanted it. He would come to the set like that, and Christine would have a conniption. Fun to watch, but I wouldn't admit it. We all had to focus on our characters and Mickey had very definite intentions about playing Boogie. And he was on the money. We got to meet Boogie, who was a legend in Baltimore. Boogie had founded Carousel Jeans, which, if the rumors are correct, made an enormous amount of money. He was rich and famous, had a wonderful personality, and was a neighborhood guy.

Diner was the perfect movie. Everyone was at their best on this film. We all would visit each other's scenes while we were filming, which was rare in the moviemaking world. Watching each other work was another plus that I recognized only after doing other films where you go to your own trailer when you are not in a scene. I got to watch Danny do a scene in the appliance store where he sells a television to a customer who wanted to know if *Bonanza* would be in color. Mickey and Danny talked about the scene and Mickey suggested that Danny rub his nose during the dialogue. If you watch it you'll see Danny flick his nose. And Barry cast a civilian, a nonactor, Ralph Tabakin, as the customer. This guy was so good that he became Barry's lucky charm in many of his films. Danny was so loose and real, his acting flowed with the nonactor so well, you do forget it's fiction.

When you shoot in a non-show-business town, people want to know all about it. They're looking for famous movie stars.

"What are you making?" someone would invariably ask as we actors stood around a trailer.

"*Diner.* A movie."

"Never heard of it." The person would want more. "Who's in it?"

"We are."

"Who are you?" They could get a little irritated if they weren't fed information they could bring home. We would say our names.

"Never heard of you. What have you been in?"

And it would go on every day. Kevin would invariably save us, as he was the best known. "Hey, yeah, Tim the alcoholic. You're really good." But aside from Kevin, it was a blank look in their eyes, and disappointment. I tried something different one day.

"What are you filming?"

"*The Godfather.*"

"No."

"Yes."

"No, couldn't be, where?"

"Down the street, in one of those houses."

"Oh no, really? My wife will flip. Who's here?" He was buying it. Finally something to bring home.

"De Niro, Pacino, all of them."

"James Caan? Sonny?"

"Yeah, they're doing the toll booth scene later."

"With the guns? I love that scene."

This really happened. Give the people what they want. He wanted movie stars, not unknowns. His wife came out after he went in and told her. She figured it all out, got a kick out of him believing it, and actually asked me to come to dinner one night, which I did. Their whole family listened as I told stories about the famous people I had met. That's all they wanted, some Hollywood.

The location of the actual diner was near the water. It was one of those prefab silver bullets that was at home in its perch the second it was placed there. A diner has a look of its own. Anyone seeing a diner from a mile away knows, "Hey, there's a building where I can get eggs, a hot meal, or even French fries and gravy." Ours was the epitome of a diner. The storyboard artist became the "owner" of the diner and with his thick accent it was all the more believable. It looked real from the outside, and it looked real from the inside. And the most fascinating work happened in about ten square feet inside. The booth.

When there are boundaries any actor will bounce off those restrictions. And if he's lucky, he could do some good work. He doesn't need much space. Just someone to hit the ball back. And here were six guys fighting to be brilliant. The competition was encouraging. And maybe, just maybe we were doing something that would be seen.

Somehow, some way, there was a working telephone in the back of the diner. It had a long-distance line that anyone could use. These were the days when calling across the country, or even across town, was expensive. So if you had business or a wife across the country, then you wanted that phone. Two of the guys needed to make cross-country calls often. One day we were filming and heard them arguing off-stage. The fight escalated, and suddenly we heard the kitchen in an uproar of pots and pans. They eventually worked it out, but it was some more excitement that added to the tapestry.

There was a group of scenes that didn't get into the film in which Kevin would be ambushed by a character called "the Grip," played by Arnie Mazer. If the Grip grabbed your hand, he never let it go. He was constantly trying to catch Kevin's character, Tim Fenwick. There were scenes in front of the diner, and around Baltimore, when the Grip would come upon Kevin and just ask for his hand.

"Come on, Fenn, just grab my hand. Let me have your hand, nothing is going to happen." And inevitably Kevin would give in and the Grip would pulverize his hand. Kevin has made a reputation as a dramatic actor, but he was also in *Animal House.* He knows how to be funny. The scenes were well done, even if never seen.

In the original screenplay, Mickey and I had no scenes together. We really got along well and wanted to do some work together. So we decided to ask Barry.

"You guys want a scene together? That's a good idea. What do you want to do?"

"We don't know, maybe something about Boogie knowing more than Eddie," Mickey said with that smile.

"Let me think about it." And about an hour later Barry said he wrote something in his trailer that he wanted us to see. It was the scene at the counter where Mickey asks me about my sexual prowess and my character admits that he's a virgin. "Technically, technically I'm a virgin." Now that might have been enough for the scene but Mickey steals it. And if a scene can be stolen, then it is in all probability a wonderful scene. He picks up the sugar jar, pours himself a mouthful, and then washes it down with Coca-Cola. Done, finished, scene. Score.

When Tim and I did the sequence at the strip bar, that was when I felt like we had a hit. All the work that was being done, all the scenes I had been in and watched, reached a crescendo in that bar. The scene was about us having a night on the town, and giving each other support. Tim was so relaxed and in control, and Barry had taken us to a strip club a few nights before to get in the mood. He kept getting us closer as a cast. And it kept working. We got to know each other off the set, and brought that friendship to the work.

Barry had wonderful dialogue and a clever and human story. He set the scenes up, told us what he wanted, and said action. He let us loose on the material, and we ate it up. We would do the written words, and then the cameras would keep rolling so we could improvise. Then the improv would sneak into the scenes. It was one of those rare experiences when everyone was in tune. For the characters, the diner was a place to meet and talk. For us actors, it was a racetrack where we could show off. And improvise.

Paul and I had a good relationship. He has a big heart, and is quite generous. He gave us laugh after laugh, and would inject his own view of life into Modell, his character. He would throw you a line, a look, an attitude, and give you an opportunity to hit back. So in one of the many improvs that went on, he turned and asked if I was going to eat the roast beef sandwich in front of me. "Are you going to eat that?" And that hit off some of the best moments on film I have ever had. My character was stubborn, and his character wanted more, and they went together like Laurel and Hardy. With Barry leading the way, we parlayed that very real moment into a comedic through line that hit a nerve with the audience. It was called back in later scenes, and the audience loved it. We respected the audience in *Diner,* and knew they could follow us. Paul is a wonderfully gifted guy, and I am lucky to have had those moments with him.

The script to *Diner* is just brilliant. A work of art, and it gave the film room for improvisational riches. Barry would direct us after each take, shape the scene and the improv, and let us do it again and again. His eyes and ears were able to choose which dialogue should stay, which should go. He incorporated a new sound style as well. Usually when actors are offstage, they have to avoid "overlapping," which is stepping on the dialogue of an actor on-screen. Barry miked everyone, let them talk offstage as equally as the onstage actors. We didn't have to mime when off-camera, giving all of us a freedom that had never been allowed. Now we were able to have all the actors do their usual thing onstage and off, and it created a realism and creativity that couldn't be achieved on a regular sound setup.

Danny didn't trust anyone, not even a maid, to enter his room. And he ultimately had good instincts about this. He came into makeup one day pale white. It seems that while he and Laure, his wife, were sleeping, someone had burglarized them. I had never heard of that, someone being a few feet from you, taking your belongings. They lost money and were scared. My apartment being robbed was nothing compared to that. But Danny had an ability to focus better than most actors I know. He was so upset about the robbery, but once the camera was rolling, and we were shooting, he ran the scene.

At the end of the day we would all do one of two things. If we were shooting days, we would end up at the Holiday Inn bar. The guy who stuck out was this grip who had a coke spoon hung on a twenty-four-karat chain around his neck. Today, it would be impossible to wear that. But then it was hip. He often sat at the bar telling me his exploits. He loved shooting nights, it's when the spoon did its thing. And we had lots of night shoots. Our routine after the night shoots was to go to a diner and have breakfast. Exactly what our characters did, and the art met reality over coffee and eggs. There is an enchanting atmosphere when you have been up all night. Intimate conversations occur, and they build relationships. Those relationships transfer back to the work, and the acting is better. We liked each other, pulled for each other, wanted for all of us to share in the shine. The competition was there, but it only made us more creative. It was as healthy as it gets.

There is something unique about being in a first-time director's film. You only realize how exciting it is after the experience. Directing a film can be taught, read about, and talked about, but nothing prepares a person for the first time they say "action." The story goes, and I'm not sure it is true, that on the first scene we filmed, all the cameras, sound, and Tim and I were ready to film. The first assistant set it up and gave Barry the nod. But he didn't say anything, he just watched. Someone had to whisper to him, "Barry, say action."

Barry had a calm, even-tempered demeanor. He couldn't be messed with, but was open to you bringing new things to the scenes. It was his vision, ever since he told the stories of the diner to friends and people he worked with, like Mel Brooks. They told him that *Diner* was a movie. He wrote it, and knew every inch of what should be on-screen. As good a director as has ever been in the business. We were all lucky to be in his directorial debut. And he only improved on each film he did. *Rain Man, Wag the Dog, Tin Men, The Natural, Quiz Show,* the list goes on.

Diner wrapped slowly, each of us doing our scenes, every one of them memorable and a gem. I really believe it was the perfect movie. As show-business traditions go, one of the best is the wrap gift. At the end of every film, the cast, director, producer, and some crew give gifts to one another. Tim's gifts were outstanding. He got trophies from a local shop. Each one of us had an engraved silver trophy, like ones given out for Little League. They had personalized sayings on them. Mine was THE STUD, THE KING, THE MAN, which was something that I, please don't laugh, used to call myself. Please forgive my youth. But it was funny when I said it because I wasn't any of them. Timmy remembered everyone's idiosyncrasies, and put them in writing. We had a dinner where we exchanged our gifts, and Tim's were the hit. They were perfect, for a perfect film.

At wrap, I ran to a pay phone and called Wally.

"It's really taking shape, Wally, I think we have something."

"Then let's get you on the phone with Army Archerd."

Army Archerd was *the* columnist. He was the voice of the business, having the inside page of *Variety.* He was Page Six before Page Six. He knew everybody, and more important, everyone wanted to know him. He and his friendly wife, Selma, were in the know about every film and every actor. He loved meeting new talent, and he loved unknowns, and breaking them before anyone else.

"Guttenberg? What kind of name is that?"

"Austrian."

"Any relation to the Gutenberg Bible? Or the printing press?"

"I think so. Maybe." It's important to be interesting in interviews. I wasn't.

"Well, is there anything going on there that I can use?" Army could get to the point.

I couldn't think of anything but, "I'm wearing Robert De Niro's shirt."

"What? Robert De Niro lost his shirt? This is good. What are you doing with De Niro's shirt? Does he know you have it?"

It was a shirt that I wore for one of the scenes, and it was labeled DE NIRO, and the costume designer knew that it came from one of his films. A head full of set stories and all I could come up with was that. But that was all he needed. Army was so good at what he did that he was able to make anyone seem interesting and full of some sort of glamour. Wally called me later.

"I heard you and Army had a good talk. He loved you. Thought you were charming and had panache. And what's this about De Niro?"

"What's this about panache?"

I was invited to a screening and met Wally Beene and Dick Guttman there. I watched as every scene unfolded and melded into the next. The story worked, the characters were compelling, and when the film came to a close the audience was elated. Then, MGM would not release the movie. What? The perfect film won't be shown to the public?

Barry told us there was an executive who felt it had no car crashes, no sex, no teen comedy, and no appeal to the audience. That's it, there wasn't even video then for it to be released on, so the film would be shelved. Good try, kids, we'll write it off. I was devastated, as was the rest of the cast. How could something so good be unreleasable? Dick and Wally both loved the movie, and my managers Larry and Jay thought that Barry was the new bright star in the directing world. He was Mike Nichols, and this was his *The Graduate*. MGM thought they had a turkey.

Paul Reiser described this: "There's a story that Barry always told afterward when the movie came out, how executives didn't know what to do with it, the studio guys, and they watched a rough cut of it, a screening, and they said, 'Look, like that scene in the diner when they're arguing about the sandwich—why doesn't he just give him the sandwich and get on with the story?' and Barry said, 'Because there is no story. That is the story. The fact that they were hocking each other for fifteen minutes over a sandwich is the story.' "

It was the first time I heard the term "shelved." But it wasn't over. The filmmakers lobbied for the film, and it was Barry who showed it to the mega film reviewer Pauline Kael, who wrote for *The New Yorker.* And this was one of those magic, lucky times when a reviewer can actually change the course of a film's destiny. Kael was going to run a review of the film, whether MGM released it or not. And it was going to be a glowing review of a movie no one could see. Ellen Barkin said that the studio was embarrassed into releasing it. And lucky for us, it worked.

A hit is unlike anything you know, or I know, or anybody knows. It comes from a deep, intense energy on the production, and a lot of luck. Luck that you have the right script, the best director for it, the perfect casting, and a studio that has the money to release it. Wally would tell me it is hard just to make a movie. But to get a hit, well, you can imagine the odds.

And you are rewarded. Really rewarded. All the filmmakers, the cast, the crew, everyone got the shine. When you are in a hit, you have heat. And everyone in town wants some of that heat.

Everyone got calls. Everyone got meetings. Everyone got work. Things changed for all of us. All the meetings you couldn't have, you got. You were on the short lists, you skyrocketed to every studio executive's assistant's watch list. And not only was *Diner* a hit, it was beautiful art. It was compelling in its storytelling and characters, and it got respect.

For an actor, things start to turn around. You start doing the choosing. What film or television show do you want to do? Do you want to work with this or that artist? Do you want to meet Francis Ford Coppola about a film? At his suite at the Sherry Netherland in New York?

But I get ahead of myself. Before all this happened, as I packed my bags at the Holiday Inn after we wrapped, preparing to get on the plane to L.A., the phone rang. It was my friend Larry Richman, my get-me-into-clubs-even-though-I'm-underage friend.

"Do you know that there are people staying in your house?"

"Yeah, Billy and Ken."

"Well, they aren't there. There are about twenty people staying there, and they have a dog."

A dog? I called Berger and Stovitz, no answer from them. I got on the plane, and got a taxi. I got let out at the corner and saw my house. Lots of cars in front, none I recognized. My key still fit the door but that was the last thing that was the same. It was 2 A.M., and in the moonlight I saw disaster. I headed toward my bedroom and saw two people sleeping that I didn't recognize. The guest bedroom, filled with more sleeping people I didn't know. My office, filled with bicycles.

I kept my cool, and wrote a note.

Dear whoever you are, I am the owner of this house. I will be back at 2 p.m. today. Please be gone.

I went to Larry's apartment and slept on the couch. It's funny how casual you are in your twenties. Crashing on couches, no problem. I went back to my house at 2 P.M., and found my small wine collection empty and the people gone. But there was a full dog dish, and a note: *Sorry.*

Berger and Stovitz's story was that they gave the house to someone to watch because they were going away, and then mayhem ensued. They both felt bad about what happened, and all is forgiven. These guys are both good guys and successful players today—Stovitz runs Will Smith's company—but man, the things that happen when you are young and stupid.

It was fun to hear about my costars getting big jobs and becoming celebrities. It's wonderful knowing someone before the whole world does and a thrill to read their names in the paper, or the trades. Your other teammates are cleaning up, and there is enough for everybody. Barry's next film was *The Natural* with Robert Redford. Mickey was on his way to do *Rumble Fish* with Coppola. And my pick? I did a 3-D comedy thriller. Sound like the right choice?

Bruce Malmuth, the director, had done a pretty good film, *Nighthawks,* with Stallone. The film was being done by Paramount and Frank Mancuso Jr., son of distribution giant Frank Mancuso and a success in his own right. He produced all the *Friday the 13th* films. It seemed like a good bet. It wasn't. Another lesson. It's about material. The script just wasn't there. It wasn't good enough and there is a curse once you know it.

I got to know Frank and his family. They were Hollywood royalty. I was invited to his house on Outpost Road. This is a very swanky address; in fact, Frank was renting it from Gore Vidal. Frank always had something going on at the house. There were directors, producers, actors, writers, successful big shots. And Frank Sr. was there a lot. Frank Jr. is a class act, and one of the first top-shelf guys in the business I got to know. He had style, quiet class. You knew he had a big job and lots on his mind, but he was always friendly. He had the charisma of a movie star. In fact, lots of successful executives have that. Look at Alan Ladd Jr., son of leading man Alan Ladd. Laddy was the force behind *Star Wars* and hit after hit. It doesn't hurt if you're good-looking on either side of the camera.

But the gist of this is I got to be around Hollywood heavyweights. I was able to watch how they graze, relax, and in turn do business. Frank Jr. would inevitably say to someone, "Read anything good?" Which is Hollywoodspeak for "How ya doing? Want to find a movie?" The rich were at his house daily and the important technicians were there too. In Hollywood, business is conducted as much at home as the office. Especially if you have a ten-thousand-square-foot showplace.

"Beautiful places make people feel beautiful, and more apt to make something happen," someone once told me. It's true. And Frank did business there, very smartly.

But all the smarts in the world couldn't make the movie work. It had everything, even the support of Michael Eisner, the president of the studio and my made-up father who had gotten me through the Bronson Gate. It was a sweet karmic moment when I knew that I was working for Paramount a second time, but I wasn't sneaking on the lot, I belonged there.

I still had some heat going afterwards and the phone calls were still incoming. My agents and managers were getting interest from the networks. If you get hot in one area, the other sectors of the business notice. So, I'm hot, and what project pilot did I choose? Of all the offers, of all the top producers in town, of all the incoming calls, I chose the most offbeat show I could find. *No Soap Radio.* Why? Because nobody knows anything.

The pilot's show runner, the most important person on the set, the rainmaker, was Mort Lachman. Mort was a big shot, he worked with Larry Gelbart, Bob Hope, wrote the film hit *Yours, Mine, and Ours,* and was an in-demand talent. He had heat, I had heat, and the executive on the show, a man whose name I can only remember as Merrill, had heat. We were all adding up to hot. A hit? No. We filmed six episodes, and were canceled. Disappointing? Yes. It takes as much effort to make a flop as it does a hit. You love the project just as much. The bright note on most shows is that you get to meet talented, generous, and kind people. Bill Dana, the comedian who made his fame playing José Jiménez on *The Danny Thomas Show,* had a role on *No Soap,* so did Fran Ryan, and Gary Owens, and Edie McClurg. You may not know these names, but you would know their faces. I would have liked the show to go on, just so these fine and hard-working actors could make some money.

In February 1983, California had some of the most torrential rains the state has seen. The streets were flooding, the hills were collapsing into mud piles, and all of that didn't matter because it was . . . Academy Awards time. The town turns into a wonderland of parties, dinners, and hoopla. It's the real Christmas in L.A. and you can't help but get in the spirit of the season. Or, if you are not in the invited crowd, the Scrooge can come out in you.

I got a call from Wally. "Young man, I have some good news for you."

"I'm reinstated at the Playboy Mansion?"

"Not that good, but almost. You are presenting an Academy Award. You're going to be seen by billions of people all over the world. It's tuxedo time, you have one?"

Silence. The Academy Awards. Oscar. The big one. *The* show.

"You there, Steve?"

"How much is a tux?"

There you have it. I was above the clouds. Breathing that rarified air. And I was concerned with how much it would cost.

"We can get everything gratis, free, you are going on the star ride, boy, you never put your hand in your pocket. We'll take care of everything, including getting you into the supreme show of shows, the afterparty at Swifty, correction, Irving Lazar's party. Just don't call him Swifty. Got it? He is not fond of Swifty, I should never have told you."

"Swifty, big deal."

"Kid, just don't call him Swifty."

"Don't call him Swifty, got it." I forgot it as soon as I said it.

"Steven, do you have a date?" Dick Guttman was always picking up an extension if he wanted to chime in. "I have someone for you to go with. It'll make news, and that's what you want. Do you know who Genie Francis is?"

Did I know? She was only the biggest soap opera and tabloid star of the moment.

"What would she want with me?"

Dick paused. "Not to underestimate your masculine charm, but you're going to the Acadamy Awards. Anyone would go with you. What do you say?"

I said yes. It was a good idea to go with Genie. She was a giant star, with lots of coverage on her every move, and she was in television. She was able to mingle with a film crowd, and I was able to have someone friendly, attractive, and famous on my arm. I think I got the better end of the deal. I spilled a drink on myself in the limo. But it was an incredible time. Every media outlet on the planet covers the Oscars, and I suspect there is a planet outside our solar system that watches it too. If you like stars, you will have a conniption when you step on the red carpet. There is a line of limos a mile long, and it is so well controlled that you arrive promptly and get to work the flashes and microphones. Dick and Wally were there as I stepped out of the limo with Genie. They represented both of us so it was very easy. If we had had separate publicists it could have been a battle of the photo ops. There are other actors that the publicity mavens would want us to try and get a shot with. And always stand at the right, facing out. That way you will be written up first. And try not looking like a sleaze doing it. The great thing is, everyone is nervous, and everyone is in the same circus. I don't think there is a person who attends the show that doesn't get butterflies. We all saw it as kids on television, so when you are in the middle of it, it's a dream for everybody.

The shouts for Genie were one after another. There had to be hundreds and hundreds of photographers, and live and tape cameras. Genie was good at the interviews, she knew what they wanted. I had some things to talk about, and Genie made sure that the press listened. Dick and Wally were clever to pair us up. I've been at the awards on different occasions, sometimes without the cover of a publicist. There is no comparison. Dick and Wally knew everyone, and if they didn't, they met them. All the stars were there, in one room, all there to mingle. To be one of them! I see

Charlton Heston, say hi, and tell him that he had told me to take a walk when he was doing the sub movie at Paramount. James Mason is there with Pamela, and he treats me and Genie to a drink. Kristy McNichol is there, and I ask her if she remembers me. Yes, she does. Jane Russell is talking with Robert Wise, who directed *The Sound of Music,* and I ask if I can say hello. I met her at Michael's beach house in Montecito. Does she remember me? Yes, she does. The biggest shmoozefest on the planet, and I'm there. In a rented tuxedo, but I am there.

When you get to your seat you look around and it is as if your imagination came to life. John Travolta talking to Billy Wilder; Sissy Spacek, Mickey Rooney, and William Shatner bunched among the seats, leaning over and cheek-kissing. I'm sitting with Genie who is getting stared at by those stars, and we are staring at them. There is Cher and Matt Dillon and Jamie Lee Curtis. The music starts and the crowd quiets down.

And the thing takes forever. It is the longest show in history, and I can't believe I'm telling you this, I can't believe I felt it, but I wanted to get out. It's sitting in your seat for over three hours, and the time goes slowly except for when the seat filler taps you on the shoulder and tells you it's time.

A cherry bomb went off in my stomach. I put on a good face as I left Genie sitting next to a man from Pacoima who sat in my seat and half of hers. It was like I was the president and I was being swept into a safe room. The security surrounded me and we jetted to backstage where I was touched up by a makeup artist and I saw Ann Reinking, my copresenter. We had met at the rehearsal a few days before, and she was kind and giving. The fact that she was Bob Fosse's muse said a lot. She was the original Roxie Hart in *Chicago.* She danced at the Kennedy Center Awards. She had her own *Great Performances* special on public television.

"Tie your shoe." Ann pointed. But I had no time, we were on. She grabbed my hand and we walked onstage and presented the Best Costume Design award. I looked out to that sea of fame, that living, breathing room full of people that could change my life if they chose. Every important person in the industry was watching. I fell over a few lines. I fell in a stare with Paul Newman. I looked at the front row, which was only for the crème de la crème, and I fell in love with each and every one of them. We completed the presentation. "And the Academy Award goes to . . ." Some of the sweetest words to say. You know you are changing their lives. The designers of *Gandhi* were thrilled, and we walked offstage and into the arms of Dick and Wally, who walked us over to another media room filled with the print reporters, who need three words out of the thousand you say. Done with that, I said good-bye to the beautiful Ms. Reinking, and went back to a seat that is still warm from the seat filler.

The show is a dichotomy, with both thrilling moments and tedious minutes of waiting. But it is in the breaks in live broadcast that you have the pleasure of seeing people run from their seats to speak with someone across the aisle. Once the show is back on the air, there is no walking or scurrying. They are doomed to crouch or stand to the side. Seat fillers to the rescue.

The show comes to a close, and the main event occurs. Getting the limo.

Now, getting your limo means arriving at the afterparty on time, so that you can get through the line, get the good press, and then go inside, stake out a free table, and meet and greet. But if you miss the flag that your driver holds, bye-bye to on-time arrival. The veterans have a system. The accomplished attendee decides who will slip out of their seat before the best picture is announced. One of them sacrifices that moment, crouches, and steals up the aisle. He or she (take those high heels off) speed-walks through the lobby and to the front of the auditorium and spots his limo driver's flag, literally a handkerchief tied to a bamboo stick. The limo driver sees the connect and leads the attendee to the limo. They then drive to the front as the hosts are saying their closing remarks. The other lucky attendee walks out and is picked up, and they are on their way. Avoiding the insane traffic that occurs. Genie and I didn't do that.

When we finally did make it to the limo, Genie told the driver to take us to the biggest party in town: "Spago, please. Pronto." This was the legendary Irving "Swifty" and Mary Lazar's party to end all parties. Every star in the solar system showed up. There was a red carpet out front, and Irving and Mary stood at the door as a young and eager Wolfgang Puck served the arriving royalty. Genie and I were seated behind Don Rickles and Bob Newhart, to the right of John Lithgow, to the left of Peter O'Toole, and smack in front of Paul Newman. The crowds were more insane than at the awards, if that was possible. There were hundreds of revelers, and Irving said hello to each and every one of us. He had someone next to him telling him who we were if he wasn't familiar. He came over to our table and shook hands with Bob Seger and his wife. He looked at me and Genie, extended his hand, and introduced himself. "I saw you in *Diner,* brilliant material. And of course Genie, Mary and I are big fans of yours."

I extended my hand. "Nice to meet you, Swifty." He and Mary stopped in their tracks. There was, imagined or not, a silence. It was the only time that Newman looked over. Irving looked at me with frost in his eyes, smiled, and forgave me.

"It's Irving, Irv if you like, but not Swifty." He gave me a pat on the head as if he were patting a puppy. "Eat, have fun, enjoy yourselves." He gave a shake of his finger and a wink. "Only one guy could call me that name, and it ain't you."

In the early fifties, a young Irving Lazar lived in New York and had an apartment on Central Park, a driver, and a thriving business. He was one of the best literary and talent agents on the East Coast. He liked to stay out late, meeting writers, directors, producers, and working the business like no one could. Irving had class. He dressed the part, in only the finest from Savile Row. He ate at only the top restaurants in town, and it was there he saw the big one. The main event of movie stars. Humphrey Bogart. He had just left his agent and the word was out.

Irving had to have Bogie on his list. He had to be able to say to his cronies, "I just signed Bogie." He approached the table where Bogart sat with two women.

"Mr. Bogart, I'm Irving Lazar, and I would like to represent you." Irving was very direct.

Bogart looked up at the five-foot-three Lazar. "Thank you, young man, but as you can see I'm busy, and I am already represented."

"Mr. Bogart, what would it take to represent you?"

"Kid, get me three offers, in one day, and you represent me. Heck, if you do that, you can represent everybody."

And Irving did just that. He got three film offers all in one day. He found Bogie at the bar of the Players Club on Gramercy Park.

"I have them, Mr. Bogart, three offers, with hours to spare." Irving gave him the three offers written on separate deal memos.

Bogart looked at the papers and squinted. He put his glasses on and after a few minutes looked up and said quietly, "Kid, these are real offers. At real money. Swift."

"Yes, sir, I can have you working in a month, at good pay, and have you go back-to-back till Christmas." He paused and stood as tall as he could. "Am I your agent, sir?"

"You are indeed, Irving. You did it. Swift. Swifty. Swifty! That's your name now, kid. Swifty Lazar."

It stuck. Everyone in the business called him Swifty, everywhere but to his face. Irving allowed no one but Bogie to call him that. Period.

Irving and Mary entertained all of Hollywood at Spago's, and if you had an invite, you were a player. You could dine out on that all year, just by being seen at Swifty's Oscar Party. Swifty was no dummy. If he had a need for you, you were probably at his party. If you wanted to be invited next year, it would be good to give Irving what he wanted. He was a premier player in the industry for all his life.

Genie and I mingled. She was good at it and encouraged me. "You've got to meet these people, why would you be here?" I was wound up by the thrill of it all, standing near Ben Kingsley and his Oscar. I just loved the glamour, the stars, the flashes of light. The tinsel. But Genie was a pro, and knew as well as any player in the room what makes the whole shebang work. Relationships. She found me talking to a busboy.

"Isn't this incredible?" The busboy nodded, not speaking English. She pulled me away.

"You've only got a few hours and we all turn into pumpkins. Let me introduce you to Joanne Woodward." And there was the connection. I shook hands with Ms. Woodward, and sitting with his chin in his palm was Paul Newman.

"Paul, this is Genie Francis and . . ." She didn't know my name but it didn't matter. I got to meet Newman. Or Newman nodded to me. I think I met Newman.

I woke up the next day with souvenirs in all my pockets, napkins and place cards, and the limo sign. I looked at my invitation on the kitchen table. Proof. Massapequa went to the Oscars.

I knew I had to start getting into the town mingle sessions. Wally and Dick told me there was no better place than Morton's, the restaurant that sets the pace in "relationship dinners." It was co-owned by Allan Carr and Monday night was the big night, the main schmooze, everybody is there. I pulled up in my Toyota Corolla and felt so good that I gave it to the valet, walked in, and the first face I saw was Larry Mark, having dinner with an executive from Fox. He introduced me and congratulated me on being on the awards. The room had a buzz, a definite atmosphere. I walked around and saw several faces that I recognized, and was shown to my table. There were my managers, Jay and Larry, who were talking to faces that I recognized from *Variety* and *The Hollywood Reporter.*

Another man in a dark sports coat, pressed jeans, and a beard came up to the table and greeted Jay. They had a very clubby exchange and then Larry said something funny and they all laughed. The man must be important; Larry and Jay introduced me.

"Steve, this is one of the most important producers in Hollywood—

for that matter, the world, the universe. This is Don Simpson. From Alaska."

Don put out his hand and shook mine. Of course I knew who Don Simpson was. He and Jerry Bruckheimer had just made a partnership, and that past Friday, their movie *Flashdance* opened to monster money. They were the hottest producers that week. Where else would they be but at Morton's on Monday night. Everyone knew the grosses and they were like kings. He was already looking for the next person to talk to when he laser-focused on me.

"*Diner,* brilliant. Someone in one of the reviews called you 'a revelation.' You know that. Pretty good. Congratulations." And he was off. I didn't have time to give him kudos about his hit. But he didn't need them from me. He had his first big hit. He was like a big, hungry brown bear in a pool of salmon, and everywhere he put his paw, he caught a fish.

Larry and Jay had something interesting to talk about. They had got a call from Hank McCann, the casting director on *The Day After,* which was going to be one of the biggest events on television. It was going to be directed by Nicholas Meyer, the screenwriter and filmmaker responsible for wonderful films such as *The Seven-Per-Cent Solution, Time After Time,* and *Star Trek II.* Nick was smart and had the attention of the industry. ABC gave him the go-ahead to do a risky movie about the ramifications of nuclear war. It was pushing the envelope. Nick was conducting interviews for this project and wanted to see me. Momentum, nothing like it. I walked out on air and gave my ticket to the valet captain. I stood there waiting while big shot after big shot got his car delivered. After forty-five minutes my Corolla dribbled in. As I drove home I counted all the open parking spaces on Melrose Avenue. I knew I should have parked on the street.

The meeting with Nick Meyer was like an interview with an MIT professor. Nick knows a mega amount about most subjects, and is one of the best screenwriters in the business. He also is well known for doctoring screenplays. This film was his message about the nuclear question.

"Did you read the script?" He sat with an unlit cigar in his hand.

"I loved the script." You always say that if you're a smart actor.

"What exactly did you like?" That's what a smarter director says.

So I explained that I saw it as a metaphor for the changing generations, and how I saw it as a shattering movie that could change some minds. He knew I was talking to get the job.

"Let's read, if you please." He and the casting director watched as I read.

"Do you know who Jason Robards is?" Nick sat back.

"I do." Of course I did, *The Iceman Cometh*.

"Well, you just might get to meet him." That was one of the nicest things that anyone has ever done for me on an audition. Hinted that I might have the job. It made waiting for the call a tiny bit easier. A day later I had a call-back and both my agent Peter Meyer and managers Larry and Jay got on the phone. When it's good news, everybody wants to share the win.

I arrived in Kansas and could tell this was a big film. The budget was enormous, complete with special effects, in person and on-screen. The landscape that this film had was bigger than anything I had been a part of. I did get to meet and work with Robards. John Lithgow was on the set and I got to know John Cullum, the Broadway star. But the best part of this film was that in the middle of the schedule, the day we "broke the back of the film," Nick rode up on a white horse and directed from the saddle. It was so out of the ordinary that it made playing those particular scenes more theatrical, while still being realistic. The character I played was one for whom radiation caused him to lose his hair and start to deteriorate. I know it may be out there, but by Nick being bigger than life, I was able to put more reality into the whole sequence. I used it to get there. The worst part of the film was that I was using Method to totally immerse myself into the story, and the nightmares of nuclear bombs were horrible.

Nick said something to me that I will never forget. "I made this film to fulfill promises that I make at cocktail parties. I talk about the nuclear threat, then go home to my cushy bed. I needed to do what I say I'm going to do." He made good on his promise. The whole country tuned in to the broadcast; it was the highest rated television event in history. So real and alarming was the film that the network invited a panel of military leaders and politicians, including the Secretary of Defense, to explain what would actually happen in a nuclear war, and how we were prepared for it.

But what mattered to my war chest was that I had another hit, and that was good. More incoming phone calls, more parties, more premieres, more popularity, more ego. I was going from talk shows to dinner parties to art openings to charity balls. My publicists made sure I got out there, met everyone who was important at an event, and made sure I got invited to the next one. I was on the advisory lists, the cochairman lists, the honorary board lists. The who-is-hot-today lists.

"So, Mr. Bigshot, we watched this *Day After the Day Before . . .*"

"*The Day After,* Mom."

"Yeah, yeah, *The Day After,* and I don't know what day after that could be. It reminds me of the day after your Father's and my honeymoon."

"Mom, it's a serious movie. Did you read the reviews?" I was so full of myself you could have pricked me with a pin and I would pop.

"Yeah, yeah, I know. Your father likes that JoBeth Williams."

"I like her, she's a good actress." My father shrugged on the extension. I could hear him watching television.

"Your father is losing his mind, he sits and watches that television."

"That television has given our son some good jobs. I like television." And there it was, my Dad gave me a small high five. He kind of liked what I was doing. I had some, if small, smattering of his approval.

"I like it too, but Steven, if it ever gets too much, I want you to come home. I don't care if it's the day after or before or whatever. You are not of that place, you are from here."

I had a nice little life going. At twenty-three, I had my own house, car, and food in the refrigerator. Just being able to support myself, and put some money away, was an accomplishment. I still thought that this life would be temporary. I never thought it would last forever. My friends from home were all going to university or graduate schools, and I thought I was falling behind. I dallied out in Los Angeles while they were building foundations for good and solid lives. I was standing in the middle of a dream factory that gave no guarantees. No degree you can hang on a wall and say, I can do that anywhere.

I knew that I was getting hooked on the action. The calls, the notes, the messenger services that came to my door with scripts. People were investing in me, their time and their contacts. My managers and agents, publicists and attorneys were all putting their efforts into making me more famous, and ostensibly all of us rich.

Chapter 13

One of the wonderful parts of being with a big agency, and having some heat, is that other agents also work for you. I had a primary agent, Peter Meyer, whose trusty assistant, Elaine Goldsmith, was sharp as a tack. They talked to everyone about me. And I thank my lucky stars they spoke to David Schiff, who had been an assistant at the agency and was now an agent. He told Peter about a film at Warner Bros., being produced by Paul Maslansky and the Ladd Company. The same company that did *The Right Stuff* and *Once Upon a Time in America.* Hugh Wilson, the creator of *WKRP in Cincinnati,* was directing. I didn't hear any of that, I just heard that they were sending the script.

I loved to read scripts. Some screenplays are good technical or passionate works. Some are just crap. But reading a screenplay takes an ability on its own. You have to surrender to the storytelling enough to give it a chance, but still be able to watch the characters, the story, the act breaks, the quality of the work. And then, once in a while, you get a lightning bolt while reading something, and you think, "This is a hit."

I told my girlfriend LeeAnne that I had read this really funny script that reminded me of *Stripes* meets *An Officer and a Gentleman.* If you need shorthand for movies, you use the cute and disgustingly trite "this meets this." But it really did make me think of those films. I had a meeting at Warner Bros. the next day.

I keep saying there is something thrilling about having a gate pass to a Hollywood studio. "Yes, sir, Mr. Guttenberg, park in any of the spots that don't say reserved." The Ladd Company is a beautiful building in Santa Fe style, with a courtyard and its own lobby. Next door is Malpaso, Clint Eastwood's company. Walking into these offices gives you a feeling of intimidation paired with desire. The waiting room had a few guys waiting to be seen. Some straight-looking, some odd. Fern Champion and Pam Basker were casting and I got called in.

Paul Maslansky, the producer, was a bear of a man with a giant appetite for stories and life and making movies. This script was his baby. He had the idea while doing an Amy Madigan movie in San Francisco. He was driving to work and saw, on a street corner, a tall policeman chewing out a young recruit. And he had it. The lightning bolt. *Those are Funny Characters. Like the Keystone Kops.* And he went on with his day. But when he got back to the Ladd Company, he asked Laddy to let him develop a film. "I call it *Police Academy.*"

Laddy was known for not getting too excited about anything. He had an even temperament and made classy films. This was way out there for him. But he wanted to make it. He was making film after film, *Chariots of Fire, Outland, Blade Runner,* he had lots of power, and was able to take chances. Paul hired Neal Israel and Pat Proft to write it. They were getting a reputation as very funny guys. One of Laddy's development executives was put on the project. John Goldwyn, as in Sam Goldwyn, as in Metro-Goldwyn-Mayer, as in Hollywood royalty. He was smart and a force behind the film. Hugh Wilson was at a peak of his Hollywood power, a television big shot wanting to get into film. There was a momentum, the pieces were coming together. Nothing was getting in the way, which is rare.

Hugh was from Atlanta, and had a folksy but intelligent manner. He had that thing that the great directors have when they are on a hit. That sense that every choice is carefully and correctly made. They know what they want. Hugh knew what he wanted. I read for him. I knew this role. It was James Garner in *The Great Escape,* it was Bill Murray in *Stripes,* it was Humphrey Bogart in *The African Queen.* Well, maybe not to you, but that's what gave me some juice.

"Thank you, that was good." That's all I got, and I walked out. The waiting room was filled with actors, and as I left I saw a friend. He told me that the part had been offered to Michael Keaton. *Well, that's it,* I thought. *Michael Keaton was in* Night Shift, *Ron Howard and Brian Grazer's hit. I can forget about it.*

The phone rang early the next morning and it was my father. I told him about the audition, and he told me not to think about someone else getting it. "You never know, Steven." The phone rang a few minutes after I hung up with my Dad. Larry and Jay were on the phone. "You got a callback at nine today. I just got a call from casting, they are moving quickly on this." Larry was excited.

"I never get up this early, so I know that it's important." Jay probably was still in bed. He was a swinger, Hef style.

Around that time there were other auditions, like the one for *Splash.* Ron Howard and Brian Grazer were taking over Hollywood. Brian was so smart and persuasive, and Ron so talented, that they were setting up films all over town. *Splash* was written by Babaloo Mandel and Lowell Ganz. They had worked with Ron on *Happy Days* and wrote *Night Shift.* I really wanted to work with them. I had a good meeting and reading and was very excited about it.

Peter called. "I got good news, and bad news, which one do you want? I have David Schiff in the office. And Elaine, are you there?"

"Yes, I am." Elaine was on the assistant's learning line.

"The bad news is they don't want you on *Splash.* But the good news is they want to screen-test you for *Police Academy.*"

And all I can say is "Why don't they want me for *Splash*?"

"Steve, this is David Schiff. I'm handling both projects and, well, they're going in a different direction for *Splash.* But it's good they want to screen-test you for *Police Academy.* We had a lot of guys up for the Mahoney role."

Peter said, "It's between you and a numbnuts from this movie *Spring Break* that opened to good numbers last week. He sucks but he is in this cockamamie tittie movie."

"I don't have a chance at *Splash*? It's such a good script, and Ron and Brian are on fire."

Peter asked, "What the fuck's going on here? Steve, you got a screen test on a Ladd movie. Goddamn actors!"

I backpedaled, and thanked them for what they were doing, but I had the actor's lament, I wanted to be wanted. By everyone.

Dressing for any audition is a task. You have to wear the right clothes, clothes that remind the decision makers that you could easily be that role, while looking good, while not too flashy, while respectable. Then try to wear your lucky outfit too. I wore one set of clothes till they refused to do another audition.

This time, I looked through my closet for something military-like and there was my father's shirt. It had NEW YORK POLICE ACADEMY on the shoulder.

"Is that a real police academy shirt?" Hugh Wilson looked at the shirt as I came on the set of the screen test. They had already tested the guy from *Spring Break.* His movie was making gobs of money, and that made a lot of people like him. I liked him because his movie was making money. Who wouldn't?

"Yeah, my father was a cop."

"Well, that'll make no difference. You have to be good, be the part. I need Mahoney to be everything that is a rascal, and then some." Paul loved this movie. "Mahoney is the drive, the engine. He sets the pace of the movie, the boundaries, and the timing. He has some of the biggest jokes, and, hopefully, laughs. This is a very important character. I should play him, except for this." He pointed to his bald head. That was the energy around there.

"Your father was in the academy in New York. Geez, that had to be dangerous." Hugh was fascinated by the city cops. He gave me a few suggestions and we did a few takes. That was it.

I walked out of the dark stage to the glare of the Warner's lot. I was the star of the screen test, and then I was just another shmegegge walking down Warner's Smalltown Street, wearing my father's shirt. I was mistaken for a security guard three times before I found my car.

The story I heard was that it was a stalemate. The executives and producers met, and watched both screen tests. The guy from *Spring Break* was, I was sorry to know, a very good actor. *Spring Break* was to him what *Nightmare on Elm Street* was to Johnny Depp. A start. And the executives loved him. He was funny, sexy, and charming. Next was me. Wonderful.

The room had just seen a great performance. And the projector broke when they started my footage. When it started again mine was good, not Marlon Brando testing for *The Godfather* good, but good enough to make it a game. The arguments flew, they got spicy. There was passion in the room. I'm really building this up. But it was close. Until, as lore has it, Jay Canter, an executive at Laddy's, stood up and yelled, "I want the Guttenberg guy." And it was settled. They were on to their next blockbuster, and Fern Champion and Pam Basker called my agents and managers. Who in turn called me, and told me news that would forever give me pleasure. "You've got ten weeks of per diem coming. Cash, all cash."

Police Academy was one of the first films to start the gold rush to Toronto. A film company could take advantage of the currency exchange and tax laws and hire a crew for three-quarters of what they would cost in Los Angeles or anywhere in the United States. Warner Bros., to their credit, found the gold there first.

I asked if I could stay in a hotel separate from the cast. I thought Mahoney was a loner, and liked to have a good time, so I thought I could accomplish both at the Hilton on the water. It was the best accommodations I had ever been treated to, a twentieth-floor view of the lake's coastline. I felt like a somebody.

The next day was the reading. I was going to get there early. I wasn't the only one to have that idea.

Bubba Smith was a gentle presence despite the fact that he was six foot eight and a champion professional football player. He was so aware of being a star. His sheer size guaranteed him that. He stood up when I walked in, and leaned into me.

"Well, you must be Mahoney. Nice to meet you." His Texas drawl comes out of a sweet face. He laughed as he met me, and told me straight off, "I have been following Hugh, and this cat knows what he is doing. He rewrote the script, kept the good parts, put in his own too. This guy can write, this guy can direct. I'm telling you."

Yeah sure, I thought. *What the heck does this guy know about movies?* But I said, "I agree with you, he is really talented." I would have said anything that I thought would appease him, he was enormous (but very well proportioned).

The room started to fill up with all different types of performers. It is the most exciting moment when you meet all the people who will be playing the roles you imagined while reading your own. They look different than you imagined, but sometimes the stars align, and you get the perfect people for the job.

Bird noises, drilling, a skipping record, voice messaging, and a taxicab driver. These all came from Michael Winslow, who was a catalog of noises. He had a talent that was something to behold. Is it a recording or for real? He must have been asked ten times "Is it real?" just by the cast. He took suggestions, and took over the room in an instant.

Donovan Scott, way ahead of his time, filmed home movies. Rudimentary video and super eight. He wanted to document the whole experience.

Leslie Easterbrook was a statuesque Playboy bunny right off the farm. An accomplished singer, she was well educated and had the manners of a princess. She couldn't help how she looked, but she was class all the way.

David Graf, who played Tackleberry, was full of vim and vigor. He was laughing and enjoying the fact that he had work. We all were. It's a great feeling for actors, to know there are checks for the next few months. And an opportunity to shine.

Then Kim Cattrall walked into the room.

Kim was a shy and humble lady. She was most famous for being one of the stars of *Porky's,* a film that made *Spring Break* money look like chump dinero. But she couldn't have been sweeter. She was serious about her role, and took the work seriously, but her laugh was big and honest. She was able to be one of the guys, and held her own. In only a few minutes everyone liked and respected her.

As a general rule, the villain is always the nicest guy on the set. As the "good guy," I was waiting to meet the villainous Sgt. Harris. I expected an unlikable John Wayne. And in walked the nicest guy on the set. G. W. Bailey, with bags of seafood for his gumbo party, which would commence that night. He was full of laughs and compliments, smiling throughout our first meeting. How could this man play the despicable Sgt. Harris? Acting, just good acting. By the way, G.W. is starring in *The Closer* now, and he eats that role up. His acting has only gotten more interesting, and I feel lucky to have been in the vehicle that gave him his commercial start. He was an acting teacher, and at that first party, we talked about the fact that our relationship in the film would probably mirror our personal relationship. We grew to be close on the set, and the dynamic became the foundation for our on-camera relationship. I really loved G.W., and Mahoney loved Harris. But the twist was, Mahoney loved to annoy and bother Harris, and I loved to visit and learn from G.W. Please don't think I'm spouting acting jargon or dramaturgy, but I think the reason Mahoney worked so well was that Harris was the perfect Archetype of Campbellion Myth to oppose him. He was seemingly more powerful and dangerous than Mahoney, and Mahoney had to elevate himself to his level. It's preposterous, but it worked. There is nothing in a story that makes a hero more believable than a good villain. And G.W. was that. He made Mahoney look good.

The first day, we had "getting in and out of cars" and long shots. Very well planned. Make the first day easy. The cast got along well, and I noticed all the friendships that were brewing. Bubba Smith became the beacon of light that all us moths danced around. He and G.W. were from the same area of Texas, so they kept the stories going. Through G.W. we learned that Bubba was over six feet tall when he was thirteen. Along with that came an early entrée into adult life that none of us had. Because of Bubba's sheer size he got recognition, but it was his character that gave him his popularity. He was as comfortable with billionaires as he was with blue-collar people. He entertained friends on the set, and they in turn regaled us with Bubba stories. Like the time when he was in college and parked in the dean's space. Bubba was a football star throughout school and went on to the NFL. And there is nothing bigger than a football star in Texas, or Michigan, where Bubba made a name for himself. Movie stars had nothing on Bubba. He had seen it all, met them all, and kept his head through it.

I think *Police Academy* worked because the cast was full of actors who gave of their talent, but wanted to make each other look good too. And how did we all get into one film? A myriad of reasons, but the director is the center of it all. Hugh was a major talent. Those words are tossed around like a sack of potatoes, but he really was. His show *WKRP in Cincinnati* was a hit because of the writing and the cast. Comedies boil down to that. Hugh got along well with everyone and made them feel as if they mattered. Accordingly, everyone worked just a little harder, adding to the recipe for success. And Our producer and leader, Paul Maslansky, made the film a hit and was its energy.

The test of a comedy director is whether he can shoot a joke that becomes the scene people use as the benchmark of the film. In any hit comedy, there is "The Scene" that is described in concert with the story of the film. We were setting up for, I kid you not, the scene where G.W. flies into the horse's ass. Yessiree, this was a Warner Bros. film, the studio that brought you *Superman* and made you believe that a man could fly. Hugh had to make the audience believe that a man could fly into the behind of a horse. I was sitting on the curb with Charters, Hugh's wife, and just watching how he was setting up the shot. There was a fake and live horse, a crowd of extras, and G.W., who wasn't so keen on this idea. He was a classically trained actor used to Molière, Chekhov, and Shakespeare. He was now going to be thrown into the rectum of a pony. Ah, the things we do for art.

Hugh was setting up the joke and started to film it. He knew every cut he needed to make, and worked the joke like a thriller director works suspense. I turned to Charters and told her that Hugh was going to catch lightning with this film. He was in the right place, in love with Charters and in love with his work. A recipe for a success. She laughed and rolled her eyes, neither of us knowing that it would be true. Hugh would get extraordinarily hot after the film came out, but today, he was putting G.W.'s head into a plastic booty. Everyone starts somewhere.

It was in the daily grind of shooting that Hugh showed his true colors. He knew the rhythm of the film, the characters' arcs, and where the beats were. He was able to glean a joke from a moment, and make it pay off down the line. There were so many funny scenes shot that the film could have been *Dr. Zhivago* in length. Much had to be edited out, but as it stands, there were laughs all the way through, and when the lights came up, the audience wanted more. And more. And, well, a billion dollars later, more.

I was lucky to be part of one of the biggest laughs in the film, the podium scene. The setup was that Georgina Spelvin, a wonderful actress who just so happened to be one of the biggest porn stars in the triple-X business, was supposed to pleasure the Harris character under the podium. Instead she got the commandant, played by George Gaynes, a very proper man in real life, famous for many roles, such as the soap opera actor in

Tootsie with Dustin Hoffman. George was, among other things, an opera singer, and had a deep resonating voice. He practically sang his lines. And when Georgina's character gave him some oral delight, George can be heard singing his surprise and satisfaction. But it was the button, when his character later sees Mahoney come out of the podium, that gave the audience a bonus laugh. And the audience wants that, they are used to that rhythm. And Hugh did not disappoint. The joke went over so well that in test screenings, the crowd asked for more podium jokes. The Ladd Company legend is that Laddy saw the film and suggested putting the podium joke again in the last scene. Except this time Mahoney would be getting the pleasure. It worked, and the audience rolled out of the theater laughing. Hitsville.

Kim Cattrall is a very polite lady and was genuinely shocked at this gross-out comedy. It was a plus for us in two ways. One, she had the sensibility of a lot of our audience, viewers who appreciated a guilty pleasure. She would cover her face with her hands as she watched some of the bawdiness that filled the set. And that was good. A comedy is again like a horror film; we want the audience to turn away and then peek back. Two, her character was a straight and proper recruit. She played by the rules. That was Kim. She had more on her mind than doing incredibly commercial gross-out films, but knew that it was a step. *Porky's* got her part of the way, and *Police Academy* was going to give her another boost. We all know that Kim went on to carve herself a signature role in *Sex and the City*. It's what every actor who is worth their salt wants, something that people can point to and say that she is the very best at it. No one does sex siren like Kim. This time it was a police siren (sorry about that). Kim recently got rave reviews for Noël Coward's *Private Lives* on Broadway and in London.

Every time I am asked about *Police Academy* by red-blooded American males, or international ones for that matter, they want to know about Leslie Easterbrook. How hot is she? Who got to sleep with her? How does she look, and hug, in person? One of the greatest surprises I like to reveal is that she too is classically trained as an actor and a vocalist. She sings like Maria Callas. The first thing you see when you meet Leslie is her smile and her good nature. Her character, her personal character, is what overshadows everything physical. The last thing you notice are her curves, though she has plenty.

We shot in an insane asylum. Really, it was a mental hospital that the Canadian government had let go empty except for a small outpatient detail. The rest of the thirty or so acres, complete with some sort of dungeon, were ours. Building after building, all empty, all full of hospital relics. Undoubtedly, some strange things had gone on there, but I thought it had good energy. It was ours to shoot in and create anything we wanted. The studio rarely visited.

The story goes that poor Hugh, who really was the engine of the film, was going to get fired two days into filming. Somebody didn't think the film was going to be funny under him, and the jury was out for a few days. Hugh was rich off of *WKRP,* but everything he had was going into the film, and he couldn't afford to make a bad move. He kept at his plan, and every day poured his entire reserve of funny into everybody, cast and crew. And he didn't get fired. Donovan kept filming as well, and there is a very funny, touching, and unreleased documentary that he made of the shoot. Oh, and the unit publicist had an idea that we should take a group photo on the steps of our beloved insane asylum. No big deal. We stood on the steps while the photographer asked us to do different poses, funny and goofy. But I remembered what Karl Malden told me on *Miracle.* He, Andrew Stevens, and I were taking publicity stills. The photographer asked us to do something goofy. We did but Karl didn't. "No goofy poses." He turned to me. "Don't do anything goofy in a still picture." So I chose to let everybody do the goofy, and I played it straight.

We finished shortly after, exchanged gifts, said good-byes. G.W., the master of every party gumbo, was going to make sure we all kept in touch. *Police Academy* was one of the most satisfying experiences on a film set I had ever had up to that point. I left Toronto with all my souvenirs of the filming, my unspent per diem, and real appreciation for working as the lead in what I thought was a funny idea for a movie. I got to put some money in the bank, and I was off to the next job. That's all *Police Academy* was, a job, just like all the others. So I thought.

I once heard from a smart actor, "You work as hard on the flops as you do on the hits." It's really true.

The executives' offices at Warner Bros. are the epitome of California film glory. The offices of Hollywood executives far outdo, for taste and style, any office of any business. Only the top of the business walks in here. And me.

I walked into the office of the VP of Publicity and Marketing, Cheryl Boone Issacs, and felt like I was in the Plaza Hotel. On the wall was a proposed one-sheet for *Police Academy.* It was from the shoot on the steps of our asylum. All the characters were on it except Kim. I thought she should be on it. Kim is one of the biggest stars around today, and at that time the decision was to leave her out of the one-sheet. Things change so much in showbiz.

Anyway, I thought it looked like a movie I wanted to see. Warner Bros., like all the top studios, has artists and executives that make marketing work like gangbusters. I knew I was in the clubhouse, and I appreciated it. From what Cheryl was telling me, the movie was getting a good response in the tests all over the country. Everything she said led me to believe that the studio was high on the film, that it was going to roll out on a spring date, and convulse the entire country with laughter. There was a screening coming up that she wanted me to go to, at the theater on the lot. I could bring anybody I wanted.

Sandy Gallin was one of the most influential managers in the business. He talked to every studio boss and successful producer that walked into Ma Maison, and lunched with Barbra Streisand and Whoopi Goldberg. He was smart, savvy, and knew the way things worked and how to make them work. He was my manager, too, and agreed to come see the film with me. I met him at one of his two offices. I walked into the reception area at 4:30. The walls were lined with Dolly Parton gold albums. His very attractive assistant brought me back to him, and I heard Sandy talking.

He was stretched out on the couch with his shoes off. "You look like a dancer out of *Oklahoma!*" I had on tight jeans and cowboy boots, a gift from Randy Jones, the Village person. His assistant put another call through and he went on to the next conversation. Eventually he got back to me. "We have this thing tonight, right? This police movie?" On came his saddle shoes and sport coat. I followed his Jaguar onto Sunset Boulevard and through the Warner gates as if he owned the place. He knew everybody at the screening. He sat with some executives and I opted to go upstairs and watch with the projectionist. The film started on time, and it got lots of laughter. It was an industry crowd, so it was reserved laughter, the good, jealous, envious kind. The best you could ask for in Hollywood. I asked the projectionist if it was funny, or if I was crazy. "Definitely funny." He switched reels and played with the sound. "I see everything; listen to me, it's funny." I walked out of the room with my feet hardly hitting the ground. I went downstairs to find Sandy standing with a group of sophisticates. We walked into the parking lot.

"Biggest piece of shit I have ever seen. What were they thinking? It's not funny, it has lousy production value, and it isn't funny. I mean this is the Ladd Company, *The Right Stuff,* Warner Bros. What were you thinking when you did that?"

I looked at him blankly, shocked. I opened my mouth; nothing came out but a squeak.

He walked toward his car. "I'm putting you in a television series right away. I mean, what is going on here with this movie?" The Jaguar door closed and he was off. I stood in the middle of the Warner Bros. parking lot with my mouth open.

Later I met with Hugh and his wife. "It's working and there isn't anything that can change that. This movie makes people laugh and it isn't going to change." I was so eager to know that it was funny like I thought, not unfunny like Sandy thought. Now Hugh was adamant that the film had a very broad reach and was going to be a smash. Charters knew it too, and gave her very dignified "The thing works." She meant it. I figured Hugh knew what he was doing, *WKRP* was a well-done big hit. Meanwhile Sandy had a meeting set up. For a pilot.

Blake Edwards was probably, irrefutably, one of the most talented artists to ever glide around Hollywood. He was a choreographer, a writer, a director, and a producer. He directed a little movie called *10* as well as the Pink Panther series. He was married to Julie Andrews and, oh, he directed *Breakfast at Tiffany's*. He also did *The Great Race* with Jack Lemmon and Peter Falk. His office compound at MGM was as big as it gets. He had a private dining room. That's all you have to say about that.

So I sat there with Blake, who was charming and interesting and confident. He wanted to do a spy series with a father and son. His president of production, Tony Adams, a strikingly dashing Englishman, sat with us. They had the supremely talented Robert Loggia and I was to play his son.

And the filming was delightful. I was so lucky to be able to watch Blake direct. He knew camera and movement and story and had all the charm and influence of anyone who had led an army and won. He explained to me that he was being sued by some people and that they wanted a few million. He very cutely declared that he would only have three hundred million left. Rich.

Robert Loggia is one of the finest actors that we have. He worked with every great artist, his résumé is a who's who, and he lives life with gusto. He's a tennis player, and plays almost every day. It was easy to act with Bob, he had his Academy Award nomination, and was so at home with himself. The shoot was first-rate, and Blake had the crew treated like gold. Many he had worked with before. And they were loyal to him and gave him any shot he wanted. There was also one of the finest Shakespearean scholars on the film, Sam Wanamaker, known for *The Spy Who Came in from the Cold*, and *Private Benjamin*, playing the role of the villain.

Sam was universally loved and respected, and had such dignity and a twinkle in his eye. The whole show had pros in it, and I hung on for the ride. It was easy.

Sandy called. "You're going on tour for this film, because exposure is good, but I don't know what you're going to say about it. I mean, it's not funny."

"Hugh Wilson says it's funny." Sandy's opinion was so important. I wanted him to love it.

"That is the director. He has to love it. It's true. Directors, of all kinds of films, love their films. Their babies." He put on his coat and said, "Ask Billie, ask what he thought of it." He got on another call. Bill Sammeth worked with Sandy and was Joan Rivers's and Cher's manager. And he wanted to talk to me about the tour.

Billy had a way of talking that was both theatrical and smart. He had that detachment that all successful representatives have. "We can erase the invisible man movie. I mean what was that film? You know when they talked about it, with Paramount and Frank Mancuso, *Friday the Thirteenth,* and his father on the board at Paramount, I thought we had a winner. So, it didn't win. Anything, not even a speck. But what I did like, more than Sandy, is the *Police Academy.* I thought it was very funny. You, Mr. Guttenberg, are a little rascal. That part is a star maker. And I think Warner Bros. is really going to push it." He had these big blue eyes that just were intense.

"So what do we do?"

"We go on this f-in' tour."

Again on the planes, from city to city, seeing the same guys, the same reporters, the same limo drivers. By this time I was comfortable with the press, and what their jobs were. There was self-promotion on both sides, yet both have to appear sincere, with little agenda.

I checked in. "Sandy, did the pilot sell?"

"Blake will know in a few days. I want you in a television series, that's where you belong. Not in a bad way, in a good, James Garner way. But you need to be on television."

The week *Police Academy* opened in 1984, I stayed at the Plaza Hotel. I had a suite overlooking Central Park and it was just starting to bloom. Spring was coming to New York, and I saw Bubba walking by Central Park South. He was admiring the trees, the flowers. He was almost like his role, a florist. I yelled down and he looked up with that big smile of his.

Bubba came up to my suite and sat down with LeeAnne and me. When he got comfortable, he told me, "You know, Warner Bros. thinks it has a big hit on its hands."

"How big?" I had no idea what I was talking about.

"Very big. And Paul is going to be a millionaire."

"Really?" Paul Maslansky was no millionaire.

"Yup." Bubba had something up his sleeve that night but wouldn't say what he was doing.

The phone rang the next morning, Saturday, at 3 A.M. Paul: "Stevie, I'm a millionaire."

I put the phone to my other ear. "What?"

"Warner Bros. can estimate the weekend grosses from the first few shows of Friday. The film is going to take the weekend, it's going to be number one. Everyone from Warner Bros. is calling me. It's their smash hit. It's going to be an enormous moneymaker."

The phone kept ringing and ringing. The flowers came in, the telegrams. The business has a few companies that it uses to track the grosses. There was a secret phone number that only a select few knew, and once you called it the numbers would be bestowed on you. This was way before IMDb and Box Office Mojo. Through this phone line you could know who was hot, who was cold. Who could help you, who couldn't do a thing. And that weekend, and for many more, *Police Academy* was the first film mentioned on the box-office bonanza line. Money, pouring in on a small investment, some eager, hungry talent, and some luck. The country, the world ate the film up. They couldn't get enough of it.

The junkets and follow-up junkets. The magazines and television chat shows. The evening news. The morning talkies. They all wanted a piece of this phenomenon. Talk show hosts referred to it as a money machine and found jokes in that. There were a lot of films released that year, and *Police Academy* was the underdog, the oddball that made people move. It made its play overseas and became more popular (if that was possible) there.

Then, from across the pond, the mother of all film festivals came calling. Cannes wanted *Police Academy,* and we went. Well, basically Michael Winslow and I went. We showed up at event after event. The ego boost is overpowering when the photographers are yelling your name. The flash photos. The attention. The women. The foreign women. Michael and I were being squired around the festival like two oil sheiks. The Hotel du Cap only took cash, we had suites and never saw a bill. Napoleon built it for Josephine and now Michael was making his famous noises in the lobby entertaining the king and queen of Sweden. We loved it. But there was work too.

A woman walked into the press lounge, looking like a combination of Gisele Bündchen and Marilyn Monroe. We had been doing interviews for the past few hours and we were done.

"Just one more?" the European press agent asked. He had on a scarf that Cary Grant had given him. He motioned toward this beautiful cub reporter with a mike in her hand, hoping to get a word out of us two. We stared at her for what had to be a minute. This was a beauty.

"She doesn't speak English very well." He motioned to her again. She put her cherry red lips together and mouthed, "Please."

"Well, I'll give this poor girl an interview." Michael sprang toward her and they walked off to some corner. A beautiful girl, who could hardly speak English, and he had the universal language. Cars, planes, typewriters, animals, and the machine gun. She was laughing and he was loving it. The press agent and I headed out of the hotel to some enormously wealthy person's yacht. Dinner and dancing, models and booze. Later Michael arrived aboard a speedboat captained by a spectacular-looking blonde. She gave him a peck, and was off. He had on an Armani suit and sunglasses. At night. And the boat and all the occupants were his. "Please, Michael, let us hear you do the machine gun."

I walked back to the hotel and there in the lobby was Miss Bündchen-Monroe napping in a chair. She woke up and saw me. "I wait for you, can I have interview?" It was some sort of Nordic accent. Are you kidding me? Some Scandinavian beauty sat and waited for me? Well, not me, but what I represented. Hollywood. Success. Power.

I looked at her, and thought, *Should I do this? Use my power to get this girl up to my room?* It took about two seconds to decide.

I put the key into my door and walked into the suite with her. It was lit like a movie set, soft and yellow. Double doors led onto a balcony. The night sky was lit with klieg lights from across the way.

"Can I get you a drink?" I asked in my best Cary Grant.

She stared at me. "Only vodka. Only."

Okay, I thought. So I went to the bar and poured a healthy glass of vodka. In my best Ronald Colman I served it to her on a silver tray. She drank it like water.

"I wait for you, can I have interview?"

Okay, it's down to business. I could accept that. "Do you need somewhere to write or set up your tape recorder?" I pointed toward the table and poured another vodka, which she shot down. I don't think there was even a swallow.

"Only vodka. Only." She leaned over the back of the club chair.

"Yes, but do you want to use the table?" Something was amiss.

"I wait for you, can I have interview? Only vodka. Only." She lit a cigarette. Her eyes focused on me and she blew the smoke out like Lauren Bacall in the famous "Just Whistle" scene.

"Do you speak any English?" Hmmm?

"I wait for you. Only vodka, only." She got up and squeezed past me to the bar and picked up the bottle of vodka. She smiled and winked at me as she swallowed what was left of the alcohol.

"You want to go to the Louvre and see the *Mona Lisa*? This is a test."

She shook the bottle upside down with a frown and put her arms around me. This woman looked even better up close. We kissed, mouths open. She pulled back, grabbed my hand, and led me to the bedroom. "I wait for you. Can I have interview? Only vodka, only. I wait for you. Can I have interview? Only vodka, only."

She threw me around the bedroom like a rag doll. Here, there, she wanted it everywhere. On the balcony, on the floor, in the closet, and in the hallway on the way to the ice machine. She screamed and yelled, but could only say those two lines. Did she really know she was asking for vodka and an interview?

The next morning I woke up and Only Vodka was dressing. She had already ordered breakfast, eaten it, and was on her way out. She turned back to me and smiled, blew a kiss, and went through the door in a flash.

What a big shot I was, a beautiful girl who couldn't speak any English and all she wanted was me. The next day was a blur of premieres and food and drinking and photos. After that experience with the two-line lady I tried to take it easy.

Two days later, I made my way downstairs and there was the American contingent standing around the lobby. The talented director Rob Reiner, my pal Jerry Weintraub, and a slew of other prominent filmmakers and executives. They were raptly paying attention to one famous lothario, and he had them spellbound. I came a little closer to hear the story. He, the famous movie star and cocksman, was describing his evening. "And she came up to my room, see, and she grabbed my ass and said, 'I wait for you. Can I have interview? Only vodka, only.' That's all she could say, and she kept repeating it. She was taking care of business, and my business mind you, with her mouth, and still saying it." He put his fingers in his mouth while he laughed. "'I wait for you. Can I have interview? Only vodka, only.'"

When I stopped in New York on my way to Los Angeles I got grilled by my mother.

"Who was there? Oh, can you believe it, Stanley, who he is mingling with? The biggest in the world. The class, the style. But remember, Steven, what I have said for years, you don't need money to have class. But who was there? Don't tell me, it's just too much. You walking down the red stairs, talking with foreign filmmakers, hobnobbing with the stars. And the starlets. Did anyone recognize you?"

"A few people, but I—"

"Did you see a lot of girls on the beach? They always send back pictures of girls on the beach at the Cane-ez." My father.

"Cannes, like in con, or conjob. Stanley, don't you watch the news? Anything?" My mother started to vacuum. "You use Lysol in those hotel rooms overseas? They can be filthy with all those people from all those countries. You should spray it on everything. Stanley, ask him about what we talked about."

My father shook his head. "Your mother wants me to ask you about the women over there. That you should be careful. And I should have had this conversation with you before." He shrugged his shoulders. "What do I know?"

On cue, my mother yelled, "What do you know? You knew the Wolf sisters in Germany when you were over there. And you know what happened there? Your father dated both of them. Those dirty Wolf sisters."

"I did not." My father smiled.

"You did. And you should have told him to be careful over there."

"I didn't get anything when I was there. The army keeps you pretty busy, and besides I didn't get anything." He smiled again.

"Well, that's your father. He has that Guttenberg animal magnetism. You get that from him, from me you get broad shoulders and good thighs." She shut the vacuum off. "Are you still happy doing this? This Hollywood thing?"

I thought of the Nordic woman. "Yes, all in all I like it."

"How much did you make for *Police Academy*?" my Dad yelled as he put away the vacuum.

"Eighty thousand."

"In how many weeks?"

"Eight."

"Ann, I like it too. Continue, son, and grab as much as you can."

Los Angeles was different the second I landed. As I came out of security there was the paparazzi. I practiced the art of appearing as if you don't care about the photos while still promoting yourself. I was getting used to it, being treated like a conquering hero everywhere. Unless you grew up with it, the adulation is intoxicating. This is the drug that gets mainlined.

I sat back in the stretch and let it glide down the freeway toward Sandy's office to meet with Billy. I couldn't wait to see them and share the success.

"Now, we have some news for you." Sandy sat with Ray Katz, his partner.

"Where is Billy?" Billy was always there.

"Billy is gone. He went out on his own." Sandy laughed. "But don't worry, Ray and I will be handling you and soon we will get a very good piece of manpower in here from ICM. Keith Addis. And he is very good."

"Why did Billy leave?" This guy was a friend to me as well as my co-manager. I spoke to him every day. We were very close, and then he was gone. That's how it happens in show business.

"He left because it just wasn't working here with him, but you will love Keith. He will bring a whole different energy in."

I just sat there. I had left agents and managers, but no one had left me. I had a hit movie and momentum. And my manager leaves.

"Don't worry. Let us handle this." One of the rare times that those words were true. "You can come in tomorrow and meet Keith."

Billy answered my calls, and was quite emotionless, but in the same moment, caring.

"Dollface, it was just time for me to leave. I love Sandy and Ray, but our styles conflicted."

"What conflicting? I just had a hit movie, and everything is working. I need you, Billy. You can't leave now."

"I know, doll, but I'm here for you whenever you want. I just had to leave. Sandy was just, we rubbed each other the wrong way. But I love Sandy. I do."

"Then why are you leaving?" This must be the conversation between a child and divorcing parents.

"Because I have to. Besides, you're doing fine. And Keith Addis is good. You can call me anytime, doll. And don't love Keith more than you love me."

I couldn't sleep. I walked around Ventura Boulevard, wondering who this new guy would be. Would he understand me? Would he care?

The next day, I sat in Billy's empty office waiting for ten o'clock. On the dot a man walked in looking like he stepped out of the English *GQ*. He had thick wavy hair, a mustache, and a suit that had to be handmade. He walked by me and put his expensive leather briefcase on the desk. It was filled with scripts.

"You're Steve Guttenberg."

"I am."

He leaned across the desk. "I'm Keith Addis. We are going to do good work, have a lot of fun, and we're going to make a lot of money together."

Chapter 14

"Do you always dress that way?" He looked me over. I had Wranglers, a T-shirt, and work boots on. "You need style." And he proceeded to show me around the fashion world. He had absolute charm and was able to listen. A very rare trait in people in general. People in show business, the attention span might be eight seconds.

"Dress British, think Yiddish." Keith Addis had a way about him. Educated at Columbia University, he dresses like a duke, and has an insatiable work ethic. To be successful in this business, it has to be an all-day-all-night thing. Especially for agents and managers. You never know when and where lightning may strike.

He put up a photograph in his office of a man spinning plates. Underneath it read, MY LIFE. "That's sometimes how it feels, Steven, like I'm spinning a million little plates and trying to keep them all spinning. Clients, producers, studio heads, women, maître d's, especially the clients. I want to make their dreams come true." And he meant it.

"I can find a scale job in a thunderstorm." He loved, like most players do, the feeling of scoring a job for someone. Despite all the "no holds barred" that goes on in getting people work, there is a noble quality attached to it. The rep will keep a client fed, and a roof over their head. He will feed their kids, and clothe them. There is a feeling in all the good reps I know, that there is some higher purpose to it all. That it isn't just getting jobs. It is a whole life that they can make better. Keith liked to know everything about his clients, and take care of anything and everything they needed.

My agent at the time was Peter Meyer at William Morris. Then suddenly I got a call from one of the senior agents at William Morris.

"Steve, it's William Morris." Names are changed to protect the innocent. "We know how happy you were with Peter but Peter isn't with the company anymore. We would like to put you with someone else. A couple of people here like you. Can I have them call you? Then you can decide.

And remember, 'Put it in writing, always put it in writing.'" That was the William Morris credo. All the older agents lived by it.

I was set to meet with two stellar agents. Toni Howard, who was smart and charming, and Alan Badiner, slick and type A. Who did I choose? Alan. About a week into our professional courtship I got another call.

"Steve, Mr. Morris on the line. Are you here for Mr. Morris?"

"Yes."

"Steve, it's William. We know how happy you were with Alan but Alan isn't with the company anymore. We would like to put you with someone else. Toni Howard likes you. Can I have her call you? Then you can decide. And remember, 'Put it in writing, always put it in writing.'"

"Mr. Morris."

"William."

"William. What happened to Alan?"

"He left the business, married a guru, and is in India on an elephant somewhere."

"My agent?"

"Your former agent. Put it in writing, kid, always put it in writing."

Toni was none too happy that I had chosen Alan over her. She was very well liked in the company and the town, and was doing the bigger thing by meeting with me.

"So, it didn't work out with Alan, huh? He ran off on a camel or something?" She took a long puff of her cigarette and smiled, a wistful smile. "He is one weird guy, isn't he?"

"I heard it was an elephant." I'm sitting there groveling. Had to. I pick an agent because mine mysteriously left, then the new guy gets a wild hair and goes to India. I have to go back and get on the good side of the agent I spurned, who was the right agent after all. And she was.

Toni and Keith worked well together, and they had something to work on. I was in demand, the flavor of the month, and that was something they could sell. At the same time, the bigger players were around, Sandy Gallin and Ray Katz. When Keith and Toni got stuck somewhere on the phone call ladder, Sandy and Ray could call any network head or film studio president. And when there is blood in the water, metaphorically (or sometimes not so metaphorically), the really big fish come out.

Enter Stan Kamen. Stan was *the* number one agent at William Morris. A gentleman, who had in his stable Barbra Streisand, Goldie Hawn, Warren Beatty, Walter Matthau, Gregory Peck, and the stellar director Alan J. Pakula.

I sat in the outer office of the executive offices of William Morris. Office placement is one of the symbols of power. Stan was in the corner office of the most sought-after real estate within the building. His assistant's chair was always filled with the smartest young person in the building. Everyone in that chair went on to achieve success in their own right. One of his assistants was Rick Jaffa, who, along with his wife, Amanda Silver, wrote and produced *Rise of the Planet of the Apes*.

"Stan will see you now." A beautiful girl with glasses and a no-nonsense attitude held the door open. I saw an office that was all wood and brass.

"I'm Stan Kamen. Steve, please sit down. Did anybody ask you if you wanted something to drink?"

"This looks like a lawyer's office." It really did.

"That makes sense, because that's what William Morris hired me as. I'm a lawyer."

"An agent lawyer?"

"Yes, I'm a double threat. I can make the deal and keep everybody honest. And make some good films and help you get to the next level. Pronto."

"Pronto?" Stan Kamen was using "pronto"?

"As soon as we can. This business moves quickly, and so do we. We are going to keep you working. And stay away from independents, they are fly-by-night. Let's keep working with the studios. But most of all, let's keep you working. One more thing. Write thank-you notes, it's very important."

He was very kind and very well connected. When he called, things got done. He had built up an enormous amount of power and loved the action. The business was all he was, he had no other life. He was somewhere between a Mafioso and an attorney. Whatever he was, he was effective when he called on my behalf. And I always wrote him a thank-you note.

Ron Howard and Dick and Lili Zanuck and David Brown were making something called *Cocoon*. I got the script through Toni.

"This film is about old people and no one wants to see a movie about old people." That is what one of the top film agents in the office told me as Toni handed me the script for *Cocoon*.

"I kind of like it." Toni wanted me to do it. Keith wanted me to do it. But this senior agent was against it.

"Who is going to see this? *Cocoon,* what is that? I say you do something with more zing to it."

Howard Borris, my business manager, liked the idea of the film, but wasn't sold on it. The guy who parks the cars at the airport liked it. You have to ask everybody. Then I sat down at a meeting with Ron, Dick, and Lili. Ron was coming off *Splash* and I really believed he was going to be a superstar. He had such a presence the second you met him. His grasp of moviemaking was masterful, and he described the making of the film with as much vision as it probably takes to put someone in space. Dick and Lili were enthusiastic and focused on making this movie, and making it a hit. They both have such intense drives, ability to get things done, and good taste. These are common qualities among successful filmmakers, drive and good taste. Dick was born into the business, the son of a Hollywood pioneer. His wife, Lili, is a very kind lady with ambition and intelligence. She was reading galleys from book publishers when she came upon the novel of *Cocoon*. It was she who convinced Dick and David Brown, Dick's partner and husband to Helen Gurley Brown, to make the film. She was the driving force. She knew what she was doing.

We talked about what the film meant, and about the possible incredible moments there would be to the film. How it was going to be a challenge to get everything in the script in the fifty days scheduled for shooting. The discussion got to the point, which every meeting has, when it is time to go. I wanted them to know how much I wanted to be in the film. This was a crowd that knew how to make good movies. "I am such a fan of your work. The movie is going to be really incredible."

If one is lucky enough to sit in a room with such a brain trust, and discuss performing in their film, it is really one of the high points of a career. Of course doing the films, and being on the set, is like a daily New Year's Eve, but when you sit with brilliant people and listen to their plans, how they propose to accomplish art, it is thrilling. A gigantic high to be in on the ground floor of a masterpiece. And that's where I was.

From what I remember, Ron was supposed to do another film, and exited that movie to do *Cocoon*. He loved the project that much. And on the producing side of the table, the Zanucks and Brown were making the perfect movie for them. This was the team that made *The Verdict* with Newman, and *Jaws* with Spielberg. They talked not about the logistics of the film, which were quite complex, but the heart of the film. How it meant something while still being commercial. This was a movie about one world influencing another, with science fiction and comedy. The story was tight and the script worked. It was written by Tom Benedek, who coincidently has a brother named Peter Benedek who is a partner in the United Talent Agency. Ron was going to bring in some of his writer colleagues to look at the script, which is a usual part of filmmaking. A director will have a reading of the script, invite some talented writers and have them look for places to improve it and create some moments.

If a film can get a few wonderful moments, it improves the audience's experience exponentially. And, for that matter, the cast and crew also. There is a sudden rush when a moment works and you know you got it in the can. Take two, try it again, but you already have one really good one.

Ron worked closely on many projects with the brilliant team of Lowell Ganz and Babaloo Mandel. *Splash, Night Shift,* and the one they met on, *Happy Days.* They attended when the cast and key department reading came about. Most of the actors were there for this meeting. If there is some magic to this whole show-business life, then it is displayed when looking at the group I was lucky enough to gaze upon. There was Maureen Stapleton, so alive and aware, it was as if she had ESP. She knew what I was thinking the second we met. She reminded me of Geraldine Page, whom I worked with on *Something for Joey.* They were both intense, dramatic actresses known for their passion. As a kid I had watched Maureen over and over in *Airport,* where she played the beleaguered wife to the master actor Van Heflin. Their portrayal of two struggling people was for me the best part of the film. How about her performance in *The Rose Tattoo*?

Maureen pulled me aside. "Steven, how long are you going to be on the film?"

"The whole thing, I think. Why?" Did she know something I didn't?

"Just keep a lookout for me, I live with my daughter and this is far for me. I really didn't want to leave home but I hear Ron is very good and the Zanucks of course are wonderful, but if I need you, you'll be there for me?"

Be there for Maureen Stapleton? Are you kidding? "Yes, of course, whatever you need." She hugged me and went back to the table. There sat Don Ameche, Wilford Brimley, Brian Dennehy, Hume Cronyn, Jack Gilford, Jessica Tandy, and Gwen Verdon. Tahnee Welch sat down at the end and there was my seat next to hers. There was hundreds of years of talent sitting there. The greatest in the world. The actors were joking and loose, and I suspect were as excited as I was. They had admired one another over the years, and now had the chance to spend some time together on set.

Ron introduced himself and the Zanucks welcomed us. Then it was time to go around the table and introduce yourself. Just listening to those famous voices for the first time as they announced themselves was entertainment.

Ron started the reading with the stage direction and the actors chimed in. The reading was like a five-star production, with only cups of coffee as props and a folding table as the set. Even with them holding back, you could just see in your mind's projection room that this was going to be some film.

We took a break in the middle. Dick and Lili had a comfortable intermission planned, with gourmet catering and an open atmosphere. There was a quiet as everyone ate and talked, almost a reverence to what we were doing. It wasn't so much the material, but a commitment to the craft. They all took their profession seriously. These people weren't going to waste any energy until the reading was through.

Brian made an announcement. "I just want everyone to know how honored I am to be here. You have all been heroes of mine since I can remember. You have given me hope, and inspiration, entertainment, and made me understand some of the more important lessons in life. All through your art. And I say with all sincerity, you are damn lucky to be working with me."

Everyone laughed heartily. Brian is an imposing figure when you meet him. He must be six foot two, and depending on the day, 250-plus pounds. He is book- and street-smart, having gone to Columbia University and been a slugger in the Marines. He was coming off some good films and preparing to shoot *Silverado,* directed by Larry Kasdan, next. Brian is utterly confident, and his presence is unmistakable. Such bravado and force. He was ready for this experience, he had waited his whole career to be in this company, and he'd earned it.

My favorite moment of the reading had to do with my part, of course. We were up to the part of the film where the character played by Tahnee and I had some extraterrestrial sex and I would have some sort of out-of-body orgasm. I was shy and reluctant to really go into the action, so I sort of mumbled that I would do it on the day.

"Oh, for Christ sakes, get on with it. Let's hear some howling." Maureen slapped her palm on the table. I launched into an orgasm that lasted far longer that was humanly possible. But the cast egged me on, and I complied. Jessica made a few catcalls and Gwen whooped it up. Everyone was laughing, and we all had a good time with it. That moment, and not because of me, was a bonding one. Everyone was looking forward to seeing how I was going to do it on the day, and it gave us a view of how entertaining this film could be.

"If you can do that halfway, I've got a hotel key with your name on it, kid." Maureen laughed.

"Maureen, you better check your blood pressure that day, you could explode!" Hume yelled.

"Don't worry about Maureen, she has more in her than you think." Jack was a pal of hers.

"Yeah, under this muumuu is a lady raring to go."

"But Maureen, do you remember where to go?" Wilford joined in.

"Oh, don't worry, honey, she knows." Jessica had her head down and was shaking, she was laughing so much. And the table exploded. This was just the start of our adventure. A room full of masters at their craft, an exciting director and producing team, and a script that had all the ingredients for success. Now all we had to do was make it.

"'Rod the Bod,' that's what I want to call you." Tahnee yawned and watched as the skipper untied the lines to the fishing boat that my character, Jack, owned, a thirty-five-foot fishing-tour job out of St. Petersburg.

"That's fine with me. As long as they pay me with movie money, you can call me what you like." Rod was the boat's real captain. He ate Tahnee up with his eyes, and had a self-effacing laugh that apologized for his lasciviousness. "I hear your mother is Raquel Welch. Is that true?"

Tahnee sat up in her bikini as she stretched across the bow. "Maybe. What's it worth to you?" She loved to put the heat on people who came into her space.

"No, nothing. I just heard that and you kind of look like her."

"Without the boobies, right, Rod the Bod?" Rod turned red and went back to his captaining. That was the first I had heard of her movie-star pedigree, and Rod wasn't the only admirer of Raquel. That *One Million Years B.C.* poster with Raquel in a fur bikini was etched in my brain. And I was going to have a love scene, be it alien, with her offspring. The funny thing is the other young alien was played by Tyrone Power Jr., whose father was you-know-who. These two legacies and the great-grandson of Joseph Guttenberg, not a movie star.

We spent days with Rod, cruising around the warm waters of the Gulf. He taught me how to pilot the boat, and gave me lots of character details that I was able to meld into my work.

If you are lucky on a film, you get rehearsal time. Time to do costuming and makeup tests, and get to know the other cast members and the crew. The director can use this preproduction for anything he wants, but the smart ones always make sure they rehearse the actors. Ron did something very much like what Barry Levinson did on *Diner.* He brought the cast to the locations early, during the rehearsals. Production thought that it would be an endeavor trying to get us all together to travel from location to location, but it was surprisingly easy. The actors, no matter what their age, were professional and thoughtful. There was so much attitude that could have come along with this group, but they climbed on the boat and rehearsed in the nursing homes with the real residents looking on and took time to talk with them. It was heartening to watch Gwen Verdon teaching a few dance steps to some thrilled women. They swooned when Don Ameche came in.

"Don Ameche, the Ameche Phone!" they would yell to him as if he were one of the Beatles. "You know, they named the phone after him when he did *The Story of Alexander Graham Bell,*" one of them confided in me. Don loved that kind of adulation and stood ramrod straight, signing autographs and giving kisses on the cheek.

"I sat around the racetrack and my Santa Monica apartment for twenty years without a phone call. Nothing, just flat. Then John Landis hired me for *Trading Places,* and my career took off again. Twenty darn years." Don loved the horses and told me he was separated from his wife for many years, but still married. He was a staunch Catholic and went to church every day.

Don had been in the studio system, where his career was cared for and maintained. His friends were names like Carole Lombard, Clark Gable, and Tyrone Power. He was a giant star and headlined film after film. You say "Don Ameche" to anyone born near the '40s, and they just about have a conniption. Don had a low, baritone voice that just sang when he spoke. He had such elegance about him, years of being a Hollywood leading man.

Wilford Brimley was one of the most interesting people I have ever met. He had met Sydney Pollack on *Absence of Malice* with Sally Field and Paul Newman. It was the start of his really successful career. He was a blacksmith by trade, and in the '70s he lived in Utah and worked at different ranches. He was all cowboy and rugged outdoorsman. One of his pals was Robert Duvall, and they both, Wilford told me, loved to "moon" people.

Wilford is tough, and he can be demanding. I heard that he had a meeting with a talented director who wanted him to read. He asked why. "I don't audition, I don't like it." The director said he wanted to see if he could act the role. Wilford replied that before he read, he wanted to know if the director could direct.

Wilford does what he wants, and I think that is part of his likeability. He was the youngest of all the elder actors, and wanted everyone to know that. And he did his homework. He spent lots of time with the cast, getting to know everyone. Oliver, the boy who played his grandson, was keen on fishing, and they spent days together, fishing and talking. When it came time to film their scenes, they were like two peas in a pod. If you see those scenes, they are effortless. That's Wilford.

The rehearsal weeks were full of dinners in the St. Petersburg Hilton restaurant, which was a revolving room that spun at a slow enough speed that you thought you were losing your mind when you looked up from your soup. Most of us didn't know where we were sitting when we came back from the restroom. There was no age restriction then on dizziness. But the dinners were historic. The names that were bandied about were sensational. The gossip, the asides. There wasn't anybody on the planet that someone at the table hadn't met. Or slept with.

I walked Maureen back to her condo many nights. She got tired by the end of the dinners, and one of us always saw to it that she got home. Gwen loved Maureen. They talked a lot, and knew each other from lifetimes ago. All the ladies, Gwen, Jessica, Maureen, and Herta Ware, knew the same people. There was professional respect going on, and a girls' club too.

Gwen was a gifted performer in everything. If there was an opportunity for Gwen to be in Cirque du Soleil, she could have done it with ease. She was Bob Fosse's muse and his wife, a dancer, singer, actress, and beauty from another world. She was Lola in *Damn Yankees* and the original Roxie Hart in *Chicago.* And as sweet as they come. She still was in good shape, able to dance and move like someone half her age. She was beautiful, with a breathy voice that made you take notice. When she would look at you, you could melt. I don't care how old you are.

I would look around the van that shuttled us to work each day. No prima donnas here, everyone rode the van, and no one was late. I would stare at the elders, wondering how they lived their lives. What they did. What they were thinking. And how much I didn't know about everything.

The first day of work was simple. In and out of cars, establishing shots. A few scenes with a few of the couples. The day was twelve hours, Ron liked to stick to that. The weather was pleasant, the sky was blue, and the cast and crew knew how to make this movie. I sat back knowing that the movie would be a success. It had the feel of something that the whole world would want to see.

Something surprising was always happening on that set. Like when Hume Cronyn punched Ron's brother, Clint, out cold. Hume was in his seventies and a former Golden Gloves contender. Fifty years before, but a right cross is a right cross. He was supposed to air-punch Clint after Clint's character mouths off. But Hume really connected. Word was that Clint was out for a minute or two. Even though it was a pain for Clint, it made for another good story at the dinner table.

The scene when Don did his break-dance was just an inspired sequence. Ron shot it with the rhythm that it required to make it something to remember. As Don's character feels more youthful, he shows his physical prowess and busts a move. It is one of the scenes that brings the house down. Don won the Academy Award for Best Supporting Actor, and the scene really gave us Academy members some sizzle along with his elegance. Someone from our group was going to win the award that year, the talent in *Cocoon* was overwhelming, even for an Academy audience.

I had the honor and joy to spend time with Jessica Tandy and Hume Cronyn. Jessica was the original Blanche Du Bois in *A Streetcar Named Desire.* And I'm sitting with her while she orders eggs over easy. Hume was a legend. He worked with Hitchcock, even wrote the screenplay for *Rope.* He won the Tony for playing Polonius opposite Richard Burton as Hamlet. Jessica and Hume had the utmost respect for one another, and knew each other's likes and dislikes. He was so attentive to her, and they showed what kindness and admiration do for a marriage.

She and Hume, like all the actors, did everything without drama. There were so many different locations, bus rides, small trailers. It was a long schedule, and plenty of time for all of them to swap stories. The elders gathered in chairs, placed there by a watchful crew. The set was always watching the actors, making sure all the locations were comfortable. But they asked for very little. They were there to do their job. You knew you were in the presence of the learned ones. I couldn't take it all in and realize how lucky I was, but I had an idea. The twenty-five-year-old mind is rarely focused. I can tell you that many times I would look at Jessica and marvel at how beautiful she was. At eighty. Just beautiful.

The film had two teams that created effects. What the audience calls "special effects" is actually called visual effects. Makeup and on-set effects are called "special." The visual effects crew, from George Lucas and ILM, were the best on the planet. Greg Cannom's special effects crew could do anything on-set to create the illusion the film demanded.

These artists are improving their craft and technology on every film they work on. *Cocoon* was no exception. It was wonderful to watch them create new tricks every day.

I was fortunate that Tahnee and I had our love scene, be it out of body, require both the visual and special effects guys. Before each scene Ron would have a meeting. His advice and visualization were intense, and he took the time to teach anyone who needed guidance. Yet it all was done so simply. He was able to run the scene, tell the director of photography, Don Peterman, how he needed the camera to move, and collaborate with the effects team. I remember how he described the fireball of an orgasm that was going to hit my character. He acted the whole thing out, with so much passion and intensity that it even got me more excited than I was when I came to the set. I knew the scene was going to be magical, but as I watched Ron put it together, it became one of my moments, and a signature scene for the film.

It's a good sign when people talk about a scene years later, and especially satisfying because I have met countless people who say the scene was filmed a block from their house. From San Diego to Houston to Key West. There is even a catering hall in New Jersey that boasts in its brochure that its pool house was used in *Cocoon.* When a film spawns urban myths, you are lucky.

I really like Brian Dennehy. It's hard not to. He is so smart, well educated, and persuasive. Brian has definite opinions. We differed on subject after subject. He was right, I was wrong. But we agreed on one thing.

"Guttenberg, you worry more than anyone I know. You are the only twenty-five-year-old sixty-five-year-old in the world. You worry more than anybody."

It was true. I always worried about the next job, the next year, the next decade and beyond. I wasn't one to really enjoy a carefree movie-star life. Brian had the gift of being able to have a good time. He would chide me that I wasn't loose enough, that I couldn't go out on the town, paint it red, or even pink. I was such a worrywart, I wanted to be in bed early, be ready for the next day. Then one day I had a chance. We were about to start the dreaded night shoots of all-night filming, 6 P.M. to 6 A.M. Another cast member, Mr. X, called me.

"Guttenberg, we have all day off tomorrow, are we going out or what?" This esteemed cast member stood in the door of my trailer, completely blocking the light.

"Yes, but we have a six P.M. call tomorrow, I want at least to get in at a decent hour."

"You worry too much, Guttenberg. Relax, I'll meet you in front of your condo in an hour. I'm driving."

He met me as promised and we started out at the local Bennigan's. That was supposed to be the first of many watering holes. My castmate walked in like he owned the place, ready to have a good time. The locals came over and said hi to us, and then the women came on, having heard about our film in their city. We were having a great time. There was joke-telling, glory stories, and dancing. And drinking, and more drinking. We bought dinner, drinks, snacks, pickles, deviled eggs, and everything else on the menu. Not just for us, but for all the folks that recognized us. The cast member and I had a long-threatened drinking contest, which he won by about a bazillion to one. It was a rip-roaring time. But our first stop? Our only stop. I actually got pretty inebriated, but my compadre got blahooey. We both stumbled out of the place at about 2 A.M. He leaned on me and I had a month's worth of workouts in the twenty-yard walk to the car. We stopped at the car and both of us looked at it like a calf we had to rope. I knew neither of us were in any condition to drive, but I was a bit more on the ball than Mr. X.

"Mr. X, give me the keys, I'm driving." I held out my hand.

"No, no fuckin' way." Getting the keys from Mr. X is like wrestling a bone from a Doberman. We played "Mr. X holds the keys above his head while I drunkenly jump for them," "Mr. X runs around the parking lot doing football plays like the buttonhook," and "Mr. X holds his entire fist around the keys while I vainly try to pry open Fort Knox." He won them all. We got in the car.

"Mr. X, we are both drunk, and we cannot get picked up by the police. We are only a mile from our condos, let me drive."

"No fuckin' way." And with that he put the car in drive and ran over the parking space's cement tire stopper. And he didn't drive over just one, he hit many. We finally got out of the parking lot. Mr. X was sweating, I was sweating.

"Open the windows." I was getting the spins.

"No fuckin' way." He locked the electric windows. So there we were swerving along the two-lane highway. Minding our own business. Then there were lights. Red ones, behind us.

"God damnit, fuckin' cops." Mr. X kept driving.

"Mr. X, we have to pull over, but let me do all the talking. Do not say a thing. You are wasted. Do not talk, let me do this." We pulled over, the window opened, and there was the policeman's friendly face.

"Do you know that you were swerving all over the place? Do you know . . ." He looked in and flashed his light. "Holy shit, you're Mr. X. And you, you're the guy from the police movie, the academy. Holy shit." We had a crack of a chance. The movie-star thing stunned the guy into listening to my tale of how I would drive us home, that I was sober, that the cop could follow us home, that we would autograph anything and he could visit our set, or any set in America for that matter. I was winning, he was tipping toward our side; we would drive slowly and he would let us go. We are movie stars, regular laws don't pertain to us. We were two yards from freedom and then Mr. X spoke.

"So, are you going to fuckin' arrest me or what?" And it was over, the cop turned from an adoring fan back to a law-abiding policeman.

"Get out of the car, Mr. X."

And so began a twelve-hour saga that started with Mr. X having his head held while he rolled into the backseat of the police car and me being allowed to follow him from jail to jail.

"Your friend is a bit particular about his jail, so we are moving him to another one." The deputy directed me to another jail, twenty-five miles away. I hadn't slept in a day and I was still waiting for Mr. X to be released. I paid his bail and was told he wasn't getting out for a few hours. I went home and slept until there was a pounding on my door. I opened it to see my very worse-for-wear buddy. He had been up all night, had a splitting headache, and needed the keys to his condo, which were in his car. I gave him the keys, asked if he was all right, and watched him walk to his rental.

We were both feeling lousy about it. I yelled to him, "Don't worry about this, it's over. Never to be heard from again. Just you and me. Go home and forget about it. It's nothing."

He turned to look at me and just sighed.

I got a few hours' sleep. The next knock on my door made me jump out of bed. It was Tyrone Jr.

"Hey man, the van is outside. We are all waiting. It's the six o'clock call." I threw together my clothes in my bag and stumbled to the van. I didn't notice everyone staring at me. I played it like nothing happened last night.

"Everybody okay today?" Hume turned to me. I nodded my head yes. "Good."

"Yes, good," Jessica chimed in. "Yes, very good," Maureen agreed. "Good, good, good." All the elders kept repeating it as we got to Mr. X's condo.

"Go get him, Ty." We all watched as Ty knocked on the door and Mr. X walked out, fresh as a daisy. And I couldn't keep my head up.

We got to the set and everything was normal until Ron pulled me aside. "Hey, what happened last night?"

"Nothing." I was keeping my vow of silence.

"Steve, it's in all the papers, you two were thrown in jail. What happened, and I want to know everything." So I spilled it. Ron already knew a lot from the news. A celebrity sighting, much less one in jail, was a big deal. A few minutes later everyone was talking about it. Mr. X felt badly about the whole thing, and Wilford really gave him a shoulder to lean on. Wilford was like that, really a good guy to talk to. The incident became a joke on the set, and it got lighter and lighter, till it was forgotten. Mr. X has since spoken about it publicly, and it was just a blip on the radar screen.

We shot that night and Mr. X was letter-perfect, as wonderful as he always is. I had a hard time keeping up with everyone, and fell asleep in my cast chair, drooling.

Jack Gilford and his wife Madeline were an event every time they showed up. Jack has such a recognizable face, from Broadway and film and television. He was "the Cracker Jack Man" on commercials. He was Zero Mostel's best friend. He knew everyone and Madeline was the perfect partner. He was able to really work knowing she was in his corner. If he was on the set, you knew something wonderful would unfold. And he was just that way on our film. Jack moved his way through a scene like the talent that he is, but he was also a writer. He knew when to button something, or take a few beats. He knew how to use silence. That was fascinating about him. He was supremely talented, and so humble about it. A very generous man. And sly. He loved blue jokes.

Throughout filming, all the elders asked Jack to do "The Pea Soup Routine." He would beg off, but at one point, I think it was Maureen, who said, "Just do the damn thing, Jack, we wrap in a few days."

Jack smiled. "We wrap in a few weeks." We did.

Maureen stood up. She was wearing a very casual muumuu of sorts. "Jack, if you don't do 'The Pea Soup' now, I'm going to brain you." She shook her fist. "Besides, I've seen you do it, I think I can perform it if that's what it takes."

So Jack launched into his famous interpretation of Pea Soup boiling. It was about three minutes long, and we witnessed true old-time talent and training, craft and showmanship. It was one of Mostel's favorite bits. The small crowd just ate it up. I was amazed, but I had heard of the act for years, like the elders. It was famous among the theater pros.

We ate dinner a few times at a dramatic hotel on the beach, very art deco, built by Al Capone. It was a treat for me to sit and talk with Lili and Dick Zanuck. I remember telling Dick that I wanted to get very tan for the role, and he suggested this new tanning gel that made me look sun-drenched for days. No body makeup needed, which was good. Standing half naked in an early morning makeup trailer is okay, but the tanner from Dick really cut down on time. Tanning, boring? I guess my point is that he was helpful, and a good producer. He came to the set the next day with the tanner. That's how these very successful guys run in the business. If they say something, it gets done. And fast. The smallest detail. They are on it. Dick was that way. That's why he and Lili are in such high demand as producers. They can be trusted with a budget, and turn in a top-grade film. From tanner to millions of dollars in negative costs. Dick gets the film in the can, on time, on budget.

I was so lucky to shoot with them.

The lobby of the St. Petersburg Hilton was virtually like a movie studio front gate. Both cast and crew were always there. When a movie company takes over a building, it is all-encompassing. The local employees really get into it and became a part of production, and couldn't be more helpful. They knew what was happening on the film before we did.

"Steve, phone call for you from your agent and manager. It's Hollywood, isn't it." The operator was giggling at the front desk while I stood talking to Ron and Dick. I took the call.

"Steve, it's Keith and Toni." Keith laughed into the phone.

"Hi, Steve, it's Toni. We have something to tell you." When reps get on the phone together it's either very good, or not so good. *Oh shit, what does this mean?*

"Warner Bros. wants to do a sequel to *Police Academy.* They want to do it soon, they want you in it. We also want a sequel, we want to do it soon, and we want a lot of money for you to do it," Keith said with a flourish.

"A lot of money," Toni punctuated.

I didn't know what a sequel was, how much a lot of money was, and didn't know what was starting. A hit, once in motion, tends to stay in motion. Toni and Keith had such excitement in their voices. A rep battles to get you in a film, and if by the one-in-a-gazillion chance it is a hit, and the one-in-a-trillion chance the studio wants to make a sequel, all the talent has to do is show up. And the rep has the pleasure of negotiating the deal.

I got off the phone and went back to Dick and Ron. I asked them what they thought of doing another *Police Academy.* They were quick to answer. If the script is good, do it. Everyone is entitled to a sequel. Both were enthusiastic about it, and had a feeling it would work. Dick knew about sequels, he had produced *Jaws* and that had many. A little conversation with two smart guys can help make a decision. I called Keith and Toni back.

"I'll do it. When does it start?"

This is the fun part. No audition, just a phone call. They want to hire you. No interviews necessary. What a feeling. I went upstairs, lay back in my bed, and stared at the ceiling. I thought about where I was, how incredible it was. *I'm on an A film and I just got offered a sequel, and there are more films asking about my availability. And what my price is. My price?* I never had a price. I worked, and whatever I was paid I accepted. Gladly. Now Keith and Toni could reap the benefits of the heat that *Police Academy* was generating. We could name a price, get it, and that became my quote. When other films called, and wanted to cast me, they asked for a quote. They asked if it was backed up, as in did someone pay it? And if the answer was yes, that was your quote. I tried explaining this to my parents.

"Quote, like a quote from a book, like a saying?"

"No, Ma, it's a number they use to get me other salaries for future films. The agents can use it as ammunition."

"How much is this quote?" My father filled the silence.

"Stanley, who cares what it is, if it's a thousand or ten thousand, what is important is that he is working. That people want to have him in their films, that he is happy."

"Steven, how much is the quote."

I told them.

"Oh my G-d, you're kidding. Oh my, oh Jesus, oh my. Stanley, did you hear that. Steven, say it again."

I did.

"Oh my G-d, Steven, Stanley, Jesus Christ. Really. You're kidding. Are you kidding?"

"I'm telling you the truth, Ma."

"Oh, my G-d, Stanley, can you believe it."

"That's a lot of money," my father whispered. "You get paid that?"

"If I do a movie, yes, Dad."

"Ann, that's a lot of money."

"I know it is. Do you still have to pay the agents and all the Hollywood people?"

"Yes, Ma, of course. Thirty percent."

"Stanley, how much is that?"

He told her.

"Oh Jesus, that's still a lot of money. Steven, do you have to pay taxes on that?"

"I do, Ma."

"Stanley, how much is that?" After my Dad figured it out, just how much I get to keep after reps and taxes, he told my Mom. There was silence.

My senior prom, with marshmallow platforms. Two days after graduating, I flew to L.A. *Author's Collection*

Michael Bell, my sisters Judi and Susan, and Michael's and my friend Susan Tolsky. I owe so much to Michael for helping me get my start. *Author's Collection*

Steve Guttenberg

Height: 5′ 11″ / Weight: 160 lbs.
Hair: Brown / Eyes: Brown
Age: 18

TELEVISION:
Something for Joey - CBS movie of the week - MTM Enterprises
The Last Chance - NBC Pilot Film

FILM:
"The Chicken Chronicles" - Arco - Embassy Films
"Rollercoaster" - Universal Studios

TRAINING:
Four years at The High School of Performing Arts
The Herbert Berghoff Studios N.Y.
Scholarship to The Nassau Cultural Arts Center, N.Y.
The "Groundlings" Comedy Inprovisational Group

COMMERCIALS:
The "Welcome Back Kotter Show" Game
Stanley Tools
Windex
Kentucky Fried Chicken
Shower Massage
Dentyne

This was my first calling card. I went on what seemed like thousands of commercial auditions. I was told "Just smile." *Author's Collection*

My family came to visit me while I was filming *The Chicken Chronicles.* They loved the filming at first, but like all set visitors, they got bored. Notice my Dad's Hollywood outfit! The lady on the left is Alyse Schram, my across-the-street neighbor from Massapequa. *Author's Collection*

James Mason on the set of *The Boys from Brazil.* He and his wife, Pamela, often shared their lunch with me. *Author's Collection*

ABOVE: Chatting with my *The Boys from Brazil* costar Gregory Peck and his wife, Veronique, at the pre-filming party. No one told me to wear a sport coat. *Author's Collection*

LEFT: Greg's daughter Cecilia became a friend of mine and we explored Lisbon together. Their whole family had an air of royalty. Here we are with stuntman David Branson. *Author's Collection*

I said I wasn't interested in *The Boys from Brazil* at first. Then I found out who Franklin Schaffner (pictured here in the hat) was. My answer became a reverberating yes. *Author's Collection*

I traveled to Mexico with Dino Martin to shoot Robert Evans's *Players*. Dino was every bit as charming and charismatic as his father. (Who the lucky lady is, I don't know!) *Author's Collection*

Even my Dad started to catch show business fever. *Author's Collection*

Allan Carr (far left) threw me a 21st birthday party at Studio 54 while we filmed *Can't Stop the Music*, with Bruce Jenner (top left) and Valerie Perrine (second from left). *Author's Collection*

On the advice of my business manager, Howard Borris, I bought my first house at twenty-one years old. *Author's Collection*

The first scene that Barry Levinson (left) shot for *Diner* was with Tim Daly and me at the pool hall. *Courtesy Warner Bros.*

ABOVE: Clockwise from top: Mickey Rourke, me, Tim Daly, Kevin Bacon, and Danny Stern while shooting a setup that eventually became the poster for *Diner*. Everyone was at their best on this film. *Author's Collection*

TOP RIGHT: Paul Reiser just happened to be out buying underwear and wound up at the *Diner* audition. Lucky for me he did. *Author's Collection*

RIGHT TOP MIDDLE: Kevin was a serious and accomplished actor but kept getting recognized for being "Tim, the Alcoholic" from *Guiding Light* wherever we went. Ah, stardom. *Author's Collection*

RIGHT BOTTOM MIDDLE: Tim and I were the first to connect when we arrived in Baltimore. He came from a classic acting family – as opposed to my family, which was mostly improvisational. *Author's Collection*

BOTTOM RIGHT: Mickey and I got along so well, we asked Barry to write a scene for us together. *Author's Collection*

My family and I while I filmed *Miracle on Ice*. I dyed my hair for the audition, and it all fell out. But I got the part. Thank you, comb-overs. *Author's Collection*

6/22/83.

A view of Toronto, Ontario, Canada showing the main down-town commercial area in its blazing night time glory. Toronto is Canada's second largest city, boasting a population of almost 3 millions.

Dear Gary, Police Academy has proved to be quite a pleasure to work on. The Canadian crew is hard working and helpful. And Hugh Wilson is a creative and very funny man. I think his direction is terrific. As you can tell I am very happy. Enjoy the summer and thanks for all your help. God Bless

Steve Guttenberg

P.S. Please make sure Peter doesn't bowl for a while!

Mr. Gary Luchesi
c/o
William Morris Agency
151 El Camino Drive
Beverly Hills, Ca.
90212
U.S.A.

Printed in Israel

A postcard to my agent reporting on *Police Academy*.
I knew I smelled gold. *Author's Collection*

For the shot that became the *Police Academy* poster, I remembered Karl Malden's advice and played it straight. *Courtesy Warner Bros.*

LEFT: Kim Cattrall was genuinely shocked by some of the humor of *Police Academy*. She was a really good sport, though – classy and funny. *Courtesy Warner Bros.*

RIGHT: Bob Goldthwait was on his way up when we did *Police Academy*. At some point – I don't know when – Bob became Bobcat. *Courtesy Warner Bros.*

One of the fun parts of the business is meeting actors before they hit it big, like David Spade and Sharon Stone, who both appeared in *Police Academy* sequels. *Courtesy Warner Bros.*

When success hits in Hollywood, they send you a Rolls-Royce AND a helicopter. That part is fairly irresistible. *Author's Collection*

Just a few of my friendly admirers on the set. *Author's Collection*

Getting the chance to host *Saturday Night Live* was a seminal moment for me. Phil Hartman was a superstar on the show at the time. I knew him from the Groundlings, and he was still a thoughtful and kind guy. *Author's Collection*

Some of my agents advised against it, but I decided to do *Cocoon* anyway. Here's a shot of the recording of the soundtrack, with one of my scenes in the background. *Author's Collection*

ABOVE: Ally Sheedy was the top star on *Short Circuit*. The talented Fisher Stevens (far left) played Ben Jabituya, an Indian scientist. Austin Pendleton, a brilliant actor-director, is in the middle. *Author's Collection*

AT RIGHT: On *Three Men and a Baby*, Tom Selleck and Ted Danson were wonderful to become pals with. We had dinners on the town after every day's shooting and proved "What's done in pleasure is done full measure." The film was a hit from the first day Leonard Nimoy said "Action!" *Author's Collection*

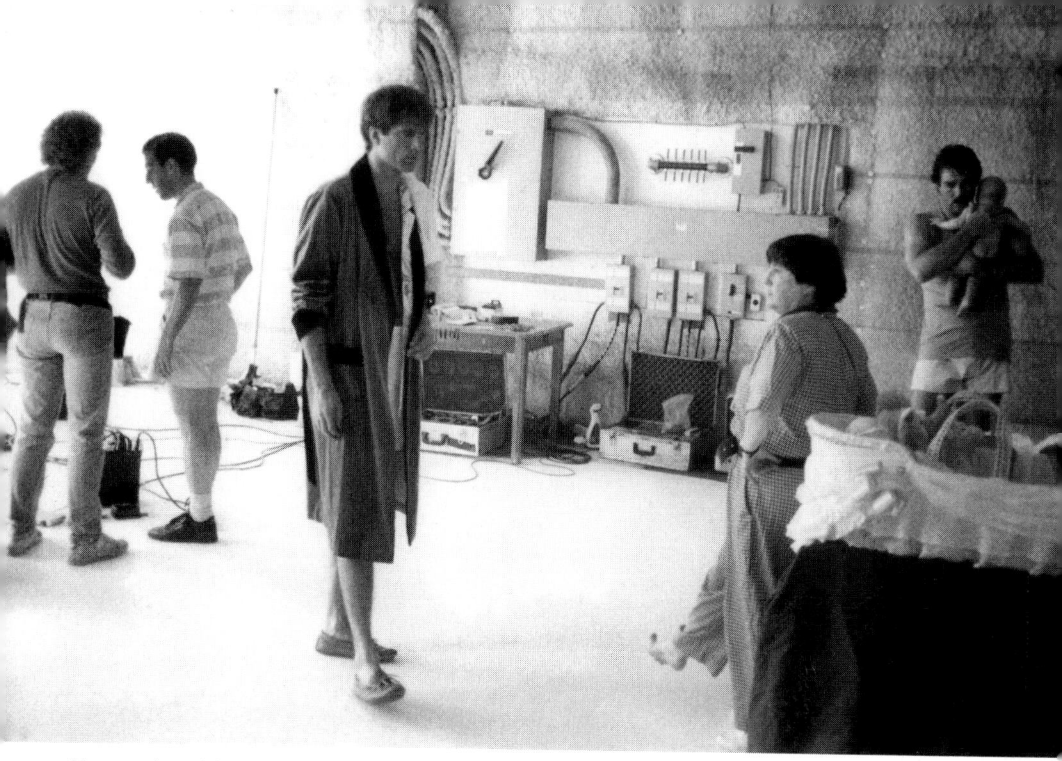

Tom and Ted had kids, so they knew how to handle the babies. They both kept watchful eyes on the twins. *Author's Collection*

Ted gave me one of the best gifts I could ever receive, an introduction to my friend Woody Harrelson. I liked him the minute we met. *Author's Collection*

Massapequa at the White House, with Tom and Vanna White. *Author's Collection*

"And he gets to keep that?"

"Yes, Ann."

"I like this business."

We wrapped *Cocoon* a week later, and it was such a professional ending. Our last day was on the boat, inside a warehouse made into a shooting stage. The cast and crew exchanged gifts and phone numbers. Everyone understood the way it goes.

The day did have some drama. One of our castmates had been having run-ins with the first AD. They were very different people, with different ways of working. Now, one of the rubs for a working actor is to be called to the set too early. Many actors despise it. This particular person really had a dislike for it. And for one reason or another, it happened to him often. The antagonism built up until on one of the last scenes on the boat, that cast member and the first AD almost came to blows. Not good. That actor was asked to leave the set. It stunned everyone, but the elders understood it, and agreed with his dismissal. Only a few yards from the finish line, and this very talented person had to storm off the set, and leave without a proper good-bye. It took the high out of the day. This person apologized, but it was not the same. This person was such a talent. It was a shame it happened.

But otherwise I felt really good about the experience. I knew how lucky I was to work on it. It was a good portrayal of a character and I also knew that it would be a hit. I could breathe easy. I think it was Gary Cooper who said, "You can have five bombs to every hit." I had in front of me at least five or ten more films.

I walked into Warner Bros.' executive offices and it was like I was in the company of best friends. I truly mistook the enthusiasm as being for me. It wasn't. It was for *Police Academy.* But the foolhardy egocentric in me adored the attention.

Keith and Toni were good at getting me in to see all the important, talented people. Starting with Warner Bros., I met most of the executives at all the studios. *Police Academy* opened a lot of doors. The sequel made everyone's mouth water, including mine. I was going to make some real money, get a big check every two weeks, and have a ball doing it.

The confidence of having a hit in your pocket can make a person cocky. It started to have an effect at home too. My parents were getting recognized when they said our last name. My father would get kudos at work and my mother had an experience at the doctor's office. The gynecologist.

She was ushered into the examining room and asked to prepare for the checkup. The doctor came in and he seemed very excited. The nurse was hopping up and down. They put my mother in the examining position (I want to be polite, this is my mother, but she does tell this story often) and the doctor started the examination.

"Can I ask you a question, Ann?"

"Yes, Doctor?"

"Is that your son, Steve Guttenberg? The one in *Police Academy*?" The doctor keeps examining.

"Yes, that's my son."

A moment went by. "So *this* is where Mahoney came from!"

As I said, the best thing about being famous is sharing it with your family and friends. Mom was a star wherever she went, the grocery store, the pharmacy, the shoemaker, the bank, and the department stores. Once the salesperson saw our name, he or she would ask my mother if we were related. And let the good times roll.

I drove to downtown Los Angeles and there is the *Police Academy II* set, a much different animal than the first. The mood was upbeat with money, as opposed to just upbeat. The trailers, the catering, the camera crew, the set, the production had an air of "We are making a hit here, folks, no ifs, ands, or buts, and if we want a masseuse for my iguana, we're getting it." The crew was upscale. Our DP was the award-winning Jim Crabbe, who did *Rocky, The Karate Kid, Night Shift, The China Syndrome,* and I knew him from *Players.* I felt like such a big shot, the second time around with the DP and this time I am the lead.

Hugh Wilson, the director of the first film, had opted out of directing. Then, it wasn't usual for the first director to direct the sequel, while now, the director wants to make his sequel. Hugh wanted to do other things. I remember him telling me that he knew he could direct Dustin Hoffman and actors of that level, and was working with good people like Nicolas Cage, Jessica Tandy, Tom Berenger, and Whoopi Goldberg. So the studio had to choose another director.

The first director—yes, *first* director—was Jim Signorelli. He was to become famous for the films he would make for *Saturday Night Live.* He had an infectious laugh and was a high-energy guy. But he had an edge to him that just didn't fit the tone of the film. It was an example of a very talented guy just not working. And an example of how sometimes only one person could have made the hit. Hugh had given him giant boots to fill. Jim was very talented, but I don't know if anyone could have made those first few days as funny as expected. There was so much expectation. So many people were depending on a hit. A very funny hit. A very funny, money-making hit.

Jim got let go. But to Paul's credit, he kept everyone calm in the time it took to get a new director. Paul and the studio had to come up with a director who knew comedy like Hugh, and knew what to shoot and how to shoot for a studio and a distribution company that had a mandate for a hit. The exhibitors were counting on it, the fans were counting on it, and the banks that loaned the money needed it. The guy had to be a superstar, and he was.

Jerry Paris flew onto the set in his lucky red sweater. "This is what I wore for the first day of every show of *Happy Days.* That I directed. And I directed every show. Every show of *Happy Days.* Yes, Ron Howard and Henry Winkler *Happy Days.*" He grabbed my face. "You, Guttenberg, you just worked with Ron. How was he?" I started to speak. "Don't tell me, I don't want to know. I taught Ron everything, everything he knows about timing, comedy, showmanship. Me and Garry Marshall. Ever hear of him? Garry Marshall? He only created *Happy Days.* What have you done? One film, one measly film that a few people saw." He shrugged at Paul. "Sorry, Paul, I have to bring him down then I'll bring him up. I like this Guttenberg. But he'll be better in my film." He grabbed my face again. He pulled me up on a table and made a speech about the start of production under his leadership with my face in his hands. He was part P. T. Barnum and part filmmaker. "I only directed thousands of *Happy Days* and I was also on a little show called *The Dick Van Dyke Show.* Ever hear of that?"

Jerry was good, very good. He had a different attack on the comedy. The setups were important, as important as the payoffs. He knew where the jokes were and knew how to shoot a joke. That's a talent, a specific talent. He rewrote the script along with two of the funniest guys in the business, Barry Blaustein and David Sheffield. They made a script that worked, and tailored it to the day-to-day shooting. They made it funny. Jerry was crazy, outspoken, honest, and interesting. And interested in Leslie Easterbrook. And she in him. They had similar passions, and by the middle of shooting those two were an item.

Jerry's rehearsals went like this.

I would do my take on the scene.

"Kid, is that how you're going to do it?" he said in a whisper that everyone could hear.

"Yeah, I think so." I did.

And he grabbed my face again. "Well, it's good, but Henry Winkler would be better."

That's how the movie worked. It essentially was funny enough to give way to another sequel. And another. Jerry and Paul created the perfect balance of fresh ideas to well-worn bits that the audience delighted in.

Bob Goldthwait started in Boston doing comedy clubs, got some attention, and came to L.A. The crack casting directors Pam and Fern had cast a wide net for talent and caught him. Bob was on the way up, and people were liking his act. He agreed to do the film, and we were lucky to get him. I met him the morning of his first day. He was the villain, and what a look he had, like Johnny Rotten in a broad comedy. He was really good, and Paul was looking after him, he knew Bob was a large talent. At some point, I don't know when, Bob became Bobcat. I kept forgetting to call him Bobcat instead of Bob. Many comedians have a different demeanor than their act. It is an act. Bob was charged up when he was playing "Zed," and very real and down to earth off the set. He had a sense of right and wrong, and was actually a very moral guy. He fell in love on the set, that was nice. He also moved his bowels in my trailer and I tell you, I didn't think it was funny until a few years ago. But now I realize it wasn't shit, it was performance art, done by an artist.

Creative passion and politics play a big role in casting. There are reasons that certain parts don't get brought back, and I don't know all of them. But G. W. Bailey wasn't in the second film. I spoke to him about it and he said that it just didn't work out. That was hard, as G.W. really created a camaraderie, and on every set where that happens, you have a better time making a better film. Instead, a new nemesis to Mahoney came on board. Art Metrano played Captain Mauser. I recognized him from a very popular commercial that he did. It was another time that I looked at this guy who I had seen on my television screen and now was acting with. It still gave me a thrill. Art came from stand-up and was just a brilliant raconteur. What I saw from Art is what I see in a lot of successful lifers. He had an enthusiasm and seriousness for his role and the movie. I know it's *Police Academy,* but everyone put their expertise into making their part work. Art knew how to build a joke, and delivered every time. Jerry loved him. (Just a side note: We were shooting a shower scene and Art had to be naked. He launched into a nude stand-up routine, twisting his privates into balloon animals. Paul yelled, "Roll the cameras," and got it all on film. Art was a pro, and gave the camera flattering angles.)

Paul asked me if I got anything in the mail. Anything from Warner Bros. I shrugged. He showed me a copy of his check, his first profit participation check. His cut of the enormous financial pie. It was gigantic. He had more net points than you can imagine, and they were paying off.

He was a working producer before these films, and now he was a net point success story. That's what Hollywood's supposed to be. Someone coming from nothing and scoring. It's the American Dream. Paul bought Linda Ronstadt's home in the Malibu Colony. He had new Range Rovers, he had a personal trainer, and he went to all the best places. He was generous, really took care of many surfer buddies who needed some cash, and fell in love with a warm lady named Sally. Everything was rolling for Paul. I hadn't seen my check yet, so I called my business manager.

"It's not that much, Steven, but if this thing keeps playing like it does, you'll see money for a long time." Howard said William Morris had mailed the check to him, after they took their commission.

"I think it's a lot, it's a lot to me," I said.

"Yes, money for not doing anything. You are a lucky boy, Stevie. If your management is smart, they will put you in some good films. You must have good material." So I went and saw my management.

Keith looked at me over his gorgeous art deco desk. "You can only do what you are offered. I would love for you to have been in *Ordinary People.* I would have loved for you to work with Robert Redford."

"So would I," the speakerphone said.

"Toni?"

"Yes. Steven, we are all trying to get you in the best movies. It's a little hard because *Police Academy* wasn't exactly a tour de force of acting. But it's a very successful and printable movie. We can get you in."

"But you have to have the chops." Keith was blunt.

"And the movies will come. Meanwhile, let's get some jobs."

"I wholeheartedly agree. Talk to you later, Toni." Keith hung up, and looked at me. "Let's have some fun with all this. It's show business. Some of it is show, some of it is business."

My friend and brother Joseph Pappalardo has a pizza place in North Massapequa that is the crown jewel of the area. Everyone knows Joey, and he put the word out that I was coming home. I had a hero's welcome at the airport and went to the family's house. That night I went to the Pizza Cove and assembled there were all my friends from high school. I was greeted by the real friends, and hugged and kissed by the too-cool-for-me friends who were now sycophantic. I loved it. We all went out from club to club. *Police Academy* got us in everywhere with free drinks and free food. There was that buzz that comes when someone famous is in the room, and that person was me. The power of fame. I was called the most likely to do nothing in high school, and now I had a couple of ex-cheerleaders purring on me. It was a testament to the rule that if you're famous, you can date five levels above your natural category.

I got back to L.A. on a flight with the most beautiful flight attendants. They all had seen the film and were falling over each other to get me my next drink. I got off the plane to a waiting limo and gave the girls a ride home. The studio gave me the car for the night, and we went to On the Rocks, the private bar above the Roxy. It was a late night.

The next morning the phone rang and it was Keith. "I have to talk to you."

Howard and I met Keith in the dining room of the Beverlywood Holiday Inn on Pico Boulevard near the Orthodox Jewish part of town. A place where no self-respecting show-business person would go. That's exactly why Keith chose it. We had to be incognito.

"I'm leaving Sandy, and I need to talk to you both."

Keith was blunt, Howard more so. "Keith, what do you want?"

"I'm leaving Sandy and I want Steven to come with me. I can do a better job than Sandy. Hell, I've been doing everything. Sandy has other projects."

"You need him to open your office. You need his commissions." Howard looked Keith in the eye. "Give him a reduced commission."

"I can't do that."

"Then he's not coming. Let's order food." Howard grabbed the menu and Keith stopped him.

"Okay, I'll see what I can do, but it will hurt me." We ate the whole meal. After, Keith went to the restroom and Howard asked me what I wanted to do. I knew Keith was responsible for a lot of the action that was coming my way, and I didn't want to cheat him out of commission, just because I could.

"Keith, we are going to go with you, at full commission. But just take care of this kid."

"I will." Not missing a beat. "Can I become a client of yours, Howard?" There you have it. Keith became a client of Howard's and I left Sandy's office to go with Keith. A common occurrence in Hollywood. The young upstarts take some of the talent from the established companies and start their own. It's the way of the representatives since the beginning.

So I went to Keith's office and met him and Toni there. It was rare that I saw them together, so this was important. They both cared about me and my career. They both had a few projects that they were interested in for me. Keith was working on a comedy about foreign med schools that Fox was doing. He was friendly with Larry Gordon, president of Fox, and knew the director Harvey Miller. Harvey was known as crazy, but brilliant, a comedy maven. Toni had a few movies she thought I could get offers on. Nike was calling and wanted to know if I would go to their celebrity-only store and pick out merchandise. This was a different level for me. Calls coming in were a third of the activity on me. There were people coming to the door with offers. Keith had a saying: "First you get the wrong offers at the wrong money. Then you get the wrong offers at the right money, then you get the right offers at the wrong money, then you get the right offers at the right money." It was a slow climb.

"Want to go to Spain?" Keith asked. Gordon okayed me for that medical school comedy, now I just had to meet with Harvey, the writer-director. I went to his house in the valley. He lived alone, a bachelor.

"I love women. I love them. I'm wild about them. But I just can't seem to get a really good one. But I am dating, I am dating. Just not the great ones. I bet you are, aren't you, you movie star. You guys get all the girls. When are they going to wake up and realize it's the brains that are sexy. This business. Sheesh." Then he looked at me sideways and smiled. Very smart guy, but a bit twisted. It made him funny. "I told Mike Nichols that I was directing and I asked him for some advice. He said, 'Just wear comfortable socks.' So I went out and bought a shitload of socks. I'm washing them now. Really going to get them clean." He kept smiling. Harvey was on the border. But he had a movie, *Bad Medicine,* and I was the lead, and I appreciated not having to audition to get it.

It really is the best job in the world when you're working. There is a line from Mel Brooks's *My Favorite Year,* that Peter O'Toole says: "I'm not an actor, I'm a movie star." The fact that people will pay to see you is just pure, unadulterated luck. Talent comes into play, but there are loads of brilliant actors working who aren't movie stars.

The limo picked me up and I was on the way to the airport. I was traveling so much that BLS Limo had a regular driver for me. I flew first class, a drink in my hand, a job ahead and a sequel coming. And I was going to work with Alan Arkin. *Catch-22* Alan Arkin, *The In-Laws* Alan Arkin. He directed Dustin Hoffman in the Broadway play *Eh?* and was an original member of Second City. I was a fan of Alan's, like so many people, and I got the chance to watch him work. That was worth the price of admission. And that price was working with Harvey, who was talented and eccentric.

Harvey drove Alan crazy, and Alan made Harvey nervous and nuts. I just sat and marveled at Alan. Even him ordering breakfast from the PA was a treat. His distinctive voice and delivery are like no one else's on the planet. Maybe Walken or Nicholson could give him a run for his money, but that's it. Alan is one of a kind, and smart. He knew everything that was going on, no matter how crazy it got. And the set got crazy. But the friends I met on the movie were wonderful. I got to work with Julie Haggerty, Taylor Negron, Joe Grifasi, Gilbert Gottfried, Curtis Armstrong, and the brilliant Julie Kavner, who, along with being the voice of Marge Simpson, was recently in the Broadway play *Relatively Speaking,* by Ethan Coen, Elaine May, and Woody Allen, with me. All really good actors, flown in to Valencia, under the direction of Miller. It was controlled chaos most of the time. Except the time that Harvey got the gypsies we hired as extras so angry that they revolted and the set became dangerous. We were all instructed to stay in our trailers and not open the doors, especially for anyone with an accent like Peter Lorre's. Harvey was very funny, though, and in between him telling me that he liked my girlfriend and would like to have her, and stressing about writing new scenes, he was very charming. He could make you feel confident and relaxed, and was very sincere when he was doing it. But he took it away from you later, telling you he was only joking. He was constantly fighting with the studio, and lamenting that he was getting eaten alive by Fox's restrictions. But it was the arguments with Arkin that were the most dramatic.

Alan was very spiritual then and still is. He spent a lot of time meditating and working on his own things. Harvey didn't see that Alan needed to be treated delicately and with some deference to his instincts. After all, Alan was much more accomplished than Harvey. I have found that when a newcomer of a director gets a seasoned actor in his grasp, he tries to mold him into what he wants. That rarely works. The older director realizes that he hired the actor for what he can do, so the best thing is to let him do it. To stifle an experienced actor is a recipe for drama. Harvey was on Alan throughout the film, asking him to deliver dialogue in a certain manner, and to basically just listen to him. Alan had other ideas for his character and wanted to play it his way. They often argued on the set, and Harvey wouldn't back down until Alan got so crazy that he had to take a walk off the set. The volcano erupted when Alan misplaced a certain black velvet bag that had some very meaningful items in it. Alan needed to get the bag back. He felt he needed it in order to work. It was another disruption that Harvey didn't need, but it became a big situation. They had some choice words and both cleared out of the set. No director, no actor, no filming. The crew, by the way, whiled away the hours as they had done at lunch every day, in the bar between the sound stages. The Valencia Studios had a bar smack between Stage One and Two. The crew would load up at lunch on beverages of every kind and alcoholic content, and then go back to work. The days that Harvey and Alan had their tiffs, the crew retired to the bar. I went with them by the end, and found a small aperitif comforting as the production got rocky. Jeff Ganz, who is Lowell Ganz's brother, was brought in to help produce and write the scenes that needed help. Jeff was very talented, but had an enormous load saddled on him. He did what he could, and kept the production moving forward. But it was not easy.

I drove back to the hotel with Alan after one rather nasty day of both Alan and Harvey telling each other to fuck off.

"You know, Steven, this film, I have a prediction. I predict this film will make a million dollars." He said it with such a flourish that it seemed like a big accomplishment. He repeated it. "A million dollars."

I thought about it and at first became comforted that a guy like Arkin thought that the movie was going to be profitable. Then it hit me. "Wait a minute, Alan. If this film makes a million dollars, it will be a disaster."

"Exactly, my good man. Exactly."

I returned to Los Angeles, and *Police Academy 2* came out and had a giant box-office weekend. Again this gross-out comedy actually satisfied the audience. A tall order for a sequel, and it had that all-important big second weekend. It felt as if I were covered in tinsel. But again, it wasn't me that was getting all the attention, it was the film, or more important, the money that the film was generating. It was delivering on its promise, the exhibitors had another hit, and the foreign theater owners were anticipating their share of this golden goose. The video companies were happy, the distributors were happy, everyone was making money. Paul had another enormous pile of points, and he shared them with all of us. Warner Bros. couldn't do enough for the cast. I was told I was in the "Warner Bros. Family." And the family wanted to do another *Police Academy.* The second wasn't out of the gate for more than two weeks and they already had a start date for the third.

"Steve, I have Toni on the line." Keith was on.

"Hi, we have some good news." Toni laughed.

"Warners wants you for the third, they only need you for sixteen days, and they will pay us whatever we want, basically. Toni and I are going to talk to Howard, see what is best for you, and get it done. Don't take any calls from Warners until I tell you to."

"Definitely no calls. They will try to make you do things we don't want you to. Oh, and I got that beautiful leather briefcase you sent over. Thank you." Toni hung up. Keith was still on the line.

"Briefcase, she got a briefcase?"

"Keith, when I send the commission to Toni, it goes to William Morris. When I send the commission to you, it goes to you. You're getting better than a briefcase."

"I still want a briefcase."

In Hollywood, gifts are essential. I bought him a briefcase.

And so, *Police Academy 3* was rushed into production. We were back in Toronto, where the first was shot. The film got whatever it wanted, including Miss Universe, Shawn Weatherly. Just walking her universally loved body all over the set.

"Dad, I'm working with Miss Universe."

"Who's that, she from Spain?"

"No, Dad, from the contest, the beauty contest."

"The contest on TV? The one that has mostly bathing suits and gowns and none of that hokey talent bull that Miss America has? I like that contest. Is she the girl from Oklahoma or something?"

The other extension picked up. "Of course, Stanley, you perk up when your son mentions anything with other women, a beauty contest. Stanley, you want to go with Miss Universe, go. Let her deal with you."

"Mom, he wasn't saying anything about it, I was telling him about the cast. They put in a pretty girl and it's really fun. I mean, she's Miss Universe. I didn't have any Miss Universes at Plainedge High School."

"Is she the one from Louisiana? The dark-haired one that had a stutter?" My Dad was excited.

"Stanley, you remember what the girls looked like? He doesn't know how to load a dishwasher but he knows the contestants on Miss Universe."

"It was just on a few nights ago!"

"Dad, Shawn wasn't from this year, she was from a few years ago."

"Oh, then I don't know her."

"You better not, Stanley. Your father is a chick magnet, I'm telling you. I leave him alone for a second at the mall and I come back and he's talking to some woman."

"That was only one time. I knew her from the office."

"I don't care. Next time I'm going to leave you and Miss Universe to talk while I get a bus home."

One of those the-world-is-small occurrences happened on the set. A wonderful actor named Ed Nelson had a role of a politician. I had met Ed when I was fourteen, visiting Michael for the first time. Michael was guest starring on a show called *The FBI,* and Ed was also on the show. I'd had an autograph book, and Ed was the first to sign it. The first film actor I had ever met. And I walk on the set and he is sitting way up high in a stunt boat, filming his scene. That's the delightful part of this business, you always run into people again.

The production was just fun and games from the beginning to the end. Bob had become Bobcat, and had enjoyed a lot of success from the second film. He was becoming a hot commodity around town and was seen as someone who was very on the edge. His stand-up was smart and topical. It was abstract at times, but he used classic timing for the punch lines. Bobcat really knew his comedy. But he didn't like the films. He went on show after show ridiculing the movies, his part in them included. Still, he accepted another, the third, and was paid fairly and handsomely. But damn if he didn't put the series down as often as he could. Even on the set, he had a dislike for what we were doing, and gave the rationale that he was there for his kids' educations. I understood that. I understood taking the money. But we were in the middle of creating another one. No matter how lowbrow and cheap he thought the films were, he too was acting in this one, and needed to be funny. Jerry, still with Leslie, was able to work with Bobcat. No matter how bad Bobcat thought the film was, he listened to Jerry. He delivered a good performance, although I know he bites his tongue at the mere mention of an academy. Any academy.

There was truth in what Bobcat was saying. I felt it too. I had the feeling that we were dipping into the well too much. We were working this animal without giving back to it. The studio saw it as a cash cow, and it was, but we still needed to give it the quality care it needed. It was just showing up, mainly, the movie just needed to get completed. The audience already wanted more. You could sail on just the uniform and a smile. That momentum carried over to the material. There was a split between truly creative comedy and the fact that a lot of people were depending on this film to do business. Certain jokes worked overseas, certain didn't. That had to be accounted for in the script. There were more restrictions during filming, and it became PG-13 as opposed to R-rated. So a natural inclination to do some sexy stuff was squashed, to keep it PG. They were broad comedies, silly movies, but there was a method and classic structure that they had to follow. Jerry's work on those two films was excellent. He stuck to tried-and-true comedy rules, but on the third film even he felt stifled. Jerry liked raunchy comedy. But he too had to color between the lines for a PG rating, and made the most of it, to his credit. He loved having Leslie around, she made him calm when something, or someone, made him crazy. Paul tried to keep a hold on the film, but it had a life of its own. Instead of being a little under-the-radar low-budget film, it became page one in the trades. Everyone knew it was being made, and everyone was watching for its first week's box office.

Everything was moving fast now. Keith and Toni were keeping me in the mix for projects all around town. I was on everybody's short list. I bought a Ferrari. I drove it to the supermarket. It was ludicrous. I went to the dermatologist, a very kind man at Cedars, and got shots in my head to keep my hair. I joined a private gym instead of working out in the garage. I dated above my natural category. I went to award shows and mingled with other celebrities. My ego was eating every day, getting bigger, fatter, uglier.

I started to buy what was being sold to me.

Chapter 15

"Twentieth is calling it a 'life-affirming' movie. It's something that comes around once in a lifetime, twice if we're lucky. Barry Diller has personally seen to it that the film will garner major attention. They are talking Oscars. What does that mean for us? It means offers, lots of offers. It's going to get really fast now, I already have guys coming at me that want you in their films. We have to be very careful not to piss anybody off." That was one of my reps after getting a call from an executive at Fox. *Cocoon* was testing with high numbers and screening successfully around the country. Every meeting I had, every lunch I took, every party or premiere I attended had the buzz. In Hollywood, as in the stock market, anticipation is the thing. Once it's out, it's out, but it's in the waiting that the buzz is built.

Dick and Lili were always communicative with me, telling me where the film was at, and what the next step was for its release. They had a screening one night and called me excitedly to report in.

"Steve, we had an industry screening the other night and every executive in town came. The place was packed. The movie played well and when the curtain came down it was silent. I tell you, Steve, you could have heard a pin drop."

"No one said anything, Dick? No applause? Isn't that bad?"

"No. That's good! They are all jealous as hell."

We filmed trailers designed specially for certain waves of publicity and release. The studio knew it had something that was going to work. When a studio has a hit, the sky is the limit on what it can do. How much it can gross, then how well it can pick up the ancillary monies. A hit pays for a lot of flops.

The president of distribution, Tom Sherak, and president of marketing, David Weitzner, were eloquent when they introduced the film to the cast. (Tom and his wife, Madeleine, have become among my closest friends.) Everyone was flown in for a private screening. Ron, Dick, and Lili watched with the cast as the film rolled out. When the lights came up, there were smiles and wide-open mouths. We were all just bowled over by the beauty of the experience. The cherry on top was that its leads were senior citizens. The same old people that an agent implored me not to act with were getting accolades all over the globe. This was the biggest group comeback the business had ever seen. These were stars, real movie stars, and they were reignited. "Once a star, always a threat," Lew Wasserman said. It was a delight to go on a publicity junket with these people. We had not seen each other for some time, so the reunion was wonderful. There is that understanding that you can have with people you have worked with that is universal in the business. And if you are lucky enough to have done a worthy piece of art, then all the better. We had a hit, and as Jessica told me, "I'd rather be a shit in a hit, than a hit in a shit." She was a hit in a hit, they all were.

The film had a successful opening weekend, it looked like it had legs, and the studio was already whispering about a sequel. Enter Marvin Davis.

Marvin bought the studio in 1981 and just loved being involved. This Denver-based oil tycoon was bigger than life. Three hundred or more pounds of raw energy and drive. He had his own chair at Spago, an actual throne, that would be put at his regular table when he fancied a meal made by Wolfgang Puck. He had the town in the palm of his mighty and thick hand, but when I saw it, it held pastrami on rye with a little spicy deli mustard.

He had summoned me to his office. Or airplane hangar, as most would describe it. This guy was personal friends with the president. Not of Fox, but the United States. He and Reagan were in pictures all over his walls, when I finally got there. I swear the walk from the security check, the first receptionist, the bank of assistants, anterooms, side rooms, personal dining room (which looked bigger than my house), and his personal assistants and their assistants, must have been a football field. All leading up to the office that had a walk-in refrigerator. Marvin stood halfway between the fridge and his desk. He had a bagel with cream cheese and lox in his hand.

"You want the pastrami or lox? I like the pastrami but I will be happy to get more pastrami if you choose the pastrami. Then I'll eat both and you can have the second pastrami. Guttenberg, you like pastrami?" And so our meeting started. He was interested in actors, he liked to talk to them. You wouldn't think that this tycoon would have anything in common with a Long Island Sammy Glick, but we had similar parents, shared lots of stories, and had a colorful first meeting. His door was always open to me, and I would visit him when I was on the lot. One of the perks of that relationship was going to some event or restaurant, and seeing him holding court. He would stop his conversation and bring me over to be introduced to whatever important crowd he was entertaining. Sometimes it was his family, and he loved to reintroduce me to them every time we crossed paths. His grandkids were enjoying the wealth, they were the "old" money, to his and his wife's "new" money. Marvin was generous and always gracious. I heard he was a beast in business, but I never saw that. I was lucky.

I became a regular at all the industry places, some that had an unlisted phone number and where only a select few were permitted in. The watering holes of the very rich and very famous. These were shadowy night spots, with entrances through the kitchen, and it wasn't unusual to see a superstar winding his way through the pots and pans into a waiting limo. I got the ultimate invitation, which was to Helena's, a downtown club that was owned by an actress of aforesaid name and her close friends, one being Jack Nicholson. The place was comfortable, dark, and reeked with opportunity of the naughty and fun kind.

I was invited everywhere, and I went. There were Cher's famous roller-skating parties, Outpost Road mansion parties, Venice and Santa Monica get-togethers. I still talked to my father every morning. Unless I overslept, and called back fibbing that I had been out for a run.

"Steven, Steven! Pick up, it's your father, Steven. Where are you? It's six thirty."

I fumbled as I picked up the phone.

"Dad?"

"Yes, it's your father. Where have you been, Steven? I have been calling for two days and can't find you. Your mother is worried and wants to fly out there if I didn't get you today. What the heck are you doing out there? You have to stay on the program, work during the day, and get to sleep early."

I would mumble something about working out early and feel terrible that I was wasting time enjoying the party. Later I confessed to my mother.

"Your father doesn't know what he's talking about. You go and enjoy yourself. You're young, it's the time to do these things. It's the time to do crazy things, to get your wild oats sown. And what better arena for a young man than Hollywood. I know you won't do something stupid, or I'll kill you, you know that. So go have fun, and don't tell your father anything. He's as straight as an arrow."

I went out, I stayed out, I came in late, I came in early. Sunset Boulevard had party after party. My buddy Mike Binder was doing a set at the Comedy Store on Westwood Boulevard. He asked me to come down. He had a bit about Disneyland in which he had a loudmouth, a plant, in the audience heckling him. The real fun about coming to see him was being part of his act. That little part of yelling from the audience felt good, just being able to do a scene with my friend. But I went time after time. The Comedy Store—both locations, east and west—were hangouts for talent. I remember Jay Leno coming into the parking lot on his motorcycle. There was Robin Williams, Eddie Murphy, Steven Wright, and Howie Mandel, and a cast of characters from a good ensemble comedy. These were the funniest guys in every city and town across the country, and they all ended up here.

Keith and Toni called about a really high-profile film. The director of *Saturday Night Fever* and *WarGames* was making a movie about robots. That's all they knew. The script was being kept secret, and only a few people could see it. This was quite common before computers. The only way an actor, or anybody for that matter, could see a script was if they drove down to the casting office and read it in the waiting room. This was a secure way not to let drafts out. Often there were competing scripts with similar ideas vying for the studio's blessing. A stolen idea could mean millions in profit gone.

This script was unique, but used a formula that had been around forever. The fish out of water that changes the people in his new environment, like *E.T.* and *Splash.* When I went to read I saw a mockup of the poster. A human hand reaching for a flower held by a robot hand. The title read *Short Circuit.* I read it at seven at night, while the casting assistant waited.

"Are you done yet? I have a life, you know." She hovered over me. I kept reading. "Hello. Anyone there?"

I looked up at her. I looked at the poster. "This is a hit, isn't it?"

"I don't know, a robot, Ally Sheedy, John Badham. I don't know. Maybe. You done?"

"Ally Sheedy from *The Breakfast Club*?" That sounded good. Ally had a good reputation. The movie was commercial material, and her involvement classed it up. John Badham was doing good work and in demand. And the movie was like *E.T.* I went after it the next day.

"Steven, you up?" The answering machine shouted my father's voice.

I was up, dressed, and on my way out the door. I wanted to be at Toni's desk as soon as she got in. I grabbed the phone.

"I'm up, Dad. I read a really good script about a robot coming to life. Really good."

"Not like that movie *2001: A Space Odyssey,* I hope. Your mother and I didn't get the banging and the yelling with those apes. Is it that kind of movie, because I don't know if that's a good move. Does your robot movie have apes?"

"It's not my movie yet, Dad."

"Well, make sure it doesn't have apes. It'll destroy the whole thing."

I drove to the agency, looking for a meter that had time on it along El Camino. It was 10 A.M., the time that all agents are back from their breakfasts and at their desks.

"Steven, how did you get in here? I'm still getting organized." It wasn't usual to have a client sneaking past the receptionist and not being announced. But that was my routine. "You know you can check with the receptionist. They won't throw you out." I wasn't too sure.

I sat on a chair with a pile of coats on it. "I read *Short Circuit.* I would love to be in that movie."

Toni never raised her voice. "You're sitting on my two-thousand-dollar Chanel coat, thank you." I sprang up, seeing the multicolored shoulder of the coat crushed. "Give it here. Thank you. And you don't have to say it. You have a meeting with John Badham tomorrow. He is really smart and the next Steven Spielberg. Just don't talk too much at the meeting."

The next day, Badham sat back in his chair underneath another mock poster of the film. "You do talk too much."

I couldn't stop telling him why I should play the role of the scientist who brings the robot, Number 5, to life. I told him why the movie would work, why it would have universal appeal, and why it would be a hit. I told him why I would be perfect for the role, why I needed to play it, and why I would do anything to be in this movie. I also apologized for talking too much.

"But I really liked the way you dealt with fantasy in *Cocoon.* You were very believable, and I need that same leap of faith taken by this character. Would you mind reading a page or two?" I did, and waited for him to tell me I had the part in the room. It didn't happen.

"We have to talk to Ally." Ally was a very big star because of *Breakfast Club* and *WarGames,* and had approval of the cast. So I waited.

I called Keith. "Nothing yet."

I called Toni. "Nothing yet."

So I waited. And waited. How could I not get this part? I was perfect for it. I had a few hit movies. I told them how much I wanted it and how hard I would work. I told them why I thought it would be a hit. I told them and told them. Maybe I *did* talk too much.

The phone rang at ten o'clock the next morning. I leapt for it.

"Robert Evans calling for Mr. Guttenberg." What was this about?

"Guttenberg, I'm having a get-together at my house. It will be good for you. Come at eight tomorrow night. You know where the house is."

"Sure, Bob. Can I bring anything?" I still didn't get the Hollywood social scene. You don't bring marble cake to a showbiz get-together.

"No, my boy, just come and have a good time. It's a Mardi Gras theme, very festive. I'll have my assistant get on the line and tell you about it." In a flash a friendly woman was on the line giving me the specifics. I couldn't bring anyone, and Bob really wanted everyone in Mardi Gras attire. As I searched my closet for something that would fit the bill, the phone rang.

"You got it." Toni giggled and hung up.

There is nothing sweeter than going to a Hollywood party where everyone eventually asks what you are working on, and having a job on a studio film with a big director and a major star. It started in a few weeks, on location, in Astoria and Portland, Oregon, with per diem. I pulled on a multicolored sweater that my aunt knitted, and headed out with something to say that night. I was working.

When you see Evans, it's like meeting a king. For all his success, he keeps humbleness and a well-mannered air about him. He is funny and makes you feel as if you are the only thing on his mind. I have noticed that the most successful have two qualities: they make you feel interesting and they call back that day. Evans calls back. And his personal life has always been colorful and exciting. This party was just that. There were stars like Nicholson and Beatty walking around and nibbling on caviar. A studio president was getting tips on his tennis swing from Bob's pro. A beginning actor, unknown but spectacularly handsome, sat next to an agent who wouldn't give him the time of day, until a superstar came up to the kid and hugged him. All of a sudden the agent was interested. Two beautiful girls who looked like they were from Sweden, just off the boat, were sitting next to the pool in what looked like nightgowns. The music was Sinatra and Tony Bennett, and I even heard that one of them was there. There were two men there interested in the same woman, and Evans asked me to talk to one of the guys about baseball and get his mind off the other suitor. I circled the party a few times, bumping into people

I knew, some who didn't want me to see them. It is such a funny thing, when someone acts as if they don't see you but you are right in front of them. People are at Hollywood parties to work. Everyone is looking for business. Who can help me? Who do I spend time on? Who do I talk to and wiggle the conversation toward business? But I had something that stopped them in their tracks.

I kept my usual souvenirs, napkins with Evans's logo on them, and a necktie that a film financier from New Jersey gave me. I stayed late and then Bob said it was time for me to go home. "You are far too young for the rest of tonight."

I drove up to my Sherman Oaks hill home. I still had that silly red Ferrari. My neighbors thought a plane was landing every time I pulled up. And there she was. My first stalker. Now, this is quite an achievement. And this one was beautiful. She was tall, blond, voluptuous, and dressed to the tens. Miniskirt, high heels, and a smile like a teeth-whitener commercial. I stopped the car and opened the window as the garage door opened. She stood on the stoop.

"Can I help you?" I shouted.

"You are him, aren't you? You're Steve Guttenberg." She had a Southern accent.

I hesitated. *Do I say I am or I am not?* She was hot. "I am."

She ran down the stairs toward the car. "Oh my goodness, I can't believe it. I told my friends I would get to meet you, they didn't think I could. I'm Cheryl, from Kentucky. I drove all the way out here. Didn't you get my letter?"

Red flag. I knew that there was something crazy here, and possibly dangerous. I should cut this short immediately. But she was hot. "I don't know if I got the letter, but—"

"Oh, you are just as cute in person. This is a little uncomfortable standing outside and all. And chilly, it gets cold at night here in California." She rubbed her shoulders. Her boobs started to wink at me through her halter top.

"Steven, can you shut that darn car off, people are trying to sleep." Standing next to my stalker was my neighbor, eighty-year-old Mrs. Fitzsimmons. She had her hair in curlers and a robe over her flannel nightgown. My Amazonian stalker shook her head and agreed.

"It is loud. Oh, here is the picture you sent me." She pouted as she pulled out a picture sent from Twentieth when I was doing *Billy*. It was a stamp of my signature.

"Shut that damn car off!" My other next-door neighbor, Bob, hung his head out the window not twelve feet from my driveway. "We have kids!"

So there I am with my stalker, Mrs. Fitzsimmons, and Bob in his pajamas, holding a two-year-old who was watching all this with eyes wide open. I shut off the motor.

"Who's your friend?" Bob wrote for the Bob Guillaume sitcom *Benson.*

"I'm Cheryl from Kentucky. I drove all the way out here to meet Steve." She beamed.

Mrs. Fitzsimmons made a face and walked away. Bob raised his eyebrows and flashed me the thumbs-up. "Ah, stardom. No one drives across the country for writers." He went inside and pulled the shade down.

I looked at Cheryl. I could hear every intelligent voice in my head telling me not to do anything with this woman. This person was not healthy in the mental department. I mean who would send a letter and then drive all the way out to California? A loony, that's who. A stranger that could do horrible things to you. A kidnapper, a nut job. What moron would take such a risk? Put everything on the line for some cheap sex?

I slept with her. I couldn't even respect the koo-koo-loo-loo law: Don't fraternize with the stalker.

"Success and failure are both illusions." Born in England, educated at Yale, John Badham was one of the most informed and brilliant directors I had worked with. He loved to listen to people's stories and their philosophies. He came from a pedigree; his sister was the young actress in *To Kill a Mockingbird.*

John had a night-before-the-first-day dinner. He presided over the dinner with the producers, Larry Turman (who produced *The Graduate*) and the father-and-son team of David and Gary Foster, who were really in the nuts and bolt and making the movie. Ally, the top star on the film, was there. She had an ephemeral shine to her and always looked like she was in on a private joke. And my favorite, Fisher Stevens, who played Indian scientist Ben Jabituya, showed me his accent and demeanor during dinner. He wanted to have dark makeup. He was brilliant in that role.

John had a flair for the dramatic, and announced that a special visitor was going to make his entrance. It was "Number 5," the robot. He wheeled in, controlled remotely by the puppeteers and special effects people. It was a magnificent puppet, sophisticated and intricate. It had so many individual movements that it actually appeared to be alive. It had a smart-aleck voice that was also done by remote control. John bantered with Number 5, as did Ally, Fisher, and me. Then the puppeteers did a funny bit with the headwaiter about the bill and who was going to pay it. The waiter didn't know what to make of this contraption talking, waving its arms, and wheeling about the dining room.

"But I am not going to pay this bill! Who had the flounder? That was nineteen dollars. Highway robbery! And you can't steal from a robot. It's against all decency!" Number 5's eyes lit up and he waved the bill in his hand. "You are certainly not getting my credit card today, sir. I am one tin can you will not take for a ride." The waiters all laughed and got such a thrill seeing the puppet up close. A movie company always brings magic to the town it is filming in. And this was no different.

"I'll remember this the rest of my life," a busboy shouted as he shook hands with Number 5.

"I will too, and mostly because of your sweaty palms. Yecchh!" Number 5 was pretty G-rated.

Ally, Fisher, John, and myself had a small powwow back at the hotel about the way John likes to shoot. John had worked with Ally before on *WarGames*. "So, basically, this is all for you two." John pointed at Fisher and me. He didn't like to shoot more than a twelve-hour day and needed everybody on cue, as the puppet was going to be the most difficult thing on the set. John hoped to meet each morning to go over the day's work with the cast and crew. Then take the time to walk the first set and go over camera moves. He gave you only a vague idea about blocking, not because he wasn't prepared, but he wanted us to breathe, to discover things on our own, and then he would add to that.

The filming was incredibly smooth. John was a techie but foremost a dramatist, so his interest in making this movie work came from many directions. It was a big film, lots of production value and scale. John would present each set and it would be either some thrilling scenery or the robot doing something extraordinary.

Acting with the puppet was a different experience than doing green screen, where you act basically to air. The puppet had specific actions, and you had to bend yourself and your performance toward those actions, which would mostly be on cue. But it often needed some management. You had to be ready. It reminded me of what Jack Lemmon used to say about acting with Marilyn Monroe. He said that he did take after take with her, and the director printed it when Marilyn got it right. So he had to be "on" in every take. That's the way it was with the puppet. It was always near the mark, but when it was perfect, that was the take. John was smart; the robot was the heart of the film, it had to be paid attention to. We humans just had to know our jobs.

I really enjoyed getting to know Fisher. He won an Academy Award in 2009 for producing *The Cove.* But he was a star from the beginning. He was a very bright guy, with a love for good material and beautiful women. He was so confident, and outspoken. I remember when he was looking around my room and saw in the bathroom that I had all these face-care supplies. Cremes and moisturizers from the facialist I was going to. He really got a laugh out of it. "It looks like a girl's."

After wrapping, I returned to Massapequa to enjoy some home cooking and the company of my family and friends. I hadn't been home for a while, so it was especially good to be able to relax and really be myself. There is a discipline that you must have when you are on the road, on location. You have to adopt an armor. And you can rarely take it off.

"Bullshit. Bullshit you did a scene with Miss Universe." Terry, the coolest guy in my high school, lit up a joint and blew smoke. It was a gathering of "the boys" from Plainedge High School. Joey had put it together. They were all there. Bob, the strongest kid in the school, Dean, the toughest guy in the school, Billy, the basketball star, and me.

"I did, and she was unbelievable. Blond, blue-eyed. Like out of a magazine." I wanted to brag. I mean this was Terry, who was reported to have had a three-way in twelfth grade. And here he was, his eyes popping out, straining to hear anything I said about Miss Universe.

"She smelled different. Different than any girl I have smelled." I was lying.

"Like what, like one of those dancers on *Soul Train*?" Everyone looked at Bob.

"No, you idiot, like from another world. She's Miss Universe. Out of millions of women, they chose her to represent the universe," Dean said.

"So in an intergalactic contest, this would be our entry. Okay. And you had a kissing scene with her?" The crowd leaned in.

"I did." Arms crossed, proud.

"Bullshit. Next time call me, I'll do the romantic scenes."

I loved being home. I could visit with all my old friends. Some lived with their parents, some rented apartments, a few had wives and some kids. I was making movies, they were making lives. There is an underdevelopment that can come from a life in the pictures. You start to mark time by the projects you work on the way other people mark time by their kids' school years. You become isolated.

"I got you a one-day job. For a million dollars." Toni was on the speakerphone. Keith sat back in his chair and stroked his mustache.

"Toni, tell him who it's for."

"Uh, thank you, Keith. This isn't my first time talking to a client." Toni could have a bite. Only five foot five, she was a force. "It's a Seagram's wine cooler commercial. Bruce Willis, Woody Harrelson, and you are each doing separate ones. They have a great director and it's one day for a million dollars. Is that okay?"

Keith, ever the negotiator, "Can we keep it to a twelve-hour day, and anything over that is prorated?" He winked at me. "Toni, it is pretty incredible, isn't it."

"I would say so. I mean Bruce Willis, Woody Harrelson, and you. Good company. I'll see if I can keep it to twelve hours. Can I let them have thirteen?"

"No. Talk to you later. Bye, Toni." He hit the speaker button. "So, we aren't doing too badly. A commercial for seven figures, a comedy franchise, and some more movies on the way. I'd say we were doing okay. What are you wearing?" I had on my regular cheap jeans, work boots, and T-shirt. "You need to start dressing like a movie star, not like a town worker from Massapequa. And I want you to start attending these dinner parties that I throw. I have very influential people there, filmmakers and studio execs. You need to start to mingle with these types. Your old friends just won't do anything for you. You will outgrow them, you need to start doing that now. Who are your friends? Failed actors and some regular Joes from home? You need to be seen at the hot places with the talented people. I need people to think you have the chops. If you spend time with people who are talented, the good directors will meet you through association. I know you hate the social scene."

I did. The scene is, as Eli Broad said about Los Angeles, a "meritopolis." The importance of success far outweighs character. Whoever has the most toys gets the most respect.

The schmooze, as ridiculous as it may seem to the civilian, is very important. I don't get that. I don't participate like I should. A producer friend referred to Hollywood meals as "relationship dinners." You have no real personal attachment to your fellow diners, but they are a way to move along an affiliation that, someday, will produce results. It is important to socialize, to get to know people, but not too well. One of the most talented of the directors I've worked with told me he can get close to people, but not too close. "You may have to turn them down someday."

Keith gave me a script to read, and walked me out. "I'm going to stop inviting you if you don't start to come. You can't stay in Massapequa your whole life."

The whole ride home I thought about it. I needed to hang out with the movers and shakers. I needed to have relationship dinners and schmooze. I needed to expand my horizons past Massapequa and on to a hipper, celebrity scene.

Epstein was on the line. He was my old friend. From where? Massapequa. Since seventh grade I have known him. A Cornell grad, and now attending Stanford Law. He was wildly intelligent and singularly eccentric. And coming to Los Angeles.

"I'm bringing a few people and we need to stay at your house, you being a movie star and everything."

"Bob, I'm not a movie star."

"You are."

"I'm not."

"Steve, you are, and you need to act like one, at least for a few days. I told everyone here about you and you need to come through. Don't be a wuss. We'll be down in a few days. We're driving."

I knew that a visit from Epstein would be two problems, absolute chaos in the house and more of me relying on old friendships, rather than playing in the film pool. *Just one more time before I go Hollywood,* I thought.

This car wheezed and sputtered up my driveway. It was full of bodies, all writhing to get out. Half-naked men and women fell onto the driveway. They had been drinking for a while. "Oh man, is that a Maserati?" One of them lumbered zombielike toward my car.

"No, no. It's a Chevy, but still don't touch it." They surrounded the car, oohing and ahhing as they got close to the door handles.

"Can I open the door?" a guy in a tank top and no shoes asked.

"I have some weed and booze upstairs." That got their attention. They turned toward the house and Epstein beckoned them in.

"I told you, he's a movie star. He gets all this for free." Epstein laughed and headed upstairs. I caught up to him once the car was no longer in danger.

"Bob, this is way more than a few guys. There are like fifteen people here." The car they came in was like a clown car at Ringling's.

"Idiot, these are Stanford people. Ivy League, something you don't know about because you went to Albany for like two seconds. Steve, these are the future leaders of America." We walked into my kitchen, where one of these future leaders had his whole head in a pretzel barrel. There were half-clothed people looking through the cupboards. Someone was in his underwear in the backyard. People were showering in both bathrooms. The stereo was on, and Epstein was into tequila, pouring it out. "There's more where this came from, he got this in movie-star school."

"Bob, cut it out."

"Idiot, I've been telling everyone here that you are a movie star. So we have to take advantage of that. If you haven't noticed I brought down girls too. We picked them up in the valley. You have to do the movie-star thing so I can get action. Don't be an idiot."

There was Al, who got perfect scores on the LSAT, future head of Telemundo and a billion-dollar media fund, sucking down his third Corona and laughing with some girls. Pete, future top litigator for Fortune 500 companies, who looked like he was carved out of marble, coming out of the shower. Willy, future sought-after top attorney, also perfect scores on the LSAT, a Golden Gloves champ from Wisconsin, dressed like a modern-day pirate, and trying to lift the dryer off the ground. "Willy, don't do that. But show Steve how you can eat a light bulb." Epstein turned to me. "He can do it. Want to see him?" Willy was reaching for a floor lamp.

"No, no, just, Bob, you got to get everyone out. I can't put up this many people."

"Steve, it's for three days. Besides, it's just going to be Al, Willy, Neil, Pete, and Steve." He pointed to Steve, who looked like an accountant. "He'll keep us straight. Steve wants to be president of the U.S. so he can't be around anything naughty."

But just the opposite happened. It was mayhem. These guys wanted to go out, they wanted the movie-star perks. "Steve, take us to the clubs. We want to go out. Where's the limo?"

"Bob, I don't have a limo."

"I promised these guys a limo. You're a movie star. You should know these things."

"Bob, it doesn't work that way."

I somehow managed to get a car for the night, and I took his crew out. That night we were able to get into not one but two bar fights, an eating contest that ended with Willy smashing and eating a cockroach, one encounter with the law, and a strip poker game in Westwood at a coed's apartment.

The phone rang at 6:30 A.M. I had just gotten into bed. The answering machine blared, "Steven, Steven, where are you? It's your father. Steven." He had that military voice that he used when he was angry. I picked up the phone.

"Hi, Dad." Frog in the throat.

"You sound out of breath, are you out of breath?"

I cleared my throat. "No, Dad, just getting up." Someone yelled from the hall. "I love the poonani in L.A.!!!" I cupped the phone.

"What was that? Did someone yell they love the pool? What pool? Did you build a pool? Steven, I told you to save your money. That house doesn't need a pool, you won't use it. Steven, what's going on out there? I hear yelling." One of the guys was singing.

"Epstein came over. He brought some friends."

"Is he staying long? And what are you two doing? I hope you aren't going out late and wandering the city with him. I know Epstein can be crazy."

"He's with guys from Stanford Law School. They're all pretty serious, really quiet guys." Someone turned my stereo way up.

"What is that, rock and roll? You're playing music at six thirty? Steven, you've got to get up, go for a run, and get to work. You can't fool around with these guys. And aren't you doing *The Tonight Show*?"

"Yeah." I stretched the phone cord so I could go into my closet and shut the door. My father always knew my schedule.

"Then get up and get ready. And don't bring Epstein to the show."

"Why would I do that?"

I fell asleep as the sun came up on Sherman Oaks. I slept for three hours and there was a phone call that got intercepted by Epstein. "Steve, you have to take us to *The Tonight Show.* This is a once-in-a-lifetime opportunity for me. And you have to take the guys. Besides, you owe us from last night. We should have had tons of girls sleeping over. Because—"

"I'm a movie star?"

"Yes, and you should use that to help your friends."

I took my Dad's advice and went alone to the show.

I got to the studio and saw Keith and Wally Beene and Dick Guttman. My other life. The show-business life. It runs at a different speed, it's faster. I liked it. I liked the action. The addiction of it. Something new every day, maybe every hour. The fame and power, the recognition. The talk shows where you are playing yourself. The limo rides and the importance of it all. People say it isn't real, but it's real all right.

One of the best things to come from *The Tonight Show* was the pleasure of getting to know Freddy de Cordova. He was the producer, the voice behind Johnny Carson. Fred reminded me of Howard Koch Sr. A pro, confident enough to be kind and serene. He enjoyed my appearances, and encouraged me. He wanted to have me back, just as long as I was hot or had something good to promote. But he made it clear in no uncertain terms that there was no way Johnny was going to interview me. He didn't like my work and it just wasn't going to happen. I went on that night with Steve Martin, I think, and had a good time. It was always extremely nerve-wracking. Having to really deliver, so that you are asked back. The guest hosts were always very forgiving. They wanted you to look good. So they caught you if you fell, if you forgot a part of the story you rehearsed with the preinterviewer. I always wondered if there was some meaning behind it if the host talked to you when they go to commercial. That moment can wreak havoc on your ego. If the host did give me the time of day when we went to commercial, I felt I was in the club. If they didn't, I got the idea that I wasn't liked. Thankfully, Steve talked to me during the break. Doc Severinsen shook my hand and saw me backstage. I felt good about myself that night.

Whenever someone from Long Island would show up in Hollywood, I ran to meet them. Epstein wasn't alone. A few of my high school classmates wound up in L.A. and got an apartment not far from where I lived. But ultimately these guys became L.A., Massapequa disappeared. They weren't in L.A. to meet up with other homesick Massapequans. They were there to make a fortune.

"This has been brewing for a while; first they wanted you, then they didn't, now they do. You have the mother lode," Keith said when he called. He had that slow delivery that meant he had something juicy. An offer.

"Coppola is considering me?"

"No, I'm talking bigger. Think which show you watch on Saturday night, late. That you think you wouldn't be hip enough to be on?"

I was stunned. This was one of the pinnacles of show business. Every generation has its "Show of Shows," *The Steve Allen Show, The Ed Sullivan Show,* or of course *The Tonight Show.* But this show was different. It was the boldest and most daring and most innovative comedy on the air. I was in awe of what I was going to jump into, and I really had no idea. *Saturday Night Live* was going to eat me for dinner, live.

I mean that in the best way. Everyone there was far superior to me in most things. They are such a tight, intelligent, and classy think tank, that a new specimen put into the room gets fed on for what he or she can offer. They know exactly how to make the show, and you exercise and contribute everything you can. These guys are fast. And they work forever. They have a day off and then it's six days straight of intense writing and creating. And you have a week to get everything out, you're on, there's a party, and you're done on Sunday.

The musical guest was Chrissie Hynde and the Pretenders. I stayed at the Berkshire House advertised on the show. The initial sit-down in Lorne Michaels's office with the writers and performers is a wonderful experience on its own. Lorne has created hundreds of careers, on and off the screen. The talent in those offices is the best in the world. They filed in, this group of on-the-edge intellectual hipsters. Everyone seemed to have been the coolest kid in their school, and carried it on to clever and distinguished adulthood. If you don't have strong self-esteem, you would have some challenges there. They sat around the very elegant and comfortable office, and the conversations were about sports, the one-day weekend, last week's show and party, and just stuff. Really low key. In came Phil Hartman, who I knew from The Groundlings. He was a superstar on the show. Lorne comes in and starts the meeting off and the crew and he start to slowly trade insights, ideas, and jokes. It's a very smart room, and Lorne could be considered the smartest there. He was very attentive to my understanding everything and being as much a part of the week as I wanted. I could talk with the writers or not, stay and create or not, whatever I wanted. He just wanted me to show up when I had to and have fun with the week and Saturday night.

So I dove in. And hit my head on the bottom of the pool the first day. I thought I was quick, that I had a reasonable idea of how to play scenes, get laughs, create strange and hopefully memorable moments. I didn't know anything. The people on *SNL* know more about comedy, pace, rhythm, story, and funny in their little fingers than I know with my whole body. I noticed that, like most interesting people, they were always engaged in mental gymnastics. "What if" was a favorite. They had surprising outside-of-the-business curiosities. Out of the blue someone working on the show would tell me about their hobby, like fly-fishing or calculus. These were really clever and heady people, and their interaction with the world didn't stop at show business.

I was carried through the first few days, reading some skits that had been written quickly or carried over from another time. The writers would pitch ideas at various meetings and readings. The real bravery is in failing in front of this bunch, and once through that you're in the club. I had to suck in a few skits so the writers and performers could know where to put me. I did suck, but I got the rhythm of the week and started to spend time with the writers and cast.

Jon Lovitz and Phil were really good friends. Phil was so generous and sincere, and he really had affection for Jon. Phil had gotten so much more educated in comedy since he'd been in The Groundlings. Just full of funny lines and takes on characters. Jon kept up with him in the mock situations that they would play out, and just sitting on a couch and seeing their acting, reacting, and improvising was mesmerizing. And when Dana Carvey would start to work, it was fantastic. He was quiet but when he did his characters, it was like watching an artist do a drawing or a sculptor molding clay. That may seem way too poetic for a late-night comedy show, but these guys were artists. They created living, breathing presentations that the audience believed enough to laugh at. Week after week. New material every day, and nothing is set until hours before the live show. So the week was to get all the ideas on the floor, and Lorne then edited and chose the bits. No wonder it shot out so many film and television stars. The education, along with the work, is a lucky break. So much material in every show, so many different and challenging characters. Such an opportunity to do everything you've ever wanted dramatically, and have most of the world watching. I wanted to go the distance. And so one of my scenes with Lovitz was banned from ever being replayed.

The banned sketch was about a blind man bringing home his date, who he thought was a woman, but actually was a gay man. Jon's character, the blind man, gets furious at my character, and throws him out, but my character keeps sneaking back in and surprising the blind man. It was a sketch that made you laugh out loud while wincing. The crowd went crazy and NBC got so many complaints about the blind man that they never repeated it. But it *was* funny.

I got to be in another sketch with Jon, Phil, and Dana. It was a 1940s newspaper bit, with fast-talking streetwise reporters. You saw how good these guys were, and when you are in a scene with them you have to keep up or they will run you over. They have to, especially on live television.

As the week went on, a good thing happened. People became less polite, not in a destructive way, but more honest about the work. It happens whenever you are in a new job. People don't want to say "you suck" until they know you a little better. In this case, you have a week to get to know each other. So things progress quickly. I wanted to open the show playing a tuba, an instrument that I played in high school. It didn't work back then and I still sucked playing the thing. But the musical director, G. E. Smith, was so easygoing that he made it work.

The office at *SNL* always had something going on. I had some conversations with Dennis Miller that I really enjoyed. He had a wit that could sting. He hit me a few times, but I liked it. Like a fan, anything Dennis said I laughed at or agreed with. I was an admirer, and I would just wilt around him.

At some point in the week you first visit the set at the spectacular, historic Rockefeller Center. So many famous feet have walked that set. That's what's great about the stage, film or theater, others have walked there before.

"You better not stand under there, he has a propensity to drop lights," a beautiful woman in work boots and gloves yelled at me from a ladder. She pointed to an electrician above me. I walked out of the way and toward her ladder. I introduced myself. She gave me a firm handshake and a pat on the back. A real New Yorker who looked like a prom queen.

Her place was a loft downtown and I was amazed by the size of it. She played the guitar and spoke about Roman history, her hobby. She had gone to Dartmouth and private schools. She put on her Gucci heels when she took her work boots off and slid into an Oscar de la Renta. This was no ordinary grip.

The next morning I walked back to my hotel, looking at the fish markets and flower markets. I slid into the hotel, had some breakfast, and went to a ten o'clock rehearsal. Exhausted, but what could I do? Say no to a grip? Not smart.

The day before the live show is when some of the cutting and editing of the scenes occurs. The set was cold in temperature, and there was a surprising feeling of excitement. They did this every week, didn't it get to be old socks? Not at all. It was only sharp-shooting here.

I started to get nervous. I started to realize that I was going to be on *the* show and I was the host and I was going on live. I didn't sleep well on Friday night, but I couldn't wait till we were on.

Having my family come to a set consistently seems like they are going to the moon. Maybe not for them, but for me. My Mother and Father making their way over cables and lights, through a back door to my dressing room. It just looks so out of place. The honesty of my parents and sisters contrasted to the illusions of show business. But there they were with two giant security guards making sure they had everything they wanted. My father didn't show much emotion, he was looking around and just staring. I think it impressed him. He was nervous for me but didn't show it. But his hug before he went to sit with the audience was long. "Ann, we gotta go." He tried to pull my mother out of the room. She couldn't believe I was on the show, and was just so happy. I introduced them to some of the cast and thought my sisters would faint. My pal Joey came with his wife, Joyce, and so did my friend Kenny Bakst, a member of the Stanford Wild Man group. They brought some of the neighborhood guys. My regular life colliding with my Hollywood masquerade.

"You know, there will be a time when you won't have those old friends around. I know you love them, but there will be just no room for them." Keith said after he watched this family-and-friend stuff. He'd flown out to New York to be there. "It happens to everyone. Once you get really busy, once you have a firm hold on your stardom, there just won't be room."

It was icy cold, but it wasn't malicious. Years ago Mike Ovitz was famous for having his agents at CAA read *The Art of War.* You can imagine what that was about. I saw that viewpoint in many a representative and executive. But something else was happening here. Keith had a powerful effect on my career, he was building a business, and I was an important part of that. My business manager Howard Borris says about reps, "You grow through your clients." Keith was growing through me and a few other artists on the rise. He lobbied for me to do this show, he lobbied to get me work. He was a twenty-four-hour full-service manager, and one of the pinnacles is having a client host *SNL.* This was his accomplishment as much as mine.

When the band plays the theme song, the overture to the show, it hits you square in the face, no matter how much you smile. I took a deep breath, gathered my courage, and told myself to have fun. They called my name. ". . . starring Steve Guttenberg. Ladies and gentleman, Steve Guttenberg!" I walked down the stairs and took in the crowd. There were a few hundred people, including my family and old friends. The lights were white, the sound in the studio disappeared, and I heard nothing but me and the show. I was floating through it. I just let go and went with it till the end. It had a small-town theater feel when I had to change costumes on the side of the stage, and a big-time feel when I watched Lorne sip his wine and give his directions to the director and crew. It reminded me of the Teen Repertory Theater that I joined when I was thirteen. Lots of energy and always the possibility of something going awry. As I went from scene to scene, I knew that afterwards I would turn back into the pumpkin that I was on Monday. We had some flubs, and some laughing, but it just rolled along until it came to the part where the guest host thanks everyone and says good night. That is such an iconic moment, and being inside it is hard to believe. It was over, I did it, and the cast was around me for that familiar shot as a party happens on stage. Maybe that's a parallel to what Hollywood is. Hard work and a party better than anything in the real world. And the *SNL* party didn't disappoint.

The mad dash for the dressing rooms and the limos is the same on every show. When it's over, everyone wants to get out. The regulars at least. Me, I wanted to stay a bit more in the dressing room, say thank you to the crew, suck in as much *SNL* as I could before I went. I took every imaginable souvenir I could. Keith rolled his eyes as I took my nameplate and the fruit plate. The socks and anything with *SNL* on it.

We walked to the elevator and saw Lorne in his expensive overcoat and fine leather gloves. "A double. I think you hit a double." Lorne was friendly and laughing. He liked what I did; it wasn't brilliant, but I did my job, what I was supposed to do, and a little better. I was relieved, I'll take a double.

At the party, Keith was able to do what he wanted to do, mix with Lorne and the *SNL* talent. He was doing what is important in this business, building relationships. He was growing through his client.

My family and friends were in nirvana. They sat at a table at the party just ogling the crowd. *SNL* brings so many people there, sometimes just for the party. It is a bit like a salon and creates an atmosphere for interesting people to congregate. Lou Reed was talking to Billy Baldwin, another Massapequan. His mother worked at the Sunrise Mall, and Billy and I both loved the ice-cream sodas at a luncheonette named Kriches near the train station.

Then in walked John Travolta.

"Tony Manero." My mother put her hand to her mouth.

"Vinnie Barbarino," my father whispered.

He walked right up to me and said, "It is such a pleasure to meet you. I'm a fan of your work. I'm John." He explained that he and his wife were in the area and knew that Lorne had a party after every show. He hoped I didn't mind his coming.

I jumped from person to person, laugh to laugh. And I came upon Phil sitting at a table. We talked about how far we had both come, and how much we were still the same. About The Groundlings and about how he loved doing the show and having a job. He had his glasses on and was quiet. The night was over for him. He wanted to go home. He liked what I did, especially in the scene with Jon, and hoped that we would work together again. And then he moved on.

Keith came up to me and pulled me aside. He was calm and controlled, but I could tell he was excited, in his own way. "The phone is going to ring on Monday. A lot. Congratulations, my friend. I'm going to name the new wing of my house the Guttenberg Wing."

Chapter 16

He wasn't kidding. Keith knew that he had a talent that was in demand. He and Toni put me in contention for most films being made. They were relentless, and they made hay when the sun shined. I knew that I was being worked like a horse but I also wanted to grab as much as I could. Greed and fear kept me grabbing at the next bunch of fruit.

"You can only do what you are offered. So let's get offers." Keith knew there was money to be made. Toni was homing in on the projects and directors that I should meet. I was put in the room with talented-name directors. One of my favorites was Francis Coppola for *Peggy Sue Got Married,* which went to the brilliant Nick Cage (who I beat out for *Cocoon,* see how it plays?). He made my all-time favorite film, *The Godfather.* For the few moments I was before him, I had the part, and asked every question under the sun about the film. He was quite ready to get rid of me when our talk ended, as he is a busy man, but he was kind and patient with me. I found out that the screen test for Marlon Brando was actually disguised as a makeup test. I think Brando put cheese in his cheeks and stroked a cat during the test. I asked about the rumors that Paramount didn't want Pacino or Brando. I told him that I worked with Bob Evans and he told me that they both had bad backs and were in traction together during the editing. I am a fan of the movies, and being able to chat with one of my most admired was one of the perks, the vig of the business. That's what makes it so palatable, the surprises that come up. You never know who you will meet. In another life I could only dream of being around these talents, and here I was in his Sherry Netherland apartment asking him if the house they shot in was on Staten Island. One of the all-time greatest filmmakers, talking with me and exchanging ideas. The whole meeting lasted probably ten minutes, but to me it was all day.

A good time can be had when you're in the famous actor department. Everyone wants to help you, everyone wants you to be around. And you get to be around some stupendous people. Intellectually, you are able to trade stories with the greats and the near greats, and those who think they are great. And then there was the night life. The sex and drugs and all that. There was the fellow from the Middle East who had hundreds of girls around. There was the famous lawyer by day and the house party impresario by night, who had the hottest of girls at his parties. Insanity, I tell you. But I didn't lose my mind.

I had a friend, let's say his name was Lenny. This guy had it all when I met him at one of the premieres. A hit show, money, women, the hottest parties, and the most up-to-date drugs. He drove a Mercedes and had my unwavering respect. He and another major movie star had a party in the Valley at this star's girlfriend's home. Or I should say parents' home. The backyard was laid out like a Ralph Lauren ad. A beautiful pool, mountains of food, a bartender, girls, and movie stars. It was a very well-behaved affair. And then Epstein walked in with Al and the Stanford collection. They were visiting again, looking for Hollywood thrills, provided by their favorite local thespian. The party turned upside down, starting with a food fight. Then came skinny-dipping followed by tossing the outdoor furniture in the pool, followed by chugging with a famous television star. Lenny reveled in getting this matinee idol drunker than drunk. Willy got in a fight with an enormous guy. But the fight was only two seconds long. The giant was on the ground and Willy was licking a cloth and dabbing a cut above this guy's eye. A keg was thrown into the pool house. It was a free-for-all. I stumbled around the house and found the girl's grandmother in bed reading a novel.

"Hello, I bet you kids are having good old-fashioned fun out there." A crash came from outside the house.

"I gotta go, have a nice evening." We ended up on Sunset Boulevard. at the East Gate of Bel Air, where I hit a brand-new Datsun Z.

The driver leapt out. "My baby!" he screamed.

Epstein whispered to me, "This guy loves his car, this is not good."

"I just got this car. I saved every nickel I had, I can't believe it." Then he looked at me, "Are you drunk?"

I owe the rest to Epstein. He was in his first semester of law school and wanted to try some stuff out. He negotiated with the guy and I was able to pay cash, no report. Epstein, attorney to the stars. It's silly, really, but being alone, far from home, the comfort of a neighborhood guy felt good. Sharing the tinsel with these guys was a thrill.

All this while the release of *Police Academy 3* was in process. This is where a bit of the gluttony started. Going to the well one too many times. Dick Zanuck and Ron Howard said, "Everyone deserves a sequel," but this was a sequel of a sequel. Once you start doing sequels of the sequels, then you get into a series, and a series spawns a franchise. And that's the tent pole every studio wants. And the actor is such an integral part of this franchise that he gets his ass kissed far more than he deserves. I once heard George Lucas, who Ron so kindly introduced me to, say that there are ten or twenty guys that can play any role. It's true. I happened upon an international hit, and everybody dined off this enormous moneymaker. The third installment was going to have its premiere in the spring, as the other two had done. The question on everybody's mind was "Will this weekend work?" And after that, "How long can we do this?"

That first weekend, the lines were around the block at theater after theater. Like a madman, I drove from multiplexes to Westwood credibility theaters to the Valley lone standings. I drove home in my ludicrous Ferrari, and pulled up to see my stalker. She was pissed. I hadn't called, as I promised months before, and had not had the decency to take her out. This was not good. I had to beg her off and ask her to please, go home and sleep this off.

"If you think I'm going to sleep with you and then never talk to you, you have another think coming," she warned. I slinked into my house, pleading for her to leave. Stalkers are a part of the business. I do believe that until you've had a stalker, a nice one, you aren't anybody. Get a stalker, that means you are happening. But this one was a cuckoo, and I did the no-no.

She threw the patio furniture through the sliding glass door of my bedroom. Like I said, she was pissed. "I want a few moments of your time, please."

"Sure, just let me make this call." I went for the phone.

"No, I want to talk now." She had a fireplace poker. *How'd she get that?*

"Okay, let's talk outside." *Keep her out of the house.* We sat down on the outdoor furniture she hadn't thrown through the window and I focused on this woman. I thought she was out of her mind, but there was some reasoning behind it. She had wanted to meet me from the films. In a heartfelt manner, she explained that she thought we were a good match.

"But you know me from the movies, it's not real. That's not me."

She wasn't buying it. "But that has to be you, you play those people. That's you." That was the weird thing about acting. The illusion may not have anything to do with your true personality, but it doesn't matter to a fan.

There is a story about an actor on location at an air force base. (I would love to say who it is but he would brain me.) The officers put a party on for the actors and crew of this very successful television show. The actor went to the party and met a wife of one of the officers. She made an advance, the actor accepted, and they found their way to his hotel room. They made love and the woman kept yelling the actor's character's name. Let's call him "Frisco." Not the actor, but his character.

Finally, he grabbed her. "My name is [Bob]. You keep calling me Frisco. That's my character."

She bent down low to him. "I don't care what your name is, you're 'Frisco.' Now fuck me, Frisco." He lost some of his verve and escorted her out. She didn't care if it was him, or the next celebrity. This was a notch for her.

As a guy, being used for intimate exploitation doesn't happen that much. But if an actor gets a famously popular part, the fanatics find you. There are those parts a lucky few get, and it can help make their career. I was sitting on a plane with Bill Shatner a few years ago, and he subscribed to an appreciative outlook on being a well-known character. He was very balanced and sensible about the business. Committed and passionate about his work. Good actors like Harrison Ford, Sean Connery, Peter Sellers, and Sylvester Stallone did series of their popular characters, and used that power to leapfrog to other films. It made them more famous, which is a form of compensation, and monetarily they got to participate in the business of the film. So a few bad moments are far outweighed by the perks.

By the way, my stalker left that night without further incident, and all was forgiven. There was a bit of strange pride in having a stalker, someone who would risk their reputation just to get close. An inappropriate pride, but pride nonetheless.

One of the perks that never disappoints is walking or driving onto a lot. They all have their own veneer of importance and pageantry. Warner Bros., with its circular driveway, gave me the feeling I was driving into the studios from the Lucy and Desi or *Godfather* era. It's all about access. Access to the powerful, the successful, the guys in the know. Those guys were Bob Daly and Terry Semel, who ran the whole shebang at Warners.

I walked down the very plush carpet to their offices. Movie executives' offices are always the best. These offices can have anything and everything. From pool tables and a bar to a bed and a barber chair. Bob and Terry had tasteful, well-appointed lairs and were as nice and thoughtful as any gentlemen come. They had wonderful relationships in town, and it was no wonder. They ran the studio for twenty years, and knew how to make it work. They made a fortune and deserved every cent.

"We would like to make a fourth, and we would love you to be in it." The fourth. Soon.

The next morning I told my parents. "I know who those guys are." I heard my father rustling some papers.

"Who, Dad?"

"Got it right here. Semel and Daly. They run the studio."

I heard the extension pick up. "Now he's a show-business expert. First he doesn't want to hear about it or talk to you." My mother was washing dishes.

"I did not."

"You did too. Now he's a regular Hedda Hopper. He knows everything about who's doing what and to who."

"I'm just taking an interest in my son's profession. It's good to know what's going on in Hollywood. Steven, you know Spielberg is going to make another film, you should get up for it. Pronto."

"Dad, did you just use 'up for it' and 'pronto'?"

I am now "Mahoney." I travel around the world doing publicity. Wherever I go, someone has seen the films. The little old man in a village in Italy, he knows *Polizia Academia.* The distributors are so good at what they do that a good film, a commercial, broad comedy, can get to every theater or TV antenna in a country. And what's important, to the people who really make movies.

"Dino De Laurentiis is one of the major players in this business, and Toni and I have convinced him that you are the one to be in his next thriller. Toni?"

"Yes, I'm here. Are you going to make me wait or can I tell him?"

"Of course, Toni, you give him the news."

She laughed and said, "Dino De Laurentiis is one of the major players, and whatever Keith said, and you are going to be in his next thriller. But you have to go meet him. Dinner, his house. Be talented and charismatic. And tell me what they serve." She had been a secretary for the legendary casting director Lyn Stalmaster, heartily worked her way up to successful casting director, and then switched over to the other side. "Do some research on Dino, he's a character."

Dune, Ragtime, Serpico. Anyone I asked attested to this man's power. He was a big deal in town, an independent producer who knew how to get things made at the studios. He had the Academy Award. He had the enthusiasm of Toni and Keith. And he had a thriller that I was close on.

Truthfully, I wasn't the best guy for the part, but I was hot, and that goes above "best" any day. Luckily or unluckily for me and for Dino. But he, like most producers, wanted to be on the way up with talent. Ever wonder why you keep seeing the same actors over and over? Heat. That's all. The heat is what Dino wanted.

The gates to his mansion were enormous. There was a guard, and a dramatic and lengthy driveway. Not like Massapequa, I tell you.

"The floors are marble from Firenze, see the pink and green. Taken from a house not far from the *David.* The walls are copies of frescos from the Vatican and the food you may be smelling is from Lake Como, and Mr. De Laurentiis's private chef. In fact everything in this house is Italian. Including me." A delightful butler walked me down a massive corridor to the football-stadium-sized living room.

"Ahh, there he is, the *Polizia Academia.*" A little man with glasses and an accent so thick I couldn't understand him until the butler whispered to me what he said. I was happy to greet this man, but among the people sitting on the couch must be Dino. I was looking for an Anthony Quinn type. "Hey, hey, I'm a-talking to you." He grabbed my lapels and kissed me on both cheeks. "I-a like you. You good in that movie. You be good in my movie?"

"May I present Mr. De Laurentiis," the butler whispered to me.

"And this is my wife, Martha." He pulled over a beautiful tall blonde. "She will produce with me, and you will be good just like the police movie. If Curtis approves. Curtis, here he is."

"I know, Dino, I know." This was Curtis Hanson, the writer-director of the film, laid-back and smart. He liked Dino, and was amused by Dino's nature. Dino wanted to make the movie, but only with someone who was hot in foreign territories. That would be me.

"Let's have some drinks, eat some food, and get to know this Steve Guttenberg. And the name is too long, but that's *amore.*" He laughed.

The food kept coming. The ten or so waiters, chefs, and maids brought dishes in and out. What was unusual was that they stood around the table as we ate. Crystal, sterling silver, and fine Italian fabric engulfed us. It was hard not to get lost in the opulence. I knew to talk to Curtis, as he needed to be sure that I was someone he could work with, whether Dino needed me for foreign sales or not. He wrote the film and it was a big opportunity for him.

"Steve, do you know who Robert Towne is?"

"I do." Who didn't know Robert Towne? He wrote a little film called *Chinatown.* He wrote *Bonnie and Clyde* and *Shampoo.*

"Bob helped me with the script and will be there for some of the shooting. He is a friend."

That was it. I had to get this freaking part. Towne was connected to everyone from Warren Beatty to Barry Diller. He was a genius in this business, or as close as anyone comes.

"You like him yet? I need to know, Curtis, make up your mind." Dino made no bones about it, he wanted me in the film.

"Can I decide after the spumoni?" Curtis was jockeying.

"Spumoni is crap, we have gelato. From Roma. Sent from Roma." Dino's food was ahead of its time. "After you have the gelato, you be a-happy, and you make me go to bed-a a-happy because we say yes to this Guttenberg."

"Maybe." Curtis was cautious. "I just want the best guy for the part."

"And I just want a good film that makes money. Let's agree soon. I want to-a shoot this picture."

The five-star food didn't stop. I think Dino was trying to whittle Curtis down, course by over-the-top course. By the time the gelato came, Curtis was relaxed and very funny.

"We hire him, yes?" Dino smiled.

"Maybe." Curtis laughed and put on his hat and coat near the front door. It had turned chilly, as California nights do. "Let me talk to Bob." And he was gone.

I stood there with Dino, Martha, and the army of servants. "I think he liked you," the butler said.

"Eh." Dino put his hand to his chin.

"I don't-a think he is convinced." One of the maids took a stand.

"Eh," Dino mumbled to her.

"He doesn't know what he wants, like all of them," said one of the small men with thick accents who were roaming the house.

"I make Fellini, John Huston, and *Conan the Barbarian*. I know what to do. I know."

"He liked the food." Martha smiled and grabbed Dino's hand from his chin.

"Eh. Now we go." And he kissed me on both cheeks and looked at my Ferrari in the driveway. "Is that yours?" Dino put his hand on my shoulder. What was he going to think of the car? Would it hurt my chances for the part because I was an egotistic ass?

"Good car. Italian. Good color, red." A tap between my shoulder blades and he turned away with the beautiful Martha.

The butler walked me to my Ferrari, which for the first time looked like it belonged. He wouldn't let me open the car door myself. "Was that kiss a good one or the one that Al Pacino gave Fredo?" I asked him. "Fredo got the ax."

"It was a very good one. Mr. De Laurentiis's favorite color is red. You are a lucky bastard."

I think it was the first time in a year of owning that red phallus that I appreciated the machine. It was a muscular drive, you could feel how powerful it was. The leather, the stitches, the smell. I had taken it for granted. I was taking a lot for granted. How easy it was to maneuver through the business. The interesting, talented, and kind people I met. The access to events, concerts, and restaurants. The free clothes and freedom to act like you wanted. However egocentric or eccentric, it's all accepted. My good friend Woody Harrelson said something to me years ago: "If you can't dress like you want, what good is it being a celebrity?" You can do what you want to do. Want to go to Dodger Stadium and hit balls? Want to go to Disneyland and have a private guide, no lines? Want to meet anyone at a party? Want to meet any woman? It's all there. For as long as you are hot.

The VIP room. The greenroom. Actors, rock-'n'-rollers, and famous people mingling. You never know who will be standing next to you. An odd part of meeting famous people is if you know about their personal life through the media, it feels unfair to already know these things. In the real world, I don't know anyone's business, but in this world, you can know everything. It always felt wrong. I got into the habit of averting my eyes from the rag stands in the supermarket, just in case I met someone who was in the papers. Give them a chance to be themselves without me knowing their business.

The Bedroom Window was as difficult an assignment as a fairly new director would get. Curtis had a very big shot with this film. It was based on an excellent novel, *The Witnesses,* by Anne Holden. He adapted the script with Bob Towne next to him. He was up to it, in a quiet and methodical way, rarely if ever shouted, and knew how to make this movie. Or at least which direction to go in, and when he got to certain points, redirect the course and get closer to what he wanted. He had to stop and do that several times. The production was a challenge for cast and crew.

"Hi, it's Toni. Do you know who Isabelle Huppert is? I think we can get her, Curtis wants her. She would be wonderful for you to work with, she's a real big-time lady. International star, can you handle that?" She laughed. Isabelle is one of the greatest actresses in the world. The Meryl Streep of France. The butler had been right, I was a lucky bastard.

The phone. The tool of the business. It can make you. If you know the etiquette, the grammar, the silent signs, the rhythms. There is a time to have small talk—and that is an art in Hollywood—but usually small talk is just the overture. Sometimes it contains foreshadowing of the meaning of the call, sometimes it is a proving ground for awareness of current events. Sometimes there is a reference to what the studios are making. And a joke. Very important to keep things light. The more subtle the joke the better. Don't leave out the private-school pedigree if you can.

The phone rings, and an assistant asks you to hold for a colleague. So you wait. There is the short wait, which the big shots do. They get on quickly. Then there is the middle management, who makes you wait for a few minutes, while he called you, and then his assistant gets back on: "Can he call you back, this other call is taking longer than he thought."

"He had you call me while he was on the other line? Why didn't you wait till he was done?"

"Thank you, oh, he's off, here he is." You wait and then she gets on again. "He'll have to call you back, just took a call." Hollywoodspeak for he has someone bigger on the line. He'll get to you when he sweeps up the few small calls that he has to make. An axiom of Hollywood, though, and this goes to the work ethic. Return every call. That day. That's the way the top has done it forever. Be consistent. Be there. Be steady. That's who people want to work with. Not the fly-by-nights. The middle guys are so swamped that they get back to you if they need you. If not, good luck. Except for those middle guys that are going to the top. Then there are the little guys. The guys just starting out. Hungry. They, like the big guys, return every call.

Then there's my favorite. The guy finally calls you back, and after his assistant announces him, he gets on.

"Hey man, how you doin'? How about that Laker game, man they were on. I went with the guys from NBC. Floor seats. Hey man, how you doin'?" A few beats go by. "Now, why am I calling you?"

When you speak to a very busy and important top dog, you let them guide the conversation. These are the phone experts, honed over thousands, maybe millions of these calls. There is the overture, which is usually sincere, then they bring up the meaning of the call. And just when you get into the meaning of the call, they move on to the good-bye. At first I found myself stepping all over these big shots' words. I treated these like neighborly calls, until an actor friend of mine told me, "Man, they don't want to talk a long time to you. You are on their list, business, just go with their flow. These guys have hundreds of calls to make." He knew what he was talking about. Really famous guy. Been on tons of movie executive calls. So go with the flow and they'll tell you when to say bye.

The oddest change that happens once you get some heat is that when you speak to an executive you are used to the minute phone call and its course, but they don't make those signals to get off the line. They keep talking, changing the meaning of the call. The meaning becomes not to get you off their call list, but to get to know you better. And you get to say good-bye when you like. The call can go on forever. Why? Because you can do them some good, and they you. Those phone calls establish a notch on your belt, that they have come down from the mountain and want to meet you. Temporarily an equal. Pure show-business cocaine. Feeds the addiction. It's that way with everybody. Try being in a conversation with someone who turns away a call from a big shot while you are in the office. "Tell him I'll call him back." To his assistant. "President of NBC, he'll wait." Whether it's true or not, even if his assistant was told to do that before you showed up, it feels good.

Lenny Hirshan, who was and is Clint Eastwood's rep, looked after Isabelle. Lenny was trained by the William Morris founders, he was an agent through and through. He cared about his relationships, and I noticed after knowing him for a while what a solid, truthful guy he was. A good agent had to be. It wasn't about this deal, it was about tomorrow's deal. About the relationships. About the access. About the tenacity meeting opportunity. Lenny was known to drive across town dozens of times to get a job for a client. He would camp out in people's offices. He would call. He would pound away. The guy was unbeatable in the long run.

"Steve, this picture could be very important for you. This director, he's very well liked here at the agency. We don't represent him, but we would like to. If he asks about us, you'll know what to say, won't you?" I admired his straightforwardness. Lenny wanted what he wanted.

Lenny walked me down the first-floor office hallway past secretaries and more secretaries, guarding offices that just got more well appointed and luxurious. At the agency, the first floor was the elite. The carpet seemed to get thicker, and the smell of expensive leather started to fill the air. Lenny turned toward me and smiled. He had an agenda. He wanted the president, Sam Weisbord, Lenny's elder, the main man of William Morris, to meet me.

"Feel my arm. Go on, feel it." Weisbord came from behind his ornately carved desk. He pulled tight the cloth around his flexed bicep and pushed it toward me. "Go on, feel how hard it is."

I looked at Lenny, who looked at me and shrugged. "Feel it, Steve, it's hard as a rock." Lenny was serious. So I felt it. The president's bicep.

It was hard as a rock. Sam stepped back and put his arms up in the classic muscleman pose. "I'm seventy-four and strong as an ox. Do you walk?" He winked at me.

I didn't know what he meant. "Walk?" I winked back at him.

"Yes, walk, fast and at a good pace. Power walking. Do you drink juice?" He winked again. He was all over the place in the office. "See this, a Picasso. And a Chagall. Not bad for a Jewish boy, huh?" He was walking out the door. I followed with Lenny behind me. I tried to catch up so I could return his winks.

"Yes, come catch up, boy." Sam walked down the plush carpet and went out the front door. Lenny grabbed my arm. "Get him to give some heat to the television department. And it wouldn't be bad if he made some announcements at the motion picture meeting. Oh, and he has a tic. He wasn't winking at you." He turned and went upstairs.

The area around the agency is the heart of Beverly Hills. South of Wilshire, where the affordable expensive is. It's where I.A.L Diamond wrote all those classics with Billy Wilder. The homes are ornate, with maids and staff, landscaping is impeccable, and the streets are built for luxury strollers. Couples and babies. Sam and me, walking at a clip.

"I love this. The fresh air, a brisk walk, and good conversation. Turn here." We walked down El Camino to Charleville, where he grabbed my arm. "We'll go straight for a while." We walked without talking for a block or so. "What do you want from this whole thing?"

I started to talk, but stopped. I thought about it. He stopped and grabbed my arm. "Kid, you got to know what you want from this business. What do you want?" He winked.

I thought, *A. What do I want? B. Do I wink back?*

He looked at me, waved to someone in a Mercedes that went by. "What are you doing it for? For the broads? The money?"

"For my family." That just came out. It's all I could think of saying.

He stared at me. No winking. "I did that too. I bought my parents a beautiful place that had a maid for my mother. My father could wander around the house fixing things and they could relax, do nothing. I know the feeling." We walked by the Beverly Wilshire. "We own that land. We're proud of this investment. We make more in real estate than show business every year. William Morris is the richest agency in town. We don't need nuthin'." He laughed and punched my arm. "And I like women.

You know how old my girlfriend is? She's thirty. Thirty!" I tried to keep up with him, he lost me on El Camino.

"He liked you. Really liked you. But you didn't ask him about anything. No favors. Nothing? You didn't ask him to do anything?" Lenny sat forward in his chair.

"I forgot. I got shaky when he started telling me about his conquests."

"He's a rascal, that Sam, isn't he? I'll talk to him, it's just we could use a good oomph from the other agents. Get everybody jazzed up about Steve Guttenberg. Did he tell you about the girls?" Lenny raised his eyebrows.

"That's what got me shaky. The man's an inferno."

"But he can do a lot for us if we get him on our side. That's what it's all about. Getting people to say yes."

I still parked on the street at a meter, I wasn't going to use the William Morris parking lot and pay the attendant. That was the lot where in the '60s a jealous producer shot a studio executive in the balls for fooling with his woman. No charges were filed. Probably no valet charge either. I headed down Wilshire past the Beverly Wilshire. One of the best hotels in the world, the land bought by representing Al Jolson. Jack Lemmon passed by in his Excalibur or some extravagant car, much more movie-starrish than my common Ferrari. He waved. I waved back. Was it me or the car? Who cares. It was Ensign Pulver.

Elizabeth McGovern. Famous and beautiful. In movies with Robert Redford, Robert De Niro, and Sean Penn. Nominated for an Oscar. Keith told me they were trying to get her. Isabelle, Elizabeth, and the talented writer-director-actor Wallace Shawn. Curtis Hanson directing, with Bob Towne and Dino De Laurentiis watching the helm. Good group. Tough movie to film. But it was in my lucky city, Baltimore, where we shot *Diner.* I was an old hand at the city, and I knew where to stay and where to eat. I also knew where "The Block" was, where the strippers were for the out-of-towners. When you have a handful of per diem, a few hours, and a desire. Something to do if you were lonely, or randy. Location can be a playground for actors, and the naughty side of theater does have its relation to legit theater. Ever notice that the strip clubs of Eighth Avenue are right next to the proper theaters of Broadway?

This time I stayed at an upscale hotel, a stone's throw from the Holiday Inn that we all stayed in for *Diner.* We came out of that okay. Let's see if my luck holds up. This smelled like a good one.

Curtis, for all his planning and organizing, couldn't help the problems we had, almost from the beginning. His first camera crew was fired or quit the first week. They were replaced by a crew that Dino worked with in Rome. We waited by the set for them to arrive, kind of like mail-order brides. Onto the set came the Italian camera crew. They greeted us in Italian. I didn't know what they were saying. Neither did Curtis. Neither did our first AD. They spoke *only* Italian. And fast. But they were delightful and charming. Friendly and patient. And so we shot the day with hand signals and a sketch pad. As the day went on, there was a communication, an artistic and sometimes crude language constructed, so that there could be forward movement. Curtis had such a good attitude, he laughed a lot, relieving the tension. He shook his head a lot and said, "Dino," who overshadowed the production. Now this wasn't a bad thing, more the norm. Every production has an alpha dog. Sometimes it's the director or the star. But sometimes it's the producer. Dino, while being a friend to the artist, also had a business to run, at a profit. And if he had to squeeze a little to get it, he did. And so we got a new camera crew that couldn't speak English, had no preparation time, and had no idea what Curtis's vision was. They even had their scripts in Italian, not English. That's the way Dino read his scripts, in Italian. He had been in the country for thirty years, and the scripts were still translated for him. Power, baby, power.

Dino wanted us to shoot faster, and make our days. Here's where the tough part comes to a production. The first AD carries the schedule on his or her back. Big accountability. Millions of dollars, every day is a fortune. Every day we get behind is worth their paycheck. Nerves get frazzled. People freak. And quit. Which is what happened.

The weather in Baltimore had been unpredictable, raining one day, calm the next. A production uses their interior scenes as insurance against inclement weather. If the weather doesn't cooperate, the first AD has tough decisions on his hands. I would wake at five to a production assistant calling me about the change from the call sheet. "Prepare the interior scene, the weather looks bad, unless it changes, then be ready for the exterior, but have the interior ready, but who knows. Just memorize the entire script. We'll call you back." Now, that's a confused assistant. The AD has been up since 2 A.M., hoping that he doesn't have to use up an interior, and can shoot outside. And shooting at night just exacerbates the whole thing. This was a thriller, so lots of nights. After enough of them in a row, it's nervous breakdown time.

We were shooting outside. An important shot panning from the architecture of a government building down to me and Isabelle on the dark and moodily lit street. It was windy and the rain came in. We had our Italians on camera cranes, shouting to each other. The wind was whipping the crane back and forth like a palm tree, fifty feet in the air. We couldn't understand what we were supposed to do. Back in the tent hastily converted into headquarters sat our first AD, melting down. Questions about what to shoot next, what to do about the rain, whether to go to an interior. The actors were getting wet, should we put them back in the motor homes? Dino called and said Martha was coming down. What was the problem? And nothing from the first. Nothing. Not an answer. Just a slow rise and a walk out.

Both Curtis and I just started to AD the show. I knew enough of what we had to get done, and Curtis knew what he wanted. We joined forces with the AD department and started to put the set together. We got the shots, at least most of them. The crew went along with it. Slowly, the Italians started to make more sense, their speech was peppered with some English. Curtis was getting what he needed, we were close to on schedule and a new AD was flying in. This was around the first week. Jose Rodero, my first assistant director from *The Boys from Brazil,* came on. Then the brilliant cinematographer Gilbert Taylor took over the camera leadership. Only five more weeks to go. Two in Baltimore, and then we would fly to Dino's personal studio, in Wilmington, North Carolina. Dino had several sound stages, production offices, and all the hardware for making films. He even had a backlot. William Petersen was filming the first of the Hannibal Lecter films there, called *Manhunter,* directed by the great Michael Mann, then of *Miami Vice* fame. On the other stage was *King Kong* starring Jessica Lange.

Isabelle Huppert. My buddy. A nicer lady you couldn't meet. She is beautiful, authentic, and sincerely friendly. Smart as a whip, and knows everything about making films. She is a dedicated artist, with such focus and diligence to get everything there is to get out of a scene. And I got to be naked with her.

Now, I'm joking, but not joking. We had a love scene, a nude scene. A few. Several. Cary Grant had a great line when referring to love scenes. "My dear, excuse me if I get excited, and excuse me if I don't." And there are several ways to approach a nude scene. First would be of the immature, try-to-get-anything-you-can-in way. This poor actress is stuck with you, there is no escape. Like hunting a deer tied to a stake. This is a rare but occasionally observed attitude, and it is disgusting. Then there is the scared-shitless attitude that makes your privates invert. There are forty or so people on the set, a large microphone near your head, and you just can't do it. And then there's the road less taken, which is how Isabelle did it. She was just so cool about it. Let's get the robes off and get on with it.

Now, there *was* underwear, and flesh-colored protectors, but the act of getting intimate with someone at work is uncomfortable. Isabelle treated it like any other scene. She was discreet and protective of her dignity. She wanted things on the set how she wanted them. No one allowed except the necessary key department heads. Then she was comfortable and ready to work. And on top of all this, I was having an affair with an equipment driver. With Isabelle being so comfortable, and this beautiful young driver watching my every practically-naked move, I decided to jettison the flesh-colored patch and go commando. It was daring and chilly. I was enjoying the illusion of sexuality with Isabelle confronted by the realism of the equipment driver affair. You've heard the countless stories about how difficult it is to do love scenes, how embarrassing, how you feel nothing. Untrue, folks. It's a ball. And don't let anyone tell you different.

"A-Steve, I-a need you to be a more funny. Like you were in *La Polizia Academia*." Dino stood next to me in front of his mansion on the North Carolina beach. He had sandals and sunglasses on. "Happy, funny. You know, like the Mahoney. You do, and the movie be better. It's too serious now, not funny."

"But Dino, it's a thriller."

"Yes, but we have to sell this thriller." He raised his eyebrows. "Eh?"

The Americans left the production one per week and were replaced by Italians who spoke English. They still had scripts written in Italian, but were speaking English. It was a multinational production in the heart of Southern hospitality. There were actors and crew everywhere, Dino had so many productions going that it became a little bit of Hollywood South. Per diem, and free time. There were lots of affairs going on, interfilm and intrafilm. If anything, people had a good time. Except I think for Bill Petersen. Bill had to crash through a window in a scene—candy glass of course. But this being a new studio, some things fell through the cracks. Bill went through a plate-glass window, and rumor is he went to the hospital, got stitched up, and went back to work.

Robert Towne visited. The private plane brought him to Wilmington and the driver took him to Dino's studio. Here was the master, one of the greatest screenwriters, and he wants to see rushes. He then wants to see Curtis. Then he wants to see me.

"I like what you're doing. What are you doing?" He had thick gray hair that flowed like that of Charlton Heston's Moses, and angular features, which made him look inquisitive. This was a guy who directed Jack Nicholson. He wanted to know what I was doing.

What *was* I doing? Playing a cad, playing the antihero? How do I answer the smartest guy on the Hollywood planet? "Playing scared, but he won't show it. Not playing anything."

"Bingo. If you keep doing that you'll be fine. Don't let anybody see you doing anything. Let the story play you." He rested his chin in his hands and stared at me. "Capisce?"

I hadn't heard anyone talk about film acting that way. Letting the story play the character made sense. Especially if it is a strong story, which *The Bedroom Window* had. An architect, me, has an illicit affair with a married woman, Isabelle. On one evening when they are together in his apartment, she sees an assault go on in the street below. She sees both the victim and the criminal, but by the time the architect gets to the window, the villain has disappeared. Her sense of right tells her to call the police and give a description, but because she was in her lover's apartment she can't. So she asks the architect to lie to the police, say he saw the assault, and the ruse begins. Curtis was such a talented artist and went on to do *L.A. Confidential* and *8 Mile*.

Hitchcock had a theory, called the "bomb under the table," that said there were two ways to include the audience in a film. One, let the audience know all along that there is a bomb under the table, even though the characters in the film don't, or two, have the bomb under the table be a surprise to the audience, which some of the characters already know about. In this case, Curtis chose to let the audience know details that the characters didn't, and slowly tricked the audience to give them a twist at the end. There was so much going on that you needed to let the audience follow you while not getting in their way. This was their mystery to figure out.

Bob stayed in town for a few days, counseling Curtis and making sure it was going well for Dino. Bob gave Dino his word that Curtis could direct this film. He flew out on his private jet that probably crossed paths with a flight from Hollywood bringing both Toni and Lenny.

When a representative leaves their office, their routine, to fly to where you are shooting, it is the equivalent of an executive staying on a phone call. How much they want to show you how much they care. It does feel good when someone visits from the home office. But it never fails to be odd. The agents are the ones that procure the employment. They talk about these movies for months, sometimes years. Tracking them from development to when a director gets on board to when the studio gives the film a green light and the active casting begins. They know more about the history and details of a film than the director. The film is theirs, especially when they get their clients in it. But why is it that when an agent walks on a set or visits location, they look totally out of place? A set is a construction site, no matter how you slice it. A hard hat would be a more fitting uniform than Ralph Lauren. But movies wouldn't be made without them. The business runs because of the reps. They work their asses off. There is no other way for them to keep up. It's a very fast business. They don't have the time to visit a set, unless it really is productive. So for Toni and Lenny to visit was a big deal, and I knew it.

The best thing about the film was Curtis's ability to keep everything together, and complete the film that he wanted. He was a writer, and he took that talent and wove it into directing. There is this thing in the talented directors, a calm of sorts, a certain absolute confidence that they have. But it's only noticeable in those moments where the unimaginative would just throw it together. The good guys give the scene or story a lift to another level. I know it's a bit over the top, but a good director breathes life into a film. Why do you think Spielberg, Lucas, Boyle, the Scotts make consistently imaginative and sometimes very successful films? They're different. That's just it. They think in a certain way that you and I don't. They think cinema. Not just point and shoot. They know how to let the camera tell the story. I don't know where or how, but I started to be able to tell if the guy was good. And Curtis was a master, even early on. For such a relatively new guy to guiding sets, he knew how to place the camera. Either the director knows, or he doesn't. Some guys can get it straight off, and that was Curtis.

What I remember was that there never was an argument. Except one. After the first difficult week, Curtis asked for a different cinematographer. The task was just going to be easier with Gil Taylor. And it was. His credits were *Star Wars* and *Dr. Strangelove*. Lucas and Kubrick. There he was on our set, looking through his viewfinder at us. That's a great thing about this business. The people you get to meet. You wake up, go to work, and there is the guy who shot *Star Wars* and he wants to know if this light is too much for you. Not too bad, I tell you.

The shoot was a lot of fun and the acting was what I have always loved. Those magnificent thrillers like *North by Northwest* and *Body Heat*. And the acting has to be on. A misstep will throw the audience right out of the dream. But the secret, which Curtis was kind enough to bestow on me, is that the audience wants to be fooled. "No one goes to a movie wanting to hate it. At least not civilians, but showbiz people, yes." Curtis knew the audience would be watching this movie, and not just like they watch a kids' film. "The audience for this film is smart, and they are going to look for signals that you are lying." That was the challenge in

Isabelle's and my roles. I had to do more experimenting with the style, but that's what is so wonderful about film acting, you are always learning. If you want to. I had the fortunate occasion to talk to Clint Eastwood about film and the business, and he very humbly and sincerely said he was still learning, and won't stop.

And Dino was happy. "I-a like what I see. First, I no like that you were so serious. 'No, no,' I think. 'This is the happy man.' But now I see what you do, I like. And we have a good movie. And we sell it." Dino slapped my face a little, grabbed my hair, and shook me. "Now, let's eat." He walked toward the mansion with his butler, leaving me standing there not knowing if I was invited for dinner or the two-minute talk. He yelled, "Come Steven, Stefano, come." The butler mouthed to me without speaking the words, "You lucky bastard."

It had to happen. *Police Academy 4*. The vulgarity of it all. We knew it was coming. We didn't know when, but it was coming. We would joke about it, like an impending doom. We knew we would want to do it for the money, but what artistic piggishness. The call for the third worried me, but the call for the fourth, all that greed and the feeling of duping the audience. They were so rabid for more, especially the international guys. Doing sequel after sequel sometimes has a slow and degenerative effect. It's like a drug that you build up a tolerance for, doesn't have the same hit to it. And if you get caught inside it, well, you become it. But my Mom would remind me of what Wally Beene told her in his Hollywood office. "This is a wonderful profession. They are racehorses, and the business will ride them till they don't need them anymore. Then it's off to the glue factory."

Keith and Toni got on the phone. "We got the call, they're doing it," Keith said. "I'm going to see what they want you to do. They are saying that they don't want you for that many days, sixteen or around that. But we have some negotiating to do. They don't want to spend a lot, but they know they have to. We have them where we want them. And Steven, this is show business. Sometimes it is the show, and times like this, it's the business."

"Keith, you sound like a Mafioso killer. Warners are professionals, we are professionals, and we have Howard Borris." Toni said that as if she was talking about a huge gorilla we keep in the closet that we let out to jump on people. But they were right. Every negotiation has a leader. Someone who is willing to put their relationship with the buyer on the line. Someone who has the power to say no.

"How far do you want me to go, Steven?" Howard had a slow and deliberate style. It's the business managers who have the secret but formidable power. They have the client's ear, and most important, his pocket. What Howard always wanted to know in a negotiation was how far he could push the other side, and whether he could create a "deal breaker," a take-it-or-leave-it position. I'm telling you, when millions of dollars are being negotiated, the brinksmanship is what can move a deal to where you want it. I'm sure all negotiations have the same universal moves, but in Hollywood they are especially cunning. And loads of fun. Negotiating a deal for an artist, especially a well-paid artist, is a lot more exciting than doing a deal for a house. It might be because the representatives involved know they will be getting their taste of the pie, maybe it's because it is literally flesh being sold, and that is so exotic it tickles even the coldest of souls, or maybe because the numbers are so ludicrous that no one can believe what is being paid for a person to show up. Whatever the reason, a corps of lawyers has to be enlisted to put in their comments. Both Keith and Toni started the discussion with Warner Bros., and then Howard continued the conversation. In person. Now if the negotiation gets to the point that the parties are in the same room, either you are buying a truck from a craigslist ad, or you are buying an artist. In a special room built for such chats, Warner Bros. created an atmosphere that hopefully they would win in. The Warner Bros. chairs are slightly elevated, to give them some advantage, at least in height. They negotiate these deals all the time. Howard was probably sitting in the same seat where, hours before, Tim Burton's agent sat wheeling and dealing.

Howard has a style that to this day amazes me. He is able to walk away from a deal, give the impression to the other side that they had come to an impasse. He's good at packing up his papers and collecting his things and walking out. And patiently waiting for the call that opens the negotiation up again. To his advantage.

That's what these dealings come to, playing chicken. Who is going to walk away first. Who will come back to the table. Howard met with the Warner Bros. lawyer, Keith Fleer, and they sat in the special room and bounced ideas back and forth. They came to an impasse and Howard walked away. Instead of a phone call, Fleer walked after him, and asked Howard to come back. By the end of the negotiation, Howard had a deal, and Keith had a date with Howard's cousin, who eventually became Keith's wife. Howard was very good, and nothing was off-limits. Not even procuring a family member for a date with the enemy.

Now we had to film it. The director, Jim Drake, had a mountain of pressure on his back. He had to save a flagging franchise, after number three didn't perform as well as the studio would have liked. He was under scrutiny from the producer, production company, and studio. There was gold in them there hills, and he had to get it. The problem was, there was a formula to the films that neither the producers nor the studio wanted to deviate from. Jim was a creative guy, and had some terrific ideas. Very few were able to surface, though. The fourth film had to perform, Warners wanted it to be a hit, but wasn't willing to commit the writing to it. Gene Quintano, a very able and intelligent writer, was commissioned for the script, but he wasn't able to complete his task, as the film had to be shot, and there was a release date already set. The international division of Warners wanted the film more than anything, and we had to shoot. Paul Maslansky, the producer, had made a fortune on the last three, and believed, and he might have been accurate, that he was the only one who knew how to make the series work, now that Hugh Wilson, the original director, was doing his own films and didn't want to be a part of the series. All in all, it added up to a formula for disaster. A rushed script, a director with his hands tied, and the studio giving the production budget a short haircut.

But every film comes with surprises, some you want, some you don't. Two pleasant surprises were the inclusion of Sharon Stone and David Spade. This was before everything happened for these two, and it's one of the great luxuries of this business, meeting folks before they hit. Unencumbered by stardom, you can really get to know them, and share some normal moments. When success hits in this business, everything changes. No more burger joints, it's Spago or strictly upper-class vegetarian.

David played one of the skateboard punks that were rehabilitated into helpful citizens. (I didn't write it, I just read it.) He was a quiet guy, really, which is hard to believe. He was just starting out, and I thought he was funny and had a good heart. And get this, one of the other skateboard punks, in a smaller role than David's, was Tony Hawk, also at the start of his career, preinternational skateboard superstar. Tony stood around the coffee cart like everyone else, just another guy with potential. But he wasn't just another guy. He was polite and fast, really fast on his board. He did some stunts for the film, and doubled a few of the actors. I think he even doubled for David, who was a horrible skateboarder but a very good actor, and committed to the role. Really, I said committed. David can act, and had such ambition and promise. And heart. We palled around on set a lot, as I knew Toronto well and this was his first foray. In fact it was his first film, maybe even his first job. I felt that for him the set and the production was a tough atmosphere. He really wanted to make something of himself, and was frustrated at the small part he had. I saw in him some of myself when I first started and I thought I could do for David what Richard Widmark did for me. Watch him and save his ass if need be.

David was another cog in the wheel, and got the rough part of production often. He couldn't skate, which was a detriment, even though Tony was around. David was playing a sidekick to a very good actor, Brian Backer, who won the Tony Award for Woody Allen's Broadway play *The Floating Light Bulb.* So his first time doing anything and David has a pro next to him and Paul wanting him to be funny and fulfill the sidekick role. David was nervous. Paul had already let a few actors go, and David didn't want to be fired from his first job. We had one day a week off, and I picked him up at his room to take a stroll in Yorkville, an area that was like Westwood in Los Angeles. It might seem like a corny thing to take David Spade window-shopping, but he did have a big heart, and it got beaten up pretty good that week.

"A watch? You want to buy me a watch?" Spade and I looked into a jeweler's window, and there was a beauty sitting there, with David's name on it. We went in, and he tried the thing on. It looked great on him, and his smile knocked me out. He had a grin from ear to ear, one that I hadn't seen on him since we started shooting.

"It's yours, Dave, wear it in good health." Can you believe we had sincere conversations? I see him rarely, but still have a fondness for him. And he always is proud of the watch. Nothing like having money in your pocket, and nothing like sharing it. David wore the watch almost every day during the shoot, and I think it gave him a bit of a boost. One thing that started to come out after that was his confidence in adding lines and improvising. David has a quick mind, and in the few instances that the script had spaces open for him to riff, he took full advantage. Although not much is in the final cut, he had the opportunity to test his chops a bit, and it was wonderful to watch. He's really funny and knows how to weave bits into story. The little we had together on camera made me feel good. Widmark saved my ass on *Rollercoaster,* and maybe I pushed David a little further than he would have been without me. It's all a circle, especially in show business.

Paul was particularly excited about the "beautiful girl" that was cast in the film. "She has star quality and she is thoughtful and easy to work with. Not a bitch at all, and that's rare. Besides, she thinks I am a very handsome man." That last line stopped me in the middle of my breakfast burrito at the catering truck. On this film, there was no rehearsal period, and no table reading, so I didn't meet the new cast members till the day of filming. "When you meet her, you'll see, she's a pistol. And did I tell you she thinks I am a very handsome man." Paul loved being flattered. He was the producer, and one of the untold jobs of a working actor is to compliment the producer. Since I already had my role, I could tell him the truth. "You look too thin, Paul." Maybe he was handsome, in a thin and tan way. He looked quite a bit different from when I met him in that little apartment on the beach.

"Paul! You handsome devil!" Out from a van that carried the makeup people and a few rough-and-ready crew members bounded a beautiful blonde. She had a big, and I mean big, presence. Talk about charisma and charm, this girl had it in spades. She ran to Paul and gave him a longer than average hug. Paul winked at me. Not the uncontrollable Sam Weisbord wink but a satisfied wink, like "There you go, boy, I told you." Why shouldn't he have a little sugar.

Sharon broke from her embrace and smiled about a thousand watts. She was all teeth and body and hair. Paul introduced her around and it was the first time I saw that intense ambition in a woman. Not malicious or conniving, but pure, honest "I want it and I'm going to get it." Sharon had her sights set on becoming a star, and you could just see it. Still, she was likeable and friendly.

"I'm Steve." I extended my hand and she took it like a politician campaigning for reelection.

"You certainly are." She had a sense of humor about this whole thing. She knew she was spectacular-looking and very impressive in person, but she disarmed you. In the movie-star game, having devastating good looks is a weapon. And Sharon had them. But she was also a buddy, a friend. She took the time to get to know you, and listen to you. And she knew how to have fun.

We were shooting a hot-air balloon sequence, and the two of us, a driver, and cameraman were a thousand feet in the air. If you've ever been up in one of these things, you know you don't want to hear anything negative.

"Uh-oh." The balloon driver was looking up.

"What do you mean 'uh-oh'?" Sharon was on it directly.

"One of the flaps isn't working. It's going to be hard to land." The driver was pulling at a cord with a bell on it that started to ring.

"Well, what the hell does that mean? What flaps?" Sharon had her hands on her hips, fists clenched, and was taking center stage in this four-by-five basket.

"I don't know if I can land us now, without a rough bang of it. Or we can wait for the winds to bring us down, kind of hard, though." He kept pulling the cord, and the bell kept ringing.

The cameraman leaned back against the side of the basket. So did I. If this got ugly, I wanted to be out of range. Sharon looked like she packed a punch.

"Look, what's your name, please?"

"Herman."

"You're kidding. Herman the hot-air-balloon driver. We have to shoot a few scenes and then land. Can you do that?" She grabbed a walkie-talkie from the cameraman. "Guys, is anyone there? Herman says we won't be able to land this thing. What should we do?"

Silence and crackling. Sharon's beautiful mouth was pinched tight. She was in charge. I whispered to the cameraman, "I think she'll get us out of here, unscathed." He just looked at me blankly. "I really do." I did, this woman was fierce, and it looked like she got what she wanted.

"Look, I'm going to have Herman work on this while we shoot. And then if Herman can't get us down, we will need a plan. And *I* will deal with Herman."

Herman quickly went to work on fixing the flap. He didn't want his ass kicked. Sharon looked at the two of us. "Let's shoot." We scrambled, the cameraman set up, and Sharon and I went over the script pages while talking to the director on the walkie-talkie. One of the scenes had us kissing.

"Let's just do it." Sharon took out a small mirror and adjusted her hair and makeup. "Ready." She took over the marker, and really ADd the sequence. We got two takes of everything. In between she would yell, "Herman, you can get us down, can't you?"

"I'll do my best, ma'am." He was sweating. Seeing him sweat, I started to sweat. The bell kept ringing.

"Herman, that's not what I want to hear." She turned to me. "Now let's do the kissing scene." Gulp. Funny thing about the kissing scene, she went from this in-charge lady to a soft and blithe spirit. We shot the whole sequence in about a half hour. And got everything that was on the schedule. And then we could land.

"I think it will be a little bumpy." Herman was correct. We overshot the landing area by about a half mile and landed in a field with enough cow pies to build a skyscraper. We bounced along, cow pies flying, bell ringing, and us rolling over the wet mounds of grass and dirt.

"Herman, land the thing!" Sharon grabbed Herman's shirt with her hand and with her other held her purse. A woman and her purse are never parted.

We finally came to an abrupt stop not far from a low fence. The bell stopped. We struggled out of the sideways basket, into the cow dung, mud, and Sharon's surprising reaction.

"Good one, Herman, I knew you could do it. Now where's the truck?" She just got up, dusted herself off, and walked toward the arriving vans.

I ran up to her. The poor thing must be discombobulated. "Sharon, you . . . ?"

"I'm fine." And she stepped over the fence. I did the same but the landing had banged a knee up so it didn't lift high enough. *Zap,* what felt like a thousand volts went through my body.

"Hey, that's electrified," Herman called out quite helpfully.

I sat in the van with a constant vibration in my leg. "It'll go away in a while, meanwhile tell me if you have a headache tonight. That could be nerve damage, and we don't want you to fall into a coma." The set nurse was passionate about her job, and it was the only thing that happened for her the whole shoot. This was her chance to shine. "Or it could be something else."

"Honey, it's nothing that a stiff drink and a hot bath won't cure." Sharon turned around from the shotgun seat. Damn, she was spectacular-looking.

We got back to the campers and were all in a rush to get back to the hotel. Bubba Smith was throwing a party, and you don't disappoint Bubba. "Steve, can I ride with you, the van back to the hotel is full. And I'd have to wait another half hour." What a difference a few years makes. Sharon Stone having to wait for a van back to the hotel. And me giving her a ride in my car. And her getting changed out of her wardrobe in the back-seat as we sped along the thruway. I thought the driver's eyes were going to pop out of his head. I didn't look, this was my buddy. Sharon talked a mile a minute as she put on stockings and a dress, and new heels. A brush through her hair, some lip gloss, and sitting in the back of my car was a superstar. She had won the lucky DNA contest for certain.

After we wrapped and went home, she would send me home-baked cookies and such. A real buddy.

There's a pallor that casts over your face when you look in the mirror knowing you did a job for the money. It's done a few times in a career, by almost everybody but the truest of artists. Lawrence Olivier did Polaroid commercials. Orson Welles did Gallo wine. I stepped into a police uniform one too many times. But the money was sizable, and I took it. We all took it.

The day we wrapped, I knew that it would be the last. If there was a fifth, I didn't think they would be willing to pay me. So I took a few of my mementos, the badge, the billy club, and a few other things. As I was leaving the dressing room, the phone rang. It was Dick Zanuck. We talked about what was happening in our lives until he blurted out, "Steve, I have to tell you, *Short Circuit* is testing through the roof. My boy, you may just have another hit." Pretty serious words from a guy who knows. And indeed, when I got back to Los Angeles, Keith and Toni were over the moon.

"We are in the 'getting almost-the-right scripts with almost-the-right money' phase." Keith was confident. His client base was getting more powerful. I, along with his clients Whoopi Goldberg and Jeff Goldblum, was working constantly. Keith was making money, and was in demand.

"Well, I think we are getting the right scripts for now, and getting the right money for now," said Toni. "I mean, Keith, did you see what this kid is making? It's good. At least I think it is."

"I want just a little more." Keith wasn't being a jerk, he just wanted what the business is built on. More.

And more there was. In came the offers. I started going from movie to movie, changing wardrobe and planes as fast as I could. Wrap in Pittsburgh on a Wednesday night? Steve is available Thursday morning. Mexico? No problem, he'll be there. I flew, I changed, I ran, and I did. Between 1980 and 1990, I shot more films than any other member of the Screen Actors Guild, tying only Gene Hackman. I schlepped to movie after movie. New people, new women, new money.

What wasn't new was the time I spent away from my family. Not seeing my Mom and Dad for months, missing my sisters' graduations and other important milestones. I started to feel disconnected. Connected to the business, which was generous, but let's face it, not sincere. But it was so good to me that I believed in it. I believed the love it was giving was real. I bought it. I wanted to buy it. This was my fantasy of Hollywood. Parties, money, beautiful and influential friends, and beautiful and inspirational women.

I noticed myself getting comfortable with a certain Hollywood style and lingo. A too-cool-for-you manner. I got into the habit of not saying good-bye, a flavor-of-the-month telephone move, also played on me by those I respected and admired. When the conversation is over it's "hang up, time to roll some calls." I was becoming a Hollywood animal.

It's a wonderful thing to be so popular and world famous. Like a toy, like a pet, like a trophy, people want you at their parties, get-togethers, and home screenings of the latest masterpiece. You are in with the in-crowd. Within this popularity, there is a loneliness and self-imposed psychological isolation. "They can have my image, but the real me, they ain't getting." You tend to keep some things to yourself. I was getting in way over my Massapequa head.

Tristar sent us all out on tour for *Short Circuit*. It seemed like old hat now, I knew every reporter in every city. I saw these guys more than my dentist. It was easy. And *Short Circuit* was getting buzz as a hit.

"How's it goin'? You liking all that press?" John Badham was on the phone. He was calm and excited in a quiet way. "I'm getting kissed every way till Sunday. How about you? I mean I'm flooded with scripts and I am a wanted man. It feels pretty good, but I know it's not real. A few weeks ago, before anyone knew about how the film has been playing, the phone was quiet. Success and failure, both illusions."

This illusion was insane. Unhealthy for the ego, too much adulation. Autographs, photos, and hugs from the ladies. Here's something strange you learn after taking thousands of fan photos. The women, well, they want a little squeeze too. There is a little cheap thrill in being squeezed by women you don't know while posing for a photo.

I wound up in Dallas. When they throw down the party for you in Texas, it's all big. Big place, big crowds, big hair, big people. And me in the middle. I started to feel a bit omnipotent and floated around the party like a conquering general. The women were coming up to me to chat, making conversation easy. The organizer of the event, a very smart interior designer named Steve, was going to have a fashion show with models start as soon as everyone was seated. "Sit on my lap, Yankee," was the war cry from some overzealous oilmen's wives. I sat with the biggest donors, which is part of their repayment, getting to sit with a star. By the end of the show, there were thirty models onstage and me, King Kong without the chains.

"And who wants to bid on Steve Guttenberg?" the auctioneer spit out as the models walked here and there around me in figure eights.

"I will, a thousand dollars," a tall buxom lady in a shimmering dress yelled from a table.

"Fifteen hunert, and I ain't kiddin'. I'll take him home and show him what Texas barbecue is all about," said another tall brunette, with earrings that looked like the Swarovski ball in Times Square.

"Ten thousand dollars, wrap him up, I'll take him home tonight," someone yelled from the back. Silence and then the auctioneer hit it.

"Uh, ten thousand going once, going twice." He took a beat. "Going three times, I can't believe it, what a whopper. Sold to the lady with the big money." Out of the fray came a ten-foot-tall beauty, glimmering in bling, walking toward the stage to claim her prize. She went straight for me, grabbed me, and hugged me to her bosom.

"I gotcha." That should have been the first red flag.

I spent the rest of the evening at my table. "Doris" sat next to me in some other girl's seat. "Well, dear, you look single, I'm sitting over there, mostly bankers. Go on, see if you can catch one." She didn't let go all evening. Fine with me.

The evening wrapped up and I was in some sort of sports car, barreling up the Texas highway, in the rain. We stopped in front of a house. Where was I? I didn't care. This was an adventure, sure to become a sexual adventure, a conquest, and then it would be back to my own hotel bed at the Turtle Creek Hotel.

I ran with my coat over my head through the door to the foyer. Lights off, just some light coming from a small room through another doorway.

"Let's go upstairs." She took my hand and pulled me toward the right. Fine with me.

Bang, bang, bang. "I'll kill you, you bitch. I'll kill you." Someone, or something, was hurling itself at a closed door, about a foot from us, hitting it so hard it was bowing. "You lousy bitch, I hate you. I'll kill you."

I was frozen, and sweating. "Who is that?"

"It's my brother."

"Your brother is saying he wants to kill you? Is this safe?"

"Of course it's safe. He wouldn't hurt a fly." She turned toward the door. "Oh fuck you, you bastard." She kicked the bottom of the door with her foot and turned toward me in the sweetest way. "Come with me, honey." I followed her, holding her hand as we went through corridor after corridor of the dark house. She led me up some stairs and into her room. A room of a thousand candles and one cat. She lit every candle as I sat patiently on the bed.

"Your, uh, brother can't get loose and get us up here, can he?"

She ignored my comment. She walked around the room, before going behind an old-time changing screen. "Let me get into something more comfortable." Cliché, cliché. A good sign that this girl doesn't know what she is doing. Time for me to pull out my Hollywood-style seduction. I know the signals.

"Why don't you come and sit here next to me." Cary Grant.

"Why don't I." The lady is now thigh to thigh with me. Time for me to close this deal. I put my hand on her leg.

"What do you think you're doing?"

I'm smooth, I know how to handle this. "I'm giving you a chance to get your money's worth."

She looked at me with some revulsion. "Do you think I brought you here to have sex with you?" She took my hand off her leg like you take a dirty rag off a table.

"I thought . . ."

"Well, you thought wrong, mister. Oh my, can't we have a civil evening?"

I went into reverse. I turned on the wholesomeness. "No, no, I of course didn't think that." I looked for the escape route. Out the bedroom door, and then what?

"Yes, you did, you thought I wanted to take my clothes off and have sex with you." She started pacing and smoking. I started sweating. I'd had too many longhorn martinis.

"No, I didn't." I heard banging from below. Was he loose?

"Yes, you did, and I am just so disappointed in you." She picked up the cat. "Are you disappointed, Peggy?" The cat didn't answer. She was nuts. I had caught a cuckoo bird.

"Well, I'm just going to get out of your hair. Would you please take me back to my hotel?"

"No." She stroked the cat.

"Oh, okay, well, may I please use the phone to call a cab?"

"No."

"Okay, well, I have to make a call." I got up from the bed to grab the phone. She stood up.

"Do not call a cab. You'll stay here till I let you go. Meanwhile you can sit there while I do some knitting and watch some late-night TV. Do you like late-night TV?"

My begging went on for about twenty minutes. Finally she acquiesced. "If you promise to take me out tomorrow night you can." She had a mental patient's smile. "I really love you."

"I love you, too." I dialed Information and had a cab on the way. "Well, thank you, but I will be going. How do you get out of here, please? To the front door, please?"

"I won't tell you. I changed my mind. I want you to stay."

"Um, thank you but no, but thank you, but no." I felt for the door handle behind me, found it, and I was out the door. Doris was behind me shouting for me to come back and then shouting some obscenities. I felt in the dark along the walls. The maniac downstairs must have heard the commotion and started snarling like a wild dog. With his "sister" behind me (I now wonder whether that was her ex-husband and they were separated but living together), I ran toward the maniac downstairs. At least he was near the front door. The rain pounding, "brother" pounding, and Doris yelling, "Leave and I won't pay my money!" There it was. I grabbed the front door handle and swung it open. I could hear Doris running down the steps as I saw the taxi pulling away from the stoop. No!

But good fortune. The house was in a cul-de-sac, and the cab circled around back toward me. I jumped into the pouring rain and the cab didn't have to even slow down. I grabbed one of the doors, pulled it open, and jumped in. The driver kept going and behind us I saw Doris run out the front door shaking her fist at me. Some dark, hunkering figure came up next to her and raised his hands above his head. We turned a corner and kept going. I still had my skin.

Westwood is the L.A. old-school Mecca of movies. The biggest premieres and the biggest movies play there. All the biggest of stars opened in Westwood. *Short Circuit* followed suit. And scored.

"I told you, Steve, you're going to have a monster of a hit there. The exit polls are through the roof." Dick Zanuck had all the legitimate inside news and he was a friend that shared it. He was right, the opening weekend was very respectable. We were full every show, with midnight shows standing room only. I had another hit. I could relax, I had security. For the moment. Until someone else had a hit.

So I have it, another hit, another way to assuage the assault on my ego that comes every day from jealousy and envy. The evil twins that land on everything the business touches. You can't avoid it. The jealousy that Dick Zanuck smelled during the *Cocoon* screening, it was in me too. I didn't have it when I arrived in town, without success. But the success that I wanted came with a footnote attached: "Enclosed please find some envy." My auntie Vera used to tell me, "You want all the toys in the room. You aren't satisfied with your toys, you want everybody's." She was on to me.

It was Christmas in L.A. It looked the same as Fourth of July in L.A., except the gas stations had Santas waving people in as opposed to Uncle Sams. It was time to go home, for those of us that had a home away from the town. First I stopped in Ohio to visit another aunt, June, and my cousin Andrea. Canton, Ohio, was gray and bleak. Big difference from sunny California. I checked with my answering service while I waited for my luggage.

"Steve, call me, it's Toni."

The gray outdoors was a contrast to the palm trees Toni was seeing. "Do you know who John Landis is? He did a little movie called *Animal House* and he's producing a comedy. A sketch comedy film like *Kentucky Fried Movie.* He wants you in it. He saw your *SNL* and wants a few days with you. It's going to be very hip, I think. Or not." Toni laughed and covered herself. Nothing wrong with that.

"I don't know, Toni, it might be like a celeb clusterbang, and I don't know if that's what I should do."

"If you don't do it, Tom Hanks will. We represent him."

"I'll do it." Nothing like the threat of another actor taking my toy.

I went on from Ohio to New York to spend some time at home. I knew now how precious time with the family was. The dearest sacrifice is your time. I had missed out on parties and small important moments. But my mother and father were good at bridging gaps. Corny as it is, your family can hold you up.

I had just a week with Landis on *Amazon Women on the Moon.* It's kind of sexy in a Russ Meyer kind of way. I read the script and it was funny. A bunch of sketches strung together. Different directors, and Landis and Bob Weiss, a comedy maven. It was also being produced by George Folsey Jr., who I worked with on *Chicken Chronicles.* The cast was a bunch of good actors. Robert Loggia was in one of the sketches. Howard Hesseman had been in *Police Academy 2.* Phil Hartman had a part, and my friend Peter Horton, from *Miracle on Ice,* was directing some of the sketchers.

It was shot on one of the no-name lots in town. They don't have a studio affiliation, they're just a bunch of sound stages surrounded by a fence and it's a lot. You shoot the same, just a bit cheaper. I met with Peter at his home a few days before. We did some wardrobe in the house that he shared with Michelle Pfeiffer. She was already shooting into superstar category, but was a very introspective and friendly person.

"You know, you're going to be working with Rosanna." Peter was showing me some of the storyboards.

"Rosanna who?"

"Arquette. We know her, she's great. Really artistic."

Rosanna, the stuff dreams are made of and songs are written about, specifically Toto's "Rosanna." You must have something to make a man, or a band, write a song about you. Who was this Rosanna Arquette?

I pulled up to the studio on game day and who walks by but Jack Nicholson. There he is with a cup of coffee. Getting something from the catering truck. The guy definitely has something, he cuts a powerful figure. Good start to the day.

On these short shoots there isn't much time to say hello and good-bye, and get to know people. You see flashes of people, in wardrobe, makeup, and craft services and catering. But if you know your job, then there is time to soak up some personalities.

"Rosanna wants to meet you." Bob Weiss led me to another set, sort of a desert with boulders. Also monkey bars. There she was. Rosanna was standing on this sandlot, backlit in a short and flattering dress. She turned and walked toward me and I was watching some sort of film, in slow motion, of this vision. I would have written a song about her too if I could.

She walked up to me and extended her hand. "I'm Rosanna."

"Yes, you are." Very Sharon Stone of me. And from there Rosanna took the reins. She can talk about anything, and had so many interests. In that half hour I heard a lot about the complexities of a show-business family and the business itself. Rosanna came from a line of actors. Her grandfather was Cliff Arquette, known as Charlie Weaver on *Hollywood Squares*. Her father Lewis Arquette was a staple in a hundred films, and her brother and sister, David and Patricia, were emerging as young actors. Rosanna was smart, well informed, and environmentally aware. She was in some really good films and knew her stuff. She pulled out her pages and we went over the scene, which was pretty funny. It was written by Michael Barrie and Jim Mulholland, David Letterman's writers. The sequence concerned a blind date, and the technology that can complicate it. Peter came in and the three of us worked on the scene.

The funny thing is, I couldn't understand where Rosanna was coming from most of the time. She talked so much about subtext, but I didn't see the scene as anything but a funny bit. I didn't think there was anything socially responsible about it. I didn't think it had a message, and I didn't think it paralleled anything that was real, except for the emotions. It was the authenticity of the emotions that made it funny. Luckily, Peter was really good at talking to artists and understanding their method. He knew Rosanna, and how to get through to her what he needed. He had an ability to get out of the way and let his actors work their craft. Rosanna and

Peter got along famously, and I tagged along and filled in the holes. I had a feeling for what would be best for the show, and the key was to make it easy for everyone else. You have a limited amount of time to get things on film, and hopefully catch a little magic.

We filmed over a few days, and Peter was kind enough to let me watch his moves and setups, allowing me to understand how he was going to make a joke work. I had been impressed with the art of letting the camera help the jokes. It's all in the camera. The audience knows what a pro film looks like, and it includes standard camera setups. Master, close-up, close-up. Peter showed so much promise in his use of light and mood. He knew how to set up the sketch and make it sexy and funny. Kind of French romantic comedy.

The shooting was easy, Rosanna was letter-perfect. For being pulled in so many directions during rehearsal, she knew what she wanted out of the scene, and was loose enough to get it. Peter got the shots he needed. And I spent those days with the song "Rosanna" in my head. When I woke up, when I drove in the car listening to other songs, and when I said hi to Mr. Nicholson.

He was shooting *Ironweed* and I caught him in the studio driveway. He was kind, patient, and had a smile that put you at ease. It's Jack Nicholson, after all. He has an ability to make you feel good, though I don't remember what we said, as I had that confounded song playing in my head.

Do you think you can play Sally Field's boyfriend against Michael Caine?" Did Toni just say Sally Field and Michael Caine, and me? I was slipping and sliding into a very good group. "They think you are too young. Do you think you're too young?" "They" and "too," words that are dreaded by the actor. *Who is this they? I'm too what? I'm perfect. What are they saying?*

I drove up to the Warner Hollywood Lot, an offshoot of the Warner Bros. company lot in Burbank. It's the uglier cousin. Same stuff, just not the pizzazz. Except this lot had something that Warners Burbank didn't. The Formosa Café, a restaurant that catered to the stars, from Bogie and Lancaster to Newman and Redford. I love that stuff. Real Hollywood history.

The building that housed the production company was a 1940s beauty made to order for a film lot. Stucco and wood, with a been-there, done-that feel. I dressed my oldest and knocked on the screen door.

"You're Guttenberg? Did you just come from school or something?" Behind the screen was a man with large glasses and a cell phone to his ear. The cell phone was emerging in Hollywood. "It's that Guttenberg kid, he looks like he's got to study for the midterm. I'll call you later." He opened the door. "Spielberg, he won't leave me alone since we worked together, uncredited, on *Close Encounters*. And on *Always* also with Richard Dreyfuss. Did you like it? A lot of people did, but it didn't do very well. I don't understand it, it was brilliant. That's what Sally Field said, it was brilliant. You look too young." He walked toward the back. "Come with me, Guttenberg."

We went into a comfortable office with lots of awards and books.

"You're Jerry Belson? The director?"

"Just because I asked if you were you doesn't mean you can ask me if I'm me. Am I correct, Todd?" An assistant appeared out of nowhere.

"Yes, you are, Jerry." Todd was dangerously Machiavellian.

Jerry started to look through his script and found what he was looking for. "Here, Guttenberg, I want you to read this." He handed me a well-worn script.

"This?" I pointed to a place on the page.

"No, this." He pointed to another bunch of lines. "Are you going to be difficult, Guttenberg? I don't care how many police academies you went to, you're going to listen to me. You hear me? I'm the commanding officer around here. I seem pretty tough, don't I, Todd?"

"Very tough, Jerry."

"Steve, do you know my credits? Do you want to know my credits? Do you care to know my credits? Let me start you off with a little *Dick Van Dyke Show*. Then we can move on to *The Odd Couple* with Randall and Klugman. And I already told you about Spielberg. Maybe can you read this now? Todd, you play Sally."

Todd took the script and read with me.

"You're too young, Guttenberg. I think you're too young, Todd, do you think he's too young?"

"Too young, Jerry." Todd had no problem with that.

"Guttenberg, have you ever worn a mustache? Todd, what about a mustache?"

"I like a mustache, Jerry." Todd coming over to my side.

"I like it. Very Burt Reynolds, who I worked with on *Smokey*. Yeah, a mustache, let me call Sally." Instead of using the landline on the desk, he picks up his cell phone and dials.

"Why don't you use the hard line?"

"I use my cell phone for everything. Sally, it's your brilliant and talented director." A beat. "Jerry!" He cupped the phone. "Academy Award actress I let mess with me. *Norma Rae,* you know?" I nodded my head yes. "Good, Todd, he knows who she is."

"He knows who she is."

"Sally, my dear star, we have Steve Guttenberg here, dressed like he's going to confession, and I think a mustache will bring him up to snuff. You think it's a good idea?" He cups the phone. "Academy Award winner thinks my idea is good." Back to the phone. "Sally, you're gonna love him, he can do this. Field, Caine, and Guttenberg. I like it, do you like it, Sally?" A beat. "She likes it. She really likes it. Just kiddin', hon, I'll call you after he leaves." He pushes a button. "You get the references, 'You like me,' from the Academy Award speech my Academy Award actress gave before she worked with me?" I nodded my head yes. "Guttenberg, now, don't fuck this up. Go home, I'll call you later. Or your agent will call you. Or someone will. If I put you in this movie, you better be good." Todd looked at me and didn't have to say anything. I knew he would agree with Jerry.

"They like you, they really like you." Toni giggled. "That was Sally's speech. She really is a good actress. Can you handle a good actress, or do you want to do *Police Academy One Million*?"

"Weren't Isabelle and Elizabeth good actresses?"

"Yes, they were, but Sally has the Best Actress award, that's pretty big stuff. Don't be nervous. And, by the way, your papers are up, can you re-sign them if I send them to you?"

Now this is an everlasting dance with the agencies. You must be signed, at least in theory, to an agency. But when an actor is hot, the signing becomes a treasure.

"Everything is a negotiation. Let's see, I'm not so sure we sign straight-away. I want to explore my options. Our options." Keith sat back in his chair, stroking his mustache. Every time I talked with him he was getting busier, more powerful. He had bigger people on the line and was moving up. There is a manner that some reps use when they hold a favorite client hostage from an agency, unless that agency trades them clients for clients. I don't know if that went on this time, but it is not uncommon.

The papers had to be reviewed by the lawyers, Bruce Ramer and Larry Rose. These were Spielberg's and Eastwood's attorneys, and they had the best definitions in town. By definition I mean if you are a working actor without a legal team, you sign whatever the agency gives you. No questions asked. But if you have legal representation, then watch out. You get a template, the same template, or the standard definition, that all the other clients have, and you benefit from their power. That's what it's all about in Hollywood, benefiting from someone else's heat.

I knew Toni really wanted those papers back, it definitely unnerved her to not have them. And she was someone I didn't want to irritate. I didn't have papers with Keith. Managers rarely asked for them, although they do about the same job as agents do. It's just a ridiculous dance that the business plays. I needed to get them back to her as soon as I could. She was a good lady, and deserved the solidarity.

"What are you doing out there? We haven't seen you. Are you coming home soon? What do you look like?" My Mom was kidding, but not. She was making dinner. My house was quiet, no one but me. "Your father said that he saw you on *Entertainment Tonight.* You did something with Arsenio Hall. Did you do something with him? No one tells me anything. Girls, dinner is served. Stanley, come down." I heard my sisters coming in. The unmistakable sound of their refrigerator opening. I looked in my fridge, some gourmet pizza and carrot sticks. The extension picked up.

"It's what they call an ensemble film with short stories. It's like *Kentucky Fried Movie.* There's an audience for it."

"Stanley, what are you talking about? Where do you get this stuff?"

"Ann, I watch those shows. I educate myself. Steven, your mother doesn't know what's happening. She's not very hip."

"I'll give you hip. Steven, when are you coming home?"

"He has to do the Sally Field film." My father knew it all.

"Sally Field, *The Flying Nun*? That Sally Field? Oh my, Stanley, she is an Academy Award winner. Oh, Stanley. This is so exciting. But that means you won't be home for another two months?"

"I'll come home soon, Ma. I will."

"Don't come back if it will interfere with the shooting schedule. Ann, he has to be present."

"Your father is crazy, all he talked about was you getting out of there, now he wants you to stay. And what do you mean 'present'? Like at roll call?"

"No, acting-wise, he has to be calm and open. I read an article."

"Steven, come home as soon as you can. Your father is acting, I mean in real life, crazy."

"I could be an actor. I could do it. People think I'm Hal Linden."

"One person thinks you are Hal Linden and now everyone does? I don't think this acting thing is so good. Steven, come home."

Isolation isn't good. But it is impossible to avoid on the road. I was going from job to job, meeting people, good, talented people, but they are short, intense relationships, and then you are on the road again. The isolation is destructive. You can find yourself floating away from some core values that you hold dear. This famous life, it's an oddity. And if you are first-generation Hollywood, there isn't anywhere to learn how to handle it. Some things you pick up are good, some aren't. I knew right from wrong. Didn't always do it, but I knew it.

I found myself in the pursuit of "more." The more I was fed the action, the calls, the jobs, the money, the attention, the more I got addicted to it. Where's the phone call? Where is the party? The dinner? The group of interesting, hot, popular people? Where is the crowd? And if one can't get that action, then the ego wants it from other places. That spotlight is a drug.

I've heard that people enter your life at certain times for a reason. I met Michael Caine at a dinner in Brentwood before we shot *Surrender.* He and his beautiful wife, Shakira, pulled up to the Twenty-sixth Street restaurant in a Rolls-Royce. He is a good-looking man, tall and unmistakable, and like Nicholson has a magic about him. He is undeniably the most interesting person in the room, wherever he goes. The table consisted of the Caines, Sally Field and her then-boyfriend Alan Greisman, the producer Aaron Spelling and his wife, Candy, and Aaron's partner Leonard Goldberg and his wife, Wendy, who was also my agent Toni's sister. Michael had the table in stitches all night. The two things that stuck out about Michael were his confidence and his love for his wife. He seemed like the perfect man, as opposed to me, with my hubris and self-confidence that seemed to go up and down depending on my amount of success. He was quite honest and straightforward and had a way of saying sincere things that were perhaps on the edge, but with a laugh. He actually told one of the producers there why he wouldn't be hired by him. And Shakira is every bit the lady that he is the gentleman. Lucky are the people who know them.

I got to know Michael in that on-set and at-dinner relationship that gypsies in the business have. He is an amazing individual, a welcome mixture of down-to-earth guy with been-around-the-world royalty. He immediately puts you at ease with his honesty and character. He is a straight talker, and knows how to phrase conversations. On the acting side, he is among the handful of master craftsmen in the business. He has been a movie star for over forty years. And none of it was given to him. He earned everything he has.

One of the most interesting things about Michael is how he acts at work. He is a pro. He is on time, and he knows the script. I walked by his trailer while we were shooting nights and there he was playing solitaire, waiting to be called to work. He comes straight to the set when called. When he gets there, he lightens everything up; there is security when he is around, in that you know everything is going to work. He listens to the director and the actors, and wants to fit in. He doesn't take a star turn, he doesn't steal, he adds and fills in the holes. And he's game for anything. Top all that off with a superior acting ability, his status as master raconteur, and his look, and you have Derek Jeter on your team.

We had one particular dinner, I think we were shooting in Tahoe, and we were talking about the career of an actor. He told me that he was frustrated at one point in his career, and someone was kind enough to remind him of "The Tortoise and the Hare." "You know what happened in the story? I'm the turtle, and I don't mind one bit."

"Your turn in the barrel, Steve." It was the first time I had heard that phrase and I had been working on film sets for years. What a jazzy way to bring me onto the set. Michael knew how to make you feel good and feel important. It was a scene where he is in one position, and then I took it over. He did his scene with Sally, and then I was brought in. You can't help but feel like a racehorse. I have always felt there was a similarity to a Thoroughbred being led into a ring and an actor being called to the set.

"It's all in how you are treated." Sally once said that to me casually, and it stayed with me. I had seen almost all her films. I remembered her as Gidget, and Norma Rae, and the hot girlfriend of Burt Reynolds. What those roles don't tell you about is her natural character. She is a hard worker, driven and ambitious. She is fair and understanding, but very, very smart. She knows this business all the way through. There isn't anything she hasn't done or won. Television, theater, and film. She studied in New York at The Studio, and is constantly learning and working on herself. She knows how to make a scene work. I don't know if it's instinctual with her, or craft, but she knows blocking and rhythm. Sally can make the scene flow, and give it a beginning, middle, and end. She is funny and knows where the jokes are. But she can find the important touching moments also. She was a teacher for me. Her knowledge is wide and deep, and she shares it willingly. I followed her lead, and it was always a good choice. Sally makes working with her an immense pleasure. And she loved the mustache.

Aaron Spelling, our producer. The guy had the largest home in California, a bowling alley in the house. Once you have a bowling alley, you have joined the "I don't live in the real world" category. "No supermarkets for me, I have a person for that." That's this guy. But very friendly and open. Never looking over your shoulder for someone more exciting, a bigger name. He was one of the richest fellows in the business, but always seemed to be stressed. He was trying to have a good time, but was so tight and rigid. You would think a guy with all that money would breathe deeply, but I don't think he did. All that money, and all that agita. Probably a lesson there for me. I don't know if I got it. I really wanted an invitation to the house with a bowling alley, but never received it.

"Aaron, I hear your house is outstanding. It must be beautiful." Hint, hint.

"It is."

Jerry was not to be overshadowed by anyone, not his actors or the crew. And he deserved most of the attention. He came from the Garry Marshall school of Brooklyn drawl. The delivery is perfect for a story. His wisdom and technique were a very sharp combination, and he came at scenes from an over-the-top bird's-eye view. He was able to see everything, and with one or two new lines or reactions, change the scene from a six to an eight. Sally loved Jerry and the way he allowed her to explore her options. She was able to try everything, without him getting impatient. "It's all in how you are treated."

Toni was still waiting for me to sign the papers and was getting antsy. The calls started coming in to me from the executive agents. Stan Kamen called. So did Sam Weisbord.

"Steve, what's going on? You don't love us? I see here, I get a list every day, of people who are still unsigned. I mean, ridiculous here. I'm looking at your name? Is this the same kid that walked with me around the block and wants to make it? Make it in this town? Come on, now, sign the papers. You have somebody telling you not to? Don't listen to those knuckleheads. You get those papers in so Toni can sleep. Don't be difficult here, I want you off the list and on the set."

It took months of back and forth, and it wasn't fair to Toni, she was doing a great job, but there were other forces in play. It had to do with growing a business. At last I signed the papers.

"Mr. De Laurentiis calling, please."

"Who? Dino? Sure, sure." I had a reading of a film script that a friend wrote going on in my house. The music was playing loud while we took a break.

"Steve, it's-a Dino, how are you?" I couldn't understand a thing he said.

"Hi, is that you, Dino?"

"Of course, a-Steve, we want to do a tour for the film, you go to the cities, go on the shows?"

"What? Say it again?"

"You go on all the shows, you do all the talking. Like *Police Academy* you go every city."

"Yeah, hi, Dino. You said how am I? I'm good. You?"

"Thank you, my friend. Ciao."

"What? Dino?"

"You agreed to do as many cities as they want?" Keith was sitting back in his chair, I could tell.

"What? When?"

"When you spoke to Dino."

"He asked me how I was and that was it. I didn't agree to a full tour. But if they want one, we should do it."

That was a ticket to a tour for a film that reviewers were ready to tear apart. Emulate Hitchcock? It was released in the winter, a tough time to sell a film. And I had seen more of these reporters than I should. There is something that happens when you see the press too much. Familiarity breeds contempt. I had done so many films and been through their towns so many times. But the mistakes were many. Everything that could go wrong, did. Planes not taking off, shows canceling or rescheduling, quick makeup sites, changing of interviews, and forgotten interviews. The distibutors were hard to get to. Just a lack of genuine enthusiasm. This is a business of hunches and feelings. This felt wrong. The film was really good, well made and with a surprise ending, which is a cherry in a thriller. Curtis made a well-crafted film, and really displayed his talents. And still we got mixed reviews.

Here's the rub: the success of *Police Academy* had boxed me in with the audience. Broad comedy makes such an impression with people that you have to be extremely lucky to switch to serious material. *The Bedroom Window,* although a fine film, didn't push me over the line to a whole new genre, and more good roles.

Thank G-d Police Academy 4 *opens soon,* I thought. *It will fix everything.*

Chapter 17

How wrong I was. Wanting a movie to fix your life is like wanting a drink to fix your life.

The movie opens well, it has fans, but in week two it falls off. The exit polls aren't up to snuff. What is uncomfortable is knowing that the first weekend was bought by advertising, and if you don't have the horsepower, it will just fade away.

When you make a movie, it is like a child. Whether it's ugly or beautiful it's still your child. If the movie doesn't perform, it takes a distant person not to care. You see it get shuffled from the A theaters to the Cs. It feels embarrassing. Keith had a point of view about it. "It's the 'hide under the covers the day it comes out' film." If the whole thing is about walking into the Grill and getting kudos, a lousy film won't do it. The studio isn't as chummy, and no wonder, the movie is bombing. Off to Siberia with you, man.

There was a glee in certain individuals, a casual reporting of the numbers to me, just to rankle my ego. It did.

"Hey, Steve, I saw the numbers over the weekend. I was really surprised, I thought it would do better. But I heard you were great in it. What's next?" An executive lightly touched my shoulder as I picked out melons in Ralph's supermarket.

What he meant was: "I love those numbers. You didn't do it, excellent, makes my disasters look better. Thanks, man. Oh, I should smooth this over with a compliment and a caring question."

My answer: "Yeah, it happens, but you know we have hefty foreign and I did my job in it, you know? I'm looking at a lot of things. Good to see you, man."

Which means: "Up yours, buddy. I know what you're doing and you know what you're doing. I'll remember this. And nothing's next, nothing." It gets pretty vitriolic. This is your kid they're talking about.

And another publicity tour comes up. Painful, painful. If you get lucky, people act as if the film works and give you a mulligan. Do over. Try again. You're still in the club. But some won't let you get away with it. "You're going to pay for all those big-money paydays, you're going to have to eat some humble pie, and eat it in front of me." And you have to. Those are the rules. You do a flop, you own up to it. You make appearances, you don't hide. And ultimately it's not so bad.

No, that's not true.

You take the money and run, and then you can't run. It's like the police legend that a criminal always comes back to the scene of the crime. I couldn't get away from the film. And after sixteen days of hard work too.

An actor I worked with did lots of films for money. When the press asked what he thought of an exploitation film he worked on, he said he hadn't seen it, but he saw the house that it bought and it was beautiful. Good answer.

I got the distinct feeling I wasn't the town's favorite son anymore. So I flew home to where I had a fifty-fifty chance of being the favorite son, depending on my parents' mood.

I pull up to my house, a split-level, three bedrooms, with an unfinished basement. Nine houses on the block, a block that fits one Dino house and a third of an Aaron Spelling. No bowling alleys in anyone's house here. The door opens and I hear, "Stanley, if you don't get down here and help them with the bags I'm going to break your legs." I was home.

It didn't get any sweeter. I was among those who loved me and those who didn't know me but knew my legend. I was hometown boy makes good. Heck, *Police Academy 4* was a success in neighborhood people's eyes. No one knew what the grosses meant. It made millions at the box office, that was enough to gauge a hit for them. I had gotten out, I went to Hollywood, I made something of myself. I wasn't a guy whose movie didn't perform, I was a hero.

Everyone was getting older. My friends were looking old. My sisters were young ladies, not little kids. I had been away for ten years, things were changing. I stayed and soaked up my family as much as I could. It meant more to me this time than any other trip. I had matured to the point where I recognized that when people really love you, and you them, you feel good about yourself.

I went back to L.A., ready to face more of the cold winds around town. I settled in to my house in the Hollywood suburbs, with my red Ferrari and professionally decorated interior and professionally landscaped exterior. *I'm twenty-eight and I feel like I've been around the block. I'm an old pro, at twenty-eight? And I'm at the bottom, a dud at the box office with almost no calls.* Except one.

"I am talking with someone very high up at Disney for you to be in a remake of a French movie. They want some other guys, but I'm going to talk them into it. You can do this role of Michael, a cartoonist. Can you draw?"

"I can. And I can take classes. I can play an artist. I can play anything, Keith." I meant to say, "I am coming off a bomb, give me a job. Disney, Eisner, and Katzenberg? The smartest executives in the business? Please get me this job." How soon you can lose your confidence. The danger of depending upon your status in the industry for your well-being. A common mistake. I'm common and fell hard.

The original film, *Trois Hommes et un Couffin,* "Three Men and a Cradle," had been written and directed by Coline Serreau. I had gone after the rights a few months before after hearing the concept of the film but couldn't compete with Disney offer-wise. So it wasn't a strange turn of events that I got the chance to meet on a role.

My automobile-shaped ego cruised up to the Disney gate and a guard with a broad smile. "Yes, Mr. Guttenberg, we have a parking space right here, closest to the building." *Special treatment? Doesn't this guy know I have a bomb in the theaters?*

I walked into the casting office and was treated like I had won the Kentucky Derby. The casting director was great to me, her assistants were offering coffee, tea, whatever-you-want, Mr. Guttenberg. Maybe they were convinced I was the guy for the job. Ms. Serreau was not so sure.

"You have seen my movie?" She sat back in her chair. She had her auburn hair up, and wore catlike glasses and colorful clothing. Her accent was thick and skeptical.

"Yes, I loved it, I loved the script, I loved your film." *I want this part. Disney, Disney, Disney.*

"But I don't know, you may be too young." She tapped a pencil and looked over her glasses at me. With a frown.

"I could wear a mustache." *Anything, anything you want. Just give me this role.*

"No, Selleck has a mustache. We don't need more mustaches."

"Selleck? Tom Selleck? I have a red Ferrari."

She looked at me funny. "Thank you for coming in. I have to think about it." She turned toward a film schedule on the wall. Over her shoulder, "Merci, thank you."

I walked out into the office where everyone loved me, to the parking lot where the guard loved me. To my Ferrari, which loved me. How could *she* not love me?

"She didn't love you." Toni said. No giggle.

"Why?" I need this job.

"She thought you were too young."

"I could wear a mustache."

"Enough with the mustache. She said that was a horrible idea."

"Jerry Belson liked it."

"Jerry Belson isn't Coline Serreau. We'll have to go around her. What did you say that she didn't like you?"

"Nothing, I didn't say anything. I told her I loved the movie, which I do."

Keith was on the phone a minute later. "Well, you did something that she didn't like, that's what the casting office said. Plus Michael J. Fox and Tony Danza are on deck. The studio likes those guys too. What did you say to Coline? You had this."

What did I do? What did I say? Did I wear the wrong color? Dino's favorite is red, but what's Coline's? The machinations of an actor's mind, ego in charge.

"You won't believe this." Keith was on the phone.

"Let me tell him." Toni was giggling.

"Tell him, Toni." Keith sighed.

"They want you. She, I think, wants you, but the studio *really* wants you. You have it. Unless you fuck it up, which you won't do. I am so proud of you."

Keith got to business. "We have some negotiating to do, but it's going to work. We have to get Howard and the lawyers in on this. I want everything to be perfect and get teeth in this one. Disney thinks this is a hit. Katzenberg really wants this made."

"Katzenberg. I'm working for Eisner and Katzenberg, the smartest guys in the business."

"Just be great in this movie. Be one of the men."

I got another job. A good job, with one of the most savvy teams in town. Katzenberg and Eisner, who make quality and artful films. That happen to make a lot of money. Katzenberg is the hardest-working executive on the planet. By 7:30 A.M. he has had three business breakfasts at the Beverly Hills Hotel. He tools around town in a low-profile black Mustang. A major player. Michael Eisner has a senior officer demeanor, wants to make good films, and has a viewpoint that blends creativity with marketing and finance. They both have been responsible for countless hits, and I had the feeling that this was going to work.

An award ceremony was going on that night and I was asked to present. There are so many of these shows, I can't remember which one it was. Maybe the Academy Awards. But I'm walking backstage and there next to me is a big guy, in shape, nice tuxedo, and mustache. It looks real. It's Tom Selleck. I've never met him, but it looks like we're going to be working together. So I say hey.

"Hey, Steve." Tom laughs. And then we both say, "You're going to do the movie?"

"Yeah, yeah. I want to. I think it's going to be great." Tom was giant-sized. And a warm, good, down-to-earth guy. "If they can get all the paperwork done? Are you going to do it?" He had ten people around him wanting him to move on. "I gotta go, I hope you do it." And he was pulled in one direction, and the one person leading me around pulled me in the other. I liked the guy, the vibe felt comfortable.

I made it a regular habit to walk the hallways of the agency and say hi to the various personalities. You cannot be a rep and a wallflower at the same time. It was an eclectic group, and each of them had superpowers of their own. Each had a distinctive outlook on life.

I stopped by the office of a very formal and smooth senior agent. His office is all IBM and private banking. He has represented the biggest action star in the business since they both started. He is respected and listened to, and he has good, legitimate stock in the company. He has done every deal that can be done, and is still ambitious and passionate. He did not like *Cocoon* and still says it was a fluke.

"Steve, I've been keeping an eye on you and I heard about the Disney film. I know how you felt about *Cocoon,* which you hit out of the park, but this Disney film, they have Selleck and they are thinking about Danson. These are TV guys. You are a motion-picture actor, you should be with those kinds of costars. The big boys."

"Selleck and Danson? Ted Danson? *Cheers* Ted Danson?"

"TV Ted Danson." He kept smiling. This guy is the ultimate in polite, it's his style. But he does bite. "I'm telling you, if you go into a film with TV actors, the movie is a movie of the week."

I told Toni later. She was quick and clipped. "He doesn't know what the fuck he's talking about. This is Disney, and that studio knows what it's doing. I don't know why he says those things to you. We want you to work, to keep working. He is out of his mind. I'll kill him if he kills this deal. This has the director of the French film, Katzenberg—arguably the most powerful executive in the business, who has lightning bolts coming out of his head—and a hot concept. I don't care who is in this film, I just want you in it." Keith stroked his mustache. "This is a leading man in a studio film. I know those guys, they will make this a hit. Also you have to start to dress like a movie star. I saw Richard Gere and his jeans were perfect. You look like your clothes are from ten years ago." He was right, I never bought clothes. I used what I had or pinched from films. I looked like everyone else in the working class.

I thought being in a film with Selleck and Danson would be good for me. I never made a distinction between actors who were popular in a certain medium. A good actor is a good actor. Theater, film, television, the work all has a commonality. The fact that an actor is used to one medium has nothing to do with success and artistic expression in another. There is still a class definition between film and television. Theater is immune, as it is the ancient foundation. But film is the holy grail in the business. The business looks at movie stars differently than they look at television stars. Is there really a difference between James Arness from *Gunsmoke,* and John Wayne from the movies? Maybe. They sure don't sit near each other at the award shows. Notice the Golden Globes, where there is a distinction between film and television projects. Television gets the second-tier seating, film gets the orchestra.

Still, I believed that working with these two guys would be a valuable experience. They were far more popular and well known than me. By being in people's homes every week, a bond is built. And especially on shows that are hot. These guys were huge stars, and I had no idea why the senior agent didn't want me to do the film. I called my parents.

"Magnum, you're going to do a movie with *Magnum*?" My mother turned off the vacuum.

"Yeah, but Mom, his name is Tom Selleck."

"I know, I know, but Magnum. You have the same car as Magnum. Did you tell him?"

"Ma, I think that car is just for the show, he probably has another car."

"Why, did he tell you he has another car? Why would he have another car if he can have a Maserati?"

"It's a Ferrari, Ma. My car is a Ferrari."

The extension picks up. "See, she doesn't know what's going on in Hollywood. Ann, the car in *Magnum* is a Ferrari, a 308 Ferrari. Like Steven has. And I read that Michael J. Fox or Tony Danza is going to be in it." I got a little tingle of nerves.

"I think I have the job, Dad." Or did I? My father kept a close watch on Hollywood.

"I don't know, I saw some chatter about those other guys. Did you do the paperwork? The job isn't done until the paperwork is done."

"How the hell do you know this stuff, Stanley? Where do you get this?" She wouldn't go upstairs to ask him. I noticed they did a lot of talking on the phone extensions.

"I told you, Ann, I pay attention to my son's business. Steven, you see how she doesn't listen to me? It's like talking to a brick wall."

"I'll give you a brick, Stanley."

"Mom, Dad, wait, do you like the idea of me in a movie with Tom Selleck and Ted Danson?"

"The handsome one on *Taxi*? I love him, he's the one that was in the cologne commercial. Aramis or something."

"Ann, where did you get that? *Taxi*? The show is called *Cheers*. How do you know he was in a cologne commercial? I'm coming down." My father hung up.

I heard him come into the kitchen. "It's going to be Michael J. Fox or Tony Danza. *He* was on *Taxi*. Ted Danson isn't doing it."

"How do you know, Stanley? Are you running a studio? I swear, Steven, he thinks he's Cecil B. Whoever now."

"I gotta go, this is costing money."

My father shouted into the receiver, "And I heard that the French director is not staying on. Rona Barrett said it on Channel 5. And the fan mags say that there is a *Police Academy Five* going on."

"What, Dad? You heard it where?"

"I'm sure it's not true, but I heard it. I love that Rona Barrett, smart girl. Ann, when do we eat?"

"Stanley, have Rona make you dinner. You like her so much." My mother hung up the phone and so did I. I sat back on the couch. So much had changed since I left Massapequa and traveled to Hollywood.

"Is Mr. Guttenberg there? Jeffrey Katzenberg calling." A very polite assistant was on the line.

"Yes, yes."

"Steve, hey, how are you? Glad it's all going to work out. Hey, we are probably going to have to change directors, that's okay with you?"

It was really a surprise, and I knew Jeffrey just wanted to tell me and get on with it. He was really accessible and easy to talk to. He has a gift for communication. No wonder he is such a success. But news like that, a director change, and not the director who directed the original. Who would know better how to make it? What does Rona say? What does my Dad say?

Coline called to tell me that she planned to leave. She couldn't tell me much, other than it wasn't working. She ended our conversation with, "Make sure they make it with good intentions. It could be very good here. But without me, I hope."

Jeffrey called within a day or two. "Leonard Nimoy. We think we are going to go with Leonard Nimoy."

I was ahead of most of the crowd, who still thought of Leonard as Spock. I knew that he directed *Star Trek IV,* and it was really well done. And I knew about his stage work, especially *Equus,* which he did on Broadway at the Helen Hayes Theatre. So immediately with Leonard, I knew he was a complex and experienced guy. Talented in the best kind of way. It seemed like the right way to go. Plus, he is an actor, and I had had luck with Ron Howard, who was an actor before he was a director.

To others, this was an out-there piece of casting for a director. There were agencies upon agencies circling Disney, trying to get their guys in there. Working for Disney, Katzenberg, and Eisner was a big deal. On top of that, Ricardo Mestres, a Harvard guy who many years later became a doctor, was our executive. He was smart, connected, and thorough. The other executive assigned to the film was Michael Roberts, now at the CW. This was the executive team that was gathering candidates for the new director, which, in Katzenberg style, was done quickly and efficiently. You have to remember, there are ten agencies, with a hundred or so agents at each. Figure twenty at each agency represent behind-the-camera people, and they each have five clients that are right for the job. So Katzenberg's team could be pitched a thousand names. Out of this pile, there has to be the right choice. And it's not like buying a carpenter. It's more like hiring an architect.

I got invited to go to Leonard's house on Stone Canyon Road, on the way to the most elegant hotel on the West Coast, the Bel Air. The house looked like a small hotel itself. Spanish architecture, manicured landscape. Leonard answered the door, and there was that face that I had watched so many times.

"Hi, I'm Leonard." He laughed and had such a deep resonance to his voice. The house was decorated tastefully, with something cooking on the stove. "My mother's stuffed cabbage, want some?" He spooned out a piece of the good stuff and we both smiled. It was a lovely way to meet. Over a stuffed cabbage. "Let me show you what we are doing."

He already had a model of the set, drawings, and all the visual tools that help a director. He either took what Coline had or ordered his own. He had only had the job for a short time, but he was prepared. His first question for me was about the character. We got into a hearty discussion. Leonard was not only an actor, he was an acting teacher, so he knew how to motivate, how to tear apart a character and rebuild it. His style was mellow and firm. He knew what he wanted. He had the characteristics of a good director. It was very easy to be around Leonard. We both had similar professional roads with commercial successes that became phenomenons, though *Star Trek* was much more all-encompassing than *Police Academy.*

Leonard told me about his relationship with the studio, and how he first met Katzenberg when he hadn't yet agreed to making *Star Trek IV.* He was doing *Equus* when Jeffrey came to visit and convince him to do the film.

Leonard spent a few hours with me, explaining his plan for *Three Men,* and how he liked to work. He had his shot list ready a while before we shot. The most important asset on his list was time. Being on time, getting done on time. And a movie set runs on a schedule. He was very aware of it and was thorough and disciplined. And honest. "Are you going to cut your hair?"

I felt as if I spent some very meaningful hours with Leonard that day. But my favorite story is one he told me about working on *Highway Patrol,* a series in the fifties that starred Broderick Crawford. Leonard was an ingenue actor and got a role as a punk slipping and sliding down the highway. When he got to work, they gave him a donut, said that was breakfast, and told him to put his wardrobe on behind the truck. What is shot in eight days now was shot in a day and a half then.

He walked me to my car. And stared at it. "Did you get this because of Selleck's show? You know he doesn't drive one in real life."

I drove down Stone Canyon, past the large homes that you can see from the street. In New York most of the large homes are hidden. Here in L.A. it's all seen from the street. And there is something inspirational in it. America is a country where anything is possible. The man who played the most famous half-alien in the universe was directing my film.

Since I was able to make some decisions as a working actor I've felt it's important to meet the people you work with before you go on set. That's just a feeling I have had. You can wait to meet the people you are supposed to love, hate, and feel for in the makeup room, or at the catering cart, but if you have the opportunity to, then a real luxury is getting a solo how-do-you-do before the production demands it. Some films, you just really don't think it is necessary, but there are those where it is essential to get to know those people as much as you can. And I have always found that they are interesting souls. Maybe it's the common thread that all actors, performers, entertainers have. Some sort of need to be listened to, to tell the audience their point of view. That's why so many actors go into politics. They have an outlook, and sometimes want to make a change, to educate. Ted Danson is that kind of guy.

I made a few calls to his agent, and it took a little doing to get through to him. Ted was, I think, the highest paid television actor in the business, and needless to say he was busy. I think I was given over to his personal office, and then got him on the phone. Ted has a very calm and easy style. He was like a cowboy on the range. "Hey, yeah, it's Ted. How you doin'?"

"Hi, Ted, hey, I'm glad I got ya." It's easy to fall into his confidence. "I thought we could get together before we go to Toronto. Maybe have a drink, or coffee or whatever. I know you're busy." I still couldn't get over the fact that I was talking to Sam Malone from *Cheers*. I was a fan of the people that I worked with. But the delightful part of that is moving on to who they really are. It is invariably a surprise. Very few actors are like the characters they play. Ted played a philandering bachelor, always on the make. So fanboy me presumed that's who he was.

"Yeah, why don't you come over to the house." *Must be a Playboy Mansion kind of place,* I thought. Can you imagine going out on the town with Sam Malone? Talk about shooting fish in a barrel. "I don't know if my wife, Casey, or our daughters will be here, but come by. It's such a good idea. When can you come? How is tomorrow at three? Let me give you our address."

Wife? Daughters? What the heck is he doing with a family? We can't go out on the town looking for women if he's married.

There was a swing set in front of the house. I pulled up to a spectacular rambling home. The size said "movie star," but it had a very homey feel to it.

The door swung open and it was Teddy. Casual and confident, dressed in regular clothes. The image of the playboy crashed into the family man. "Hey, Steve, nice to meet you." He yelled. "Casey, he's here!" And in walks a very normal, attractive lady, but not the pinup girl that fanboy me imagined. Casey extended her hand. "Hi, come on in, we just love your work."

We went into a beautiful den, with two large chairs with ottomans that Ted and Casey flopped onto. On the side of the house was an indoor pool. "It's for Casey. It's terrific physical therapy." He built it for his wife to swim in? I realized where I was, and that these were people in the real world, a real world that I had forgotten as I let my imagination run away with me. This guy wasn't Sam Malone.

And he wasn't. The three of us had a long and fascinating conversation that ranged from our careers to *Three Men,* to conservation, wildlife protection, and the ocean. These were two bright and informed citizens who also had a side interest in Hollywood. Ted was an accomplished actor, aside from *Cheers,* and had varied interests. He had gone to Stanford. He came from a well-educated family. All these things built an intelligent and informed person, who happened to be very good-looking and funny. I still expected everything he said would be buttoned by a Sam Malone joke, but that melted away. Ted didn't take his fame for granted and seemed to live his life focused on doing the best he could as a member of society. When one is in the company of such enlightened beings, one tries to contribute what one can to a conversation.

"My mother said you were the Aramis man. Was that you?" Ted was very kind to me that day, and I will forever be in his debt. He suffered this fool gladly.

As I drove away, I noticed all the homes nearby. This was a street for families, not playboys. Ted was a man with responsibilities to people he loved. And he was a very good actor.

"I told you he was the Aramis Man. Stanley, I was right, he was the Aramis Man." My mother was vacuuming, again. "I'm just cleaning up after your sister spilled Cheerios on the linoleum." I missed that. The normal life. The extension picked up.

"Your mother only vacuumed ten times today, and it's three o'clock. I was the one who told you about Aramis, Ann. He was also in *Something About Amelia*. He was excellent in that."

"No, he wasn't, that was Peter Strauss. And *Something About Amelia* was with Mary Tyler Moore."

"Mom, Dad . . ."

"No, Peter Strauss was in *Masada*. And it was Glenn Close in *Something About Amelia*. I'm sure of it."

"Stanley, how are you getting all this information? You never leave the den. Oh, Steven, your father is going into the hospital tomorrow."

"What?"

"Is the guy who plays Spock directing? I also heard that on *Entertainment Tonight* with Mary Hart."

"Dad, what? Mom, why is he going in the hospital?"

"Just some tests, he's okay. But that Leonard Something is directing? I love him, he's very talented. He has written some books. Very learned man."

"Dad, why are you going in the hospital?" I wanted a straight answer.

"I'm okay, Steven, I just have a rash that won't go away and a headache that feels like I got hit in the head with a baseball bat. But I'm fine. Nothing to worry about. You go do the movie."

"Yeah, you go do the movie with *Magnum* and *Cheers* and *Star Trek*. We'll see you when you get done." My mother started vacuuming again.

I was on a plane that night. The story was that my father had started to not feel well a few days before. It went on for a day or so before he went to the doctor. They didn't know what was wrong. The doctor did some tests, and they waited for the results. But as very typical Brooklyn-born parents, they didn't want to call me and worry me. So I only found out when it was absolutely necessary to tell me. The doctors couldn't figure out what it was and recommended my father go into the hospital for observation. It was frightening for everyone. I ran off the red-eye and got to the house in time to ride to the hospital.

I was supposed to be up in Toronto in a few days, but the company was very understanding. And so we waited for doctor after doctor, and they all came up with nothing. At one point my father started to say wacky things. Nothing wackier than at home, but an intern heard him and a psychiatrist was called.

"Mr. Guttenberg, I'm Dr. Schwartz, do you know where you are?"

"I'm at Winthrop hospital." My father was very polite.

"Do you know what day it is?"

"It's the first."

"Do you know what year it is?"

"Doctor, do you know who that is?" My Dad pointed toward me.

The doctor looked over and his eyes flew open. "It's Magillicutty! From the *Police Story* movies!"

"Dad, let him examine you." I felt pretty serious about all this.

"No, he's fine, your Dad's fine. Let me take a look at you." The doctor started touching me, grabbing my hands. "Yes, it's you!" The curtain around the next bed was closed and a nurse was giving the man an enema. "Nurse, see this guy? He's in the movies."

The nurse peeked her head out. "Oh, yeah, he was in the hockey movie. I like him." She had tubes and metal clamps in her hand.

The man getting the treatment squeaked out, "I thought it was you."

The nurse was in the middle of her business with the patient but it didn't stop the conversation. "What is he doing here?"

"This is his father." The doctor proudly displayed my Dad.

"I'm the father." My Dad pointed toward himself with glee. His chest puffed out. He seemed to be getting better.

"You should be proud, he's a very good actor. From Massapequa, I think," the man squeaked out again as he kept getting his treatment behind the curtain. We couldn't see him, but the nurse kept her head poked out.

"Were you in *Johnny Dangerous*?"

"Ow! Too much," the man yelled.

"Sorry." She was moving at double speed. "Were you in that movie?"

"No, that was Michael Keaton." I couldn't believe we were having this conversation.

"I love him too. Except I think he's getting too big for his britches." Dr. Schwartz was off my father and on to Hollywood.

"I have to say he's a good actor, though, very powerful. And yes, we're from Massapequa." My Dad stuck a lollipop in his mouth, and gave one to Dr. Schwartz. "Lolly?" My Dad handed one to the nurse.

"Can you unwrap it, I only have two hands." The nurse opened her mouth and my Dad reached across and stuck the lollipop in.

"Well, this has been exciting as hell. What are you doing next?" Dr. Schwartz got up and went toward the door.

"A movie in Toronto. But, Doctor, how's my Dad?"

"He's fine. Who wouldn't be a little crazy if you don't know what's wrong with you. Is it the one with Kathleen Turner? I heard on the radio she was filming in Toronto." And he was off.

"He's in the one with Magnum!" my father yelled after him.

Dr. Schwartz peeked his head around the corner. "I liked him in *The Sackets,* that Western. Anyone else in it?"

"*Cheers.*" My mother was back from the cafeteria. "The Aramis man from *Cheers.* He's in it."

"The psychiatrist? Frasier? He's too much." He was gone again.

"Stanley, what did the psychiatrist say?" My mother was passing out the sandwiches she brought back.

"He said he thought Michael Keaton was too big for his britches, and I agree." My Dad started to eat.

And this went on for days. The good part was that my getting recognized made it a little easier to get my Dad attention. More and more nurses and doctors came around to check on him. I saw again what a blessing being famous is, what it can do for those you love. Hollywood gave me something that I couldn't buy for my Dad. They still didn't know what was wrong with him, but he was getting the care that the president would get. He loved showing me off, and I think that made him feel better. That and the steroids.

"It's Thursday, Steven. Time for you to go to Toronto and do that movie with Spock."

"I can't leave, Dad, not yet."

"You're going to leave, get on that plane, and knock it out of the park. I liked that *Star Trek Four,* the one that Spock directed. He's good. You have good luck with actor-directors. Go, have a good time, and bring me back a Cuban cigar."

And so I went, looking forward to three months in Toronto. Hoping this trip would be worth it.

The Toronto airport was old hat to me. I had been there so many times, shooting and reshooting, that the customs agents knew me and waved me through. "Mr. G, you're almost a citizen," one of the guys said to me.

A driver waited for me outside, a guy who I had worked with on *Police Academy.* "Donny" was a really good-hearted biker with a deranged sense of humor, not unlike mine, and we got along well.

"Oooh, boy, Stevie, wait till you see what's waiting at the hotel for you." He had glee in his eyes. We pulled up to the Sutton Hotel, and standing out front was a butler. As we approached he clasped his hands together and smiled.

"Mr. Guttenberg, we are so happy to have you. Please, come. We will get everything to your room. I am Werner, your personal butler. Well, not so personal. I will also be assisting Mr. Danson and Mr. Selleck and Mr. Nimoy." His German accent was thick, Sergeant Schultz thick. "It's just magnificent that you are here. There are so many productions here at the hotel. So many of you Americans. Are you hungry? Come." And Werner took me through the lobby where the staff was lined up to say hello. Up the elevator, and down the hall. "This is the executive hallway where all the big shots will be. All of you on one floor. Oh my, how exciting." Werner walked me into my suite and showed me the phone. "You press this number, my code, and I will be here in three minutes. I have the pager. That's all you have to do. I will do everything for you. Your food, your laundry, your messages, packages, errands, dinner parties, parties of any kind."

"A hundred people? Tonight?" I wanted to play with this force of nature. He stopped and froze.

"Tonight?"

"Tonight. A hundred. Maybe more."

"I can do it. Yes, I can do it. You like Romanian food? I will call my team." He went for the phone. I stopped him.

"No, no, I'm kidding, Werner, just joking with you." He laughed and grabbed my shoulders.

"That's the funny, yes. Oh, I was going to call and get you . . . Oh, you movie star. You have all the funny. Okay, good. No party?" He was disappointed.

"Not yet, but I think there will be." I put on the stereo and popped a tape in. The Eagles.

"Hotel California, here in Toronto. Ooh, we are going to have a good time." He was rubbing his hands together. Almost making smoke.

"I think so, Werner. I'm ready for a good time."

"Me too. May I call you Master Guttenberg?"

"Steve."

"Steven. Good. Mr. Danson is here in his suite. And Mr. Selleck is coming and Mr. Nimoy is here too. What a lovely bunch of coconuts I have." He ran out down the hall and I called after him, "How do I dial long distance?"

"Eight!"

I called home every couple of hours to check on Dad. They still didn't know what was wrong, but he was improving. That's what was important.

I sat back in an easy chair and turned on the television. A man sweeping the ice in front of a moving disc and people cheering for him. It had to be a joke, a Second City show or something.

The phone rang. It was Ted.

"Hey man, I'm here. Want to get together? I can order some food up or we can go out." A really wonderful way to start a film.

We met in his suite, which was ten times the size of mine. "You met Werner?" He used the German accent.

"Ja, I did."

"Yes, you both did, and I'm sorry to interrupt but we have more of your bags, Mr. Danson."

"Ja, Verner, sank you!" Teddy said sweetly.

"I think I'm going to have a lot of calls because of you two. Do you want to sit in the elevator when Mr. Selleck arrives? We can have it furnished like a little apartment and you both can be waiting. What do you think?"

He had this fantastic idea, and he wanted us to try it, but we both shook our heads and said in unison, "No, no, we don't want to do that to him. He's just off the plane and such. Let him relax first." We didn't know Tom too well, so we didn't want to put him on the spot. Werner understood, but did lobby a little more for his bit. He had the acting bug in him.

Ted and I walked up Yonge Street, with the boutique hippie stores, Asian foodie stops, and record stores. We went into a luncheonette and as we sat down he said, "Hey man, I saw the weirdest thing on TV. A guy threw a round thing on, like, hockey ice, and another guy had a broom and was cleaning the ice or something. Did you see that?"

"Yeah, it was a skit or something. Like Second City, I think. But it went on for some time, didn't it? Some Absurd Comedy or something. I guess that's what they do up here, make these funny, short films and put them on TV."

"That was so weird." He looked up at the waitress. She just about fainted.

"Oh my, you're . . . Ted. Ted Danson. Right? Oh my, I have to, oh, I don't know what to . . ." She looked at me and started to do it again, but then she left me and just fawned over Ted. He was a very big star, TV really is powerful. And he is quite charismatic in person, charming without having to open his mouth. It was beautiful to watch how generous he was with people.

We walked out of the restaurant and down the street and it was just a recognition festival. People were so surprised to see us, but then many said they had seen other actors in town. Kathleen Turner, Burt Reynolds, Cher.

Ted and I walked into the lobby and Werner fluttered toward us. He was just beside himself. "Oh, he is here. Mr. Selleck," he whispered, and raised his eyebrows. "He came in. Ohh, he is so nice. Just wonderful. So polite, and he has a team. A driver, and an assistant, a makeup man, and a bodyguard. Oh, everybody was so nice. I think we are going to have a good time."

We both called Tom and made plans to go out to dinner. We all met in the lobby at seven. Tom is a very punctual person. It's not that he minds if someone else is late, but he doesn't want to be late for others. Very thoughtful. He's never missed a plane, as opposed to me. So I showed up my usual five or ten minutes late and Tom was there, and Ted was there before me, though after Tom. Anyway, my reason for focusing on this minutia is that we went out to dinner a lot. Almost every night, and I started to be on time.

That first night, it was the three of us, all guys with a lot going on, sharing stories, and uncovering a few layers. In a way, we are all the same guy. We grew up normally, had good childhoods, and good relationships with our families. Tom and Ted had worked together before. Ted had been a guest star on *Magnum*. That was so typical of the business. The real version of "Today you're a day player, tomorrow you are THE player." Tom laughed about it and I just sat back and listened to these really accomplished and successful and extraordinary guys talk. It was a three-hour dinner, and I couldn't believe I was this lucky. It just kept getting better.

The next day I was ten minutes late to the car, Leonard's car. Now, he being the director, he was especially on time. He didn't like the fact that I was ten minutes behind.

"That's ten minutes less that I have to work, Guttenberg." In that low growl. I think of him as a volcano inside an iceberg. He wasn't happy with my tardiness, and let me know it. Really stupid of me to think that this was a lollygag movie. It was a serious endeavor that Leonard and the filmmakers were attempting.

We got to the studio and the other guys were already in makeup. Leonard gave me a nod and I got to it. There was a head makeup artist named Barbara Palmer, she was really alternative and colorful. Tom worked with an incredible pro makeup guy, Lon Bentley. He worked with everyone and had been with Tom for years. There is a relationship between guys in the business. It doesn't really matter what occupation you have, it all comes down to who you trust. There is so much noise that having a few safe harbors is a luxury. When you are a big enough star, the circle is pretty tight. Lon and Tom were very close. And he had a wonderful preshoot style. Very calming.

That first day it was a makeup test and chat session, with hair and makeup, wardrobe and lighting all looking at how the set and the actors should be lit. It was a perk of having a big studio in charge. So Tom, Ted, and I walked up and down the set, individually, and together. Really just walk-around stuff, but it felt like we had some good chemistry. We all got along and respected one another. It really was a pretty generous atmosphere. It was a smart movie with smart casting. Adam Greenberg was the cinematographer, a really top-of-the-line guy. He knew how to shoot sexy, funny comedy. As well as everything else. And at the helm was Leonard, a very skilled and creative artist.

But there was no script. Not that there wasn't *a* script, but it wasn't rewritten yet by James Orr and Jim Cruickshank, known for *Mr. Destiny* and for being fast, talented, and easy to work with. These guys were holed up at the hotel, eating room service, never seeing the light, rewriting the film so that it was ready in time for shooting.

Later we all got calls from Jeff Katzenberg that the screen test looked great, and everyone at the studio was happy. Oh man, that was gold. Just the high of feeling like something is working. Now, when it doesn't work, you know it. You have to plod on, week after week, in something that you know will not hit. Like a walk to the gallows. But the rare luxury of working on something that you know has a chance of winning. Man, that's the jackpot.

The job for Tom, Ted, and me was to get to know one another, and have a good time on this really terrific two-week rehearsal. We went to a different restaurant every night, although we did have our favorites. There was Joso's, a Croatian-Mediterranean place owned by a shining star, Joso Spralja, a musician who toured and had hit folk records. He was also an artist and the restaurant was covered with his creations. It was crowded every night.

While the three of us were eating, drinking, and working out at the gym, Leonard, Robert Cort, our producer, the Disney guys, and the writers were figuring out the script. Now, this is not recommended, don't try this at home. Starting a film without a finished script is not advisable. But that's where we were heading as we got closer to the start of production. I also did not have a signed contract.

Keith was adamant when we spoke. "I don't care how nice Katzenberg is on the phone, he wants this deal signed and we have to get it done before start of production. You have to get Borris and the lawyers on this." He didn't want the deal blown, which could happen even while I was up there. True, very few productions with the actors on location shut down because of an unsigned contract. It can take years to negotiate contracts, sometimes the films are out and there isn't a signed contract. Just an agreed-upon, big-points deal memo.

The three of us talked about it, and Tom and Ted had the same lawyer. They too were working out the details. So there were no deals and a work-in-progress script.

During that two-week rehearsal period, we all got in the room and read what we had with everyone there. The writers took notes and went away. We went to movies, the three of us went to *Beverly Hills Cop 2,* and then back to the hotel. Across the street there was an Italian place that we made a club of our own. We had uninterrupted good times during rehearsal. Would we really have to shoot?

The hotel was mobbed by film companies. They were all up there taking advantage of the currency difference and the tax breaks. So, there were actors galore. We had an idea: Let's have an actors-only party. Ted had the biggest suite, he set the food up and invited all the actors in the hotel. He told them to invite other actors. Before we knew it, fifty or so thespians were at the party. More people slowly came in after work. Burt Reynolds, Chris Reeve, Kathleen Turner, Treat Williams, Charlie Durning. Peter Coyote told me a very useful piece of location preparation. He always brings only clothes that are black. His whole location wardrobe is black. So he doesn't have to think about it. He can concentrate on the part. Chris loved to talk about his airplanes. Treat was a pilot and they were like kids together. The actors were both big names and not, but the party was about actors, not the class system that the business dictates. We were all just actors at a party, everyone equal. It was really wonderful. We all appreciated that freedom, without production around. Actors are very much the same. We all have that same bone.

That first party went into the late hours, and we had to push people out. Ted was such a sport about it, letting it happen in his home. But the party was a place where you could express yourself knowing that you were in an atmosphere of acceptance and creativity. It might appear a little far-fetched, but it was that. A big acting and singing symposium. Complete with extraordinary food and drink.

And oh yeah, we had a few more pages. Day one was approaching and we just rolled into it. But first a press conference. It was a madhouse. Tons of reporters from all over the globe. Everyone wanted to know about the film, and the principals.

"The three of you, have you ever worked together?" a reporter with an accent yelled.

"No, but we are really getting along." Tom gave them some conversation.

"Ted, you are a big TV star, how do you like movies?"

"I've done a few films before, *The Onion Field*."

"What were you all like in high school?"

Tom said, "I was kind of shy."

Ted said, "Me too, actually."

"I was a stud." I delivered it deadpan and broke the ice. It was obvious, these guys are the studs, I'm the sidekick. The jokes started to fly and the reporters got the drift. We were having a good time. The excitement was high, people were interested in the film. Now we just had to make it.

Good news came in. My father was released from the hospital. But he was still on steroids and eating everybody out of house and home. My mother couldn't keep up with the food intake, and he was exercising like crazy. But he was home.

"Steven, I've been reading the magazines and they say that you guys are having a good time up there. What's the script like? Is it getting better?" He was talking at double speed.

"Dad, I think we have thirty pages." We had less than that.

"Don't worry. They rewrote *Casablanca* all during filming. They didn't even have an ending."

Leonard and his wife, Susan Bay, made a "night before we start to film" dinner. Susan was a film executive. Her love for Leonard was and is really extraordinary. The dinner also had our writers, James and Jim. One looking very much like an English professor, the other, a cowboy from a Western. There was producer Bob Cort, who dressed impeccably, and Edward Teets, who was line producing, who looked as if he came off a London street. It was quite a refined evening. Most important, we all liked each other, and that makes the game a lot easier.

I think it was the first day of filming that I was late again getting to my car. Why, I don't know. Just ten minutes, but I was late. I was late getting to makeup, and although it didn't slow down the day's schedule, Leonard didn't like it. And you don't want to get Leonard mad. That volcano in the iceberg. He pulled me aside and gave it to me. First day. But he was entitled. I watched it after that.

We started with some very easy stuff, the montage at the beginning of the film, me drawing in the vestibule. He shot it at different speeds, knowing that he would experiment with it in editing. That's a real director. He knew the look of the film, and wanted to set the tone immediately. In the opening credits.

I think it was the next day or so when we started on the baby being put on the bachelors' doorstep. We had incredible babies. Babies as in twins. Lisa and Michelle Blair. They were beautiful children, identical, and just superb. They had separate personalities, and they were actresses. I mean it. They loved the attention. They showed up and as if on cue we all cooed over them. Ted had kids, so this was old hat to him. Tom had a son, so he knew this game. Me, no. So I was a bit to the side. Leonard had children and he took over. He knew how to deal with these girls. He had a relationship with them. I would think they were these blobs sitting in their bassinets. But they were very aware. And in love with Leonard.

So they bring the girls on set, and we only have about a half hour a day to film with them under the lights. There are fantastic laws that protect kids, especially infants. The lights are harsh, even when dulled, and babies just can't be under them too long. Hence the twins. Tom was sensational with the girls. He was helpful and almost became one of their minders. Watching the clock for them, making sure they were both happy. It was a love fest. And I threw a stick in the mud, as I didn't agree with how a scene was being filmed. It just wasn't working for me. It worked for Leonard, Tom, and the crew. I thought we were on the wrong track. Boy, was I off. But I stuck to my misguided guns and had a few convos with Leonard. He calmed my stupidity down, and we continued. Thank you, Leonard, for not chopping my head off.

Tom, Ted, and I continued to have our dinners on the town, after almost every day's shooting. When we went to Joso's it was a party. And me being the single guy of the bunch, I was able to piggyback on their popularity. If Magnum and Sam Malone said I was worthy of attention, what woman could argue with that? I was the least famous, the least wealthy, and the shortest. But I tried my darndest to fit the bill. It was there that I met an exquisite redhead from Montreal. Only later I found out that she was married. I have always had Guttenberg rule number one, no married women and no women who were associated with friends of mine.

The film called for a party scene, in which the three confirmed bachelors invited their black books full of womenfolk. So to insure that the screen was filled with beauties, the production put out a general casting call. Beautiful ladies for a party scene in *Three Men and a Baby.* I had got to driving with Leonard almost every day, partly because he wanted to keep an eye on me, and partly because we liked it. We would talk some, read the paper some, or just be quiet. But this day was different. We drove up the main highway toward the set, and it must have been lined with cars for a mile. Cars of beauties from all over Canada. Our driver almost veered off the road twice. They were all getting out of their cars, hundreds of them, in short skirts and bar wear. It looked like the end of a night at the best club in town, but it was 10 A.M.

At the studio Leonard and I made our way through the crowd, and the lovelies started to recognize us. We just about made it with our very lives. We got through the stage door and Leonard turned to me. "Now, this is fun. But I think they are all looking for Tom and Ted." Which was true. Meanwhile, T and T were in their dressing rooms, rehearsing lines and other boring professional things. So I mingled. With a pen and paper.

To give you an idea of Ted and Tom's fame, we went to a hockey game one night. The arena was full, about 19,000 people. We walked into a luxury skybox and every eye in the place was on Ted and Tom. The hockey players stopped playing, the beer sellers stopped throwing suds, the JumboTron went black. It was as if the presidents of two major countries came in and everyone waited for them to sit. They did, play resumed, the crowd continued rooting, and the JumboTron stayed on them, even when a goal was scored. It was Danson and Selleck. A very big deal. Of course, I had my pen and paper.

Disgustingly so, I had an affair with this married lady. What I didn't know was that her husband had an office across from my hotel room, and could watch what was going on through binoculars. She brought the lingerie and wanted the shades open. I would have said yes to whatever she wanted. It was only later on that I realized I was the show. The guy loved *Police Academy* and Mahoney. And it was a strange wish for him to see his wife with that character. Hollywood isn't the only place that breeds some freakiness.

To balance this image of me that you must be building, there was the night that the three of us were at the Italian restaurant that served as our clubhouse. As opposed to Joso's, this was a quiet place where we were able to have a conversation. I think Kathleen Turner joined us for dinner that night.

"Steve, do you remember me?" A young lady with curly hair showed up to the table. That's all Tom and Ted needed.

"Does he remember you? How could he forget? Steve, get the list out."

"It isn't a list anymore, it's a novel. Steve, do you have the novel with you?"

I cut their antics short and ushered the lady to the side. I didn't remember her, but she said that we had met the last time I came up to Toronto. We made a plan to meet at my room later that night.

I came back to the table, took some ribbing, even from Kathleen, and bided my time. These three would be going back to their rooms to watch TV, while I had an adventure waiting for me.

After dinner I walked by Burt Reynolds's room. He peeked his head out. "Alone again, Guttenberg? Tsk, tsk." He laughed. I kept going toward my end of the hall. I knew something Burt didn't.

I got my room ready. The lights down low, Kenny G on the stereo, and the strawberries and cream on the nightstand. There was a knock on the door, a light, suggestive tap. I let the lovely in, and started my very tired but well-rehearsed rap. It was my ten best stories, and I started on number one.

"I had an odd-jobs business when I was thirteen, and gave all the money to my parents to help pay for food." It got more ludicrous, but it usually worked. I moved on to how I joined the Peace Corps out of the goodness of my heart. It was working, she was getting closer to me, and so I went in for the kill, story number three. Then she opened her mouth.

"David told me you were hysterical. Have you seen him?"

"David, David who?" *You know men other than me?* Egomaniac.

"David Spade, don't you remember? We double dated."

Done and done. David Spade, this was the girl that he'd adored when he was here. He wrote me about her, he talked about her. He really liked her. And she was in my arms. Reluctantly, Guttenberg rule number one came into play. No dating your pal's girl. The love den became a room again, and she became persona non toucha.

I walked her to the elevator. The doors closed and I had a good feeling. I did the right thing, rare as it was.

I walked down the hall and Burt opened his door. "Strike out, huh? Too bad, Guttenberg, better luck next time."

I went back to my room. I knew that it was a meaningful thing I did, and I should keep it to myself. Of course I didn't; I called Spade as soon as I found his number.

The Saturday night parties continued. By now, the legend had grown, and the suite was overrun by actors. Faces that you always wanted to meet were hunched over a coffee table eating roast beef. We would let the odd writer or director in, but there had to be a vote by the four of us. Fourth being Werner.

Ted had a tremendous relationship with Leonard. He is an intellectual, a global thinker . . . and loved to pinch Leonard on the ass. It really startled Lenny, every time he did it. Tom and I couldn't believe it the first time Ted did it. Leonard just about jumped ten feet. This was serious, stoic Leonard. And you just don't do that. It would be like pinching Prince Philip. But Teddy did, often. And it made us all laugh.

A scene that caused a stir was the scene with Ted and Celeste Holm, who plays his mother. *Gentleman's Agreement, All About Eve,* Oscar nominee, *that* Celeste Holm. Two fine actors doing a wonderful scene. But what is that scene remembered for? The ghost. The little boy behind the curtain, staring out at them. The legend goes that he was killed in the apartment that we shot the film in and haunted it. So much so that he went onscreen, uncredited, in his own wardrobe. The problem with that story is that we shot at a sound stage, not an apartment, and the only ghost on set was someone stealing underwear from wardrobe. But it was estimated that the rumor made rentals of the film go up in the millions, so yes, there was a ghost. And he sat next to the Easter Bunny.

What was amazing to watch was the way Bob Cort and Leonard distributed pages every day that the writers and rewriters had just finished. It would have been a precarious situation in any film but seemed like business as usual. Leonard knew where he wanted the film to go, and so did Disney. Everything just worked. I was lucky that Michael J. Fox or Tony Danza didn't take my part. I was lucky that I had an agent and manager that wanted me in it. I was lucky that I didn't listen to the agent who said not to work with TV actors.

Selleck is funny. Really has a sense of humor. He and Lon would be constantly thinking of practical jokes to play with us. Dan Helfand was the executive in charge of production, which is a long title for the studio's eyes on set. He had to be the bad guy, often, and put the kibosh on things. He was a hard-working guy, who sometimes worked a little too hard. So Tom had a goat delivered to his office, with panties and stockings on. Dan came in, and saw the goat eating some of his schedule. His diary. His notes. In lingerie. For the record, I did not know the goat.

Ted showed up one night at my door, suit and tie on, ready to go out. "We are going out." And we proceeded to meet Tom and go to watering hole after watering hole. At the end of the night the three of us staggered home, Tom got off at our floor, and Teddy and I got off to go to his room.

"Tomorrow," Ted said, "I'm going to give you one of the best gifts. I'm going to introduce you to a friend of mine."

Woody Harrelson wandered around the lobby with his bag in his hand. He had come in from L.A. and was supposed to start a TV movie in the next few days. I think it starred Helen Slater. Ted and I walked up to him and got him through check-in. Then we shuffled him upstairs to Ted's room and the three of us watched some sports and talked.

Woody was a tremendous guy, and he and Ted had been friends since Woody went on *Cheers*. It was easy to see why. Woody was a good guy, enthusiastic yet proper, like Ted. He had a mischievous side to him, but also a conservative outlook. I liked him the minute we met, though I think I scared him a bit with my propensity to go out and the pace of it all. I think that first night we broke Woody in to the night crawl of Toronto. I think it was too much for him, as he wound up sleeping on my couch. The next morning, we got up and went to breakfast. And our bromance started and hasn't stopped. When you meet someone and just fit in with him, really like the guy, there is a feeling to making a new friend that can't be beat. Better than a girlfriend, possibly. He was well read and a theater and writing major in school. He had gone to college, and I hadn't. He was a thinker, and very sensitive. Woody was a meat eater then, and Toronto has the best steaks and eggs there is.

We traded our histories. One particular story stays with me, maybe because it is so Horatio Alger. Woody told me that at one point while living in New York, he contemplated quitting the business. It had just gotten too hard for him. He was packed and ready to move back home. The next day he had an audition for *Cheers*.

We talked about our families, and L.A. He lived in Marina del Rey, and shared an apartment with a bunch of other actors. He was a true, authentic guy, and Hollywood didn't affect him. I don't think it ever will. Ted was right, he gave me one of the best gifts I could ever receive.

Being with Ted and Tom, something was always going on every weekend. These guys were flying in and out of town to all kinds of engagements, like it was getting on a bus. And people threw out the red carpet wherever they went. They were generous to a fault, and let me just tag along.

"The White House? The White House? We're going to the White House?"

Tom was putting his shoes on, getting ready to do a scene. "Yeah, the First Lady invited me and I thought you would want to go. Unless you have another plan, which is probably chasing someone around a couch."

"Chasing *someones*." Ted popped his head in.

"I can chase in Washington, can't I?"

Selleck stood up. "Now, they will have to do a security check on you, will you clear?"

"I think I got booked for robbing a dry cleaner, but I was innocent."

"They have a dry cleaner at the White House. You'll never get in." Ted popped out.

As I said about Tom, he never misses a flight. He was in his car waiting when I ran out of the hotel half dressed. "I knew I would get in."

"By the skin of your teeth." Tom grinned that big smile. "You have your passport?"

He was a bit perturbed as we raced to the airport. It had taken a while for me to go back upstairs and find my passport. But we got there on time. We flew down to Washington, and it was just pandemonium walking throughout the airport with this guy. Tom can't hide, he's too big. His driver, David, and bodyguard, Dave, who had both been with him on *Magnum,* knew how to get him through. I think the fact that Tom is so tall, bigger than life, makes people go gaga. He really looks like a movie star. He reminds me of Greg Peck.

We walked into the hotel lobby and there was Vanna White. She was also there for the tennis event that Nancy Reagan was hosting. It was getting really heady, with calls from Secret Service and all kinds of White House people buzzing around. We had this magnificent suite overlooking the city and were there a minute before we were off to the White House.

Say what you will about the government. Criticize as much as you want. That all goes out the window when you are driving up Pennsylvania Avenue and you see the building. The gates open and it gets very serious. It doesn't matter how famous you are, it's all a very rigid system.

"Good to see you again, Mr. Selleck." The marine saluted. We were in.

The place is really overwhelming, and you recognize everything. It was teeming with people, everyone in tennis white. The event was a "Just Say No" tennis tournament, which brought out all the pros. Tom knew everyone.

"Hi, Julius." Dr. J., one of my favorite basketball players, walked by. I said what a fantastic player he was. Tom told me he was an even better businessman. He had a Coca-Cola distribution company in Philadelphia. There was Catherine Oxenberg. And in the flurry, Tom and I both got dressed in our tennis whites.

"Tom, do we get to keep the sneakers?"

"Yes, Steve, we do. Meet Nancy Reagan." And there she was. A little lady surrounded by a staff and friends. Tom introduced us, and pow, no wonder this lady is such a force of nature. She looked at me with those big brown eyes, just like my grandmother's, and focused on me. A thousand people around her but it was as if I was the only person there. I notice that some really powerful people are able to do that, just block out everything around them. Make you feel like their whole concentration is on you.

"Welcome to the White House, Steve." For those few moments, I was a Republican. *Whatever you say, Nancy. Or just say no to. I'm with you.*

George Bush played tennis and Tom and I did some refereeing. Julius Erving was a terrific tennis player, being six foot eight and all, one of the only guys that made Tom look short.

"Want to go to the Batcave?" Tom whispered. He raised his famous eyebrows and pointed toward a group of suits with earpieces. We were going to see one of the most exciting secret agent places in the world. The basement of the White House was Secret Service headquarters. I can't tell the details, or they will have to kill me, but suffice it to say there is weaponry around that would make your head spin.

Next a tour of the upstairs. We walked down a hall that I recognized from pictures in magazines. This hallway led to the office that JFK played in with his kids, that every head of state has visited, the office that my mother said was decorated "too busy."

Tom tapped me on the back. "You can breathe now, Steve."

I walked around the Oval Office, taking in as much as I could. We snuck into the little side room that is the President's actual office, the one that looked like someone human worked there, and saw the presidential loo. We walked back into the Oval and I dared to walk up to the desk. And started to walk toward the back.

"Uh-uh, that's a no-no," an agent whispered from the side. I inched my way back.

The tour went through the hallways, all the public and some private rooms. "Lots of things hidden inside these walls," the agent whispered again. Then way down the hall was a big guy, suit, hair, and smile. President Reagan.

"Tom, how the heck are you?" he yelled.

"Good, Mr. President, I'm coming," Tom mock-yelled.

If you are lucky enough to meet a president, it really knocks you a hundred feet in the air. And if you think Nancy was focused, the president was a charm machine. He shook my hand and did all the talking. He loved the movies, loved the business. He said he enjoyed my films and was waiting for another *Police Academy.*

It was time for me to speak and somehow "Your office is decorated really busy" came out.

He looked at me, and I think he knew I was nervous. "Yes, well, thank you, Steve."

I thought that maybe I had given him a valuable piece of information, straight from Ann of Massapequa. Maybe I did, as he immediately whispered to an assistant and they scurried away. I hoped I didn't get a decorator in hot water.

As we drove back from the event, I watched out the rear window as the White House disappeared into the background. "Don't worry, you'll be back," Tom said. "You didn't steal anything, did you?"

I held up some presidential jelly beans.

We shot for a few more days in Toronto, and then it was time to fly to New York, to shoot exteriors. As usual, Tom never misses a plane, Ted was ready, even I was ready, but we were waiting for Woody. He was coming with us to New York to visit friends. Five minutes, ten minutes. Fifteen minutes; Tom was getting hot under the collar.

"We have never missed a plane," Dave the driver said.

"We have never missed a plane," Dave the bodyguard said.

"We will not miss this plane," Tom said. The elevator doors opened and Woody walked out. Slowly, with no baggage. Shuffling.

"Where's your bags?" Teddy knew something was up.

"I'm not going. I've had some signs. From the universe." He sat down on a bench in the lobby.

"He's sitting, why is he sitting?" Tom's eyes opened wide.

"We never miss a plane." Dave the bodyguard opened the car door, beckoning Woody.

"Well, I'm not going on this one."

"Why, may I ask?" Ted was very calm.

"Seven one four." Woody stood his ground.

"Seven one four? What does he mean, seven one four?" Tom seemed taller and bigger than ever.

"Woody, we never miss a plane," Dave the driver yelled from the car.

"Seven one four. I woke up today and the clock said seven one four A.M. I took seven steps to the bathroom, and four to get in the shower. It took seventeen steps to walk to the elevator. Today is July 7. I was staying on the fourth floor. My hotel bill is seven hundred and fourteen dollars. And look at our ticket. What kind of plane is it?"

"Seven forty-seven." Ted smiled.

Woody frowned. "And what flight number is it?"

"Seven one four." Tom gritted his teeth.

"And my ticket number, look, it has a seven and a four and another seven. I'm not going, I can't get on that plane."

Woody wriggled and squirmed in Dave the bodyguard's arms like a puppy trying to get loose. Werner brought down Woody's luggage and Dave the driver piled his suitcases in the follow car and we were off.

"You guys can't do this, I won't go. Please, it's for your own good. Turn around, let's go tomorrow." Woody was pretty good at being charming himself. But he couldn't get out of Dave the bodyguard's arms. "This is kidnapping. I'm going to tell the authorities."

We shuffled Woody toward the gate amidst his cries of refusal. "Don't be doing this in front of customs." Tom was happy we were making progress.

"I don't like this, I won't do it." Woody reluctantly went into a private room with us to meet customs. Once in a while, they make it easy for film companies, so instead of going through the normal lines, we had a very friendly agent ask us if we had anything to declare. "I have something to declare," Woody yelled. All eyes on him. Especially the agent's.

"Yes?" The agent zeroed in on him.

Woody looked at the agent, and looked at us. "We never miss a plane."

So we all got on, the flight took off on time, and everything was cool. Then the captain made an announcement. "Ladies and gentleman, we will be hitting some turbulence. Please make sure your seat belt is buckled."

"I told you guys. I told you. Now we're cooked." Woody started to pray. And indeed we hit turbulence. And each of us had a thought that maybe he was right.

A bump hit us. "Anyone have a pen and paper?"

"And why?" Ted was calm.

"I want to write a last will and testament." Dave the bodyguard gave Woody a pad and a Bic, and Woody wrote, between the shakes, his will.

"Can I have your car?" Ted liked his beat-up Chevy.

"Can I have your stereo?" I needed a stereo.

"Can I have your return ticket?" Tom was always thinking.

"This isn't funny. I told you guys." But before we landed we got Woody to leave all his worldly possessions to us. The fact that we were flying on the same plane didn't matter. If Woody went, we would all be a little richer.

We approached JFK. "You know, we're not out of the woods yet. The landing is the most dangerous part of the flight."

"I thought the takeoff was," Dave the driver said.

"Whatever, make sure this will gets to the proper people." He handed the pad back to Dave the bodyguard, and prepared for the touchdown.

We landed with a hard thud. Woody just about broke out of his seat belt. "This is it! I tried to warn you! Make your peace!" But alas, the plane evened out and we coasted to the gate. We collected our carry-ons, quietly eyeing Woody. He had this sheepish look. We walked out of the plane toward the baggage.

"I still get your car." Ted.

"I still get your stereo." Me.

"I still get your return ticket." Tom.

"Well, it could have happened," Woody squeaked out.

We walked toward the waiting town cars and wouldn't you know it, one of them was number 714. Woody just about fainted.

New York was a different place to film since the last movie I worked on there, *Can't Stop the Music.* I had been twenty years old, roller-skating down Broadway, tight white cords and a sock in my privates. That was long gone. I checked into a hotel on Park Avenue. That night Tom, Ted, Woody, Leonard, and I had dinner at Café Central, famous for its celebrity owners such as Regis Philbin and Robert Duvall. Bruce Willis and John Goodman tended bar there years before. We schmoozed with the crowd and discussed the game plan. A week's worth of exteriors and we would be done.

We started filming the day after next, and my mother and father visited the set. It was such a proud moment for them. Everyone knew how close I was with my family and how much it meant for them to visit. Tom and Ted came into my trailer, and we all waited for my parents. The door sprang open.

"Stanley, help me up the step, it's a big step." My mother's unmistakable voice.

"I got you, I'll push from behind."

"Stanley, don't yell, everyone will hear you."

"Steven, help your mother up."

I grabbed her arm and she and my Dad made their way into the Winnebago.

"How was the trip, Mom?"

"The traffic was terrible, they don't know what they're doing in this city. People drive like there are no laws. What's wrong with them?"

"I agree, Mrs. Guttenberg, the traffic is horrendous." Tom stood up. "I'm Tom."

"It's the way it is here in the city, but it's no better in Los Angeles, believe me." Ted stood too. "I'm Ted. It's good to see your rash has subsided, Mr. Guttenberg."

"Thank you . . . Ted?" My father squinted his eyes.

"Yes, and it's a pleasure. You have a good son."

"We like him." My mother was a little curt.

An AD knocked on the door. "We need you guys in makeup."

"Okay, we'll see you guys on the set." Tom and Ted went for touch-ups. I offered my parents some cold drinks and waited for their reaction. They had just met two of the biggest stars in the world. Nothing.

"Steven, where's the bathroom?" I directed my father to the back.

My mother ran her hand along the couch. "I like these seats, and the fabric. So nice. Better than the one in California for *Chicken Chronicles*."

"Mom, do you know who you just met? That was Ted and Tom."

"So?" My mother drank her juice.

"Tom and Ted, the guys from the movie."

"Which guys?" my father yelled from the bathroom.

"The guys you just met, who were sitting here just now."

My mother froze. "Those were them? Which one was Spock?"

My father banged on the door. "The door is locked! I want to meet Spock! Which one was Magnum?"

"The tall one," I yelled back.

"They were both tall, which was which?" My father jiggled the doorknob. "Get me out of here!"

A teamster had to come and open up the door. My father ran out. "Where are they?"

"Dad, you didn't recognize them?"

"Who looks at people? I meet people, I shake their hand and that's it."

"Yeah, Steven, who looks at people? I thought they were your friends or something. I didn't know they were the actors."

"Yeah, I thought the tall one was someone but I didn't know."

We went on set and my parents got a proper introduction to the guys and Leonard. This time they were thrilled.

"I love your show, but I love your show too. And I love your show. Stanley, tell them." My mother tapped my father on the shoulder.

"Yeah, *The Magnum Show, The Bar Show,* and *Star Wars.* Good stuff."

"*Star Trek.*" Leonard smiled.

"Yeah, that's what I meant, *Star Trek.* Tom, we watched you for years and let me ask you, you get a lot of mildew in Hawaii?"

Tom shrugged. "Not a lot, but I guess some."

"Yeah, it's a situation you have to keep aware of. Anywhere there's moisture."

"Thank you, Mr. Guttenberg." Tom laughed.

"Anytime, Ted."

"I'm Tom."

"I'm Ted," Teddy said.

"Let me look at you both. Two handsome guys, three handsome guys." He included Leonard. "Now, can you do a little filming? I want to get back before the expressway fills up."

And so we did. The exteriors went off without a hitch, and the day after we wrapped, Leonard had practically a finished product. That's a director.

That night I went back to Massapequa, and slept in my old room, in my old bed, in my worn pajamas from high school.

Before I fell asleep, my parents peeked their heads in. "Just like when you were a kid, like you were never gone."

"I never was gone, Mom and Dad. I was always here."

"You were always here." My father pointed to his heart.

"Well, if you were always here, why was there so much less laundry to do, and so much more food in the refrigerator?" That came from the side of my Mom's mouth.

My Dad sat on the bed. "I know you have to leave again, Steven, but just for tonight, let's make it like you won't. Like we all live together, like we did. Before Hollywood, before you learned what you learned out there."

"He learned how to survive in the jungle, Stanley. That's how I want my son to be. Tough, a man. He learned some good things there. He learned how to survive."

"I learned how to order lunch and how to use Fountain instead of Sunset to get to Hollywood. Less traffic." My contribution to the discussion.

"Let the kid snooze, Stanley, he has to go to a wrap party tomorrow. He needs to look like a movie star." My mother pulled my father's arm.

He stayed.

"No, I think I'm going to lie here in the bed with him, till he falls asleep, so he knows I'm here for him. So he knows whatever happens, whether he is a star or a regular person, he comes from here, from us."

"He knows that, Stanley." My mother walked down the stairs to the kitchen. And started to do the dishes.

My father had his arms around me, and I did fall asleep.

And I know who I am.

And I know who I tried to be.

And I know where I came from.

From them.

The Conclusion

So after all of it, all the scratching, begging, cajoling, and payoffs that got me to certain inner sanctums, what is it all about? What is the meaning of playing the game in one of the most sophisticated and immature high schools of civilized life? At the expense of everything else? After all this, why do it? I think aside from some gigantic ego monster that lives somewhere behind the intellect or the conscious desire, there is another reason for all the mountain climbing.

I was here.

That's it. That's the whole thing. All of it rolled into one. I planted my flag at the top of Everest, and it will sit there forever. Or until it disintegrates and slowly fades. But seeing the electronics that the business has at its fingertips, that's not likely. So I was here. I have proof. I did something, a few things, that changed the dispositions of people, most of them people I don't even know. So all these strangers get my sense of humor and drama. They can get what I'm trying to portray or parody. The audience can see how a joke or a scene or a story is built. And I could help that along, so the audience is sated. I climbed up that mountain, and I planted a flag.

I was here.

There's more to it. Hollywood is a ball. One of the greatest professions ever. You have to remember it is a fairly new medium, these talkies. And it has a sexiness and excitement that you only get here. Only in Hollywood. Or what it stands for. And it needs to be perpetuated. Because the movies, television, live theater, are talent, but also marketing. Put together. The overture to the show. And it is in that marketing that Hollywood made an indispensable quality for itself. The most extravagant and outrageous lives ever are lived in Hollywood. And everyone in the business has to have a love, or at least a little love, for the Babylon of it all. I mean, the power, the fame, it's sexier than computers, shipping, world politics, oil, you name it. People in other businesses want to be in show business. It's everything you can think up. It's John Ford's "Dream Factory." It is

Horatio Alger and Napoleon Hill rolled into one. If you can dream it, you might be able to do it. Between Ventura Boulevard, Pacific Coast Highway, Olympic, and Los Feliz, inside those borders is Hollywood. And inside is where you can make your play. In several ways.

There are many ways to skin a cat.

My way was unorthodox. I didn't get discovered sitting on a drug-store stool, or working on a construction site. I wasn't born into it. I didn't have an acting coach who was connected to a studio or major player. And believe me, I would have gladly accepted those leg-ups. I did it the old-fashioned way. I hoped and prayed. I hustled and waited, I was patient and I pushed. I wandered around at night, looking in windows, hoping to get to sit at those tables one day. And it's a good story, because it worked. I don't know if it would be as entertaining if it didn't. Thank you, movie angels, wherever you are.

Three Men and a Baby was released a little over ten years to the day I arrived in Hollywood. Ever since, I've worked steadily in the business, if not hitting all the box-office highs that were demonstrated in this book. It's been an emotional, physical, crazy, and comedic up-and-down life. There have been years when I made more money than I did during my start and years where no one called. I've sat in the bitter box and at the appreciation table, both illusions. But when you are there, they seem real. I've had the good fortune to share all of this, the beautiful and the ugly, with my family, friends, and business partners. And all in all, it's been a delightful ride.

People ask me what movie was your favorite? Which gave you the most satisfaction? The most pleasure? That's a touchy question, as I've done more than fifty films. And I answer that the same way. Every time. The jobs are like children, I love them all the same. And hate them just as well. It takes as much effort to make a bad movie as it takes to make a good one. And every film has its positives, and every film has its negatives. Every film. No exceptions. But they all are great. They all have the promise when you get the start date, and they all have the spin when they are released. Some grow up pretty, some grow up ugly. But I love them all the same. Which is my favorite?

The next one.

Thank you for listening, thank you for reading. I hope that this inspires you, or entertains you, heartens you, or helps you line your bird cage.

But the next time anyone tells you that you are the last person he could see doing anything . . .

Remember not to hear a word he said.

Index